LESSONS AND LEGACIES VII

LESSONS AND LEGACIES VII

The Holocaust in International Perspective

*Edited and with an introduction
by Dagmar Herzog*

NORTHWESTERN UNIVERSITY PRESS   EVANSTON, ILLINOIS

Northwestern University Press
www.nupress.northwestern.edu

Printed in the United States of America

10 9 8 7 6 5 4 3 2 1

ISBN 0-8101-2370-3 (cloth)
ISBN 0-8101-2371-1 (paper)

Library of Congress Cataloging-in-Publication data are available from the Library of Congress.

⊗ The paper used in this publication meets the minimum requirements of the
American National Standard for Information Sciences—Permanence of Paper for
Printed Library Materials, ANSI Z39.48-1992.

Dedicated to Donald P. Jacobs, dean of the Kellogg School of Business Management, in recognition for his dedication to the work of the Holocaust Educational Foundation and his continuous support and encouragement from the beginning of the foundation's work, especially the conferences of Lessons and Legacies

Contents

Theodore Zev Weiss

Foreword

IT IS A GREAT PLEASURE, ONCE MORE, TO THANK THOSE WHO HAVE made the publication of another volume in the Lessons and Legacies series possible. The essays assembled here constitute a selection of those presented at the seventh Lessons and Legacies Conference held at the University of Minnesota in 2002. The Holocaust Educational Foundation is very grateful to Professor Stephen Feinstein for his hard work as host in helping to organize the Lessons and Legacies Conference in Minnesota. Stephen was always available and committed to making the conference pleasant and enjoyable to all the participants. And to Professor Ronald Smelser, who was the academic chair for the conference, we express our gratitude for his strong commitment and excellent work in making the conference an academic success. Thanks to these individuals and their many helpers, the conference not only took varied and stimulating form but also became an integral part of the university's intellectual life. Words cannot convey our appreciation for their accomplishment and for our pleasure at being part of an educational experience in the broadest sense.

My personal thanks to all the scholars who participated and contributed so greatly to the success of the conference.

As was true regarding previous Lessons and Legacies Conferences held at Northwestern University (1990, 1992, and 2000), Dartmouth College (1994), Notre Dame University (1996), and Florida Atlantic University (1998), the sessions could not have occurred without the generous support of many patrons. I am particularly indebted to our board for supporting and fostering this very important undertaking of the foundation.

Once again, we thank Professor Dagmar Herzog for the time and energy she put into editing this work. Of course and as always, I drew strength for this project from my lifetime partner, Alice, and my children, Deborah, Danny, Gabi, and Jodi, who have become as much a part of the Lessons and Legacies family as they are of mine.

With the Minnesota conference and the publication of this volume and its predecessors, the Lessons and Legacies series has established itself as a major forum for Holocaust study and research. The Holocaust Educational Foundation is proud to have fostered this ongoing initiative and to present this collection of the scholarly results.

Dagmar Herzog

Introduction

IN RECENT YEARS, NEW THEMES HAVE COME TO THE FORE IN Holocaust studies. This volume, based on Lessons and Legacies VII: The Holocaust in International Perspective, a conference held November 1–4, 2002, at the University of Minnesota's Twin Cities campus in Minneapolis–St. Paul, emphasizes a number of crucial issues that are just now beginning to receive serious scholarly attention. Among them are: greed and theft as motives for Holocaust perpetrators and bystanders; sexual violence and what it tells us about the experiences of both victims and perpetrators; collaboration with Nazis among the local populations on the ever-moving eastern front; the durability of anti-Semitism after 1945; and the perspectives of the Soviet military and Soviet leadership on Nazi crimes.

Certainly, one main aim of the seventh Lessons and Legacies Conference was to extend the boundaries of Holocaust scholarship into national arenas beyond the central loci of the planning and execution of technologized mass murder: Germany and Poland. Thus, for example, this volume takes us into ghettos and killing fields in Ukraine and Belarus—and also into spaces whose boundaries and national identifications changed repeatedly. It includes work on the expropriation of Dutch Jews and on the exigencies of post-Holocaust filmmaking in France. And it extends our view beyond Europe, as it draws on insights from such more recent genocides as those in Cambodia and Rwanda to offer deeper understandings of the Nazi genocide of European Jewry. In addition, this volume provides new critical analyses of the course and meaning of responses to the Shoah in nations and locations that have been thoroughly researched before but where scholarly consensus remains contested, from the United

States to the Vatican. At the same time, the volume demonstrates that this expanded geographic focus provides an enhanced vantage point on the trajectory of developments in Germany and Poland themselves, and it includes pathbreaking work on such topics as the ideological indoctrination of the perpetrators, the voyeuristic and self-serving strategies of bystanders, the desperate attempts to escape persecution and death used by some Germans of Jewish ancestry, and the ongoing force of anti-Semitism in post-Holocaust Poland.

As the present evolves, so too does our understanding of what matters most about the past. The introductory essay by Omer Bartov brings into focus the numerous paradoxes structuring early twenty-first-century retrospective thinking about the significance of the Holocaust as a central theme of the twentieth century. Relocating the Holocaust's import not only in an international context but also in a *longue-durée* time frame, Bartov points out that the end of the cold war brought with it both the opening of Soviet archives and therefore an immense amount of new source material about the Shoah *and,* tragically, a proliferation of interethnic conflicts in various parts of the world that redirected our attention to the apparently close possible links between intimate familiarity and vicious violence. Insisting on the need to place Nazi anti-Semitism in the broader contexts of twentieth-century state- and empire-building projects and their connections with "scientific" and "eugenic" racism, Bartov emphasizes just as much the imperative of taking the peculiar specificities of anti-Semitism seriously, and not least because of the unanticipated resurgence of new forms of anti-Semitism in recent years. Placing current discussion of the Holocaust's potential lessons in the context of the "war on terror" and ongoing global economic inequities, Bartov notes as well the unexpected conjunctions in perspective between those who have come to identify the Holocaust as the leitmotif of the twentieth century and those who angrily object to what they perceive as an overemphasis on it. And noting the many challenges that our recently much increased understanding of cruel and self-interested individual and group behavior during the Shoah and other twentieth-century genocides present to a "liberal imagination," Bartov warns that although we must not discard the idea that we can learn from atrocities, we should not assume that such learning prevents their recurrence.

The essays in part 1, titled "Avarice," leave no doubt that we have for too long failed to understand the furious dynamism of greed as a core element in the Holocaust and in its wake. As Jonathan Petropoulos observes, "The Nazis were not only the most notorious murderers in history but also the greatest thieves." And as Jan T. Gross points out, we cannot even begin to understand the anti-Semitic violence–filled aftermath of the Nazi occupation of Poland—and the remarkable and heretofore unacknowledged cooperation between the Catholic populace and the new Communist overlords—unless we realize that what was at stake was nothing less than the economic positions once filled by the three million murdered Jews of Poland. Directly challenging the old but persistent canard that Jews had a special predilection for communism, Gross provides the heartbreaking evidence that postwar communism was built by anti-Semites and that it was non-Jewish Poles who, within five years after the war's end, effectively made Poland *"judenrein"* (free of Jews). While Gerard Aalders calls attention to the massive and intricate legal and pseudolegal apparatus facilitating Nazi control of the Dutch economy and comprehensive expropriation of Dutch Jewry, Frank Bajohr emphasizes the out-of-control pandemic corruption and patronage saturating the "Aryanization" of formerly Jewish-owned businesses in Germany; instead of a bureaucracy, Bajohr finds a bribe-taking nepotistic neofeudal community with ganglike mores. But all of the essays demonstrate that we can no longer neglect the powerful fact of gentiles' money hunger and its radicalizing impact on the deportation and killing processes, and that attending to the centrality of plunder helps us reframe our assumptions about perpetrator and bystander motivation and about what constitutes complicity.

Part 2, "Ideology," asks us to think more critically about what exactly ideology is and how it worked under Nazism. In the initial postwar decades, numerous scholars presumed a reductive understanding of ideology as a set of ideas held by a particular group of people, and they too frequently thought of repetition and coercion ("brainwashing") as the main means by which adherence to an ideology was spread to ever more individuals. More recently, scholars have begun to think more creatively and perceptively about ideology: as a phenomenon which succeeds precisely *through,* rather than in spite of, apparent contradictions; as something which is not analytically distinct from material or lived reality but rather which profoundly structures our understanding of what counts as reality; and as something that works psychologically and takes hold of selves—indeed, shapes selves—via complex identificatory processes. In addition, scholars have begun to pay attention to the "positive" and "inspirational" aspects of the work of ideology as well as the more negative prohibitions and prejudices more usually associated with the term. Jürgen Matthäus's contribution, for example, is to show that the goal of Nazi indoctrination was not so much to inculcate a specific body of ideas but rather to produce a specific "posture [*Haltung*]," an attitudinal stance characterized above all by "energetic ruthlessness" and a combination of determination and flexibility, a way of being in which constantly self-radicalizing activity was both method and goal, and in which the Final Solution was represented as a quasi-natural phenomenon that seemingly had no human agent or object.

Turning our attention to the strategies of the victims in a world gone utterly mad, Thomas Pegelow sensitively explores the ways some Germans of Jewish heritage, in order to save themselves or loved ones, sought to exploit the contradictions within the Nazis' hallucinatory but deadly system of categorization—even as, in so doing, they necessarily and however inadvertently reinforced the ostensible reality of those phantasmic categorizations. Turning back again to the perpetrators, the remaining two essays in this section offer further innovative perspectives on the conditions that made Nazi ideology so effective. Edward Westermann highlights the heretofore underresearched relevance of institutional culture for making the Nazis' distinctive combination of martial and racial ideology persuasive. James Waller offers an eloquent, devastating assessment of the twentieth century's death toll and a strong argument about the need for multifactor explanations for individuals' receptivity to participation in mass murder.

Part 3, "Gender and Sexual Violence," demonstrates how much new insight can be gained by considering men's experiences in the Holocaust as well as women's through the lens of gender. As feminist scholarship on the Holocaust grew in the course of the 1980s through the 1990s, so too did some scholars' anxieties that "a gender analysis" might somehow lead to a painful and inappropriate competition between victimized men and women, to a misapprehension of the overwhelming pertinence of ethnic identity (and also age)—as opposed to gender—in accounting for who was killed and who survived, to an objectionable exposure of shameful matters that should be left private so as not to intensify the hurt already sustained by survivors, or to an unseemly and deeply problematic tendency to titillate readers and thereby trivialize the Holocaust's horrors. But in recent years, there has been an increasing recognition that many of these anxieties were misplaced.

Not least because of the incidence of mass rapes perpetrated in the 1990s in the wars convulsing the lands of the former Yugoslavia, there has been growing understanding that sexual violence is itself a human rights violation and a frequent feature of genocides. At the same time, the extraordinary accumulation of empirical evidence from the 1930s and 1940s has led us to acknowledge just how integral different forms of sexual violence were to many aspects of the Holocaust as well. Patricia Szobar's findings foreground the intimate invasions that were such a key tactic of Nazi rule and the excruciating impact of the Nuremberg race laws and ensuing "race defilement" prosecutions on individuals' personal lives and relationships; her insights into the voyeurism drenching the police investigations and the courtroom trials give us new perspectives on perpetrators and bystanders as well. Christa Schikorra challenges prior interpretations of "prostitution" within the concentration camps as something that could be understood as either voluntary or in continuity with victims' prior professional lives; she stresses the "choiceless choice" that shaped the experiences of those who worked in the brothels and urges us to compare concentration camp prostitution not with prostitution in the world outside but rather with slave labor more comparable to the other forms of torturous coerced labor demanded of camp inmates.

Doris L. Bergen's conceptual think piece and call for more sustained investigation into sexual violence as an essential element of the Holocaust emphasizes the plethora of forms of sexual violence to which both female *and* male victims were subjected, and it emphasizes the intricate links between sexualized violence and diverse aspects of Nazi racism. Bergen also encourages us to reflect on what functions experiences of sexual pleasure and romantic attachment, on the one hand, and enactments of horrific sexual violence, on the other, may have had for the (mostly male) perpetrators. Rochelle G. Saidel, drawing from the research for her pioneering book, takes us into the particularities of the women's concentration camp of Ravensbrück. She amasses crucial information on the distinctive experiences of Jewish prisoners in Ravensbrück, a group whose contours have too frequently gone out of focus in studies which extrapolated to Jews from the experiences of imprisoned gentile political or religious dissenters.

The essays in part 4, "Collaboration and the Eastern Front," confront us with multiple difficult issues—difficult both because in fact many individuals and groups were *both* victims *and* perpetrators, especially in territories whose governance changed hands frequently, and because political considerations (both Western and Communist) have long distorted our ability to make sense of the conflicting shards of evidence the historical record offers. All of the essays, then, although informed by the methods of quite diverse scholarly disciplines, engage the important subject of contemporaries' meaning-making processes. Martin Dean provides an instructive examination of diverse types of collaborator-perpetrators in the Eastern territories and begins the challenging task of identifying these collaborator-perpetrators' motives. Rebecca Golbert, in a meditative ethnography traversing postwar and post-Communist time zones, captures effectively the confusions of interpretation we confront: in the face of intra-Jewish conflict; in cases when the shared suffering of different groups of Ukrainians became entangled with acts of savage complicity with the occupiers on the part of non-Jews; and in instances in which acts of support flipped over into betrayal.

The two final essays in this part tackle the topic of Soviet perspectives on the Shoah. Harvey Asher offers a critical survey of what the government of the Soviet Union knew about the systematic extermination by mass shooting of Jews on Soviet territory as well as how it interpreted what it knew and the evolution of its reactions. Jeffrey Herf's provocative piece charts a research agenda for the future as he assesses what the Soviet Union knew of the gas chambers at the Auschwitz concentration camp and whether it could have bombed Auschwitz if it had wanted to. The essays are contrasting but complementary in their analyses. Both, however, make clear that the systematic mass murder of Jews on Soviet territory was no secret while it was happening; the information was not only available to the Soviet government but also publicized in the media.

Part 5 turns to diverse "Dimensions of Memory" and in so doing amplifies our understanding of postwar meaning making in shaping perceptions of the Holocaust and its legacies. Michael Thad Allen provides an original interpretation of the politically compromised German philosopher Martin Heidegger's postwar self-refashioning and German elites' enthusiastic reception of Heidegger's decidedly uneven efforts to rewrite the significance of German guilt. Suzanne Brown-Fleming offers a meticulous and anguished critical examination of the

Catholic Church's remarkably successful postwar self-construction as having done all it could to help Jews during the Holocaust. And Bob Weinberg supplies a valuable analysis of the long-term suppression of information about the Holocaust in postwar Soviet historiography and the eventual surfacing of attention to the Holocaust in the wake of communism's demise.

Part 6, "Documentary," turns to Holocaust films and highlights the challenging issues of representational strategy confronting film-makers who utilize documentary footage. Stuart Liebman gives us a fascinating introduction to the very first Holocaust documentary, Aleksander Ford's Polish-Soviet coproduction on the concentration camp Majdanek, liberated by the Soviets in 1944; remarkably, aesthetic techniques used in this film have become so widely adopted in subsequent Holocaust films that most of us do not even recognize them as constructions. Christian Delage in turn provides a nuanced and deeply researched historical recontextualization of the making of what is probably the most widely viewed Holocaust documentary of all time—Alain Resnais's *Night and Fog*—and makes sense of the pressures under which the filmmaker and his scriptwriter formulated their message to viewers. With astute and perceptive attention to telling detail, Lawrence Douglas analyzes four filmic incarnations of the trial of Adolf Eichmann and the meanings conveyed to various constituencies by the footage excerpts utilized, the identificatory processes mobilized, and the visual juxtapositions and voice-overs employed. Precisely the most aesthetically experimental of the films is also the one which contains a crucial truth that too often gets missed. In it, Eichmann is shown in a moment off guard, smirking: this instant can communicate as powerfully as hours of other evidence the ultimate cynicism of the Holocaust's main organizers.

Part 7, "Historiography and Pedagogy," addresses Holocaust scholarship directly. Piotr Wróbel's essay constitutes a forceful critique of what he identifies as the limitations—in the use of evidence and in analysis—of Jan T. Gross's much-discussed book, *Neighbors* (first published in Polish in 2000), a study of the 1941 massacre of the Jews of Jedwabne, Poland, by their gentile fellow citizens. While Wróbel expresses just how important *Neighbors* was for catalyzing Poland's long-delayed confrontation with gentile Poles' behaviors under Nazi occupation, he also insists that more research needs to be done to uncover the details of intra-Polish conflict, German involvement in instigating the massacres in Jedwabne and elsewhere, and the perceptions—however false they were—of Jews' relationships to communism, which shaped gentile Poles' reactions to Jews and Germans both. In his contribution, Gavriel D. Rosenfeld pays homage to the work of the preeminent Holocaust historian Saul Friedländer. Rosenfeld explores the ongoing pertinence, into the twenty-first century, of Friedländer's many insights—in *Reflections of Nazism: An Essay on Kitsch and Death* (1982)—in instrumentalizing the Holocaust in pop cultural representations.

Eric D. Weitz concludes the volume as he revisits themes adumbrated by Bartov in the opening essay and places these in the context of his own recent scholarship on genocide. More than any of the other essays, Weitz's expressly engages the ever-changing pedagogical dilemmas of Holocaust studies. Drawing together his findings from his deliberately comparative research on the Armenian and Cambodian genocides as well as Stalin's programs of mass murder with his research on Nazism and the Holocaust of European Jewry, Weitz cogently shows how our comprehension of the Shoah is deepened when we understand the ways virulent utopian fantasies of race and of nation building functioned in other national contexts.

"This is not the Holocaust I learned about in high school." This is a frequent refrain heard from college students, gentile and Jewish alike. What they mean is many things: that they never learned that mass executions by shooting constituted almost as significant a portion of the Holocaust as gas chambers; that they had never been confronted with the pervasiveness of Jewish assimilation in Western and Central Europe and the reality of mixed identities and therefore of the significance of processes of social exclusion and "social death"; that they never knew how much self-described Christians, both Catholics and Protestants, had voiced anti-Semitic and pro-Nazi sentiments during the Third Reich; that they did not know about intravictim conflict and the sophisticated divide-and-conquer strategies that kept most prisoners unable to rebel within the context of imprisonment; that they have been given inadequate opportunities to consider the epistemological, even ontological, problems raised by torture and mass slaughter; that they can't quite visualize vast swaths of a continent soaked both in blood and in rampant corruption; that appropriate moral evaluation is often complicated rather than simple. What this reaction suggests is just how important ongoing research in Holocaust studies remains.

Although Omer Bartov is surely sadly right that learning about atrocities does not prevent their recurrence, Theodore Z. Weiss, founder and president of the Holocaust Educational Foundation, is no less right when he argues that "learning remains the best antidote to humanity's most inhumane impulses." The essays in this volume are meant to be debated and their implications energetically argued over.

LESSONS AND LEGACIES VII

Omer Bartov

The Holocaust as Leitmotif
of the Twentieth Century

THE DISCOVERY OF AND REDISCOVERY OF GENOCIDE

THE IDEA THAT THE HOLOCAUST MAY HAVE BEEN A LEITMOTIF OF THE twentieth century emerged only toward the end of the century, long after the belated appearance of the term "genocide." Introduced as an internationally recognized term in 1948, "genocide" was meant to connote the mass and indiscriminate killing of specifically targeted populations, an increasingly widespread phenomenon that had hitherto lacked a precise definition. The Holocaust was seen as one of the most distinctive manifestations of genocide.[1]

Why, then, has the assertion of the Holocaust's centrality to the history of the twentieth century come so many years after the event? Does this assertion merely reflect the zeitgeist of the current fin de siècle, or does it accurately recognize the profound consequences of an event that former generations had failed to perceive? Clearly, even now the view of the genocide of the Jews as being at the intersection of the main trends of modern history and civilization has not gone unchallenged. Indeed, a growing chorus of critics claim that what they perceive as the overemphasis on the Holocaust in current historical discourse distorts our view of the past, relegates other atrocities to a secondary position, obscures the crimes of imperialism and post-colonialism in the third world, and privileges the Jews over the rest of suffering humanity.[2]

Such criticisms are obviously related to the fact that for several decades after the end of World War II, the mass murder of the Jews—which came to be generally known as the Holocaust only gradually between the 1960s and 1980s—hardly featured even as a crucial event in the history of the war itself, let alone that of the entire century. The new focus on the Holocaust seems to displace other historical protagonists and to empower the Jews, who—despite their mass extermination—are still suspected by some of seeking to legitimize their growing influence and power by appeals to their past persecution. To be sure, the absence of the Holocaust from the general (rather than Jewish) postwar historical consciousness was arguably a product of anti-Semitic prejudice, repression of collaboration in mass murder, and nationalist and Communist political ideologies. But if these influences have been largely overcome, contemporary critics of the alleged omnipresence of the Holocaust in public discourse attribute this phenomenon to prejudices against the third world, repression of complicity in the suffering of non-European peoples, and capitalist and neocolonialist political ideologies that perpetuate such crimes even as they deny their existence.[3]

The growing influence of forces that oppose the recent view of the Holocaust as a historical event of universal significance compels us to examine in more detail some of the specific aspects of this argument. Was the Holocaust a "break of civilization" or an extreme manifestation of trends and fractures that are still present today?[4] What is the relationship between those who assert the Holocaust's centrality and those who reject it? Can we identify some continuity in both sets of arguments, and can both claim a degree of legitimacy? Does the "discovery" of the event's centrality, long after it receded into history, reflect a better understanding and a more objective view of the past, or is this a mere phase, or even fad, that will be replaced by the "discovery" of other historical events and actors who will make their own claims for a central locus in the past?

The "discovery" of the Holocaust is, in fact, closely linked to the "discovery" of genocide. When Raphael Lemkin coined the term that was eventually embraced by the United Nations Resolution on Genocide, he was thinking first and foremost of the Holocaust, although he certainly considered many other cases as "worthy" of the term.[5] Indeed, while the memory of the event was fresh in everyone's mind, and the horrifying documentary footage was available for all to see even if they had not had any direct contact with the atrocity, the absence of an appropriate term to describe that particular brand of crime against humanity became glaringly clear during the Nuremberg Trials.[6] In convening the first international court ever assembled to provide a judicial setting for indicting and punishing an entirely novel class of criminals who had perpetrated an as yet nameless crime, it became evident that a new concept had to be introduced both into legal discourse and into international relations.

Still, although it served as the incentive for coining the term "genocide," the Holocaust itself was not generally recognized as a crucial event in the twentieth century for several more decades. Moreover, despite the clear relationship between the term "genocide" as a general category and the event of the Holocaust as a specific instance of genocide, a certain competition developed between the two that can hardly be said to have diminished in recent scholarly, media, and political discourse.[7] Paradoxically, the centrality of genocide was not recognized both because it was used too loosely to denounce the actions of one's opponent and because it was so prevalent as to become almost invisible. The cold war contributed greatly both to the perpetuation of the phenomenon and to the long-term refusal to recognize its pervasiveness.[8]

This curious condition, whereby a phenomenon that had just been identified, defined, and named both kept happening and remained "unseen," also had to do with the fact that the victims of genocide were so often voiceless. Western intellectual and scholarly debates were concerned with other issues, such as the ideological split between capitalism and communism, the degree to which either of them could be described as "fascist," and the conflicts, promises, and disillusions of decolonization and liberation. The generally triumphal tone of these debates—the certainty that one was right and the other was wrong—left little room for the actual victims of genocides and other related crimes against humanity in Africa, Asia, and Latin America in particular.[9]

In the case of the Holocaust, the vast majority of the victims were, of course, dead. Many of the survivors were rendered voiceless in a number of ways. Some simply could not express their trauma; others found that the societies to which they transplanted themselves, or to which they returned, did not want to hear about their experience in any detail or, when they did, wanted to hear it expressed in a manner that validated their own identities and interpretations of the event rather than doing justice to the memories of the survivors. The urge to reintegrate into old societies or to be accepted into the new "host" countries played a role in muting the victims either temporarily or permanently. And the nature of the atrocity itself was such that it was both exceedingly difficult to represent and almost impossible to believe.[10]

The reappearance of both genocide and the Holocaust, including the emergence of competition between the two, as a central phenomenon of the past century was also related to the changing political and ideological realities of the fin de siècle. While the Arab-Israeli War of 1967 played an important role in Jewish consciousness and in changing conceptions and representations of the Holocaust, the global East-West conflict and the mass killings it generated in such countries as Vietnam and Cambodia drove home the realization that despite the vows of "never again" made at the liberated Nazi camps, the phenomenon of crimes against humanity had hardly been banished from the face of the earth. But it was the end of the cold war, the collapse of communism, and the accompanying eruption of new ethnic and religious conflicts associated with long-repressed enmities and prejudices that compelled people to look back at the legacy of the entire century and to reevaluate the optimistic prophecies made at the end of World War II.[11]

Yet just as genocide and the Holocaust were "liberated" from the straitjacket of the cold war, they were plunged into the realities of the new turn of the century. In some ways, it now became possible to debate more openly what had previously been obscured by ideological constraints. It was also possible to view documents and visit archives that had previously been under lock and key. In other respects, however, while the focus on past genocides might have provided a context and an explanation for present atrocities, it also diverted attention from the crimes that could still be stopped, by dwelling on crimes that could no longer be undone. In a sense, the obsession with the *phenomenon* of genocide came simultaneously with the proliferation of *actual* genocides. Talking about past genocide eased the consciences of those who could not bring themselves to engage in combating the mass crimes that were about to happen or were already unfolding right under their very noses (or on their television screens). Thus, between the opening of the United States Holocaust Memorial Museum in Washington, D.C., in 1993 and the establishment of the Task Force for International Cooperation on Holocaust Education, Remembrance, and Research, in Stockholm in 1998, hundreds of thousands of Bosnians and Rwandans were murdered. Outside intervention came either very belatedly (in Bosnia) or not at all (in Rwanda).[12]

The "rediscovery" of genocide and the Holocaust also brought back to mind some links that the previous decades had refused to acknowledge. Already in 1951 Hannah Arendt argued that one of the origins of totalitarianism was European imperialism. This aspect of her influential book, however, was not picked up by Western scholars during the decades of postwar colonialism and decolonization, and it was finally recognized (although it still remains seriously underresearched) only in recent years. The links are not only historical in the sense that there was a clear—albeit crooked—path between European policies of repression, "ethnic cleansing," genocide, enslavement, and exploitation, especially in the African colonies, and subsequent such policies carried out in Europe itself.[13] One can also trace the origins of such recent African genocides as the case of Rwanda to pre–World War I colonialism and its interwar and postwar manifestations.[14]

Similarly, the multiethnic roots of European genocide have only recently been recognized. With the collapse of the German, Austro-Hungarian, Russian, and Ottoman empires in World War I, the various ethnic/religious groups that inhabited the vast swath of borderlands stretching from the Baltic to the Balkans began seeking national self-determination. The nationalization of ethnicity and religion, which began in this region in the latter part of the nineteenth century, resulted even before 1914 in a great deal of violence during the liberation of the Balkans from Ottoman rule and culminated in large-scale ethnic cleansing and genocide throughout the first half of the twentieth century. To take just one example, the composition—indeed, even the location—of Poland and Ukraine changed dramatically between 1914 and the aftermath of World War II. While the Jews were mostly murdered, the Ukrainians and Poles carried out mutual ethnic cleansing. Subjected to a brutal German occupation regime that had planned to depopulate and colonize much of this area, once the Reich had retreated from the region, these populations also cleansed the ethnic Germans in their midst. Meanwhile, international agreements "moved" Poland westward into former territories of the German Reich while establishing Ukrainian and Belorussian Soviet republics in areas formerly under the rule of interwar Poland.[15]

Recent research has "rediscovered" such "population policies" as being at the root of much of the last century's violence. A number of scholars have argued that there were clear links between the demographic policies of Nazi Germany and the Final Solution, while others have maintained that Soviet "population policies," which included categorization of nationalities and stigmatization of state enemies, similarly culminated in mass incarceration in gulags, vast ethnic cleansing operations, and possibly also genocide. Indeed, it has been suggested that the entire apparatus of the emerging modern nation-state, racial state, or totalitarian state became dedicated to the process of defining enemies and targeting victims. Under circumstances of total war, especially when conducted by ruthless dictatorial regimes driven by rigid ideological dogmas, this process unleashed unprecedented state-directed violence.[16]

THE APPEARANCE AND REAPPEARANCE OF RACE

Thus we can clearly see that with the "rediscovery" of genocide and the Holocaust, much of the twentieth century has had to be rewritten. The implications of European colonialism and imperialism, of the fall of the multiethnic empires and the emergence of the new nation-states, and the determination of the modern state to define its citizens through a process of inclusion and exclusion can all be seen as related in a complex but intimate manner to the phenomenon of modern genocide and specifically to the Holocaust. The centrality of the genocide of the Jews to twentieth-century violence can, however, also be seen from another, related perspective, namely, the manner in which Jews were perceived in European society. For here was a "category" of people that could be seen as the harbingers of modernity and as anachronistic medieval remnants; as the progenitors of the nation-state and as obstacles to a homogeneous society; as the carriers of capitalism and as agents of communism; as ethnically egocentric but as disruptive cosmopolitans; as racially exclusive but also as polluters of other races. In other words, the Jews came to incarnate all evils of the modern era without thereby being able to shed their demonic premodern stigma.[17]

This brings us to the relationship between the Holocaust and racism. At the beginning of the previous century, one of the most central obsessions of the natural and social sciences—and a major preoccupation of respectable politicians, demagogues, imperialists, nationalists, prophets of doom, and heralds of progress—was the idea of race. Scientific racism had various sources, such as the study of evolution, the development of linguistics, the encounter with peoples of a different appearance and culture, the emergence of neoclassical aesthetics, and the new sciences of anthropology and criminology. But whether it was labeled scientific racism, racial hygiene, or eugenics, there was hardly any sphere of Western intellectual, artistic, and scientific endeavor that was not touched by this idea.[18]

The links between the Holocaust and racism may seem so obvious as not to merit any discussion at all. In fact, however, they have been repeatedly disputed. On the one hand, there is no doubt that Nazism was based on a racist ideology and that at the center of the Nazi worldview was the "Jew" who belonged to an antirace and therefore posed a mortal threat to humanity in general and to the "Aryan" race in particular. On the other hand, Nazism was far less consistent in its racism than it was in its persecution and destruction of the Jews. Romanys (more commonly known then as Gypsies) were not pursued with the same determination. Slavs could be seen in several ways: as *Untermenschen* (subhumans) worthy of decimation and enslavement (especially the Russians), as requiring political and cultural destruction (especially the Poles), or as allies (as in the case of the Bulgarians and Croatians). Indeed, the Nazi regime chose to drop the term "anti-Semitism" altogether so as not to alienate other "Semites" such as the Arabs, who were considered to be perfectly respectable allies. Hence while Nazism was a racial ideology par excellence, and the Nazi regime was determined to create a racial state, its obsession with the Jews far transcended its racist ideology and could therefore be seen as having an entirely different quality.[19]

Nevertheless, at least in part because of the "excesses" of Nazi racial policies, the concept of racism came out of World War II severely battered. This did not mean, of course, that it disappeared. Eugenic policies continued in various guises for decades after 1945, both in Europe and in the United States. European colonial empires were imbued with deeply seated racism, and the segregation policies in the American South continued unabated despite the contribution of African Americans to the war against the Nazi racial state. Nevertheless, racism lost its legitimacy as a scientific concept and a socially respectable term. Without the sanction of the scientific community—which had largely invented it in the first place—racism came to be associated with the margins of society rather than the centers of power.[20]

The conundrum is, then, that if the Holocaust was an extreme manifestation of general European, and especially German-Nazi, racism, then it follows that the Jews were only one of a variety of other groups that were threatened by Nazi racial and eugenic policies. And indeed, it has been argued that the Nazi regime persecuted homosexuals, people with disabilities, and even women on the basis of the same general racist worldview. In fact, however, homosexuals were never persecuted with the same vigor (and only German gays were targeted); the "euthanasia" campaign (again directed mainly at German citizens with disabilities) was at least officially stopped under public and church pressure, although killings continued by other means; and however the status of women in the Third Reich was undermined, it could hardly rate as outright genocide.[21] Conversely, however, if we disengage the genocide of the Jews from the general racist-ideological context in which it occurred, we would miss the crucial contribution to mass murder of the medical and legal elite of a modern state, which perceived itself as carrying out "surgery" on the "Aryan" body politic and strictly separating between friend and foe rather than as legitimizing, facilitating, and committing mass murder.[22] That is why the insistence of some scholars on the Holocaust as rooted only in traditional European and Christian anti-Judaism is not only misleading but takes too many key modern professions off the hook (as indeed they were in the Federal Republic).[23]

But the retreat of scientific racism in the postwar decades also meant that little attention was paid to the links between "euthanasia," the persecution of Romanys and homosexuals, and state natal and abortion policies—all of which continued after the war—and the genocide of the Jews. It is again one of the curiosities of this age that just as a growing recognition of the links between scientific racism and the Holocaust emerged in the last two decades of the previous century, so too racism as a political and scientific notion began to experience a revival. This revival has not come under the old facade of eugenics but rather as an element in the debate over genetic manipulation, cloning, and hereditary diseases and the associated issues of health insurance and records.[24] Similarly, the renewed legitimacy of the concept of race in political discourse has been articulated in a manner that strikes contemporary ears as divorced from the pernicious terminology of the past. Rather than speaking of different races, politicians stress differences in culture, religious customs, or manners of dress.[25] In

Germany one speaks of a "leading culture"; in France one stresses the necessary predominance of French culture. Europe as a whole wants to retain its identity as a homogeneous society; multiculturalism is frowned upon as something akin to mongrel American society (even as "hybridity" has become the new catchword). Torn between the demographic reality of an aging population and the reluctance to admit young non-Europeans, the European Union is surrounding itself with immigration walls that fill its cities with illegal immigrants and promote a vast industry of trafficking in humans. The foreigners thus quickly come to conform to the image attributed to them as they fall prey to international criminals and prostitution rings.[26]

When the United States declares a "war of civilization" (even if the term was quickly withdrawn) and indiscriminately goes after American residents of suspected "origins" or religious affiliations, and when Europe defends itself from the encroachment of non-European immigrants and fends off such non-European countries as Turkey from joining its union, the case of the Holocaust comes to play a peculiar role. For those who condemn the Holocaust rather than actually study it, the profession of humanitarian sentiments vis-à-vis an event that has long ended can serve to cover up the pernicious policies of a present from which such sentiments are so evidently absent. As the West keeps ruthlessly exploiting "racially" and culturally different regions of the world and blocks them from ever benefiting from its own affluence, one may doubt the sincerity of those who invoke the Holocaust in political and intellectual discourse: not because the genocide of the Jews is the equivalent of current policies, which it is not, but because the cynicism of the present does not sit well with the remorse expressed about the sins of the past.

THE STRANGE PATH OF ANTI-SEMITISM

The concept, rhetoric, and manifestations of anti-Semitism have followed a similarly crooked path. With the emergence of the Holocaust as a perceived leitmotif of the century, new questions have been raised about the impact of anti-Semitism on the event itself and about its perpetuation after 1945. It has long been accepted that there was a clear connection between the "discovery" of the "Jewish question"—which flowed from the emancipation and assimilation of European Jewry in the nineteenth century—and the emergence of modern anti-

Semitism.[27] There has also been a fair amount of consensus about the link between modern anti-Semitism (along with its premodern and religious leftovers) and the emergence of Nazism, although the nature and relative importance of this link has been at times hotly disputed.[28] As in the case of scientific racism, the extermination of European Jewry largely discredited public manifestations of anti-Semitism in Western Europe and the United States—although anti-Semitic policies and rhetoric continued to thrive in the Communist bloc, parts of Latin America, and the Arab world.[29] But especially between the 1960s and the 1990s, some of the most influential interpretations of the popular support for Nazism and of the motivation of the perpetrators of the Holocaust largely dismissed the impact of anti-Semitism as sentiment and ideology in favor of other impulses such as antimodernism, economic resentment, xenophobia, opportunism, peer pressure, greed, and fear of punishment.[30]

Curiously, the renewed emphasis in the scholarship of the last decade or so on anti-Semitism as a major factor in the worldview of the Nazis and their supporters and in the planning and implementation of the Final Solution coincided quite neatly with the recognition of the Holocaust's centrality as one of the main watersheds of the twentieth century. And yet, just as anti-Semitism experienced a revival in historical scholarship, it also began emerging from history and entering present rhetoric, demagogy, and politics.[31] The recurrence of anti-Semitism as a contemporary phenomenon has come in several guises. Most important, the perfectly legitimate criticism of Israeli occupation policies has often and increasingly served to legitimize blatantly anti-Semitic statements and actions.

Thus the desecration of Jewish cemeteries in Europe, or the refusal by a British professor to advise an Israeli doctoral student, or the ousting of Israeli scholars from the editing board of a European journal, or the refusal to publish papers by Israeli scholars in such journals have all been presented as acts of protest against Israeli policies vis-à-vis the Palestinians. The same intellectuals who denounced the September 11, 2001, terrorist attacks on the United States expressed sympathy for Palestinian suicide bombers and absolute indifference to the civilian Israeli victims. European newspapers and electronic media outlets reported false accusations about Israeli actions—such as claims about a massacre in Jenin—without checking their sources and often without public apologies even when subsequent inquiries proved them wrong.

Often Israeli military actions have been compared to Nazi occupation policies and the Palestinians to the Jews of the Middle East (victims of a Jewish-perpetrated "Holocaust"). The Israeli prime minister has been portrayed in such newspapers as the *Independent* in the shape of a bloody ogre devouring Palestinian children. And the United States, attacked by Europeans for its support of Israel, has been depicted as controlled by the Jews, whose lobbies, financial and electoral power, and key figures in the White House and Pentagon are manipulating both the American public and world politics.[32]

Some of this behavior is hardly new. In the former Communist bloc, much of this rhetoric was commonplace. Thus, for instance, Polish anti-Semitic policies in 1968 were justified as anti-Zionist reactions to Israeli aggression.[33] Similarly, endemic anti-Semitism in the European Left found very similar expressions during the Lebanon war of 1982.[34] The intersection between Left and Right, East and West, North and South in the case of anti-Semitism is again anything but new. The so-called third path of European politics in the interwar period—the creation of fascism as both criticism and synthesis of capitalism and communism—united over the Jewish "threat."[35] European teenagers wearing Arabic headscarves and carrying placards describing Israel as a Nazi state feel that they are true fighters for justice, just as other teenagers wearing swastikas and condemning the "invasion" of their continent by Arabs, Africans, and Jews feel that they are the true fighters for the preservation of their culture and race. Paradoxically, while the anti-anti-Semitic European Left has justified anti-Semitic outbreaks as criticism of Israel, the European Right has used its support for Israel as an alibi for its traditionally anti-Semitic views. The European political scene has been further complicated by the expansion of Muslim populations in Europe. Though hardly welcomed by their Christian cocitizens, radicalized Muslims, often under the influence of Islamic fundamentalism and marginalized in their "host" countries, have nevertheless become powerful political forces that must be courted by the various parties. Among these populations—in Germany, France, Britain, Italy, and others—one frequently finds a tendency to link anti-Israeli and anti-Semitic sentiments vis-à-vis their Jewish neighbors.

Another aspect of this revival of anti-Semitism stems from the perception by some European and American critics that the recent focus on the Holocaust is nothing but the outcome of what can only be described as a Jewish conspiracy to monopolize suffering, extort money, and legitimize power at the cost of others. This monopoly of suffering, it is suggested, may be used to justify the persecution of the Palestinians just as much as to obscure the Jewish dominance of political, economic, media, or academic positions. The alleged "Holocaust industry" has supposedly ranged from shaking down Swiss banks to robbing poor Polish peasants of their last possessions. Jewish professors are said to have taken over the teaching of German literature, and the canon of German classics is said to have been perverted by them into a compilation of Jewish writings concerned primarily with the Holocaust, thus once more justifying their own power and influence by appealing to past persecution and exclusion.[36]

The September 11, 2001, terrorist attacks on the United States had an especially curious effect on these attitudes. Rather than diminishing anti-American sentiments, the attacks and their aftermath actually served to further expand and enhance them—precisely as the terrorists had intended. Anti-Americanism, denials of its existence notwithstanding, has become a deeply entrenched and powerful sentiment both in Europe and in much of the rest of the world, especially Arab and Islamic countries.[37] Most relevant to the present context, anti-Americanism and anti-Semitism are far from easy to tell apart. At a time when the Holocaust is supposed to be paramount in everyone's minds, as shown by the activities of the European Union's Task Force for International Cooperation on Holocaust Education, condemnations of the alleged link between the destructive imperialism of the United States and Jewish international conspiracies are expressed more openly than at any time since the dark days of Stalin's anti-Semitic campaign of the early 1950s.[38] If Egyptian television has been airing a soap opera in which the Protocols of the Elders of Zion are featured as the historical backdrop to the rise of Arab nationalism, the pernicious idea that the attacks on the World Trade Center were initiated by the Israeli Mossad—which warned the Jews in those buildings not to come to work that day—has gained tremendous popularity in Arab and Islamic lands. Most American and European commentators have preferred to ignore the fact that the murder of the journalist Daniel Pearl in Pakistan was motivated by explicit anti-Semitism. Instead, critics in Europe and in some liberal and university circles in the United States have argued that while the attacks of September 11 were motivated by American support for Israel, the American attacks on Afghanistan and Iraq were carried out primarily in support of Israeli/Jewish interests.[39]

ECHOES OF THE PAST

Just as the Holocaust has emerged in European and American scholarship and intellectual discourse as a leitmotif of the previous century, therefore, some of its underlying causes have been given a new lease on life. Contemplating the ominous beginning of the present century, we may detect much of the hate, prejudice, violence, and destruction with which modern genocide originated in the previous fin de siècle. Eric Hobsbawn has written about the short twentieth century that began in 1914 and ended with the fall of communism.[40] But one might also speak of a long twentieth century that began with the ethnic massacres in the Balkans even before World War I and ended with the attacks of September 11, 2001. In some respects, these attacks changed the world in ways that still cannot be predicted. In other respects, they are reminiscent of the assassination of the archduke Francis Ferdinand in Sarajevo on June 28, 1914—preceded, as it was, by innumerable other terrorist attacks and followed by the mayhem of total war. One may also point out that the decade of optimism that followed the fall of communism and supposedly heralded the beginning of a better twenty-first century was actually distinguished by mass killing in Bosnia and Rwanda whose savagery and scope can be compared only to that perpetrated by the Third Reich.

As the new century forges ahead, it is carrying with it much of the legacy of its predecessor. Europe and the United States continue to pursue postcolonial economic policies of ruthless exploitation while depriving vast regions of the world of the benefits of prosperity, science, and medicine, thereby dooming them—and in the long run also themselves—to the epidemics and uncontrolled violence that must eventually erupt and spread around the globe. Conversely, especially in Europe, we see a continuing denial of the real threats facing the West, a retreat into a fortress European Union, and an escape to old xenophobia and prejudice, whereby fears of "invasion" from the third world are combined with denunciations of American political and cultural imperialism and condemnations of Israeli colonialism and Jewish influence. As scientists ignorant of history promise us a brave new world based on genetic manipulation, demagogues familiar with past racism seek new ways to advertise it as a viable political agenda. As the affluent, self-satisfied, and self-righteous societies of the West close off their borders, they are increasingly composed of a cautious, conservative, elderly majority. Facing them are volatile societies made up mostly of frustrated, disadvantaged, and progressively angrier young men and women. The proliferation of both primitive and sophisticated weapons, produced in the West and Russia and dispersed all over the globe, will ensure that the fury of these masses will not be contained for long.

NEIGHBORS TO GENOCIDE

With the "rediscovery" of the Holocaust's centrality to the past century and the growing focus on genocide more generally, another aspect of mass violence has come to the fore: the relationship between intimacy and murder.[41] This relationship could already be seen during the ethnic cleansing and mass rape campaign in Bosnia and, even more vividly, in the genocide of the Tutsi in Rwanda. But it was Jan T. Gross's study *Neighbors,* a reconstruction of the massacre of the Jews of Jedwabne by their own Polish neighbors in summer 1941, and the controversy it provoked in Poland, which made it possible to link past and present atrocities from this particular perspective.[42] For here is indeed one of the greatest paradoxes of human civilization and one of the greatest challenges to the liberal imagination. How does one contend with, how does one explain and yet avoid normalizing, the eruption of violence between neighbors? What is it that makes people who have often lived in close proximity to one another for many generations, who depend on each other economically, perhaps politically, and at times also emotionally, to turn against each other with the kind of savagery that only intimacy can seemingly unleash?[43]

This too is not a new phenomenon, although its links to the wider context of modern genocidal undertakings is novel. Already at the beginning of the last century, German settlers in Southwest Africa called upon the German Imperial Army to eradicate the indigenous population with which they had maintained good relations for decades. The ancient conflict between shepherds and farmers was translated into genocide within its colonial setting and the tools of a modern army.[44] The Christian Armenian population of Anatolia, which had lived side by side with its Muslim Turkish neighbors for centuries, was annihilated by a state keen on acquiring a homogeneous Turkish-Muslim identity, within the context of a world war and the disintegration of the formerly multiethnic and multireligious Ottoman Empire.[45] The exchange of Greek and Turkish populations in the wake of World War I uprooted hundreds of thousands of people from their homes—declaring them to be foreigners—and sent them "back home" to lands where neither they nor their ancestors had ever lived.[46] Romanys were ostracized and hunted down by their own neighbors even before the Nazis murdered them, and they are still regarded by their neighbors in vast parts of central and eastern Europe as unwanted foreign elements.[47] Neighbors, often even family members, turned their backs on the people with disabilities who were torn from their midst and gassed by Hitler's doctors. And of course one saw it over and over again in the Holocaust. German Jews such as Victor Klemperer found their colleagues and friends—with a few exceptions—condemn them to social death even when they managed to avoid deportation to the death camps.[48] Heda Margolius Kovály has written both on her abandonment by fellow citizens of Prague when she escaped the Nazis and about being ostracized by her neighbors when her husband fell victim to Stalin's anti-Semitic campaign.[49]

Indeed, Jedwabne in not an exception even within its own narrower context. As the Polish state commission that investigated this case following the controversy over the book has established, such massacres took place in several other nearby communities.[50] Moreover, even within the wider context of the Final Solution, open-air massacres of Jews by a combination of German perpetrators (made up of police, army, even firefighters), uniformed collaborators (especially Ukrainian and Lithuanian militias), local police and residents, and so on, were hardly an exception. Despite the image we have of the Holocaust as a production-line industrial murder—which it in part certainly was—vast numbers of Jews were murdered in public view of their neighbors and often with their active participation. Thus, for instance, about half of the 500,000 Jews of East Galicia were murdered in their own towns, watched by the local population.[51] Some neighbors hid and rescued Jews, voluntarily or for a fee; some denounced them; some participated avidly in the killing. Most neighbors, colleagues, friends, and schoolmates just stood by and looked on. There were many specific reasons and explanations for such events. But we would do well to remember that similar scenes and patterns of behavior were seen decades later in Cambodia, Bosnia, and Rwanda.[52]

What does all this evidence teach us about pluralism, interethnic relations, or human nature? Can we retreat to a kind of cultural pessimism or anthropological determinism that would make us akin to the fascists who were at the root of this violence in the first place? Can we remain attached to a naive liberalism that believes that all people can learn to live with each other and never fear men and women with different hair color who pray to a different God?[53] If we wish to consider the Holocaust as a leitmotif of the twentieth century, we can say, as Dan Diner has suggested, that while the event of mass killing itself was very brief, its compressed impact was so great that it was generated both backward to its origins and forward to its far-reaching consequences.[54] But we can also say that the long life of the Holocaust (including its so-called recent resurrection) is a complex phenomenon. It shows us that some of the prejudices, dangers, misconceptions, and triggers of violence that were present then are still with us today. They may look different, come from other sources, beliefs, and politics, but they share some similarities. The notion that one learns from an atrocity should not be discarded. But one of the most important lessons must be that learning about atrocities does not prevent their recurrence. On the contrary, as the number and scale of atrocities, genocides, and destructive impulses multiply, and as our belief in progress, modernization, education, and social mobility diminishes, we must think of this leitmotif not only as a key to understanding the past but also as a warning about the future.[55]

NOTES

1. Frank Chalk and Kurt Jonassohn, *The History and Sociology of Genocide: Analyses and Case Studies* (New Haven, CT: Yale University Press, 1990), 8–27.

2. Norman Finkelstein has conveniently compiled innumerable examples on his Web site: http://www.normanfinkelstein.com/default.htm. The tremendous success of his insidious book attests to the popularity of this view, especially in the German-speaking parts of Europe. Norman G. Finkelstein, *The Holocaust Industry: Reflection on the Exploitation of Jewish Suffering* (London: Verso, 2000). For the same argument made brilliantly earlier, see Alain Finkielkraut, *Remembering in Vain: The Klaus Barbie Trial and Crimes Against Humanity,* trans. Roxanne Lapidus, with Sima Godfrey (New York: Columbia University Press, 1992).

3. For the emergence of discourse on the Holocaust, see, for example, Peter Novick, *The Holocaust in American Life* (Boston: Houghton Mifflin, 1999); Henry Rousso, *The Vichy Syndrome: History and Memory in France Since 1944,* trans. Arthur Goldhammer (Cambridge, MA: Harvard University Press, 1991); Tom Segev, *The Seventh Million: The Israelis and the Holocaust,* trans. Haim Watzman (New York: Hill and Wang, 1993); Lucy S. Dawidowicz, *The Holocaust and the Historians* (Cambridge, MA: Harvard University Press, 1981); Jonathan Huener, *Auschwitz, Poland, and the Politics of Commemoration, 1945–1979* (Athens: Ohio University Press, 2003).

4. Dan Diner, ed., *Zivilisationsbruch: Denken nach Auschwitz* (Frankfurt: Fischer Verlag, 1988).

5. More in Howard Ball, *Prosecuting War Crimes and Genocide: The Twentieth-Century Experience* (Lawrence: University Press of Kansas, 1999).

6. Barbie Zelizer, *Remembering to Forget: Holocaust Memory Through the Camera's Eye* (Chicago: University of Chicago Press, 1998); Lawrence Douglas, *The Memory of Judgment: Making Law and History in the Trials of the Holocaust* (New Haven, CT: Yale University Press, 2001).

7. See, for example, Yehuda Bauer, *Rethinking the Holocaust* (New Haven, CT: Yale University Press, 2001), chap. 3; Helmut Walser Smith, ed., *The Holocaust and Other Genocides: History, Representation, Ethics* (Nashville: Vanderbilt University Press, 2002); Robert Gellately and Ben Kiernan, eds., *The Specter of Genocide: Mass Murder in Historical Perspective* (New York: Cambridge University Press, 2003).

8. For one of the earliest studies, see Leo Kuper, *Genocide: Its Political Use in the Twentieth Century* (New Haven, CT: Yale University Press, 1981).

9. See, for example, François Furet, *The Passing of an Illusion: The Idea of Communism in the Twentieth Century,* trans. Deborah Furet (Chicago: University of Chicago Press, 1999); Frantz Fanon, *The Wretched of the Earth,* trans. Constance Farrington, preface by Jean-Paul Sartre (New York: Grove, 1963).

10. The literature in this regard is voluminous. But see, for example, Donald L. Niewyk, ed., *Fresh Wounds: Early Narratives of Holocaust Survival* (Chapel Hill: University of North Carolina Press, 1998); Lawrence L. Langer, *Holocaust Testimonies: The Ruins of Memory* (New Haven, CT: Yale University Press, 1991).

11. Among general overviews of the century, see Mark Mazower, *Dark Continent: Europe's Twentieth Century* (New York: Knopf, 1998); and Eric Hobsbawm, *The Age of Extremes: A History of the World, 1914–1991* (New York: Vintage Books, 1996). The attacks on communism that followed the collapse of the USSR culminated in a controversial volume: Stéphane Courtois, Nicolas Werth, Jean-Louis Panné, Andrzej Paczkowski, Karel

Bartošek, and Jean-Louis Margolin, *The Black Book of Communism: Crimes, Terror, Repression,* trans. Jonathan Murphy and Mark Kramer (Cambridge, MA: Harvard University Press, 1999).

12. Most important, see Samantha Power, *"A Problem from Hell": America and the Age of Genocide* (New York: Basic Books, 2002); and Geoffrey Robertson, *Crimes Against Humanity: The Struggle for Global Justice* (New York: New Press, 1999).

13. Hannah Arendt, *The Origins of Totalitarianism* (1951; London: André Deutsch, 1968); Woodruff D. Smith, *The Ideological Origins of Nazi Imperialism* (New York: Oxford University Press, 1986); Sara Friedrichsmeyer, Sara Lennox, and Susanne Zantop, eds., *The Imperialist Imagination: German Colonialism and Its Legacy* (Ann Arbor: University of Michigan Press, 1998); Cornelia Essner, "Zwischen Vernunft und Gefühl: Die Reichtagsdebatten von 1912 um koloniale 'Rassenmischehe' und 'Sexualität,'" *Vierteljahrshefte für Zeitgeschichte* 6 (1997): 503–19; Christian Davis, "Colonialism, Antisemitism, and the German-Jewish Consciousness" (Ph.D. diss., Rutgers University, 2005).

14. Gérard Prunier, *The Rwanda Crisis: History of a Genocide* (New York: Columbia University Press, 1997); Jean-Pierre Chrétien, *The Great Lakes of Africa: Two Thousand Years of History,* trans. Scott Straus (New York: Zone Books, 2003). See also Adam Hochschild, *King Leopold's Ghost: A History of Greed, Terror, and Heroism in Colonial Africa* (Boston: Houghton Mifflin, 1998).

15. Misha Glenny, *The Balkans: Nationalism, War and the Great Powers, 1804–1999* (New York: Viking, 1999); Eric Lohr, *Nationalizing the Russian Empire: The Campaign Against Enemy Aliens During World War I* (Cambridge, MA: Harvard University Press, 2003); Terry Martin, "The Origins of Soviet Ethnic Cleansing," *Journal of Modern History* 70, no. 4 (December 1998): 813–61; Timothy Snyder, *The Reconstruction of Nations: Poland, Ukraine, Lithuania, Belarus, 1569–1999* (New Haven, CT: Yale University Press, 2003); Aviel Roshwald, *Ethnic Nationalism and the Fall of Empires: Central Europe, Russia and the Middle East, 1914–1923* (London: Routledge, 2001).

16. Amir Weiner, ed., *Landscaping the Human Garden: Twentieth-Century Population Management in a Comparative Framework* (Stanford, CA: Stanford University Press, 2003); Peter Holquist, "'Information is the Alpha and Omega of Our Work': Bolshevik Surveillance in Its Pan-European Context," *Journal of Modern History* 69 (September 1997): 415–50; Götz Aly, *"Final Solution": Nazi Population Policy and the Murder of the European Jews,* trans. Belinda Cooper and Alison Brown (London: Arnold, 1999); Michael Burleigh and Wolfgang Wippermann, *The Racial State: Germany 1933–1945* (Cambridge: Cambridge University Press, 1991).

17. Omer Bartov, *Mirrors of Destruction: War, Genocide, and Modern Identity* (New York: Oxford University Press, 2000), chap. 3 and literature cited therein.

18. Robert N. Proctor, *Racial Hygiene: Medicine Under the Nazis* (Cambridge, MA: Harvard University Press, 1988); Paul P. Weindling, *Health, Race, and German Politics Between National Unification and Nazism, 1870–1945* (Cambridge: Cambridge University Press, 1989); Daniel Pick, *Faces of Degeneration: A European Disorder, c.1848–c.1918* (Cambridge: Cambridge University Press, 1989); George L. Mosse, *Toward the Final Solution: A History of European Racism* (Madison: University of Wisconsin Press, 1985).

19. Eberhard Jäckel, *Hitler's World View: A Blueprint for Power*, trans. Herbert Arnold (Cambridge, MA: Harvard University Press, 1981); Guenter Lewy, *The Nazi Persecution of the Gypsies* (New York: Oxford University Press, 2000); John Connelly, "Nazis and Slavs: From Racial Theory to Racist Practice," *Central European History* 32, no. 1 (1999): 1–33; Moshe Zimmermann, *Wilhelm Marr: The Patriarch of Antisemitism* (New York: Oxford University Press, 1996), 112–15.

20. Ivan Hannaford, *Race: The History of an Idea in the West* (Baltimore: Johns Hopkins University Press, 1996), chaps. 10–11; Francis R. Nicosia and Jonathan Huener, eds., *Medicine and Medical Ethics in Nazi Germany: Origins, Practices, Legacies* (New York: Berghahn Books, 2002), 1–12, 93–139; Stefan Kühl, *The Nazi Connection: Eugenics, American Racism, and German National Socialism* (New York: Oxford University Press, 1994); Elazar Barkan, *The Retreat of Scientific Racism: Changing Concepts of Race in Britain and the United States Between the World Wars* (Cambridge: Cambridge University Press, 1992); Marc Ferro, *Colonization: A Global History*, trans. K. D. Prithipaul (London: Routledge, 1997).

21. Michael Zimmermann, *Rassenutopie und Genozid: Die nationalsozialistische "Lösung der Zigeunerfrage"* (Hamburg: Christians, 1996); Henry Friedlander, *The Origins of Nazi Genocide: From Euthanasia to the Final Solution* (Chapel Hill: University of North Carolina Press, 1995); Geoffrey J. Giles, "The Denial of Homosexuality: Same-Sex Incidents in Himmler's SS and Police," *Journal of the History of Sexuality* 11, nos. 1–2 (January/April 2002): 256–90; Adelheid von Saldern, "Victims or Perpetrators? Controversies About the Role of Women in the Nazi State," in *Nazism and German Society, 1933–1945*, ed. David F. Crew (London: Routledge, 1994), 141–65.

22. Robert J. Lifton, *The Nazi Doctors: Medical Killing and the Psychology of Genocide* (New York: Basic Books, 1986); Ingo Müller, *Hitler's Justice: The Courts of the Third Reich*, trans. Deborah Lucas Schneider (Cambridge, MA: Harvard University Press, 1991); Carl Schmitt, *The Concept of the Political*, trans. George Schwab (Chicago: University of Chicago Press, 1996).

23. Ernst Klee, *Deutsche Medizin im Dritten Reich: Karrieren vor und nach 1945* (Frankfurt am Main: S. Fischer, 2001).

24. Further discussion appears in Omer Bartov, *Murder in Our Midst: The Holocaust, Industrial Killing, and Representation* (New York: Oxford University Press, 1996), 3 n. 2; Pat Shipman, *The Evolution of Racism: Human Differences and the Use and Abuse of Science* (Cambridge, MA: Harvard University Press, 2002).

25. Paul Gilroy, *Against Race: Imagining Political Culture Beyond the Color Line* (Cambridge, MA: Harvard University Press, 2000).

26. Gérard Noiriel, *The French Melting Pot: Immigration, Citizenship, and National Identity,* trans. Geoffroy de Laforcade (Minneapolis: University of Minnesota Press, 1996); Alec G. Hargreaves, *Immigration, "Race" and Ethnicity in Contemporary France* (London: Routledge, 1995); Klaus P. Fischer, *The History of an Obsession: German Judeophobia and the Holocaust* (New York: Continuum, 1998), chap. 10.

27. Peter Pulzer, *The Rise of Political Anti-Semitism in Germany and Austria,* rev. ed. (Cambridge, MA: Harvard University Press, 1988); Reinhard Rürup, *Emanzipation und Antisemitismus: Studien zur Judenfrage der bürgerlichen Gesellschaft* (Göttingen: Vandenhoeck und Ruprecht, 1975).

28. Saul Friedländer, *Nazi Germany and the Jews,* vol. 1, *The Years of Persecution* (New York: HarperCollins, 1997); Daniel Jonah Goldhagen, *Hitler's Willing Executioners: Ordinary Germans and the Holocaust* (New York: Knopf, 1996); John Weiss, *Ideology of Death: Why the Holocaust Happened in Germany* (Chicago: I. R. Dee, 1996).

29. Jacobo Timerman, *Prisoner Without a Name, Cell Without a Number,* trans. Toby Talbot (New York: Vintage Books, 1982); Robert S. Wistrich, *Antisemitism: The Longest Hatred* (London: Thames Methuen, 1991), parts 2–3; Wistrich, *Antisemitism in the New Europe* (Yarnton Manor, Eng.: Oxford Centre for Postgraduate Hebrew Studies, 1994); Bernard Lewis, *Semites and Anti-Semites: An Inquiry into Conflict and Prejudice* (New York: Norton, 1986).

30. For an incisive survey, see Saul Friedländer, "The Extermination of the European Jews in Historiography: Fifty Years Later," in *The Holocaust: Origins, Implementation; Aftermath,* ed. Omer Bartov (London: Routledge, 2000), 79–91. See also Ian Kershaw, *The Nazi Dictatorship: Problems and Perspectives of Interpretation,* 3rd ed. (London: Edward Arnold, 1993), chaps. 5, 9–10.

31. Hermann Kurthen, Werner Bergmann, and Rainer Erb, eds., *Antisemitism and Xenophobia in Germany After Unification* (New York: Oxford University Press, 1997); Pierre-André Taguieff, *La nouvelle judéophobie* (Paris: Mille et une nuit, 2002); Amy Elizabeth Ansell, *New Right, New Racism: Race and Reaction in the United States and Britain* (New York: New York

University Press, 1997); Paul Gilroy, *There Ain't No Black in the Union Jack: The Cultural Politics of Race and Nation* (London: Routledge, 2002).

32. For these and other instances, see, for example, http://www .israpundit.blogspot.com/2003_02_01_israpundit_archive.html; http:// www.mylinkspage.com/israel.html; http://www.guardian.co.uk/uk_news/ story/0,3604,858363,00.html; http://www.rense.com/general29/rev .htm; http://www.campus-watch.org/article/id/144; http://www.president .harvard.edu/speeches/2002/morningprayers.html; http://news.independent .co.uk/world/middle_east/story.jsp?story=374145; http://www.guardian .co.uk/israel/Story/0,2763,767632,00.html.

33. Daniel Blatman, "Polish Jewry, the Six-Day War, and the Crisis of 1968," in *The Six-Day War and World Jewry*, ed. Eli Lederhendler (Bethesda: University Press of Maryland, 2000), 291–310. See also Jan T. Gross, "A Tangled Web: Confronting Stereotypes Concerning Relations between Poles, Germans, Jews, and Communists," in *The Politics of Retribution in Europe: World War II and Its Aftermath,* ed. István Deák, Jan T. Gross, and Tony Judt (Princeton, NJ: Princeton University Press, 2000), 74–129.

34. Dan Diner, *America in the Eyes of the Germans: An Essay on Anti-Americanism,* trans. Allison Brown (Princeton, NJ: Markus Wiener, 1996).

35. George L. Mosse, *Germans and Jews: The Right, the Left, and the Search for a "Third Force" in Pre-Nazi Germany* (New York: Grosset and Dunlap, 1971); Zeev Sternhell, *Neither Right nor Left: Fascist Ideology in France,* trans. David Maisel (Berkeley and Los Angeles: University of California Press, 1986).

36. Finkelstein, *Holocaust Industry;* Mark M. Anderson, "German Intellectuals, Jewish Victims: A Politically Correct Solidarity," *Chronicle of Higher Education* 48, no. 8 (October 19, 2001): B7–B10.

37. Philippe Roger, *L'ennemi américain: Généalogie de l'antiaméricanisme français* (Paris: Seuil, 2002); Jean-François Revel, *L'obsession anti-américaine: Son fonctionnement, ses causes, ses inconséquences* (Paris: Plon, 2002); Dan Diner, *"Feindbild Amerika": Über die Beständigkeit eines Ressentiments* (Munich: Propyläen Verlag, 2002).

38. Gennadi V. Kostyrchenko, *Out of the Red Shadows: Anti-Semitism in Stalin's Russia; From the Secret Archives of the Soviet Union* (Amherst, NJ: Prometheus Books, 1995); Arkady Vaksberg, *Stalin Against the Jews,* trans. Antonina W. Bouis (New York: Knopf, 1994); Louis Rapoport, *Stalin's War Against the Jews: The Doctors' Plot and the Soviet Solution* (New York: Free Press, 1990); Joshua Rubenstein and Vladimir P. Naumov, eds., *Stalin's Secret Pogrom: The Postwar Inquisition of the Jewish Anti-Fascist Committee,* trans. Laura Esther Wolfson (New Haven, CT: Yale University Press, 2001).

39. http://www.likud.nl/extr240.html; http://vigilant.tv/article/2543;

http://www.csmonitor.com/2002/1122/p07s02–wogi.html; http://www.
rense.com/general13/mosso.htm; http://www.prisonplanet.com/analysis
_lavello_050503_bombs.html; http://www.worldnewsstand.net/2001/
article/who.htm; http://biblebelievers.org.au/nl188.htm; http://www.
islamicsydney.com/printable.php?id=203; http://www.rediff.com/us/
pearl.htm; http://www.intelmessages.org/Messages/National_Security/
wwwboard/messages/367.html; http://www.berkeleyboycott.com/Pearl;
http://www.academicinfo.net/iraqcrisis.html; http://psychoanalystsoppose
war.org/iraqresources.htm; http://feralnews.com/links/iraq_war_and
_zionism.html.

40. Hobsbawm, *Age of Extremes.*

41. Donald L. Horowitz, *The Deadly Ethnic Riot* (Berkeley and Los
Angeles: University of California Press, 2001); Horowitz, *Ethnic Groups in
Conflict* (Berkeley and Los Angeles: University of California Press, 2000);
Ashutosh Varshney, *Ethnic Conflict and Civic Life: Hindus and Muslims in
India* (New Haven, CT: Yale University Press, 2002).

42. Jan T. Gross, *Neighbors: The Destruction of the Jewish Community
in Jedwabne, Poland* (Princeton, NJ: Princeton University Press, 2001). See
also Antony Polonsky and Janna Michlic, eds, *The Neighbors Respond: The
Controversy over the Jedwabne Massacre in Poland* (Princeton, NJ: Princeton
University Press, 2003).

43. See, for example, Mahmood Mamdani, *When Victims Become Killers:
Colonialism, Nativism, and the Genocide in Rwanda* (Princeton, NJ: Princeton
University Press, 2001); Elizabeth Neuffer, *The Key to My Neighbor's House:
Seeking Justice in Bosnia and Rwanda* (New York: Picador, 2001).

44. Tilman Dedering, "'A Certain Rigorous Treatment of All Parts of
the Nation': The Annihilation of the Herero in German South West Africa,
1904," in *The Massacre in History,* ed. Mark Levene and Penny Roberts (New
York: Berghahn Books, 1999), 205–22; Helmut Walser Smith, "The Talk of
Genocide, the Rhetoric of Miscegenation: Notes on Debates in the German
Reichstag Concerning Southwest Africa, 1904–14," in Friedrichsmeyer,
Lennox, and Zantop, *Imperialist Imagination,* 107–23; Jan-Bart Gewald,
Herero Heroes: A Socio-Political History of the Herero of Namibia, 1890–1923
(Athens: Ohio University Press, 1999).

45. Vahakn N. Dadrian, *The History of the Armenian Genocide: Ethnic
Conflict from the Balkans to Anatolia to the Caucasus,* 3rd ed. (Providence,
RI: Berghahn Books, 1997); Vahakn N. Dadrian, *Warrant for Genocide:
Key Elements of Turko-Armenian Conflict* (New Brunswick, NJ: Transaction
Publishers, 1999); Richard G. Hovannisian, ed., *The Armenian Genocide in
Perspective* (New Brunswick, NJ: Transaction Publishers, 1991); Ronald
Grigor Suny, "Religion, Ethnicity, and Nationalism: Armenians, Turks, and
the End of the Ottoman Empire," in *In God's Name: Genocide and Religion*

in the Twentieth Century, ed. Omer Bartov and Phyllis Mack (New York: Berghahn Books, 2001), 23–61.

46. Norman M. Naimark, *Fires of Hatred: Ethnic Cleansing in Twentieth-Century Europe* (Cambridge, MA: Harvard University Press, 2001), chap. 1.

47. On Romanys and other groups, see Panikos Panayi, *An Ethnic History of Europe Since 1945: Nations, States and Minorities* (New York: Longman, 2000). See also Gilad Margalit, *Germany and Its Gypsies: A Post-Auschwitz Ordeal* (Madison: University of Wisconsin Press, 2002).

48. Victor Klemperer, *I Will Bear Witness: A Diary of the Nazi Years,* 2 vols., trans. Martin Chalmers (New York: Random House, 1998–99).

49. Heda Margolius Kovály, *Under a Cruel Star: A Life in Prague, 1941–1968,* trans. Francis Epstein and Helen Epstein with the author (New York: Holmes and Meier, 1997).

50. http://www.poloniatoday.com/ipn-pressrelease.htm; http://www.judentum.net/europa/jedwabne.htm; http://www.civilrights.org/issues/hate/details.cfm?id=9430. See more on the debate in http://www.pogranicze.sejny.pl/english/jedwabne/index.htm; http://www.wings.buffalo.edu/info-poland/classroom/J/index.html.

51. Dieter Pohl, *Nationalsozialistische Judenverfolgung in Ostgalizien 1941–1944: Organisation und Durchführung eines staatlichen Massenverbrechens* (Munich: Oldenbourg, 1996); Thomas Sandkühler, *"Endlösung" in Galizien: Der Judenmord in Ostpolen und die Rettungsinitiativen von Berthold Beitz, 1941–1944* (Bonn: Dietz, 1996).

52. Alexander Laban Hinton, ed., *Annihilating Difference: The Anthropology of Genocide* (Berkeley and Los Angeles: University of California Press, 2002); Alexander Laban Hinton, ed., *Genocide: An Anthropological Reader* (Oxford: Blackwell, 2002).

53. In this context, see also James C. Scott, *Seeing Like a State: How Certain Schemes to Improve the Human Condition Have Failed* (New Haven, CT: Yale University Press, 1998); David E. Apter, *The Legitimization of Violence* (New York: New York University Press, 1997).

54. Dan Diner, "Gestaute Zeit: Massenvernichtung und jüdische Erzählstruktur," in *Kreisläufe: Nationalsozialismus und Gedächtnis* (Berlin: Berlin Verlag, 1995), 123–39; Dan Diner, *Beyond the Conceivable: Studies on Germany, Nazism, and the Holocaust* (Berkeley and Los Angeles: University of California Press, 2000), chaps. 10 and 12.

55. For some thoughtful essays on this issue, see "Extreme Violence," special issue, *International Social Science Journal* 174 (December 2002).

I. A·V·A·R·I·C·E

Jonathan Petropoulos

The Nazi Kleptocracy: Reflections on Avarice and the Holocaust

AS WE ARE ALL AWARE, HISTORIANS ATTEMPT TO EXPLAIN NOT ONLY what happened and how it happened, but also why. In other words, understanding the motivation of our subjects is central to the collective project. It is a daunting, perhaps impossible, task. We will never be able to comprehend fully the minds of the individuals we study—but we must nevertheless try to understand what compelled them to act.

With regard to the Holocaust, it is clear that the motivation of the perpetrators was multifaceted. With so many participants, and with such diverse social and geographical backgrounds, how could it have been otherwise? Indeed, there is a scholarly consensus that a variety of factors compelled perpetrators to kill—witness the attacks on Daniel Goldhagen's thesis about eliminationist anti-Semitism on the grounds that it constituted a monocausal explanation and his response that he recognized multiple forces that influenced the killers.[1] Among the factors that need to be considered are peer pressure, the threat of punishment, compartmentalization, bureaucratization, and a culture of obedience. This debate between Goldhagen and his critics also resulted in the acknowledgment of the paramount importance of anti-Semitism among the perpetrators. My essay here is grounded on these two premises: the crucial importance of anti-Semitism and the need for a variegated understanding of the perpetrators' motives.

In assessing the various factors that compelled acts of persecution, there has been an inadequate appreciation of greed as a motive. Daniel Goldhagen discounts it as a factor, and Christopher Browning does not mention it specifically in *Ordinary Men*—although he does discuss "self-interest and careerism," which are related concepts.[2] In his most recent book, *Rethinking the Holocaust,* Yehuda Bauer writes, "robbery was the outcome of the Holocaust, not its cause." He adds, "no serious historian has ever claimed that robbery was the basic reason for murder."[3] Well, with all due respect to Professor Bauer, it appears that he is obscuring an issue by overstating his point. Self-enrichment was not "the basic reason" motivating the perpetrators, but it was *a* reason. Theft was also not pure effect, but it entered into the minds of many perpetrators before and while they acted.

My co-panelists, Frank Bajohr and Gerard Aalders, are among a cohort of historians to address the importance of self-enrichment in their scholarly work. Frank Bajohr, with his fine book on profiteering in the Third Reich, has argued that corruption was endemic within the Nazi hierarchy.[4] And Gerard Aalders, author of a three-volume set on plundering, has provided the most comprehensive examination of theft in the Nazi "New Order."[5] All three of us have been thinking along the same lines for a number of years. I will therefore try to push our common project forward by arguing for a more explicit structural approach to the issue of avarice and expropriation during the Holocaust. I propose that we think about theft in terms of a hierarchy of constituencies.

The first group would be the Nazi elite and would consist of Hitler, the Reichsministers, Reichsleiters, Gauleiters, Kreisleiters, Oberbürgermeisters, Höhere SS- und Polizeiführer, and the like. I would query, was there a leader from this group who did not personally enrich himself during the Third Reich as a result of the persecution of the Jews? If so, he was a rare exception. The *New York Times* recently featured an article—on its front page, no less—titled "Hitler, It Seems, Loved Money and Died Rich," which explored the dictator's obsession with money and historians' recent discovery of his materialistic inclinations.[6] Of course, scholars have known about this aspect of the dictator for some time—even journalists such as Wulf Schwarzwäller have written about *Hitlers Geld.*[7] My earlier work on the dictator's art collection and his grand residences offered similar findings about his avarice, and I tried to show how other leaders emulated this behavior.[8] As Albert Speer noted in *Inside the Third Reich,* Hitler believed that his top subordinates should exhibit their wealth as a means of reinforcing their power.[9]

The situation is complicated by the rhetoric of Hitler and other top leaders. Heinrich Himmler, to take a notable example, spoke out against self-enrichment on a number of occasions, including his famed speech at Posen in October 1943.[10] In the preceding year, the deputy general governor of Poland, Karl Lasch, was charged with embezzlement and summarily executed, and Odilo Globocnik was transferred from Lublin to Trieste in August 1943 after he was found to have misappropriated victims' assets. The commandant of Buchenwald, Karl Otto Koch, was also subject to a "punitive transfer" to Majdanek due to his excessive plundering of victims' assets.[11] But these were measures to check subordinates and prevent the theft and corruption from spinning out of control. As Hermann Göring said at Nuremberg, "chauffeurs of Gauleiter must be prevented from enriching themselves."[12] The Nazi elite, however, did steal. And I would argue that this behavior was extremely pervasive. As historian Robert Koehl noted, "It was impossible to keep a monopoly in Germany of so popular and rewarding an activity as stealing from the Jews."[13]

The second category would be Nazi Party members in privileged positions—but not so elevated so as to be part of the elite. Here, I am thinking about those who implemented the plundering programs and those who became *Treuhänder* of "Aryanized" businesses (a topic where we need more research), as well as the influential businessmen who were in the party and benefited from the Nazis' policies. Concerning the first group, the overseers of the looting operations, it is indeed striking how they stole and enriched themselves. The art plunderers whom I examined in *The Faustian Bargain* frequently profited from their activities.[14] They also preserved much of this wealth in the postwar period. For example, Kajetan Mühlmann, the chief art looter in Austria, Poland, and the Netherlands, concealed assets in both Austria and Switzerland and survived after 1945 by gradually selling off the paintings and other pieces. Among the *Treuhänder* and businessmen, we might point to Oskar Schindler with his inexpensive Jewish labor as an example—although he later spent most of the profits in an attempt to save lives. More Nazi businessmen are to be found in the recent scholarship of Peter Hayes on Degussa and Hans Mommsen on Volkswagen (or in any work dealing with slave and forced labor).[15] While it is unclear how many people are in this category of privileged party members, the number is in the tens, if not hundreds, of thousands. They benefited economically from the persecution of Jews and other victims in that they could buy businesses and other assets at prices well under market value, take advantage of the disappearance of competitors, and employ slave and forced labor in a profitable manner. They were also keenly aware that the persecution of Jews might lead to additional profits in the future.

The third category would be the population at large. Frank Bajohr's numbers on "Aryanization" in Hamburg are particularly striking in this regard. He analyzed the sale of the contents from more than 30,000 Jewish households stemming from Western Europe to more than 100,000 inhabitants in Hamburg—and that is just one German city! Bajohr added, "from February 1941 to April 1945, there was hardly a day on which Jewish property was not publicly offered and auctioned off in Hamburg."[16] Even though the Hanseatic city was one of the first big cities to be devastated by Allied bombs, it was not unusual in terms of the non-Jewish population's acquisition of Jewish assets. Wolfgang Dessen's 1998 book on Cologne, titled *Betrifft: Aktion 3; Deutsche Verwerten jüdische Nachbarn,* offered similar findings, and Tina Walzer and Stephan Templ's recent book on Aryanizations in Vienna, *Unser Wien,* has continued in this vein.[17]

It was not just residents of urban areas who pursued Jewish property during the Third Reich but also those in rural settings. Jan T. Gross showed in his study of Jedwabne that there was "a core group of plunderers [who] kept moving from place to place" surrounding this village in rural Poland. Indeed, Gross devoted an entire chapter to the issue of plunder, noting that "the same people who organized the pogrom afterward took charge of Jewish property as well," and concluded, "given our growing awareness of the importance of material expropriation as a motivating factor in the persecution of the Jews all over Europe, I would think it very probable that the desire and unexpected opportunity to rob the Jews once and for all—rather than, or alongside with, the atavistic anti-Semitism—was the real motivating force that drove Karolak and his cohort to organize the killing."[18]

Another glimpse of the killing in rural central Europe has been provided by Aharon Appelfeld, who published an article in the *New Yorker* in 1998 in which he recalled how he had recently returned to the village where he grew up in Bukovina.[19] Many local residents still possessed property taken from their Jewish neighbors—books, pictures, furniture, dishes, and so on, taken from the victims who had either been slaughtered in the June 1941 pogrom or, more rarely, fled.

In a particularly poignant scene, Appelfeld found some of his family's property in the home of a villager.

The fourth and final category I would suggest encompasses personnel in uniform: SS men, camp guards, members of the Wehrmacht, and so on. This category is more complicated in that there were orders from Himmler and other top leaders that prohibited theft. Members of the various organizations were therefore, in principle, subject to disciplinary measures. We must, however, recognize that the SS, SD, guards, and even the Wehrmacht plundered on a grand scale. Men in these uniforms carried out the majority of the looting operations during the war. One question, then, is to what extent did they utilize the property they "secured" for personal purposes? My sense is that we would find a range of responses, including personnel in uniform who took valuable assets with an eye to the future as well as those who "only" used assets to improve their immediate circumstances (e.g., food and bottles of liquor). Historian Martin Dean, for example, has shown that Wehrmacht forces were involved in the confiscation of property in Belarus and the Baltic states and that "only the most valuable items were sent on to Berlin for processing."[20] This finding implies a certain degree of personal self-enrichment. And, as Dean noted regarding the historiography of the subject, "Dieter Pohl and Christian Gerlach have stressed the widespread corruption within German offices in the east, especially amongst the police and civil administration, which organized the property seizures."[21]

There were also guards within concentration and death camps who regularly "organized" property. Eugen Kogon, for example, described his time in Buchenwald where "large amounts of precious woods, copper, bronze, gold, [and] silver . . . were constantly siphoned off for the needs of the SS commander. . . . Entire living room sets, inlaid furniture . . . and sculptures drifted not only to the garrison areas, but to all sorts of friends throughout Germany and even other European countries."[22] After the war, Franz Stangl recalled mountains of plunder at Treblinka and stated "that he believed the primary motive behind the entire extermination process was plunder."[23] But their cases strike me as more a "by-product" arrangement, as suggested by Yehuda Bauer.[24] The guards deployed at camps took advantage of the situation in which they were placed. One didn't request an assignment at Buchenwald or Auschwitz in order to make money. It is also unlikely that men joined Einsatzgruppen or units of the Order Police with the intention of self-enrichment. But all perpetrators knew that the expropriation of victims' assets was part of their assignment and quickly recognized the opportunity for personal gain. Greed was a sentiment that entered the minds of many of the perpetrators early on in the genocidal process: after all, they had witnessed the expropriations and economic marginalization of Jews in the 1930s. During the war, it was perhaps easier for those outside the camps to commandeer victims' property; there was less oversight, more freedom of movement, and in a sense, greater opportunity. But even within the camps, nearly all who had the opportunity to benefit materially seized it.

So, what do we have? Well, to employ the title of this panel, we have "economic exploitation, self-enrichment, and corruption"—from top to bottom, and with strikingly few exceptions. I would stress that this description does not apply just to Germans. We see it, for example, among collaborators in the West and among auxiliaries and local populations in central Europe. Would the Swiss have been as accommodating to Nazi Germany if it hadn't been so profitable? Some scholars, such as Walther Hofer and Herbert Reginbogin, have been arguing that British and U.S. multinational corporations continued to have business relationships in German-occupied Europe in violation of the Trading with the Enemy Act.[25] But we must preserve distinctions, and in doing so, we must conclude that the Nazis were not only the most notorious murderers in history but also the greatest thieves.

I would like to return to the question raised by Yehuda Bauer: was theft only a by-product of murder, or did greed in some way contribute to the willingness of perpetrators to participate in the persecution? Of course, I am arguing here today for the latter. And here is why.

First, as Karl Schleunes, Avraham Barkai, and others have shown, economic exploitation preceded deportation and murder along the "twisted road."[26] It was part of the process of gradual radicalization. It drew people into the "networks of persecution."[27] By marginalizing and impoverishing Jews, the economic measures desensitized perpetrators and bystanders to the plight of the victims. Historian Jörg Friedrich observed, "there exists a transition in taking all of life's property from a group of people and finally also taking life itself away from them."[28] In short, it was easier to kill impoverished and destitute people.

Second, the Nazis tapped in to a long tradition of economic anti-Semitism. Yes, theirs was a fundamentally racialistic worldview, but part of their justification utilized arguments that had been around for centuries. The Nazi ideologues not only argued that Jews represented a biological threat to the "Aryan Volk" but also spoke of Jewish financial advantages that grew out of conspiracies and other "unfair" practices. Addressing the economic injustices supposedly perpetrated by Jews and taking back *geraubtes Volksvermögen* (property robbed from the people) was one of the arguments first used by the Nazis to garner support.[29] A logical response was to dispossess Jews and effect a redistribution of their assets. This idea was even suggested in the Party Program of 1920.

Third, those engaged in the economic exploitation of Jews usually made decisions in a calculated, well-thought-out, and rational manner. It wasn't just that they stumbled across Jewish assets—although that sometimes happened, especially on the eastern front. Very often, those engaged in the persecution thought about how best to exploit an opportunity. They considered who was vulnerable, how they would store and/or resell the property, how they could expand their operations, and so forth. And to return to a point made earlier, many perpetrators eyed future profits stemming from the persecution. That, for example, is what Peter Hayes has found with regard to Degussa: corporate executives identified prospects for economic gain in the future which would exceed current profits from the smelting of looted gold and silver and the production of Zyklon B, among other wartime enterprises.[30] Throughout Nazi-occupied Europe, avaricious actors made conscious and thoughtful decisions. It is difficult to characterize such rational and premeditated thinking as a "by-product."

Fourth, plunder was central to Hitler's worldview. Albert Speer, among others, noted that the dictator's megalomaniacal building programs were so ambitious as to be unrealizable with German assets alone. Art historian Otto Karl Werckmeister, citing earlier scholarship, noted, "Jochen Thies, Robert Taylor, and others have pointed out that the comprehensive building programs at Berlin, Nuremberg, and almost fifty other German cities earmarked for rebuilding according to Hitler's ideal of monumental state architecture could never have been implemented with the financial, material, and labor resources available in Germany alone, even after the annexations of Austria and Czechoslovakia, but they presupposed the resources of the Eastern territories in Poland and the Soviet Union to be conquered in the imminent war."[31]

It is inaccurate to suggest that all the perpetrators, from top to bottom, were rational actors who sought only to maximize their own "bottom line." There were many exceptions to the behavior that I have just described. But too little attention has been paid to greed as a motive. While it certainly does not deserve to be at the top of the list of factors that animated perpetrators, it was far more prevalent than has hitherto been recognized. To ignore the issue of avarice is to overlook an important variable in the psychology of those who implemented the Nazis' genocidal program.

NOTES

1. Daniel Goldhagen, *Hitler's Willing Executioners* (New York: Knopf, 1996). For examples of scholars construing Goldhagen's interpretation as monocausal, see Fritz Stern, "The Goldhagen Controversy," *Foreign Affairs* 75, no. 6 (November/December 1996): 134; and Robert Wistrich, "Helping Hitler," *Commentary* 102, no. 1 (July 1996): 28. Goldhagen has responded to these and related charges in a series of articles, beginning with "Motives, Causes, and Alibis: A Reply to My Critics," *New Republic* 215, no. 26 (December 23, 1996). These articles, in certain cases expanded and revised, can be found at http://www.goldhagen.com.

2. Christopher Browning, *Ordinary Men: Reserve Police Battalion 101 and the Final Solution in Poland,* 2nd ed. (New York: HarperPerennial, 1998), 169.

3. Yehuda Bauer, *Rethinking the Holocaust* (New Haven, CT: Yale University Press, 2001), 47.

4. Frank Bajohr, *Parvenüs und Profiteure: Korruption in der NS-Zeit* (Frankfurt: S. Fischer, 2001).

5. Gerard Aalders, *Roof: de ontvreemding van joods bezit tijdens de Tweede Wereldoorlog* (The Hague: SDU, 1999); Gerard Aalders, *Berooid: de beroofde joden en het Nederlandse restitutiebeleid sinds 1945* (Amsterdam: Boom, 2001); Gerard Aalders, *Eksters: de nazi-roof van 146 duizend kilo goud bij De Nederlandsche Bank* (Amsterdam: Boom, 2002). See also Gerard Aalders and Cees Wiebes, *The Art of Cloaking Ownership: The Secret Collaboration and Protection of the German War Industry by the Neutrals; The Case of Sweden* (Amsterdam: Amsterdam University Press, 1996).

6. Steven Erlanger, "Hitler, It Seems, Loved Money and Died Rich," *New York Times,* August 8, 2002.

7. Wulf Schwarzwäller, *Hitlers Geld: Bilanz einer persönlichen Bereicherung* (Salzburg: Arthur Möwig, 1986).

8. Jonathan Petropoulos, *Art as Politics in the Third Reich* (Chapel Hill: University of North Carolina Press, 1996).

9. Albert Speer, *Inside the Third Reich* (New York: Avon, 1970), 109.

10. Heinrich Himmler's October 1943 speech in Posen is translated in Benjamin Sax and Dieter Kuntz, eds., *Inside Hitler's Germany: A Documentary History of Life in the Third Reich* (Lexington, MA: D.C. Heath, 1992), 392–93.

11. Friedemann Bedürftig and Christian Zentner, eds., *The Encyclopedia of the Third Reich* (New York: Macmillan, 1991), 507.

12. Hermann Göring quoted in International Military Tribunal, *Trial of the Major War Criminals,* vol. 9 (Nuremberg: International Military Tribunal, 1947), 545.

13. Robert Koehl, *The Black Corps: The Structure and Power Struggles of the Nazi SS* (Madison: University of Wisconsin Press, 1983), 173.

14. Jonathan Petropoulos, *The Faustian Bargain: The Art World in Nazi Germany* (New York: Oxford University Press, 2000).

15. Peter Hayes, "The Degussa AG and the Holocaust," in *Lessons and Legacies V: The Holocaust and Justice,* ed. Ronald Smelser (Evanston, IL: Northwestern University Press, 2002), 140–76; Hans Mommsen and Manfred Grieger, *Das Volkswagenwerk und seine Arbeiter im Dritten Reich* (Düsseldorf: ECON, 1996).

16. Frank Bajohr, *Aryanization in Hamburg: The Economic Exclusion of Jews and the Confiscation of Their Property in Nazi Germany* (New York: Berghahn, 2002), 279.

17. Wolfgang Dressen, *Betrifft: Aktion 3; Deutsche Verwerten jüdische Nachbarn: Dokumente zur Arisierung* (Berlin: Aufbau Verlag, 1998); Tina Walzer and Stephan Templ, *Unser Wien: "Arisierung" auf Österreich* (Berlin: Aufbau Verlag, 2001).

18. Jan T. Gross, *Neighbors: The Destruction of the Jewish Community in Jedwabne, Poland* (Princeton, NJ: Princeton University Press, 2001), 90, 110.

19. Aharon Appelfeld, "Buried Homeland," *New Yorker,* November 23, 1998, 48–61.

20. Martin Dean, "The Expropriation of Jewish Property in *Reichskommissariat* Ostland, 1941–44" in *"Arisierung" im Nationalsozialismus: Volksgemeinschaft, Raub und Gedachtnis,* ed. Fritz Bauer Institut (Irmtrud Wojak und Peter Hayes) (Frankfurt am Main: Campus, 2000), 201–18.

21. Ibid.

22. Eugen Kogon, *Der SS-Staat: Das System der deutschen Konzentrationslager* (Munich: W. Heyne, 1974), 294, my translation.

23. Franz Stangl quoted in James Pool, *Hitler and His Secret Partners: Contributions, Loot and Rewards, 1933–1945* (New York: Pocket Books, 1997), 330–31.

24. Bauer, *Rethinking the Holocaust,* 47–48.

25. Walther Hofer and Herbert Reginbogin, *Hitler, der Westen, und die Schweiz, 1936–1945* (Zurich: Verlag Neue Zürcher Zeitung, 2002).

26. Karl Schleunes, *The Twisted Road to Auschwitz: Nazi Policy Toward German Jews, 1933–1939* (Urbana: University of Illinois Press, 1970); Avraham Barkai, *From Boycott to Annihilation: The Economic Struggle of German Jews, 1933–1945* (Hanover, NH: University Press of New England, 1987).

27. For an exploration of this theme, see Wolfgang Seibel and Gerald Feldman, eds., *Networks of Persecution: The Holocaust as a Division-of-Labor-Based Crime* (New York: Berghan Books, 2003).

28. Jörg Friedrich, "The Apartment Keys Are to Be Relinquished to the House Manager," in *The German Public and the Persecution of the Jews, 1933–1945,* ed. Jörg Wolleberg (Atlantic Highlands, NJ: Humanities Press International, 1996), 150.

29. Barkai, *From Boycott to Annihilation,* 175, 186.

30. Hayes, "Degussa AG and Holocaust," 162. Hayes writes, "In the long run, Degussa expected to profit from the brutality in which it partook." He notes, however, that the company's immediate profits from its involvement in the Holocaust were relatively small.

31. Otto Karl Werckmeister, "Hitler the Artist," *Critical Inquiry* 23, no. 2 (Winter 1997): 294.

Frank Bajohr

Cliques, Corruption, and Organized Self-Pity: The Nazi Movement and the Property of the Jews

HANS REICHMANN WAS A LAWYER FOR THE CENTRAL ASSOCIATION OF German Citizens of the Jewish Faith in Berlin until early 1939. He then went into exile in London and wrote a vivid report early that summer about his experiences in Nazi Germany. Reichmann described in detail the widespread corruption that Jews were confronted with. He wrote of high-ranking SS leaders who smuggled money from Jews out of the country in return for so-called fees. And of police chiefs who accepted so-called donations as compensation for issuing passports to Jews. And of economic advisors of the Nazi party who got rich through "Aryanization." He also stressed that it was conspicuous that corruption was not limited to Nazi officials. Even lower-level civil servants were also "seized by the corruption devil":

> This state has undermined one of its very foundations. It has cor-
> rupted its civil service. The pillaging of the Jews will one day be
> avenged according to the standards of Greek tragedy. The state that
> became culpable as it plundered the Jews, whose servants shared
> the guilt and the spoils, shall perish, because its civil servants have
> lost their honor, security, and sense of duty. An acquaintance who
> was involved in foreign exchange criminal proceedings was surpris-
> ingly released from custody. "What did it cost?" I asked him, and
> this popular expression characterizes the present situation in a Ger-
> many that once was virtuous. "From five marks upward to 50,000
> marks; from the prison warden to the highest echelons—everyone
> was on the take."[1]

Political corruption as described by Hans Reichmann is generally defined as misuse of authority for private purposes and was one of the central structural problems during Nazi rule.[2] It is therefore hardly surprising that the persecution of Jews was likewise accompanied by all forms of personal enrichment, which were typical for the corruption under the Nazi system of power.

Of course there was no lack of official decrees that admonished the use of a strictly legal procedure against the Jews and sought to suppress every kind of individual and institutional enrichment. Hermann Göring and Hitler's deputy Rudolf Hess, for example, commanded that the "abolishment of the Jews from the economic scene" was to be exclusively the "job of the state," should be carried out on a "strictly legal basis," and was to be "for the sole benefit of the Reich."[3]

Nonetheless, the state claims to Jewish property could not be fully enforced. The financial and currency interests of the Reich were in a latent state of tension in relation to individual enrichment efforts and to the interests of the Nazi Party and its representatives. Especially the anti-Semitic activists within the party and its organizations did not show any willingness to subordinate their individual "claims" to the sole title of the Reich. While referring to their "sacrifices" during the *Kampfzeit* (formative period of struggle), they demanded their personal portion of the anticipated loot and underlined this expectation in a number of individual actions with which they had already staked their claims immediately after the Nazi seizure of power. Therefore, anti-Semitic terror after 1933 not only was marked by violent attacks on Jews but was also, right from the very beginning, targeted at their material possessions. Nazi propaganda did not respect such possessions as personal property; rather, they were ideologically redefined as "objects obtained by devious means" or "stolen national assets."[4] Many Nazi activists went "hunting for spoils" as early as the spring of 1933. Nazi storm troopers, for example, robbed jewelry and money from the homes of Jews in various cities, presented fictive home-search warrants, and maltreated representatives of the Jewish community, who were ultimately forced to hand over the keys for their strongholds.[5] These acts of wild plundering occurred particularly in the spring of 1933 and the summer of 1935, reaching a sad climax during the annexation of Austria in the spring of 1938. Wild confiscations of Jewish property were particularly prevalent in Vienna. A witness reported in this connection: "Then the demolition and 'requisitioning' began, i.e., the plundering of Jewish businesses, blackmailing of Jewish businessmen and private persons. In the shops, youths fourteen to sixteen years old appeared, led by SA men in their early 20s; they 'requisitioned' food, shoes, suits, fabrics, etc. Often the loot was transported off in lorries. In this way, for example, almost all the Jewish businesses in the city center were ravaged. . . . The clearance of the department store Schiffmann in the Taborstraße took three days. Workers with swastika armbands emptied storerooms, men in brown shirts kept the curious crowds away. . . . The police refused to provide any protection."[6]

Furthermore, during these pogromlike riots, more than 25,000 self-appointed "commissioners" occupied Jewish businesses and satisfied their material needs without any inhibitions.[7] Similar excesses took place during the November 1938 pogrom. For example, in the *Gau* (party district) Süd–Hannover–Braunschweig, the SS stormed into businesses and homes of Jews, confiscating money, valuables, typewriters, and vehicles. The National Socialist German Workers' Party (NSDAP) Reich's Treasurer reported about similar events in Stettin (which today is the city of Szczecin in Poland): "Some fellow party members from the regional office appeared in the homes or businesses of the Jews and first cut through the telephone lines. Then they presented the Jew with a 'deed of donation' duly prepared by a notary, pointing out that he now had the opportunity of giving something away. If they dared to resist, they were threatened with being shot."[8]

The Nazi party in Berlin was able to combine pogrom and personal enrichment in a particularly cynical way. Using similar methods as in Stettin, the *Gau* propaganda leader Waechter blackmailed leading representatives of the Berlin Jewish community, among them Leo Baeck, into paying a "voluntary donation" amounting to five million Reichsmarks as "reparations" for damages incurred. Among the beneficiaries of these so-called reparations were political leaders of the NSDAP, who had torn their shirts and coats during the nighttime plundering and acts of destruction, while the Berlin party organization received 200,000 Reichsmarks and the SA and SS were awarded 70,000 Reichsmarks "for day-long operations, including night duty."[9]

Robbery and "wild" confiscations of Jewish property reflected not only the precarious legal status of the Jews in Nazi Germany but also the pressure caused by the high expectations of the Nazi activists who hoped for a redistribution of Jewish property, channeled into their personal possession. Great expectations were associated with the Aryanization of Jewish property. Many regional branches of the party took advantage of Aryanization in order to set up black financial funds.

These funds were accumulated mainly from compulsory "donations" extorted from the Jewish owners for the approval of Aryanization contracts. In the *Gau* Saar-Palatinate, the NSDAP Gauleiter Buerckel founded a firm precisely for this purpose. Jewish owners, some of whom had already been transported off to concentration camps, were forced to sign the authorizations that commissioned the Nazi firm with the Aryanization of their businesses. In the end, it transferred 40 percent of the purchase price to a special account in the name of a party office which then distributed the money among so-called old fighters of the Nazi party.[10] In this form of patronage and nepotism, corruption bound its beneficiaries directly to the Nazi system of power, even if patronage did not aim at the creation of future loyalty but was declared a form of "reparations" for "sacrifices" in the past. Second, the enrichment from property of the Jews had a radicalizing effect on the anti-Jewish policy as a whole, because the plunder of the Jews gave rise to a constantly growing circle of beneficiaries whose keen and pressing interest was not to be held liable for compensation by the former Jewish owners.

Many of those who participated in the deportation and mass murders treated possessions of Jews as poolable assets for their own personal use. Representatives of the Jewish communities reported in their memoirs of fictive "home searches which had the sole purpose of equipping the Gestapo people with all kinds of things."[11] Some of the Gestapo officials who plundered Jewish homes during their "visits" afterward urged a speedup of the deportation formalities for the Jewish owners, deemed "uncomfortable witnesses."[12] Others, such as Willibald Schallert, head of the Hamburg department for Jewish forced laborers, used these visits primarily for sexual harassment of women. This kind of perpetrator not only was interested in satisfying his own material and nonmaterial needs but also primarily enacted his personal power over his victims, whom he was then able to "use, exchange and remove" at will.[13] The Berlin police chief, Count Helldorff, was particularly clever at blackmailing wealthy Jews and using this lucre as a personal source of income to finance his luxurious lifestyle. He imposed a passport ban for all Jews with assets of more than 300,000 Reichsmarks. An exit permit was attainable only against payment of a compulsory donation, which was also termed by those affected as the "Helldorff donation" and often amounted to several hundred thousand Reichsmarks.[14]

Although gain and corruption formed an important side effect of the destruction policy as earlier in the "Old Reich," they were even more common in the occupied territories in which the mechanisms of bureaucratic control were hardly developed at all. During the murderous actions against the Jewish people in the occupied areas, portions of their possessions disappeared into the pockets of the murderers and of those indirectly involved and therefore did not appear in the official recorded statistics. In an inspection report, the Reich Auditing Office determined in this connection:

> The monetary values accrued and the jewelry have not been registered in numerous cases so that no-one can ever find out whether and how much of the recorded values has already disappeared before. In the GG (*Generalgouvernement*), mass shipments of confiscated jewelry were made to the SS operational force Reinhard or the SS and police chief Lublin without an individual record by the accounts unit. A particularly blatant case occurred in the branch office Stanislau in Galicia. Here, confiscated money and jewels were retained on a vast scale. During an on-site inspection in the rooms of the responsible administrative official, Police Secretary Block, the representatives of the Auditing Office discovered large amounts of cash in every possible box and receptacle, desk, etc., as well as gold coins, in all possible currencies—including even 6,000 dollars—along with entire chests of valuable jewelry, all of which were neither collected nor officially registered.[15]

The connection between racism and absolute power over the victim promoted a corrupt master-race mentality among many perpetrators, embodied for example by Hans Frank, head of the German-controlled *Generalgouvernement* (GG) in Poland. He turned the GG virtually into a private enterprise of family and friends. In order to secure enough fur coats for his wife, even the Jewish Council in Warsaw was used as a procurement agency. Frank believed that only "representatives worthy of the great Reich can maintain the administrative authority. Only true members of the master race can rule in the East. I cannot let them appear as having humble, petit bourgeois living conditions. No, I have to guarantee them a more generous standard of living. This will be true for all of the regions in our great empire."[16]

It would go far beyond the limits of this essay were I to detail any further some of the many hundred, indeed thousands, of examples reflecting the enormous proportions which political corruption took on in connection with the persecution of the Jews. Instead I would like to turn briefly to its underlying causes, to which I have already alluded when I mentioned racism and absolute power. On the one hand, corruption under Nazi rule was a typical structural problem of conditions prevailing under a dictatorship. After 1933, there was no critical independent press, and there were no independent institutions of control. Nor was there any longer a critical public sphere, a civic culture where open opinion could have been aired regarding misgovernment and abuses. The destruction of the parliament demolished the extensive system of parliamentary control. Moreover, the Nazis politicized and controlled the justice system, reining in its possibilities for action.

On the other hand, important elements of Nazi rule that stimulated corruption had emerged long before 1933 within the Nazi movement. The Nazi Party disaggregated into an assemblage of cliques and coteries not subject to any control or the need to justify their actions. The formation of such cliques inside the party was due primarily to the fact that the NSDAP did not permit any institutionalized articulation of interests. Programmatic discussion and votes on preferred policy such as are common in democratic parties were unknown in the Nazi movement. Moreover, as a dictatorial party led by a führer, the NSDAP had no internal democratic structures or procedures (such as voting), elsewhere a key element in legitimizing governance and providing a source of checks and balances on power. Decisive for individuals' position was their personal bond to their immediate superior or their integration into internal party personnel networks. Those who behaved loyally could rightfully expect proper "care" and consideration and laid claim to that "entitlement." As a result, the party's political leaders were forced to distribute jobs, posts, and functions—and, after 1933, most particularly material extras and "incentives"—to keep a hold on their retinue and to accentuate their own position of power inside the party. This practice gave rise to extended and corrupt cliques, coteries, and circles as the substructure of the National Socialist movement.[17] For that reason alone, Nazi rule should not be misconceived as a complex, bureaucratic institutional system. Rather, it was an aggregation of personnel that exhibited certain neofeudal features. The individual Nazi functionaries did not see themselves solely as a small, precisely spinning wheel inside a huge bureaucratic machinery but rather as part of a ganglike community.

A central component of the self-image of the Nazi movement also proved conducive to corruption. The movement's internal cohesiveness was based to a large extent on the way its members styled themselves as a community of persons who had made substantial sacrifice. The NSDAP provided its followers with a simplistic and persuasive interpretation for their anxieties and frustrations: active National Socialists were victims of the "Weimar system," as it was termed, and in addition repeatedly suffered disadvantages as a result of their active support of the "movement." A great many Nazi activists attributed their frustrated hopes for advancement and their plans for life ravaged by unemployment to the malicious effects of the hated "Weimar system," dominated by Jews and Democrats. They redefined their joblessness as a form of sacrifice in the service of National Socialism. In his study on the autobiographical reports of "old fighters," the German historian Christoph Schmidt has convincingly shown how this self-styled sense of being a victim, of making a sacrifice for the cause, played a central role: "According to the descriptions, more than half suffered disadvantages in their profession or at work due to their being National Socialists. Especially activists who were younger or much older talk about having made such 'sacrifices' for the movement. About 30 percent of those reporting interpreted the economic crises they had suffered in their personal lives as the result of their work for the NSDAP. In part, these reports border on delusionary tales about permanent persecution and suffering disadvantages in a totally hostile environment."[18]

For that reason, there is some justification in also terming the NSDAP the "party of organized self-pity." After the Nazi seizure of power, that basic attitude stirred great hopes for redemption among party members. The supposed discrimination of Nazi Party members was now to be redressed and "compensated" by political means. In the event, organized self-pity led to institutionalized corruption, an organized nepotism which the Nazis used to enrich themselves after 1933 at the expense of their adversaries. The connection between their alleged "sacrifices" during the "period of struggle" and their deserved "compensation" after 1933 made up an important sociopsychological element of the "redemptive anti-Semitism" which Saul Friedländer has referred to as a specifically German or Nazi variant of anti-Semitism.[19]

Alongside the clique structures and the mentality of compensation that sprang from the stylized sense of "sacrifice," there was a third element that predestined the Nazi movement for corruption or lowered the scruples among its activists. Any person in the movement who expressed formal misgivings or even moral objections quickly ended up on the scrap heap. Formal misgivings and moral reservations were enough to trigger in Hitler an immediate fit of rage. They were considered the mark of a lack of energy and self-assertiveness. By contrast, a person who simply pocketed material goods without any consideration for the authorities demonstrated his strength of will, in the process accentuating his position of power in the Nazi hierarchy. Hitler in particular looked favorably on the so-called plucky daredevil, not the person with bureaucratic qualms: a man who did not give a damn for ethical principles and who almost sensed a certain glee in violating formal regulations when useful for the movement or him personally. One could also term this mechanism a negative habitual selection in whose course especially unscrupulous functionaries had their way—men for whom the boundary between "mine" and "yours" was quite fluid. In a movement where "ruthlessness" had a positive connotation, as in the phrases "ruthless vigorous action" or "ruthless extermination," a movement in which tolerance was denounced as "sentimental humanitarianism," the purported "right of the stronger" triumphed over behavior guided by normative principles and values. "After we've won, who'll ask us about methods?"[20] was how Goebbels aptly expressed this attitude.

But the pseudoidealistic phraseology of Nazi propaganda was unable to hide the fact that National Socialism was devoid of a core of basic values. That distinguished the Nazis from almost all other political movements—conservatives and Catholics, liberals and socialists—who derived their political conceptions from universalist basic values, such as the equality of all human beings before God, the idea of solidarity, personal freedom, and so on. In marked contrast, the unprincipled cult of "men of action" in the National Socialist movement led to presumptuousness and gang morality. The NSDAP propagated an idealism without ideals which only barely veiled the material greed of many functionaries. There was an evident nexus between this lack of basic values and the absence of scruples and morality. And while in its self-presentation the Nazi movement sought to embody authority, discipline, and order above all else, the type of the unscrupulous functionary, not bound to formal rules and regulations, represented de facto an anarchist element in the mix. In this manner, authority and anarchy melded in National Socialism into a glimmering melange.

If one visualizes the extent of the plundering, the "wild" personal enrichments, the illicit confiscations and uncontrolled distribution and selling off of Jewish possessions that accompanied the National Socialist policy of destruction, then corruption does not represent an isolated marginal phenomenon but a mass occurrence immanent in the system. This fact relativizes the image of an accurately working, mechanistically bureaucratic machinery, as the Holocaust is sometimes described.[21] It is true that the mass murder of the European Jews would not have been possible on such a massive scale without the institutions of a modern bureaucratic state. But it cannot be reduced to the image of a state crime, organized coolly and objectively and implemented with bureaucratic precision. Despotism, blatant obsession for personal gain on the part of persons and institutions, radical individual initiatives and measures, occasional anarchically violent methods of expropriation, the robbing and murdering of the Jews—these were also typical features of the Holocaust. Material gain was in fact not the prime reason behind the mass murders but simply a concomitant phenomenon. Yet it constituted a substantial motivational basis for many of those concerned, one whose importance should not be underestimated. "Base motives" such as greed contributed just as much to the Holocaust as ideological fanaticism or amoral bureaucratic routine.

NOTES

1. Hans Reichmann, *Deutscher Bürger und verfolgter Jude* (Munich: Oldenbourg, 1998), 260. All translations in this essay are mine.

2. On corruption and the Nazi regime in general, see Frank Bajohr, *Parvenüs und Profiteure: Korruption in der NS-Zeit* (Frankfurt: S. Fischer, 2001); Richard Grunberger, *A Social History of the Third Reich* (London: Weidenfeld and Nicolson, 1971), 90–107.

3. Decree by the representative for the Four Year Plan, 10 December 1938, *Akten der Partei-Kanzlei der NSDAP,* part 1 (Munich: Oldenbourg, 1983), microfiche, sheet 20400474f.

4. Symptomatic of this Nazi perspective on the property of Jews was the comment by the head of the Aryanization Office in Munich, who explained in a report: "The assets which are still in the hands of the Jews represent, according to National Socialist ideology, a part of the German national heritage,

of which in the course of time the German national comrades were mostly deprived, even though this was done under pretence of the legal reasons." Quotation from the conclusory report on the activities of the Vermögens-verwertung München GmbH, 25 January 1939, sheet 2, Archives of the Institut für Zeitgeschichte, Gm 07.94/8, vol. 1, Munich.

5. Frank Bajohr, *"Aryanisation" in Hamburg: The Economic Exclusion of Jews and the Confiscation of Their Property in Nazi Germany* (New York: Berghahn, 2002), 16–20.

6. *Deutschland Berichte der SOPADE,* vol. 5 (1938; repr., Salzhausen: Verlag Nettelbeck,1980), 732ff.

7. Hans Safrian, "Expediting Expropriation and Expulsion: The Impact of the 'Vienna Model' on anti-Jewish Policies in Nazi Germany, 1938," *Holocaust and Genocide Studies* 14, no. 3 (2000): 390–414.

8. Quotation from a letter of NSDAP Reich's Treasurer Schwarz to the Stabsleiter Stellvertreter des Führers, 2 December 1938, Bundesarchiv Berlin, NS 1/430, Berlin.

9. Hans-Erich Fabian, "Der Berliner Scherbenfonds," *Der Weg: Zeitschrift für Fragen des Judentums* 1, no. 37 (November 8, 1946): 1.

10. Letter from the Reich's Treasurer of the NSDAP to the Stabsleiter of the Stellvertreter des Führers, 2 December 1938, Bundesarchiv Berlin, NS 1/430, Berlin.

11. Max Plaut, "Records on the Time After 1939," p. 8, file 14.001.1, Archives of the Institute for the History of the German Jews, Hamburg.

12. Max Plaut, "The Jewish Community in Hamburg 1933–1945," excerpt from tape-recorded interview by Christel Riecke, 1973, p. 4., file 14.001.2, Archives of the Institute for the History of the German Jews, Hamburg.

13. On Schallert, see Beate Meyer, *"Jüdische Mischlinge": Rassenpolitik und Verfolgungserfahrung 1933–1945* (Hamburg: Dölling und Galitz, 1999), 62–67.

14. Compare Rex Harrison, "'Alter Kämpfer' im Widerstand," *Viertel-jahrshefte für Zeitgeschichte* 45 (1997): 385–422, esp. 406–9; Reichmann, *Deutscher Bürger,* 103f.

15. Reich Auditing Office inspection report, Bundesarchiv Berlin, 23.01/2073/2, sheet 86f, Berlin.

16. Hans Frank to Hans-Heinrich Lammers, 10 March 1942, Bundesarchiv Berlin, NS 19/2664, sheet 24f, Berlin.

17. Bajohr, *Parvenüs,* 17–34.

18. Christoph Schmidt, "Zu den Motiven 'alter Kämpfer' in der NSDAP," in *Die Reihen fast geschlossen,* ed. Detlev Peukert and Juergen Reulecke (Wuppertal: Hammer, 1981), 21–43, quotation at 28.

19. Saul Friedländer, *Nazi Germany and the Jews,* vol. 1, *The Years of Persecution 1933–1939* (New York: HarperCollins, 1997).

20. Quotation from Goebbels's diary entry dated June 16, 1941, in Joseph Goebbels, *Die Tagebücher von Joseph Goebbels,* ed. Elke Fröhlich, pt. 1, vol. 9 (Munich: Saur, 1998), 379.

21. See, for example, H. G. Adler, *Der verwaltete Mensch* (Tübingen: J. C. B. Mohr, 1974); Zygmunt Bauman, *Modernity and the Holocaust* (Ithaca, NY: Cornell University Press, 1991).

Gerard Aalders

"Lawful" Abuse of the Dutch Economy, 1940–1945

ALL OVER OCCUPIED EUROPE THE NAZIS TARGETED MONETARY GOLD found in central banks or national reserves. Germany needed this gold to finance its war industry. Not all war-material needs could be satisfied in Germany proper or obtained in the occupied areas. Hitler thus turned to neutrals to buy commodities and supplies he needed. The German Reichsmark, however, was not convertible. In any event, neutral states preferred payments in Swiss francs, which served as a broadly accepted international currency during the war. Neutrals also accepted payments in gold, which the Nazis easily stole from vaults of central banks in occupied countries. Nazi large-scale looting of gold also occurred in the Netherlands. Theft of Dutch gold was, however, just one of several methods utilized by the Nazis to exploit the Netherlands during the years of occupation. The Germans inflicted economic damage from the first day of Nazi rule. Yet in the beginning the Dutch public remained largely unaware of such exploitation. This lack of awareness is illustrated in the case of the *Reichskreditkassenscheine,* or Reich credit bills, as well as other developments to be discussed in this essay.

The German attack on the Netherlands started in the early morning of May 10, 1940, and five days later, all Dutch forces had surrendered. The country remained under military control until May 29, 1940, when a German civil government was introduced. The Austrian-born Dr. Arthur Seyss-Inquart was appointed by Hitler as *Reichskommissar* (Reich commissioner) to lead the Dutch administrative apparatus. The *Reichskommissar für die besetzten niederländischen Gebiete* (Reich commissioner for the occupied Dutch areas) got his instructions directly from Hitler, but in the field of economics, Hermann Göring also had the right to give guidelines as he was the *Beauftragter für den Vierjahresplan* (in charge of the reformation of Germany into a war economy). The Dutch government had fled into exile in London but had instructed the secretaries-general (the chief civil servants in the ministries) to stay at their posts and continue their work, as long as it remained within the terms of the existing laws and the constitution. In effect, the occupier took over a fully operational administrative system. The secretaries-general were placed under the supervision of four German *Generalkommissare* (general commissioners), of whom Dr. Hans Fischböck of Financial and Economic Affairs was the most important.[1] After Seyss-Inquart's inauguration, no immediate steps were taken; at this early stage of the occupation the Germans did not want trouble, and they took great pains to avoid civil disturbances. Neither did they expect to encounter great troubles because the Dutch were considered to be fellow "Aryans" of the same Germanic race who might be induced to accept the National Socialist ideology and, in due course, become an integrated part of the Third Reich. The installation of a civil government had important political and psychological advantages, not least in going some way toward quelling fears that the country might be annexed. This fear undoubtedly contributed to keeping the population quiet, which had the additional advantage of requiring a relatively small occupation force to control the country.[2]

EXPLOITATION OF THE DUTCH ECONOMY

The exploitation of the Dutch economy manifested itself in various ways: from the regular buying of goods in the beginning through forced deliveries to straight looting toward the end of the war and everything one can think of in between. Initially, for the Dutch economy the occupation meant an upswing, hard-stricken as it was by the depression of the 1930s.[3] But gradually, as time passed, the exploitation more and more acquired the character of old-fashioned extortion methods. It remains a remarkable phenomenon that the Nazi regime for quite a long time—and certainly in the beginning—tried to keep up an appearance of adhering to international law and often sought to justify its actions by reference to the Hague Convention on Land Warfare (1907).[4] When Seyss-Inquart issued his decrees and measures, he always referred to the *Erlass des Führers* (Führer's Decree) of May 18, 1940 (which stated that he was directly subordinate to the head of the German state), and asserted that he derived his authority as supreme representative of the occupying power from this decree in line with the Hague Convention. Section 1 of the decree read: "Should the interests of the Greater German Reich . . . render it necessary, the *Reichskommissar* may take the necessary measures, including those of a legislative nature. These decrees by the *Reichskommissar* have the force of law."[5] That the German interests took precedence goes without saying, and it is evident that Hitler's private interpretation of the convention provided him with ample space to maneuver as he wished.

Reichskreditkassenscheine

Before outright confiscation and looting took place, subtler means were used.[6] *Reichskreditkassenscheine* (Reich credit bills) were introduced in the first stage of German rule. They were meant for use by the occupying forces, and although they were issued by the Reichsbank, they were pure military currency. The *Scheine* (banknotes) were not legal tender in Germany proper but exclusively for use by the military in the occupied countries. The notes had an inflationary effect, as extra buying power was pumped into the economy while at the same time no goods were brought in but, on the contrary, goods were taken out. In various Dutch cities, so-called *Reichskreditkassen* (Reich credit bureaus) were established to bring the notes in unlimited quantities into circulation. They gave the Germans, in the words of Dr. L. J. A. Trip, president of De Nederlandsche Bank (the Netherlands Central Bank, or DNB), "complete financial control." The notes had quite a short life of circulation; the DNB took them in (on orders of the Dutch state, which also bore the expenses) and exchanged the *Scheine* at the earliest opportunity for Dutch legal tender in order to combat the inflationary tendencies.[7] The circulation of the *Scheine* was provided for by the capitulation treaty, and the Germans repeatedly used the treaty to break down the resistance of Dutch authorities during financial negotiations: if they refused to come to terms, the Germans saw no other way out than to pay by means of *Scheine* to which they were entitled by treaty. In total, the Netherlands Central Bank, but in effect the State of the Netherlands, suffered a loss of 133.6 million guilders on the *Reichskreditkassenscheine*.[8]

Straight Looting and Selling Under Duress

Straight looting or, as it were, robbing at gunpoint hardly happened in the Netherlands; only toward the end of the war did the Germans confiscate whatever they needed. But they nonetheless exploited the Dutch economy in a variety of ways. The most tragic example is the nearly 100 percent expropriation of Dutch Jewry. Through looting by decree (*Verordnung* 148 of August 8, 1941), between three hundred and four hundred million guilders in securities and obligations were submitted under duress and subsequently sold at the Amsterdam Stock Exchange.[9] Also all other Jewish possessions (close to 100 percent) were confiscated through issuing looting decrees. Important in this respect was the "Aryanization" of the Jewish businesses that were taken over by Germans or Dutch collaborators. Small firms, on the other hand, were simply liquidated and their owners sent to a concentration camp. Aryanization figures are roughly known (about eighty-one million guilders), but they mean little because the Germans always paid a fantasy price for the companies and firms. As a rule, about a third of the company's value was paid. At least there was an estimated amount of roughly a third of the real sales price which was promised to be paid (in one hundred installments; i.e., over twenty-five years) to the expropriated former Jewish owner. In reality this policy was a sham because most of the owners (and their heirs) were murdered within a few years after the issue of the Aryanization decrees. Here, too, however, the Germans liked to keep up the appearance of legal formalities.[10] Goods, especially works of art, were also sold under duress. By means of threats or other illegal means of persuasion, owners were pressured to sell goods they would have preferred to keep.[11]

The Allied forces deemed sale under duress to be legally equivalent to straight looting. They were aware of German tactics from an early date and warned the Nazis in their declaration of January 3, 1943, that the Allies

> reserve all their rights to declare invalid any transfers of, or dealings with, property, rights and interests of any description whatsoever which are, or have been, situated in the territories which have come under the occupation or control, direct or indirect, of the governments with which they are at war or which belong or have belonged, to persons, including juridical persons, resident in such territories. This warning applies whether such transfers or dealings

have taken the form of open looting or plunder, or of transactions apparently legal in form, even when they purport to be voluntarily effected.[12]

The Allied declaration has had great influence. After the war it became the legal basis on which the restitution processes in various countries were founded. During the war, however, it had an undesirable side effect: the Germans and their neutral buyers (fencers) became more careful and tried to hide their activities as much as possible.

Kapitalverflechtung

Between May 1940 and the fall of 1941 the Germans attempted to penetrate the Dutch economy by means of *Kapitalverflechtung* (capital interlocking), an attempt to achieve a considerable participation in and influence on the economy of the Low Countries. For various reasons it appeared to be much less successful than initially expected.[13] In a letter from the Reich Ministry of Economics to a number of German banks, the aim of the *Verflechtung* (interlocking) was clearly explained:

> It should be attempted to achieve a participation of the German economy in the Netherlands to the greatest extent possible. . . . With the investment of capital should be connected as far as possible a dominating influence in the management of the enterprise and an infiltration of personnel. . . . Special consideration must be given to the important key-positions in the Dutch economy. . . . In addition I request that you find out yourself which interesting positions in the Dutch economy in the area of your competence should be considered as suitable for German participation and submit to me suggestions accordingly.[14]

That the Nazis wanted to use the Dutch industrial resources for their war efforts is evident, but it is remarkable that no effective plans had been developed to reach this ambitious goal.

Of course there had been extensive planning in the economic field (as for example through the Four-Year Plan) to attempt to make Germany independent of the supply of raw materials.[15] It seems that *Reichsmarschall* Göring had counted on a short war, and a fast interlocking of capital fitted into that vision. It was assumed that the companies in the overrun countries had little choice but to follow the directives of Berlin. Originally the Germans had three procedures in mind: (1) compulsory *Verflechtung* of particular Dutch companies with selected German firms on orders from the general staff; (2) the creation of a "friendly interlocking atmosphere" with the voluntary help of influential citizens in both Germany and the Netherlands; and (3) *Verflechtung* through private initiatives but under the supervision of the state.

Due to the resistance of the firms, the first, compulsory method had practically no success and brought nothing but unrest. The second was—with the war having just broken out—not very popular either. Only the last method seemed, after a year of predominant failure, to be a way that could bring a modest success through buying shares in the big enterprises or making use of capital increase.[16]

Above all, Berlin was interested in the shares of four worldwide Dutch concerns: Unilever (food), Philips (electrical engineering), Shell (oil), and AKU (wood fiber). Commissioners were appointed for Shell, Unilever, and Philips in order to make them work for the Reich's war economy to their fullest capacity. Philips and Unilever had taken a number of legal measures to protect their possessions and had moved their head offices out of Europe while holding companies had been set up, in territories out of reach of Berlin. A modest success was achieved in the case of Shell because of an agreement with the oil company and its subsidiary Astra Romana, on the one hand, and the Kontinentale Öl, on the other hand. This agreement guaranteed maximum capacity of oil production by Astra Romana, a full subsidiary of Shell in Romania. The majority of AKU's capital was brought into German hands, but this success was mainly due to a capital increase that resulted from the construction of a new wood-fiber factory and from purchases on the stock market.[17]

Other companies such as Koninklijke Nederlandse Hoogovens (steelworks), Stork (machinery), Heineken Breweries, Wilton Fei-jenoord (shipyards) and Verenigde Koninklijke Papierfabrieken Van Gelder (paper mills) were also put on the *Verflechtung* list. In some cases the Germans had some success: Vereinigte Stahlwerke (steel) acquired 40 percent of Hoogovens, while the shares of the Dutch aviation plant, Fokker, were taken over by the Bank der Deutschen Luftfahrt on behalf of the German Air Ministry. As of November 1941, however, German capital participations amounting to (only) fifty million guilders (sixty-five million Reichsmarks) had been acquired, and this modest amount would not be exceeded.[18]

Elimination of Foreign Currency Barriers

Much more dramatic for Dutch economic life was the abolition of the currency border. The position of the Netherlands differed from that of other occupied Western European countries because the currency frontiers between the Reich and the Netherlands had been abolished on April 1, 1941. In Norway, the only other country with a civil government, the barriers were not removed. Traffic in goods between Germany and the Netherlands was subject to myriad restrictions, which were enforced by the customs services of both countries. Import and export activities required permits and payment of the corresponding duties. Dutch suppliers did not receive payment directly from the German buyers but rather through a Dutch Clearing Institute, which dealt with its German counterpart, the Deutsche Verrechnungskasse. The two institutes settled their reciprocal debts and claims against each other. Until January 1, 1940, the Netherlands had nearly always had a claim outstanding against Germany, although rarely for more than two million guilders. The Netherlands had an ample supply of exchange and a favorable balance of payments. Currency inspection entailing government management of international financial transactions was therefore unnecessary.

The invasion changed this situation drastically. Intervention was vital to avert the capital flight and unbridled speculation in foreign currencies, gold, and securities that would devalue the guilder. The stock exchange closed, banks were instructed to suspend payments (under a moratorium), and currency restrictions were imposed that blocked financial transactions with other countries. The Dutch government's emergency foreign currency measure, issued on the day of the invasion (which intended to use the available foreign currency to fund the war effort and food supplies), was replaced by the foreign currency ordinance imposed by the Nazis on June 27, 1940 (which tightly regulated financial transactions with foreign countries).

Upon occupying the Netherlands, the Nazis enacted a series of measures to "liberalize" financial transactions between the two countries in three stages. In the first stage (from May 9 to November 1, 1940), financial transactions were severely restricted. In the second stage (from November 1, 1940, to April 1, 1941), many of the restrictions were relaxed, although foreign currency transactions were not entirely free. Instead, a few openings appeared in the currency barrier.

This period is therefore considered a time of *durchlöcherte Devisen-grenze* (foreign currency frontier with loopholes). Dutch financial circles objected strenuously to these measures. On April 1, 1941, the resistance ceased at the start of the third stage in which the foreign currency frontier between the Netherlands and Germany was lifted. Henceforth, monetary transactions in the Netherlands were subject to the same regulations as German domestic ones, although a few restrictions were introduced for certain securities. The disappearance of the foreign currency frontier signified the outright economic annexation of the Netherlands. From April 1, 1941, until the liberation in May 1945, De Nederlandsche Bank was forced to exchange any amounts of guilders in German Reichsmarks at a—particularly unfavorable—rate set by the Nazis.[19] As a result, the Netherlands was inundated with German Reichsmarks, and the sale of Dutch property began.

Hitler aimed to integrate the Dutch economy with the German one to have unrestricted access to Dutch goods, commodities, and in some cases the means of production. Thanks to the success of the abolition of the currency frontier, the relative failure of the *Kapitalver-flechtung* was not so important anymore. Such a course of action also facilitated deployment of Dutch industry for the benefit of the Nazi war effort. The measure allowed the indirect looting to continue with a minimum of restrictions. Again, every effort was made to maintain the appearance of legality and proper procedure.

The lifting of the currency barrier led to the systematic looting of the Dutch economy, albeit again without the direct knowledge of the public and companies. After all, they got paid for their goods in regular Dutch guilders. Few people realized that many of the guilders in circulation were nothing other than camouflaged Reichsmarks. The measures enabling this indirect looting required coercion from the Nazi authorities. Trip, the president of De Nederlandsche Bank, refused to take responsibility for the consequences and resigned. His successor was M. M. Rost van Tonningen, a member of the NSB (National Socialistische Beweging—National Socialist Movement, the Dutch fascist party), who obeyed the Nazis to the extreme. Upon the liberation of the Netherlands, De Nederlandsche Bank held a claim of about six billion Reichsmarks which by then were almost worthless. When the foreign currency frontier was lifted, many securities and bonds also had disappeared to Germany without any tangible compensation. Some of the German issuing institutions used the elimination of the foreign currency frontier to redeem loans ahead of schedule. Such transactions were very advantageous because of the favorable conversion rate of Reichsmarks to guilders. Many German institutions benefited from this inexpensive opportunity to repay their foreign debts.

DUTCH MONETARY GOLD

The Germans made every effort to gain control over raw materials in the occupied areas and exploit them wherever they could, but the lack of certain raw materials remained a problem, although Germany had managed to overcome deficiencies in natural resources of raw materials through scientific research. During the Hitler era the production of ersatz materials reached an unprecedented scale, but certain materials and products were impossible to manufacture in the Reich. For them, Berlin stayed dependent on imports from the neutral nations of Europe and elsewhere, buying, for example, ball bearings and iron ore from Sweden; ammunition, weapons, and precision tools from Switzerland; tungsten ore from the Iberian Peninsula; and chrome from Turkey. The problem for Hitler's regime was that these countries wanted to be paid either in gold or in hard currency (which itself could be bought only with gold).

After 1933 the published gold reserves of the Reichsbank had grown steadily lower and by 1937 came to a standstill at 31.1 million U.S. dollars, an amount that during the years of war would not alter. But the Reichsbank also had a secret reserve of gold, built up since 1933 by the then-president of the bank, Hjalmar Schacht. With the outbreak of war, its total had risen to $82.7 million. So Hitler had $113.8 million worth of gold at his disposal *plus*—due to annexations—$99 million in gold from the Austrian and $33.8 million in gold from the Czechoslovakian central banks.[20] If we convert the total amounts of looted gold to kilograms, we arrive at a total quantity of 552,000 kg. The gold originated from, respectively, Belgium (198,000 kg), the Netherlands (146,000 kg), Italy (46,000 kg), Austria (92,000 kg), and Czechoslovakia (39,000 kg), with another 31,000 kg from Albania, Greece, Yugoslavia, Luxembourg, and Poland altogether (totaling rounded-off quantities). That Germany used the looted gold for the purchase of strategic materials has already been explained. But how did Berlin loot the Dutch monetary gold?

The board of De Nederlandsche Bank had been worried about the situation in Europe long before World War II actually broke out. The Netherlands had been able to keep out of the First World War, but there was no guarantee of this in a next war. Therefore, on September 10, 1938, a first transport of gold bars was shipped from the Netherlands to New York, and many more shipments were to follow, until war broke out in May 1940. By that time most of the Dutch monetary gold stock had been brought into safety in the United States, Great Britain, and South Africa.[21]

On May 9, 1940, the eve of the German attack, approximately 35 percent (i.e., 192,360 kg) of the Netherlands Central Bank's total gold stock was still in the Netherlands: about 70,605 kg remained at the Amsterdam headquarters of DNB, with another 113,755 kg at the Rotterdam branch.

On the night of the German invasion, two freighters with the headquarters' gold on board escaped to London, but a transport of 937 gold bars (11,012 kg) from the Rotterdam branch failed to reach the British capital. The ship struck a mine before it could reach even the North Sea and sank. The Germans managed to recover 816 bars (9,571 kg). The Prize Court in Hamburg decided in 1941 that the bars were to be considered prize (war booty), and they were transferred to the Reichsbank in Berlin.[22] The missing bars were dug up after the war.

About 80 percent of DNB's gold had found a safe haven abroad, while approximately 102,743 kilograms got left behind in Rotterdam. This part, a fifth of the total Dutch monetary gold stock, was to become a looting target for the Nazis, and during 1941 and 1942 the whole stock was moved to the Reich.[23]

The confiscation of the gold was carried out in the approved German method: with reference to the Hague Convention. It was looting in disguise, spoliation behind a facade of international law. The confiscation of gold was done for the benefit of purchasing strategic materials, but it was (at least partly) presented as a victor's right under the provisions of the Hague Convention. Presenting a legalistic appearance clearly satisfied a hidden need, and straight looting happened only at the end of the war with German forces in retreat and the country immersed in chaos. The most favored pretext to draw in the gold was the cost of the occupation, which was governed by article 52 of the Hague Convention on Land Warfare (1907):

> Requisitions in kind and services shall not be demanded from municipalities or inhabitants except for the needs of the army of occupation. They shall be in proportion to the resources of the country, and of such a nature as not to involve the inhabitants in the obligation of taking part in military operations against their own country.[24]

This was a rule open to broad interpretation. Already on July 16, 1940, the Nazi decree VO 49 (*Über die Vergüting für Leistungen für die deutschen Wehrmacht in den Niederlanden*—About Recompense for Achievements of the German Army in the Netherlands) was issued. It settled, among other matters, regular deliveries of goods and services of Dutch authorities and civilians to the Wehrmacht: the so-called R-Leistungen, which was further specified in article 2 of decree 49. Seyss-Inquart never ordered the occupation costs in the usual sense of the Hague Convention, and the deliveries of goods, services, and gold had little relation to the occupation costs proper, which refer to food, housing, clothing, and transportation required by the occupying forces. The *Reichskommissar* imposed the occupation costs under various pretexts, disguised as additional war levies. For the civil German government, costs totaling 173.8 million guilders were charged (a guilder was worth $1.88 in 1940).[25] The Wehrmacht received payments of 6.356 billion. The Dutch authorities regularly protested against the imposed expenses that they considered neither fair nor reasonable along the lines of the Hague Convention, but their protests were always in vain.[26]

Operation Barbarossa—Hitler's war against the Soviets that began on June 22, 1941—furnished Seyss-Inquart with another pretext to extort a *monthly* addition to the war on communism. Was it not also for the sake of the Netherlands that Hitler waged war against the Soviet Union? The occupier decided that it was. The *Reichskommissar* and Rost van Tonningen, the newly appointed DNB president and secretary-general of the Ministry of Finance, eagerly agreed with a Dutch contribution of 50 million Reichsmarks, of which 20 percent (10 million Reichsmarks) was to be paid in gold. Seyss-Inquart preferred the term *weitere Kriegszahlung* (further war payment) for this newly imposed levy because it fitted more or less in the terms of the Hague Convention. That was also why he rejected Rost van Tonningen's wording of a "contribution to the warfare in the East": nothing, not even remotely, could be found in the convention that could make an occupied country pay for a war against another country.

The war against the Soviets had started in June 1941, but the order to transfer gold to Berlin had come nine months later, in March 1942. This order implied—to start with—an "overdue payment" of nine times 10 million Reichsmarks in gold: in total 90 million Reichsmarks in gold on top of the already claimed 10 million Reichsmarks in gold. The first gold transfer was made on April 29, 1942, the last on September 7, 1942. Then the transports stopped for a simple reason: there was no gold left in the vaults of DNB. The war on communism cost the Netherlands 68,995 kilograms of gold.[27]

The German thirst for gold was not restricted to monetary gold alone. In June 1940, under the foreign exchange regulations, all Dutch residents were summoned to register their privately held gold (including gold coins) with the central bank (in accordance with decree VO 27 of June 27, 1940, *Über die Devisenbewirtschaftung*—About the Regulation of Foreign Currency Transactions). The next step was the forced sale of this gold to DNB, which in turn got its orders from Berlin to sell this "civilian" gold against Reichsmarks to the Reichsbank. The Dutch public was paid in guilders for the submitted gold. In this way the Nazis took 28,835 kilograms of gold from the public and moved it to Berlin. This gold transaction was yet another example of sale under duress.

Most of the gold extracted from the Netherlands was sold in or through Switzerland, which functioned as a *Golddrehscheibe* (gold turntable). The money-laundering process was carried out in three steps: (1) the Swiss National Bank exchanged the (looted) gold for Swiss francs; (2) Germany used these francs for its purchases of materials in, for example, Sweden, Portugal, or Spain; and (3) the central banks in these countries exchanged the francs back for gold at the Swiss National Bank, which in many cases happened to be gold originating from the Reichsbank. The Swiss alleged to have clean hands because they claimed not to have known that the gold had been stolen in occupied Europe, and the neutrals could assert that they had obtained the gold in the normal international *Zahlungsverkehr* (flow of payments).[28] At the Reparation Conference in Paris (November 9 to December 21, 1945) the Netherlands claimed losses of $14.148 billion (25.725 billion guilders, based on the purchasing power of the guilder of 1938). The Netherlands never received more than about 2 percent in compensation of the total damage inflicted upon the country.[29]

CONCLUSION

The German occupation of the Netherlands was a costly affair for the Low Countries, which were exploited in every possible way. Jews were totally removed from economic (and also public) life, and German citizens or Dutch traitors kept the Jewish businesses as their own. Moreover, Jews lost all their other possessions as well. From the first day of the occupation, inflationary impulses in the form of *Reichskreditkassenscheine* (Reich credit bills) threatened the Dutch economy. Although the *Kapitalverflechtung* (capital interlocking) seemed promising at first, it became a failure. However, the elimination of the currency border was a great success from the German point of view because it meant the complete annexation of the Dutch economy and unrestricted access to the Dutch market in which goods and services were paid in inconvertible Reichsmarks. The non-Jewish citizens did not feel its impact directly because they got paid in the national guilder. But it was the State of the Netherlands (and so in the end its population) that bore the loss.

All the monetary gold of the Netherlands, as well as the gold in private possession, was claimed by the Germans and unlawfully transferred (contrary to the stipulations of the Hague Convention) to Berlin, where the Nazi government used it for the purchase of materials and goods in the neutral countries. A remarkable constant in the German policy with regard to the Netherlands was that it always tried to present illegal actions with reference to the Rules on Land Warfare. The Germans' devotion to sham legality was constantly perceptible in their issuing of decrees, which were utterly profitable for themselves but outright harmful for the Dutch people.

In the end, however, only the Jews (and Romanys) were systematically looted of all their property. The looting from the Dutch Jews was a highly systematic operation. The process was based largely on several regulations, which were enforced as laws. The first victims were associations and foundations, and the next were Jewish businesses affected by the Aryanization of the economy. Jews were to be excluded from economic participation. The regulation of August 8, 1941, "concerning procedures for Jewish financial assets," forced all Jews to open accounts at the Lippmann, Rosenthal & Co. Bank in Amsterdam and to deposit their cash and transfer their bank balances there. They were also required to turn in their securities and checks at this bank that was set up for looting.

Less than a year later, the regulation of May 1942 was the coup de grâce for Jewish private property. "All types of collections"—gold, silver, platinum, art, jewels, patent rights, copyrights, and concessions—had to be surrendered. Other regulations ordered Jews to turn buildings, farmland, mortgage and nonmortgage monetary claims, insurance policies, and pensions over to the occupying powers. From June 1940 on, the possessions of Jews who had fled were confiscated as enemy assets. In the summer of 1942, when the deportations began, the homes of Jews who had been taken away were emptied and sold. According to my calculation, the Nazis stole at least 1 billion guilders in assets from the Dutch Jews. This amount is the equivalent of about 14 billion guilders today, or approximately 6,700 billion dollars.

NOTES

1. Gerhard Hirschfeld, *Nazi Rule and Dutch Collaboration* (Oxford, 1988), 12–54.

2. Niod (Nederlands Instituut voor oorlogsdocumentatie—Netherlands Institute for War Documentation), Notities voor het Geschiedwerk, nr. 91, "Het ontstaan van het Duitse Rijkscommissariaat voor Nederland."

3. Hein A. M. Klemann, *Nederland 1938–1948: Economie en samenleving in jaren van oorlog en bezetting* (Amsterdam, 2002).

4. Allan Bullock, *Hitler and Stalin: Parallel Lives* (London, 1993), 336; Michael Stolleis, *The Law Under the Swastika: Studies on Legal History in Nazi Germany* (Chicago, 1998), 7.

5. *Reichsgesetzblatt* [*German State Gazette*], pt. 1, p. 778, my translation. Compare article 43 of the Hague Convention (1907): "The authority of the legitimate power having in fact passed into the hands of the occupant, the latter shall take all the measures in his power to restore, and ensure, as far as possible, public order and safety, while respecting, unless absolutely prevented, the laws in force in the country."

6. For a broad survey of the systematic systems of looting and confiscation in the Netherlands, see Gerard Aalders, *Roof: De ontvreemding van joods bezit tijdens de Tweede Wereldoorlog* (The Hague, 1999, English translation forthcoming).

7. L. J. A. Trip, *De Duitsche bezetting van Nederland en de Financiële ontwikkeling van het land gedurende de jaren der bezetting* (The Hague, 1946), 5.

8. Ibid., 17–18.

9. Aalders, *Roof,* 171–200.

10. Ibid., 135–47.

11. Ibid., 61–105, 211–28.

12. Inter-Allied Declaration Against Acts of Dispossession Committed in Territories Under Enemy Occupation or Control. See *Foreign Relations of the United States,* vol. 1, *General* (1943; Washington, DC, 1968), 443–44.

13. L. de Jong, *Het Koninkrijk der Nederlanden in de Tweede Wereldoorlog,* 14 vols. (The Hague, 1972), 4:375–80; Otfried Ulshöfer, *Die Einflussnahme auf Wirtschaftunternehmungen in den besetzten nord-, west- und südosteuropäischen Ländern* (Tübingen, 1958), 140–42; Gerard Aalders, "Three Ways of German Economic Penetration in the Netherlands: Cloaking, Capital Interlocking and 'Aryanization,'" in *Die "Neuordnung" Europas: NS Wirtschaftspolitik in den besetzten Gebieten,* ed. Richard J. Overy, Gerhard Otto, and Johannes Houwink ten Cate (Berlin, 1997).

14. Confidential circular letter from the Reich Ministry of Economics (Dr. Landfried) to the banks, 7 September 1940, Niod, Archief 264, Chief Counsel War Crimes Nurnberg, N 84/1.

15. A. (Hans) J. van der Leeuw, "Aanpassing en collaboratie," in *Samenwerken met de vijand: Verslag van het symposium over de vraag waar de aanpassing ophoudt en collaboratie begint* (Voorburg, 1981), 16–23.

16. Map B, "Niederschrift über die Sitzung des interministeriellen Ausschusses über Fragen der Kapitalbeteiligung," 23 September 1941, Niod, Archief 266, N 85/3.

17. Map C, "Memorandum on German Participation in the Netherlands, Belgium and Greece, by Rademacher (German Foreign Office/Auswärtiges Amt)," 22 November 1941, Niod, Archief 266, BBT, Box 7. For Unilever see also de Jong, *Koninkrijk,* 2:428; for Philips see also Map A1, "File note re: acquisition of the firm Philips, Eindhoven (Holland)," 30 November 1946, Niod, Archief 266, BTT, Box 7; and Frits Philips, *45 jaar met Philips* (Rotterdam, 1976), 106–14. For AKU see also Han Magnus Enzensberger, *Ermittlungen gegen die Deutsche Bank* (Nördlingen, 1985), 257–65. For Astra Romana and Shell see Enzensberger, *Ermittlungen,* 265–68; and H. Gabriëls, *Koninklijke Olie: de eerste honderd jaar 1890–1990* (The Hague, 1990), 105–43 passim.

18. Memorandum for the files Dresdner Bank, 20 September 1940, Niod, Archief 264, N 84/1; Map C, Archief 266; "Zusammengefasster Bericht über die Kapitalverflechtung mit Holland und Belgien seit der Besatzung im Mai 1940" ["Condensed report on capital interlocking with Holland and Belgium since the occupation in May 1940"], n.d., Niod, Archief 266, BBT, Box 7; "Vermerk über die am 6. and 11. September 1940 unter Vorsitz von Ministerialdirigent Dr. Schlotterer stattgefundenen Besprechungen über wirtschaftliche Beziehungen zu den besetzten Gebieten," 16 September 1940, Niod, Fin. Div. fr. collection RWM, Feindvermögen, vol. 42. For Hoogovens during the war, see also Johan de Vries, *Hoogovens*

IJmuiden 1918–1968: Ontstaan en groei van een basisindustrie [*Brith and Growth of a Basis Industry*] (IJmuiden, 1968).

19. The exchange rate was 75.36 guilders for 100 Reichsmarks. Before the invasion, the rate had been about 15 guilders for 100 Reichsmarks.

20. *Independent Commission of Experts: Switzerland—Second World War; Gold Transactions in the Second World War; Statistical Review with Commentary; A Contribution to the Conference on Nazi Gold in London* (Bern, 1997), 16–20; *Independent Commission of Experts: Switzerland—Second World War; Switzerland and Gold Transactions in the Second World War; Interim Report* (Bern, 1998). Prices are as of 1945: $1.125 per kilogram of fine gold.

21. Johan de Vries, *Geschiedenis van de Nederlandsche Bank: Vijfde deel; De Nederlandsche Bank van 1914 tot 1948; Trips tijdvak 1931–1948 onderbroken door de Tweede Wereldoorlog.*

22. Ministerie van Financiën (Dutch Ministry of Finance), "Adjudication by the Tripartite Commission for the Restitution of Monetary Gold on a Claim Submitted by the Royal Netherlands Government for the Restitution of 145.650 kgs of Fine Gold," June 9, 1958, Archief Bewindvoering, Rubriek 1514, Gestolen Goud. The Hague.

23. Ministerie van Financiën, "Nederlandsch goudbezit," Archief Binnenlands Geldwezen; Ministerie van Financiën, "Questionnaire on Gold," Archief Bewindvoering; Ministerie van Financiën, "Adjudication by Tripartite Commission." See also de Vries, *Geschiedenis van de Nederlandsche Bank,* 361. The Hague.

24. For the full text of the Hague Convention, see http://www1.umn.edu/humanrts/instree/hague-convention-1907.html.

25. The same exchange rate applied for 1941; it dropped to $1.25 in 1942, and there were no quotations in 1943 and 1944, but in 1945 the rate had gone up to $2.65 for 1 guilder.

26. Trip, *Duitsche bezetting,* 17–18.

27. Ministerie van Financiën, "Postwar Report," Archief Bewindvoering, Rubriek 1514, Gestolen Goud.

28. Jean Ziegler, *Die Schweiz, das Gold und die Toten* (Munich, 1997), 80–90.

29. G. M. Verrijn Stuart, "Enkele Aspekten van de Duitse Herstelbetalingen," *Internationale Spectator* 10, no. 15 (1956): 415–36. Compare de Jong, *Koninkrijk,* 12:293. De Jong estimates the reparation payments at 4 percent of the total damage and losses.

Jan T. Gross

After Auschwitz: The Reality and Meaning of Postwar Anti-Semitism in Poland

> *To write a poem after Auschwitz is barbaric.*
> —*Theodor Adorno*

YOU HAVE, OF COURSE, RECOGNIZED THE POINT OF DEPARTURE OF MY remarks. Regrettably, it turned out to be possible after Auschwitz to do many a thing far more objectionable than writing poetry.

A moment of realization that some unaccounted for, "difficult" past is buried in the immediate postwar history of my mother country came for me when reading a book by Miriam Hochberg-Marianska, a wartime member of an organization called Żegota, which on behalf of the Polish underground was helping Jews hiding from Nazi persecution. Hochberg-Marianska was Jewish, but she had what at the time was known as "good looks," which meant that she could pass for an ethnic Pole (although she also happened to be strikingly beautiful). She worked in the Kraków branch of Żegota and was very courageous.

After the war, on behalf of the Central Committee of Polish Jews, she traveled all around Poland, also a risky business then, to look for Jewish children who had been placed with Polish families. Many of these children had been orphaned, or else relatives who had miraculously survived the war did not quite know where to look for them. In any case, it was one of many important tasks at the time for the remnants of Polish Jewry—to retrieve its dispersed and lost still surviving youths.

Hochberg-Marianska was instrumental in this effort and soon published a slender book describing the fate of a few children and their rescuers.[1] And in the introduction to this volume she made a striking remark—"I wish I could thank all courageous Poles who had saved the Jewish children," wrote Hochberg-Marianska, but several had asked her not to mention their names. They preferred to remain anonymous. Why, I wondered? Why did those who will later be honored as Righteous Among Nations not want their role as rescuers of Jews to be known? Why were they afraid to be recognized as such in their communities? Since then, having read a number of memoirs by rescued Jews, I came to realize that it was a ubiquitous phenomenon.[2]

Independence of postwar, Communist-ruled Poland dates, symbolically, from July 22, 1944. In "People's Poland" this was the day celebrated as the most important national holiday, commemorating the so-called July 22 Manifesto, issued by the Committee of National Liberation in the city of Lublin and proclaiming the country's independence.

To be sure, the war was still going on, and more than half of Poland's territory was still under the German occupation. But Lublin was free. And it was in the city of Lublin, some two weeks later, on August 10, that a group of Jews had assembled at five o'clock in the afternoon and established an organization, a "committee"—what else, this was the word in fashion at the time—to bring assistance to the remnants of Polish Jewry that had survived the war. What would soon become the Centralny Komitet Zydow w Polsce (Central Committee of Polish Jews)—an umbrella organization put together by representatives of prewar Jewish political parties—was first called Komitet Pomocy Zydom (Committee to Bring Assistance to Jews).

In its very first protocol, produced the following day, on August 11, we read that the Jews of Włodawa need help because they are being "attacked by destructive elements."[3] The committee's second meeting on August 13 was devoted to a general discussion about "security." Should both the Polish and the Soviet (military) authorities be alerted that there are "elements inimical toward the Jews," or should this information be kept *en famille,* with only Polish officials so alerted? Should mayors of already liberated towns be asked to issue proclamations addressed to the Polish population and requesting that it be friendly toward its Jewish cocitizens? Should Catholic clergy be informed about threats and lack of security experienced by the Jews? And how to do all or any of this without making matters worse for Jews and creating an atmosphere of excessive panic?[4]

Protocol number 3, from August 14, begins with a Dr. Gelbart reporting on a conversation he had on this matter with a member of the Krajowej Rady Narodowej (KRN), the newly established National Council. Then Gelbart continues, reassuringly, that "for the moment Jews are not being threatened in Lublin," and he adds, "but loud conversations [presumably in Yiddish] and gathering in groups in the street should be avoided."[5]

In the next day's protocol, dated August 15, again we read about a constant flow of pleas for help by Jews from the provinces. Mind you, the war was still going on; Germany had not yet been defeated; these territories were barely liberated from the yoke of a long and exceedingly brutal occupation which caused suffering to virtually every Polish family; and yet local people were already after the remnants of Jewish survivors.[6]

How are we to understand these episodes? Can they be placed in the context of a well-established frame of reference which posits that Jews have a particular fondness for communism, that indeed they brought communism (or Bolshevism) to Europe and were therefore hated by the local populations in Eastern Europe which were anti-Communist?

Has it indeed been the case that the dominant postwar Jewish experience in Poland involved partaking in the imposition of scientific socialism on reluctant fellow citizens and attendant persecution of ethnic Poles? Did postwar manifestations of anti-Semitism flow from the realization that Jews were then in the driver's seat and that by striking at the Jews, one was delivering a blow to the Communist regime?

I do not think so. Rather, I am prepared to argue that the dominant Jewish experience in post–World War II Poland was fear; and that the Communist authorities in Poland, together with large segments of the Polish society, actually found a platform of accommodation with respect to "solving the Jewish problem." The society pushed for, and the authorities tolerated, getting rid of the Jews. In the Communist-controlled media, nothing special was made of the Jewish experience during the war. The history of Polish-Jewish relations under the German occupation was not revisited. The courts did not look favorably on the efforts of returning Jews to retrieve property they had left for safekeeping with their neighbors. Few were prosecuted for having directly assisted the Nazis in the mass murder of Polish Jews. And the Jews were given tacit permission, bordering on encouragement, to leave the country. Apparently, it was mutually acceptable—and few things were mutually acceptable to Polish subjects and their Communist rulers at that time—to close that chapter of Poland's history: as a result, there was to be no more "Jewish problem." Or so it seemed.

Of course the story is more complicated than that, and it is wrapped in ideological clichés. But the general thrust of Jewish experience in postwar Poland—I hope you will be convinced by the time I finish—was just as I stated.

State administration acts rather slowly, as we know, and it does not send circulars in response to individual interventions. Thus, it is fair to assume that the Ministry of Public Administration must have received a good number of complaints before circulating a memorandum entitled "In the Matter of Attitude Toward Citizens of Jewish Nationality," to all the *voievods* (i.e., chief administrators of the largest territorial units, voivodships), district plenipotentiaries, and presidents of Warsaw and Łódź. Dated June 5, 1945, the memorandum was issued barely one month after the capitulation of Nazi Germany:

> The Ministry of Public Administration has been appraised that voivodship and county authorities, as well as offices of general administration, do not always apply necessary objectivism when dealing with individuals of Jewish nationality. In the unjustifiably negative attitude of the said authorities and offices when handling such cases, and especially when making it difficult for Jewish returnees to take apartments which are due to them, a highly undemocratic anti-Semitic tendency rather clearly comes to the surface. The Ministry of Public Administration calls attention to this undesirable phenomenon and emphasizes that all loyal citizens of the Polish Republic, irrespective of nationality and religious denomination, should be treated the same, and they ought to be helped within the boundaries of existing law. Therefore the Ministry of Public Administration implores you to make sure that authorities and offices within your jurisdiction abide by recommendations of this memorandum.[7]

One cannot help but note a certain discrepancy between the benign language of this memorandum and the scandalous reality it addressed, given that events it alludes to were taking place in Poland in the immediate aftermath of the Holocaust.

So how did this "undemocratic anti-Semitic tendency" actually manifest itself in the lives of ordinary people? Let me illustrate with an item from the State Archives in Kraców Voivodship: at the beginning of July 1945 in Chrzanów, "a registration clerk at the Citizens' Militia office requested that citizen Schnitzer Gusta, who returned from a camp, prove her identity by bringing a witness who would testify as to her identity, and that she lived in Chrzanów before the war. When citizen Schnitzer Gusta presented to the clerk at said office as her witness the chairman of the County Jewish Committee in Chrzanów, citizen Bachner Lesser, said clerk stated in the presence of the witness that he had no confidence in the presented witness and that he would trust only a witness of non-Jewish extraction and that he would register citizen [Schnitzer] only when she presented such a witness."[8]

The significance of such an episode lies in being indicative of a trend. It often signaled an attitude on the part of some segment of the state administration that affected many people. It could thwart development of a specific institution, for example—such as Jewish cooperatives, which were routinely bogged down during registration procedures by the Central Cooperative Administration known as Spolem.[9] It could affect specific communities, such as when Jews were occasionally branded by zealous local bureaucrats and then discriminated against when they sought gainful employment. One of the best weeklies of this period, *Kuznica,* carried the following item on October 14, 1945:

> Third Reich is no more. Nobody knows what happened to Hitler. Himmler and Goebbels took poison. But Jewish identity cards have reappeared—in the reborn, democratic Poland. Let's be precise. It's not so much identity cards as labor certificates issued by the Regional Labor Office in Dabrowa Gornicza. One such document is just in front of us—certificate no. 102466 issued on July 5, 1945. One month after mysterious disappearance of Adolf Hitler, on this certificate, right next to the Polish seal of the Dabrowa Gornicza City Government a round stamp is visible with the letter "J"—Jew.
>
> The Labor Office explained this original manner of stamping certificates by "technical reasons" pertaining to registration. What kind of reasons could they be? As far as we know, the same rules for registration apply to Jewish and non-Jewish citizens. As far as we know, the same principles are binding in the Ministry of Labor and Social Welfare as in the rest of the country stipulating complete equality of citizens, including the Jews. . . . Who are the people responsible for this horrendous, Hitlerite scandal in a Polish state institution?

At the other end of Poland, in Szczecin, during a high-level conference with the voivods and chief executive officers of all the main enterprises in town, the Jewish Committee representative read a long list of complaints concerning job discrimination. The most glaring case, he stated, were City Tramways (the MTA of Szczecin) "where despite our interventions no Jews were given employment."[10] In yet another region of the country, we learn from a recent article of a young Polish historian, the Ministry of Public Administration sent a reprimand to the Kielce Voivodship office: "In Jedrzejów the county *starosta* [sheriff], Feliks, turns down all cases brought to him by Jews. The same situation prevails in Checiny and Chmielnik. The city council in Ostrowiec called representatives of the Jewish Committee and requested that all Jews be sent to work in a mine."[11]

State bureaucracy at the local level frequently made categorical distinctions between Jews and non-Jews, which triggered a deep emotional response from the Jewish community. The town office in Chrzanów at some point began sending daily requests for laborers to the Jewish Committee, demanding on July 5, 1945, for example, that "twelve persons of female sex be designated for washing dirty linen of Red Army soldiers." And it mattered less, in the eyes of the Jewish Committee filing the complaint, that the town office did not honor its promise to pay the honorarium than the very fact of its issuing the request in a form "emulating methods of the occupiers, which makes the Jewish Committee responsible if the labor contingent does not appear in designated time and place. Such requests are issued only to the Jewish population with the intermediary of the Committee. In this manner the town office in Chrzanów perpetuates traditions established by the occupiers who communicated with the Jewish population with the help of *Judenrat*."[12]

Sometimes tense relationships between the two groups were so badly mishandled by local authorities that an outside intervention was necessary to find a modus vivendi. Thus, the Jewish Committee in Lublin during its plenary meeting on April 15, 1945, discussed the situation in Miedzyrzecz, where about two hundred Jews resided at the time. "In order not to inflame the situation the local Jewish Committee restrained the Jews from trying to regain their property which had been robbed from them by some of the local Christians. . . . At the beginning the mayor was unfriendly toward the Jews. He didn't allow a Jewish doctor to establish himself in town. The militia didn't respond when Jewish houses were devastated. Following some complaints, a representative of the Security Service came to town and he smoothed things between Jews and Poles. Even a so-called agreement [*ugoda*] was signed. Now things have quieted down."[13]

The very term *ugoda* has a solemn significance in Polish, pointing to social distance between parties. One can use it synonymously with "treaty," for example, to designate an agreement between foreign entities. Clearly, in the perception of local authorities, Jews were distinct, a "special problem" category of the population which remained in an adversarial relationship with the rest of local inhabitants, and they had to be dealt with accordingly. What was the nature of the tension between the two groups, it behooves us to ask? Even though the *cherchez la femme* trope would be misleading in this case, I am afraid that the answer to this query, a part of the answer in any case, is just as banal, for one of the paramount underlying reasons for conflict between Poles and Jews after the war had to do with money or, to be exact, with material property.

Polish society was uniquely affected by the Holocaust in that massive killings of Polish Jews created a social vacuum that was promptly filled by the native Polish petite bourgeoisie. Sociologically this was, in a manner of speaking, a natural process. There were more than three million Jews in Poland, most of them in the lower middle class; when they were wiped out by the Nazis, the local population moved in to occupy their social space. Now the new incumbents were a social stratum with vulnerable status (if only because a Communist revolution was in the offing), traditionally anti-Semitic in outlook, politically conservative, and full of resentment. Many Polish observers contemporaneously noted its, so to speak, reactionary mental outlook. But whether one puts this situation in the sociological language of social mobility or some other objectivizing rhetoric, the long and short of the story was that before being killed during the German occupation, Jews were plundered by the Nazis, and the local population in various ways benefited in the process—often by foul play.

Again the archives of the Jewish Committee may be harvested for illustration. Its legal department kept records of numerous suits filed in courts by Jewish survivors for restitution of property. Much of their prewar property, especially items of greater value, was unrecoverable to Jews, because Polish authorities promptly "socialized" it as enemy property, taking it over from its last owner—the German state. But it is bread-and-butter issues that directly affected the lives of many Jews. "During the occupation in 1942," wrote Jochweta Rozenstein, in a characteristic example, "I left for safekeeping with citizen Ludwika Chrapczynska in Ozarow two eiderdowns and four pillows. Citizen Chrapczynska refuses to return my property."[14] The complaint closes with a sentence that repeats in numerous filings of this sort: "Please, adjudicate the case, even if I am absent." For already in May 1945, when this complaint was filed in the city court, Jews were running away from Poland, fleeing for their lives to, of all places, Germany. *Safe Among the Germans*—the title of Ruth Gay's most recent book about Jewish life in displaced person camps—is largely about Polish Jews who fled their mother country after the war.[15]

Irrespective of how personal disputes over bedding or furniture were resolved by the courts, it is telling that the returning token Jews had to use courts to press such claims. One would wish for a climate of compassion toward the few returnees, whose communities and families, as a rule, had just suffered an unspeakable calamity. But it was absent. Indeed, there was no social norm mandating the return of Jewish property, no detectable social pressure defining such behavior as the right thing to do, no informal social control mechanism imposing censure for doing otherwise. That is why the Jews who dared to pursue the matter had to resort to courts.

Apparently Jewish property was for the taking. In any case, it has been taken by people all around (not a Polish specificity by any means—Heda Kovály recounted the same phenomenon in a moving book about Czechoslovakia).[16] A courageous miller's wife from Radziłów, Chaja Finkelsztajn, left a searing memoir in Yad Vashem about the mass murder of Jews in her hometown on July 7, 1941, and about subsequent years when she was hiding with her family among the peasants. On several occasions (in one instance just as the mass killing was unfolding in Radziłów) the so-called good local people, actually women, came to her asking that she turn over whatever things she still had, since she and her family would surely be killed. And it was only right—the interlocutor argued without malice—for the good people, who knew the Finkelsztajns, to get possession, or else the killers would be rewarded.[17] To a Jewish man trying to find a hiding place with a peasant acquaintance near Wegrow, the latter's son-in-law said matter-of-factly, "Since you are going to die anyway, why should someone else get your boots? Why not give them to me so I will remember you?"[18] Communal Jewish property, such as cemeteries or synagogues, was in large measure devastated after the war as the local population carted away tombstones, bricks, roofs, anything useful for its own construction projects. Imagine the sense of bad luck among the likes of Chrapczynska (the woman being sued for the return of an eiderdown and two pillows in Ozarow). Why did "her" Jew have to come back from the dead while all the others—most of the others—disappeared and would not bother the neighbors who also stocked up on Jewish stuff?

Pronounced tension, invidious comparison, and envy existed among the lower-middle-class Poles after the war concerning which family had enriched itself, and how much, at the expense of the Jews. Indeed, one of the reasons why the future Righteous Among Nations wanted to keep wartime assistance to Jews a secret from their neighbors was because they feared being identified as recipients of Jewish largesse.

It was assumed that people who kept the Jews had enriched themselves handsomely (which was often the case). If found out, in addition to being stigmatized as a "Jew lover," a future Righteous Among Nations would get identified as a potential target for robbery—a frightening prospect, especially among those who had hidden Jews on principle, for the presumption of Jewish wealth and cunning was so pervasive that they risked being tortured by bandits to reveal the hiding place of putative Jewish treasures they did not have. When the village head in one of the places they were hiding learned the whereabouts of the Finkelsztajns, he requested that they move on—not because he feared German reprisals against the village but because, he argued, if they stayed for a long time, the peasant who was hiding them would excessively enrich himself.[19]

So, the token returnees usually would be met with hostility. On October 11, 1945, Major Irving Heymont, who ran the Landsberg DP camp at the time, wrote in a letter to his wife, "It seems that many Jews from Poland are drifting into the camp. Most of them, I am told, returned to Poland after being liberated from concentration camps to meet persecution again. Their attempts to repossess their prewar property met with violent opposition from the present owners. The local police forces, according to new arrivals from Poland, often take no action and even join in preventing former owners from regaining their property."[20]

Time and again returning Jews were greeted on arrival with an incredulous, "So"—followed by their first name, as they usually were on first-name basis with their Polish neighbors—"you are still alive?" And before long they got an unambiguous hint, or a piece of "good advice," to clear out or else. "The story of their experiences during the past six months," wrote H. J. Fishbein, director of a United Nations Relief and Rehabilitation Administration (UNRRA) Team in Berlin in the spring of 1946, "is a monotonous one as it is repeated by all refugees coming out of Poland. They tell of letters received from a Polish organization known as AK. . . . These letters threaten the Jews with outright murder if they continue to live in that locality."[21] There was no high politics behind such threats—or good advice, however one wants to call it—and wherever they came from. Token Jewish survivors, going back to their hometowns in a usually vain search for relatives or family belongings, had nothing to do with the establishment of Communist rule in Poland after the war. If they had, communism would have collapsed in the country long before 1989, because Jews promptly ran away from villages and small towns into a few big cities. And soon thereafter, in a mass exodus, they fled Poland altogether.[22]

But from time to time, people wanted to restore a semblance of normality to their shattered lives. "After the war, people lived here in fear," recalled Stanislaw Ramotowski, who married a local Jewish woman with whom he fell in love. "On one occasion about two years after the war, my wife wanted to buy back an oak family dresser. She could have a better one, but this was a family heirloom. And somebody didn't like it. We found a piece of paper stuck to our house door saying that we were sentenced to death. At that time NSZ [the national armed forces] gave out a lot of such sentences in our area. They stole, they beat people up, they killed. I went to my own people, because I was a member of the AK [*Armia Krajowa,* or Home Army]. . . . And then AK made them take the sentence back. And so we survived."[23] But not many Jews could draw on such local networks. Ramotowski was a Pole; he saved and married the Jewish woman Rachela during the war and continued to protect her at considerable personal risk.

Thus, in addition to everything else—such as socialization into anti-Semitic ideology by the most numerous prewar political parties and the Catholic Church, and wartime demoralization—a broad stratum of beneficiaries, for economic reasons, resented and actively opposed the return of Jews to their towns and villages after the war.

But unfortunately, the legacy of Polish-Jewish relations during the war was much more complicated.

It has now been acknowledged in Poland that the extent of direct involvement of the local population in Nazi persecution of the Jews was significantly greater than previously recognized. After the Institute of National Remembrance (Instytut Pamieci Narodowej, or IPN) began its thorough, two-year-long investigation of the Jedwabne murder, researchers at the institute combed through their extensive archives. The IPN took custody of documents from various organizations, including what was known at the time as the Main Commission for Investigation of Hitlerite Crimes. In these holdings there are court files of many cases that had been tried in the late 1940s and early 1950s under the so-called August laws (passed in August 1944, hence the name), which made collaboration with the German occupiers during the war a crime. They are known collectively by a shorthand designation as *sierpniowki,* or "August cases."

It was assumed by scholars that *sierpniowki* for the most part referred to prosecution of individuals who had signed the *Volksliste* during the occupation or who had served in the so-called dark blue police formation. After the Jedwabne investigation began, the IPN experts discovered that sixty-one cases from the Bialystok district court alone were brought under the August paragraphs against defendants accused of participation in killings of local Jews. And new files continue to reemerge from the archives.[24]

But since our subject is not the wartime but rather postwar relations between Poles and Jews, what interests us in this context is not that Poles killed Jews during the war but how prosecution of such behavior was handled in the courts of Communist Poland after the war. We have sources that shed light on this issue, including recollections of Jewish survivors who tried to bring to justice after the war those whom they knew as murderers of their kin. But let us instead consult the distanced-in-time, expert voice of a leading legal scholar from Warsaw University, Professor Andrzej Rzeplinski, entrusted by the Institute of National Remembrance with evaluation, from a legal standpoint, of the 1949 Jedwabne murder trial. In his interview for *Gazeta Wyborcza* on July 19, 2002, Rzeplinski first described the circumstances which led to the indictment of the Jedwabne murderers.

In December 1947, a Jew from Jedwabne who emigrated before the war to Montevideo wrote a letter to the Central Committee of

Polish Jews in Warsaw, stating, "We have information that they [the Jedwabne Jews] were killed by the Poles, not by the Germans. And we know that those Poles had not yet been brought to justice, that they still live in the same village." The letter somehow reached the Ministry of Justice, which in February 1948 ordered the prosecutor in the Łomża district court to investigate the matter.

The prosecutor's office in Łomża did not react for the next three weeks. And during the following ten months nothing was done in the judicial sense, though probably behind-the-scenes negotiations went on. Suspects in the case were arrested only in January 1949. The Łomża law enforcement apparatus—the prosecutor's office, the police, and the secret police (Urzedy Bezpieczenstwa, or UB)—as well as the Łomża County Committee of the Communist Party and the Catholic diocese all must have known about the events in Jedwabne. But the investigation started only after Warsaw made the request.

Eight functionaries from the UB office in Łomża conducted the investigation. They were very young, without professional qualifications. Only one had a high-school diploma. Investigators were trying to limit the case as much as possible from the beginning. For example, a witness said, "The following people took part in murdering of the Jews," and then only one name is written into the protocol. Probably, when the witness started to enumerate other names, the investigator changed the subject.

During questioning, witnesses specifically identified more than ninety people as participants in the crime. For the most part they no longer lived in Jedwabne or were deceased. But not one of those who were still alive was interviewed as a witness. The local priest was not interviewed, either, and he should have been asked why he didn't appear during the pogrom with a cross and the sacraments—he knew very well what needed to be done to convert that mob into a controllable crowd which could be dispersed. Poles who saved some Jews—Antonina Wyrzykowska, for example—were not asked for depositions, either.

Question: The main trial started on May 16, 1949, in the Łomża district court, and the sentence was pronounced the next day. How could such an immense crime be judged in such a short time? Answer: Frankly speaking, it is utterly unimaginable to me. During two days of deliberations (about sixteen hours altogether) the court heard testimony from twenty-two accused and fifty-six witnesses. Seventy-eight people! If you subtract the time needed for various necessary procedures in a court of law, including reading of the indictment and other documents, and final speeches, that leaves about six minutes per person.

This was a deliberate ploy on the part of the judge to make sure that witnesses said as little as possible. Prosecutors agreed to it, and defense counsels certainly thought it advantageous to their clients. Neither the prosecutors nor lawyers for the defense nor the auxiliary judges (a three-judge panel sits on the bench) asked any questions! Defense counsels recognized that if they remained silent, the trial would end sooner and their clients would get leaner sentences. Witnesses in the courtroom usually repeated the same line—"I have hardly seen anything at all"—even though they gave copious depositions during preliminary interrogation.

A vast majority of witnesses appearing in court testified for the defense. They usually stated that they saw a given accused far from the crime scene. One woman who had described during pretrial interrogation how the accused Laudanski boasted about killing two or three Jews later in court retracted her testimony. She probably feared the Laudanski family more than she feared the secret police.

Not one among the people prosecuting and involved with the case knew the topography of Jedwabne. There had been no court visit to the crime scene. This ignorance of the terrain was used by the accused and their witnesses to spin tales about what was where. A distance which in reality could be walked in five minutes in their testimonies took twenty to thirty minutes to cover. No exhumation was ordered. In a sense, in this trial there were no victims. The crime allegedly consisted in that the local inhabitants chased the Jews out into the market square and there guarded them a little. There is nothing about burning of the Jews in the trial sentence. The sentencing and its justification are embarrassingly unprofessional, not for the lack of legal qualifications of the judge but as a result of the tactic he adopted—which was to limit as much as possible the scope of the case, the number of the accused, and the accusations against them.

The presiding judge of the three-person panel, Antoni Malecki, was of peasant background. He came from the area and probably shared the prejudices of the local people. I have a special grudge against the presiding judge. Prosecutors in the case were very young, after some remedial legal tutorials, typical for the Stalinist judicial system. But

Malecki was a prewar judge, with twenty years of experience on the bench. He had to know what he was doing.

Question: Was this a political or a criminal trial? Answer: It was a political trial in the sense that the whole case was deliberately scaled down—some people beat up some other people, but in the end it is not entirely clear who, whom, and for what reason. I think that the decision to so limit and circumscribe the case was made somewhere in the voivodship offices of the Communist Party. A big trial could not bring any political benefits—there was no way it could be demonstrated that the Germans had killed the Jews in Jedwabne. Indicting a large group of Poles for the murder of Jews could result in a political scandal. Well over a hundred people should have been brought to justice, according to my calculations.

In my deepest belief, those ten Poles who were found guilty drew convictions for only a fraction of what they had actually done. And all of this after a glaringly unprofessional trial, not because legal know-how was lacking but as a result of reluctance to bring to light all the circumstances of the crime due to anti-Semitic prejudice. We can understand now why Rzeplinski prefaced his interview with these words: "I analyzed in my life some fifteen hundred criminal cases, and none has made such a big impression on me as the trial connected to Jedwabne."[25]

Lucky fellow, he somehow never managed to reach out for the really good stuff. For lest you think that this was an unusual case, an aberration of sorts, a unique miscarriage of justice (it was not, really—the case went through two appeals and the legal cover-up/incompetence was never challenged), let me disabuse you. The Jedwabne murder trial was a jurisprudential masterpiece, a paragon of diligent integrity and thoroughness in the treatment of evidence compared to dozens of trials held well into the 1950s in the Bialystok regional courts, where the issue of killings of Jews by their neighbors came up. I say "where the issue of killings of Jews by their neighbors came up" because in these trials (just like in the Jedwabne trial) it was often a tangential, sideline matter, disposed of *en passant*, with the main accusation and investigation focusing on some other transgression. The two volumes of IPN documents and reports I referred to earlier offer ample evidence in the matter.[26]

So now we know about the lingering anti-Semitic inertia of the local administration and the judiciary in postwar People's Poland.

I mean to say that the Jews were not so much actively persecuted as processed in a prejudicial manner whenever they had to transact with these bureaucracies, as one frequently must in a modern society, especially under a regime promoting etatism of collective life. Anti-Semitism, of course, was not a part of Communist ideology. In an ideal world, with Communists safely in power, there wouldn't be any anti-Semitism. But in an ideal world envisaged by communism, there wouldn't be any Jews, either. Ethnic identification was an epiphenomenon, to use Marxist vocabulary, a thing of the past that was bound to go away. Or else, if it found a political articulation and congealed into an organized movement, then it would be promptly denounced as "nationalism" and fought against—the anti-Zionist campaign that Stalin would launch in his last years is a case in point.

But Communists, and this was deeply ingrained already in Lenin's contribution to the Bolshevik tradition, were also paramount pragmatists of power. And since wartime experiences of the USSR they (certainly this applies to Stalin) understood that patriotic, indeed nationalist, sentiments of the population must be tapped to safeguard the rule of the Communist Party. And if such sentiments—among the Russians, the Ukrainians, the Romanians, or the Poles—came with an admixture of xenophobia or anti-Semitism, so be it. There seems little doubt that Stalin exhibited anti-Semitism in his later years. Others may have been more reserved, acting out of sheer opportunism or, to use the felicitous expression of Ian Kershaw, "working towards the Führer."[27] The underlying anti-Semitic impetus of the Rajk trial in Hungary and especially the Slansky trial in Czechoslovakia were unmistakable. One could point out that they came in later years. But already since the earliest phase of the Communist reach for power in Eastern Europe, the party made a clear choice between Jews and their local enemies.

"I, the undersigned, herewith declare that I was a member of the Arrow Cross Party from . . . to . . . I now realize that my activities were directed against the interests of the people and that my conduct was faulty. I am resolved to atone for what I have done. I promise to support the fight for a people's democracy with everything in my power and to devote my entire energy to the achievement of this task. I herewith solemnly pledge myself to be a faithful fighting member of the . . . branch of the Hungarian Communist Party."[28] To an American journalist who traveled all over liberated Europe in 1945, the Hungarian Communist Party leader Matias Rakosi explained the matter thus: "Look, these little fascists aren't bad fellows, really. They were forced into fascism, see. They were never active in it. All they have to do is sign a pledge, and we take them in."[29] In Romania, Ana Pauker, the proverbial, symbolic Jewish Communist of Eastern Europe, struck a deal with the Legionnaires immediately after her return to Bucharest, and the rank-and-file Iron Guardists were admitted *en masse* into the ranks of the party. At the time in Poland, the leader of the prewar fascist ONR-Falanga, Boleslaw Piasecki, was released from jail on orders of the top NKVD operative in the region, Ivan Serov, and allowed to set up an organization of "progressive" Catholics, PAX, to neutralize the influence of the Catholic Church. Two days after he was freed, Piasecki was received by the first secretary of the Polish Workers' Party (as the Communist Party was known at the time), Władysław Gomulka.[30] Serge Moscovici intelligently noted the complementary predicaments of radical Right and radical Left in Eastern European (in his case, Romanian) politics. The rightists had ample social backing before the war but did not have power and were reaching out for it. The leftists, on the other hand, in the immediate postwar years had power but no social base to speak of and had to mobilize it in order to acquire legitimacy. Hence the carefully orchestrated fusion between Communists and fascists in postwar Eastern Europe in literal exemplification of the principle *les extremes se touchent* (opposite extremes come together).

We can see now why Zygmunt Laudanski, a convicted murderer in the Jedwabne trial, a rabid nationalist before the war who managed to join the Communist Party immediately after the war, could write in his clemency plea from jail without being completely ridiculous, "I believe that on shoulders like mine our workers' regime may safely rest."[31]

Let us be careful here: the central authorities in Warsaw (or Bucharest, or Budapest, as the case may be) were not happy about this state of affairs. And they gave vent to their disapproval—the Ministry of Public Administration sent a memo, as we remember, to its subordinates, pleading to give Jews equal treatment; the Ministry of Justice from Warsaw set the Jedwabne murder investigation in motion; and so on. But then, one has to observe—as subordinates both in the bureaucracy and in the judiciary must have known very well—Warsaw did not press the issue.

Communists in Eastern Europe had their hands full. They had to pick their fights. And making sure that Jews got what they deserved was not one of the priorities. Hal Lehrman published a long piece on Hungary in the January 1946 issue of *Commentary* where he reported that "neo anti-semitism is not the Jews' chief complaint here. Its existence is obscene, to be sure, after the price paid in lives but it could have been expected. . . . What is startling and, in the opinion of Hungarian Jews, the most shocking element in their present position is the cool indifference of the new anti-fascist regime."[32]

Likewise, Communists of Poland were confronted with an overwhelming popular sentiment on the "Jewish issue," and they could ignore it or fight it only at their own peril. On August 19, 1945, in the cinema Raj (Heaven) in Bochnia, one thousand delegates assembled for a county meeting of the Peasant Party. The gathering by invitation only (*za zaproszeniami imiennymi*) brought together local activists, the elite of Stanislaw Mikolajczyk's political opposition (he had just given up the prime minister's office in the government-in-exile in London and returned to Poland). An anonymous rapporteur submitted an account of the meeting to the Kraków Voivodship Office and in it wrote as follows: "In turn the third speaker took the rostrum (his name unknown), and by analogy to a thesis from Kiernik's speech that Poland must be a monoethnic state [the matter previously discussed concerned expulsions of the German population from newly incorporated territories], put out a resolution that Jews should also be expelled from Poland, and he also remarked that Hitler ought to be thanked for destroying the Jews (tumultuous ovation and applause)."[33]

To complete the review of attitudes in matters Jewish among law enforcement organs of the Polish state immediately after the war, let me remind you also that Jewish Committees all over the country complained about anti-Semitism in the regular police, the Citizens' Militia personnel. And this fact was well known to the commander of the force, Franciszek Jozwiak.[34] In some areas local people perceived the Citizens' Militia as their natural ally in anti-Jewish struggle. Thus, a Jewish woman fleeing from the scene of the Kielce pogrom two days after the event found herself pulled from a train by fellow passengers who first attempted to lynch her and then delivered her into the hands of the Citizens' Militia—"to be shot." Actually, this happened to her twice on the same journey. In the first instance a militiaman took a bribe and let her go. She then boarded another train, was once again

identified as a Jew by fellow passengers, and was delivered to an outpost
of the railroad police, where she was threatened with execution and
witnessed a beating of another Jew pulled off the train. A group of
schoolchildren pelted her with stones through an open window while
she was in police custody until finally she was taken to a central outpost
of the Citizens' Militia in town, where her documents were checked
and she was released.[35] Actions of the militia are of less significance
in this case than the perceptions of the populace about what it was
supposed to do and, presumably, ready to do.

Archives of the Jewish Committee from Tarnów describe repeated
assaults by uniformed soldiers against local Jews and the futility of lodg-
ing complaints with the authorities in the matter.[36] Scores of militiamen were implicated in the Kraków pogrom; soldiers and militiamen,
as is well known, participated in the infamous Kielce pogrom.

Even the attitude of the Urzędy Bezpieczenstwa (Security Offices,
the secret police), the most politicized organs of the administration, often made Jews uneasy. In October 1945, a high-ranking NKVD official
who was advising the Polish Ministry of Public Security sent to his boss
in Moscow, Lavrentii Beria, a lengthy "Report on the Situation of the
Jewish Population in Poland." He described in it, among other items,
anti-Semitic attitudes among employees in the headquarters of the
Public Security Service in Warsaw. At the other end of the spectrum we
find a memorandum in the documents of Kraków's special commission
on a theatrical "revue" put on by the sports club Force in, of all places,
Auschwitz (in Polish, Oświęcim), on January 24 and 25, 1947. The
memorandum states, "The themes and content of this show were to
make fun of the Jews in various sketches and songs. We want to stress
that the main part in these anti-Jewish gimmicks was played by the
commander of the Security Police in Oświęcim."[37] For better or for
worse, the Communist organizers of public order in Poland adopted
an attitude of benign neglect with respect to "the Jewish problem."
They decided to let the matter take its course. And if anything, from
time to time, they would even attempt to ride the tiger.

From provincial towns one hears numerous stories about physical
attacks, windows being broken in Jewish houses, offensive graffiti, or
verbal threats. "It is an undeniable fact," wrote Jan Kowalczyk, who
held the title Kraków Voivodship Commissar for Productivization
of the Jewish Population, to the Presidium of the District Commission of the Labor Unions (an entirely "Polish" venue, if you will) "that

the living conditions of the Jewish population in county towns are extremely difficult. Because of the terror of reactionary elements [a phrase often encountered in the official language of the time] Jewish population runs away from those locations in order to save their lives and concentrates in larger towns."[38] Indeed, county and voivodship Jewish Committees urged the Jewish population to move to larger towns, but even there Jews were not safe. The August 1945 pogrom in Kraków and the July 1946 pogrom in Kielce are cases in point.

How many Jews had been killed at the time is difficult to estimate. One historian puts the total at around 1,500.[39] Many people were being killed in Poland at the time, as we will soon be reminded by the bishop of Lublin. There was a civil war of sorts as Communists were consolidating their grip on power. But what makes murders of Jews a phenomenon apart is that they were anticipated—as punishment is anticipated in a case of transgression. Frequently Jews would receive prior warnings, either public (I mentioned earlier a report by an UNRRA officer from Berlin to this effect) or private (Wasersztajn, for example, was saved in this manner).[40] Apparently, there was a diffused, prior knowledge about impending killings among people in a town who weren't necessarily part of a conspiracy. Likewise, it was public knowledge that Jews traveling on railroads might be pulled off a train and killed. Killings of Jews, in other words, were not a secret cloak-and-dagger operation. They were, instead, a form of social control. If Jews remained in their hometowns despite the warnings, if they traveled by trains knowing the risks, then—in the moral economy of postwar life in Poland—they had nobody else to blame but themselves if harm befell them. The following Jewish woman's account is found in the files of the Central Special Commission:

> On the third of October [1946] at seven in the evening, I boarded a train from Warsaw to Kraków. I was accompanied by my husband, Henryk Liberfreund, and Amalia Schenker. We rode in a compartment with a couple more passengers, including a nun. A candle was burning. We traveled peacefully until we reached Kaminsk station near Radomsko. In the meantime the candle burned out and passengers were sleeping in darkness. During the train stop in Kaminsk a man in civilian clothes, wearing a cap with an eagle sign and toting a submachine gun, entered the compartment. He checked the passengers one by one with a flashlight. When he reached my sleeping husband, he pulled the coat covering him and

said, "I got you, kike, *heraus, heraus, aussteigen.*" My husband drew back, unwilling to get off the train, and the man pulled him by the arm but could not budge him. Then he whistled and immediately another man appeared, whom I did not see very well, accompanied by the conductor. I started screaming terribly, and then the first assailant got to push and pull me using the words *heraus, aussteigen* [out, get out]. I pulled myself away; in the meantime the train took off, and the assailant pushed my husband off the train and jumped after him. I continued to scream, and I don't know what happened afterward. I wish to add that nobody's documents were checked, not even my husband's. *Other passengers and the conductor did not pay much attention to the whole episode; quite the opposite, they laughed and behaved rather improperly*" [emphasis mine].⁴¹

It may be hard to believe, but there is a silver lining in this story: the manifest attitude of the upper crust, the uppermost layer, of the creative intelligentsia. There were a number of outstanding literary and public-interest weeklies and periodicals at the time—*Kuznica, Odrodzenie, Warszawa, Tworczosc,* and *Tygodnik Powszechny,* to name the most important—and a climate enough unfettered by censorship through 1947 to give people a chance to speak their minds on issues of importance. And speak they did about anti-Semitism, especially after particularly vicious public outbursts of anti-Jewish violence—for example, in the aftermath of the Kraków (August 1945) and Kielce (July 1946) pogroms. The moral pitch of their articles is so high, so dramatic, so full of exasperation that one reads them as mourning prayers that have never been uttered by Poland's clergy and people at large. Wyka, Szczepanski, Zagorski, Andrzejewski, Ossowski, Jastrun, Nalkowska, Rudnicki—all of them spoke in print, forming the *republique de lettres* and humanities of postwar Poland. Some in the chorus of lamenting and warning voices—but no more than a third, I would say—were assimilated Jews, as Polish as Heine was German. And several were officially Catholic—the *Tygodnik Powszechny* milieu in Kraków, for example, and many of its distinguished contributors.

Jerzy Turowicz, the longtime editor in chief of this extraordinary weekly, must be recognized in particular. A most literate clerk from whose repertory, nevertheless, *trahison* (treason) was missing; who never betrayed his calling. Imagine: after Stalin died, *Tygodnik Powszechny* (Turowicz was already editor in chief) refused to publish an obituary. It was all so unexpected, it all happened so quickly, the tide turned in Moscow in the right direction, and this unprecedented act of defiance (I am pretty sure there was no other similar case in the entire Stalinist bloc) ended up with but a dismissal of the editorial board. After 1956 Turowicz and his colleagues were reinstated, but at the time they had to be prepared for immediate imprisonment.

And it gets better. Turowicz never discarded any scrap of paper. One entered his apartment, I've been told, at one's own risk—you had to walk carefully between mounds of books, manuscripts, letters, and newspaper clippings piled to the ceiling. He never left a letter unanswered, and he kept a diary noting every day, however briefly, every conversation.

Through careful and loving archaeological work of his grand-children, friends, and collaborators, a chronicle of the noblest, the best, and the wittiest in the second half of the twentieth century by Polish intelligentsia is being put together. Various treasures are being unearthed all along, such as previously unknown poems by Tadeusz Borowski, a former Auschwitz inmate, who left the remarkable liter-ary testimony to man's inhumanity, "This Way for the Gas, Ladies and Gentlemen."

No reflections on postwar Polish anti-Semitism can leave aside the Kielce pogrom. As this is a well-known episode, I will only briefly mention the circumstances. The most deadly assault on Jews in Eu-rope after the war, the pogrom lasted for almost an entire day, July 4, 1946, and involved the participation of hundreds of Kielce inhabitants resulting in the murder of forty-two Jews. It began with a made-up accusation by a young boy who—at the instigation of his father, it seems—declared that he had been held captive for a few days in the basement of a building where Jewish survivors and returnees lived in Kielce (presumably in order to have his blood harvested in a ritual murder). Under the circumstances, it didn't matter that the building did not have a basement. A squad of Citizens' Militia (i.e., the regular, uniformed police) was dispatched to search the house and investigate, and the pogrom started. Both militiamen and soldiers on the scene took part in the killings.

Yet it is not just the event itself but also public reactions to it that are very revealing about attitudes toward the Jews in various milieus of the Polish society. One needs first, in this respect, to mention a nonreaction, the absence of curiosity, as it were, in a certain milieu about the Kielce pogrom.

If we were to scrutinize the archives of the leadership of the Ministry of Public Security for this period, or of the leading bodies of the Polish Workers' Party (as the Communist Party was called at the time), or certain post-Soviet collections such as Stalin's special files (the so-called Osobyje Papki) which include NKVD reports from Poland, we would not be able to tell that the Kielce pogrom ever took place. We have it on the authority of a well-known scholar who is recognized as a most knowledgeable specialist on matters pertaining to the history of security police for this period. "I looked over all the protocols, even though some were incomplete, from the regular meetings of the leadership of the Ministry of Public Security with chiefs of the Voivodship Security Offices," stated professor Andrzej Paczkowski during a conference about the historiography of the Kielce pogrom, on March 12, 1996, in the Jewish Historical Institute in Warsaw. "The issue of the Kielce pogrom was never addressed in this forum (*Sprawa pogromu kieleckiego nie byla w tym gremium poruszana*)."[42] As Paczkowski pointed out later in the discussion, this was a busy time for the party leadership and the security apparatus: they were really hard at work falsifying the results of the June 30, 1946, referendum, which was construed as a vote of confidence in the Communist rulership of the country.

Had all the files pertaining to the Kielce pogrom been purged so successfully that no trace of any remained in the archives of the decision-making bodies in the party or in the Ministry of Public Security? It seems unlikely. A more plausible explanation was ventured by another well-known historian participating in the discussion. Professor Jerzy Tomaszewski suggested that the absence of relevant documents in Poland's leadership files was due to lack of interest in the matter among the highest government officials. The Kielce pogrom was not an event bearing on the issue of holding onto, or consolidating, power by the Communists. According to Tomaszewski, "Whether five Jews had been killed, or one hundred, either way the grip on power by the regime was not threatened by this. And therefore this was not interesting for the authorities. Other things were much more important."[43] The matter was presented during a July 5 meeting of the presidium of the country's National Council (Krajowej Rady Narodowej, or KRN) by Boleslaw Bierut followed by a report of the Minister of Public Security, but that is the extent of documented interest in the matter at the highest echelons of power.[44] The same body, the KRN, shelved during its meeting six weeks later a project of a decree to "combat anti-Semitism." Its chief legal expert, one Itzak Klajnerman (Naczelnik Wydzialu Praweneg Biura Prezydialnego KRN), argued that all the requisite laws were already on the books, and that "it seems unnecessary to issue a new decree, specifically devoted to combating anti-Semitism. It is not only unnecessary, but counterproductive (*wrecz niecelowe*), perhaps even harmful, as such a decree would certainly become an excellent pretext for energized agitation against the Jews and against the Government. Reactionary underground will offer arguments about privileged position of the Jews, and the government will be accused of protecting the Jews with special care."[45]

Thus spoke Klajnerman. But bigger men occasionally also addressed the subject. Amos Elon recounts, "In a letter from prison on February 16, 1917, [Rosa Luxemburg] wrote her friend Mathilde Wurm: 'What do you want with these special Jewish pains? I feel as close to the wretched victims of the rubber plantations. . . . I have no special corner in my heart for the ghetto: I am at home in the entire world, where there are clouds and birds and human tears."[46]

Many a Jewish Communist would have said the same. But personal views aside, Communists in Poland, as a matter of policy, were running away from the putative association between Jews and communism that they knew was on the public's mind. Jewish Communists routinely were made to change their names. A commission that took care of this matter was run by the wife of the first secretary, Władysław Gomulka (who was herself rather homely looking and Jewish). Turning around a phrase she apparently often used when assigning people new names—"wyglad w porzadku, ale co za nazwisko . . ." (looks, i.e., external appearance, is OK, but what a name . . .)—she was referred to as "nazwisko w porzadku, ale co za wyglad" (name is OK, but what an external appearance . . .).[47]

As to the purported association between communism and Jews in east-central Europe, it may be equally worth noting that the vulnerability of the Jewish population or, to use the term then employed, security of the Jews—which was so generally compromised in Poland at the time (a condition repeatedly brought to the attention of the authorities by the Jewish Committees)—was never discussed as a separate issue during the periodic high-level meetings at the Ministry of Public Security that I mentioned earlier.[48] Norman Salsitz, who as Tadeusz Zawadzki was in charge of the security police for the Kraków county until August 1945, has never heard the issue of Jewish security being raised during periodic meetings held every ten days at the UB's voivodship headquarters. Whatever affinity Communists may have had for the Jews in Poland after the war (whatever affinity Jewish Communists may have had for the Jews in Poland after the war), they certainly did not share their concerns.

But let us move into a more congenial environment and leave conference rooms in Warsaw's Ministry of Public Security for reception rooms in the Lublin bishop's residence. In the files of the Legal Department of the Central Committee of Polish Jews we find a memorandum reporting the conversation between the then-bishop of Lublin, Stefan Wyszynski, and a delegation of local Jewish leaders some two weeks after the Kielce pogrom. The Jewish Committee was desperately trying to get influential members of the Catholic hierarchy to condemn the event and the anti-Semitism which brought it about. This is how their pleas were received by Stefan Wyszynski:

> The bishop did not agree with [our] assessment [of the Kielce events]. He argued that the causes are much deeper, that they are rooted in the general dislike of Jews who are taking active part in the current political life. Germans wanted to destroy the Jewish nation because it was an advocate of communism. According to the bishop, Jewish input into the life of Poland is minimal. The Polish nation is grateful to Jews for Fitelberg [a renowned conductor and composer] and some others, but for many other things it cannot be grateful. The bishop stresses that the horrors of Hitlerite camps had their model in Siberian camps. They were the primary school of Hitlerite barbarism, which has its follow-up also at the present time. Jews, according to the bishop, should work hard to get a state in Palestine, or some colonies in South America. . . . In Poland, Jews are not the only ones being murdered; also Poles suffer that fate. Many are in prisons and in camps. The bishop condemns every kind of murder from the point of view of Christian ethic. In the specific case of Kielce, the bishop has nothing to add or deliberately condemn, because the idea of condemning evil is always spread by the church.
>
> During the discussion about exciting the crowd by the false legend that Christian blood is necessary to make matzo, the bishop clarified that during the Beilis trial, a lot of old and new Jewish books were assembled, and the story concerning blood was not definitely settled. In the end the bishop declared that he cannot

issue an official statement about the Kielce events, but during a soon-to-be-held meeting of priests he will explain this matter in the spirit of calming down the faithful.[49]

With this state of mind on the issue of "blood libel" among the most distinguished churchmen in Poland (Wyszynski after a long career is hailed today as the Primate of the Millennium, and his beatification process just began in Rome), one cannot be at all surprised that this medieval prejudice brought people into the streets in postwar Poland on many occasions and in many towns—in Kraków, in Kielce, in Bytom, in Bialystok, in Szczecin, in Bielawa, in Otwock, or in Legnica. On occasion the whole matter was treated, one is tempted to say, with a disarming simplicity: on October 19, 1946, a few tipsy fellows were looking for a lost child in a building where Jewish returnees lived in Kraków, at 10 Stradom Street. A small crowd began to assemble in the street, and when guards of the building proceeded to disperse it, "the head of militia patrol [which in the meantime had been called by alarmed residents] told one of our guards that 'if your child got lost, citizen, you would also be searching around' [*gdyby obywatelowi zginelo dziecko, to obywatel tez by szukal*]."[50]

A Jewish person in those days could not appreciate this militiaman's earnestness or dry sense of humor. They would be paralyzed with fear instead. The chairman of the Jewish Committee in Częstochowa, Brenner, thus wrote in the first issue of *Glos Bundu* (*The Voice of Bund*) in August 1946, "Lately, an eleven-year-old Christian child, accompanied by his mother, walked on Garibaldi Street, where a lot of Jews are living, and pointed at a house where allegedly Jews held him for two days. This time Christian neighbors laughed at the boy and chased him away. . . . And even though the danger has passed, and people start calming down, this episode had a horrible influence on our neighborhood. People started to close up apartments, businesses, dropped what they were doing, and fled. But where to? Nobody knows and cannot give a clear answer."

We need to acknowledge that there were also voices uttered in public which conveyed the sense of deep pain and shame over what had happened in Kielce. Among them, also a lonely voice of a prominent churchman—the bishop of Częstochowa, Teodor Kubina, who made a forceful statement condemning the perpetrators.[51] A whole panoply of Polish intellectuals wrote dramatic texts in periodicals that I mentioned before. Yet the general thrust of commentaries which circulated at the time, and later stuck in public consciousness and historiography, was not to address the issue directly but instead to instrumentalize it. The notion that the Kielce pogrom was a provocation by the security police gained wide acceptance—presumably the Communists did it in order to divert attention abroad from a recently falsified nationwide referendum. This interpretation allowed various journalists, and later also historians, to conveniently forget who took part in the pogrom and instead to speculate as to who set it off and with what purpose in mind. Numerous condemnatory commentaries published in daily newspapers and during public meetings immediately afterward also put an instrumental spin on the tragic events. As noted by the Jewish weekly *Opinia,* coming out at the time in Warsaw, "During protest meetings held after the Kielce pogrom Polish speakers often put out a question—What will public opinion in foreign countries think about us? How one would rather want to hear the simple and so pleasant-sounding words—What will our Jewish fellow citizens think?"[52]

Postwar anti-Semitism was widespread and predated any Communist attempts to take power in Poland. It was firmly rooted, among other things, in medieval prejudice about ritual murder. The ancient canard made rounds after the war also in an updated, modernized version, stating that the blood of Christian Polish children was drunk by Jews in order to fortify themselves after they came back emaciated from concentration camps.

For true believers in communism, and such were the leaders of the Polish Workers' (i.e., Communist) Party taking over in 1944, the Holocaust was not a real issue. It could not be told as an autonomous story for lack of a requisite vocabulary. The Holocaust of the European Jews (in this case, Polish Jews) did not fit into conceptual categories employed by the Communists. It was a side effect of something different, greater, and more significant. It was an aftershock, yet another manifestation of class conflict, a tremor registered during the last "dying" stages of capitalism. So, fascism, colonial expansion of Hitler's Germany, racist imperialism of the Third Reich—these were the proper, universal categories capturing all facets of the conflict which murderously played itself out during World War II. And the mass killings, the genocide of European Jewry, could only be subsumed under these categories along with everything else that had happened.

Such a Weltanschauung was not espoused solely by unimaginative party bureaucrats. It was an element of the emerging cultural paradigm propagated by sophisticated intellectuals. The foremost Marxist literary critic of this epoch, Jan Kott, thus commented on the story "Easter Week" (*Wielki Tydzien*) by the foremost contemporary Polish writer, Jerzy Andrzejewski: "I know both versions of Andrze-jewski's novella. . . . In the first version the Jewish tragedy [the action of the novella is placed at the time of the Warsaw ghetto uprising in April 1943] was one of a people deprived of any empathy (*odartych z braterstwa*) and condemned to a hopeless struggle. . . . In the second version a rich, correct, and differentiated analysis of the social situation of all the protagonists put back on its feet a world that was previously turned upside down. Jewish struggle in the ghetto ceased to be a mystical drama of the chosen people but became an element of the general struggle against the German occupation. In the second version of 'The Easter Week' the word 'fascism' for the first time made an appearance."[53]

Of course, we must be careful to properly historicize this discussion. At the time, *nobody* was talking about the Holocaust. Jews themselves were not able to articulate the issue for a long time. But the momentary silence of communism was of a different nature than the silence of the Jews, of the Germans, of the French, of the Dutch, or of the Poles. All, except the Communists, were rendered speechless because of varying degrees of collusion with the Nazi-organized crime. Even the Jews, as is known, shared in the sense of guilt as individuals in the form of survivor complex: why have I (you!) been spared the horrible fate which befell all my (your!) relatives and coreligionists? And, as a facet of community life, there was the deeply ambiguous issue of the *Judenrat* which could not be addressed for a long time and, frankly, still awaits its historian.

Communists by and large were not implicated in this particular wartime crime. This was yet another characteristic feature which set them apart from the East European societies where they operated. And it did not facilitate the legitimization of their postwar rule, either. (Remember that Righteous Among Nations would be estranged after the war amid their own communities.) The Communists wanted at all costs to authenticate themselves as the only organizational embodiments of the true national interest of East European societies, and they did not shy from drawing on xenophobia and ethnic prejudice to mobilize support. Władysław Gomulka, a leading Communist who would soon be shunted aside for the so-called nationalist deviation, labeled the legal anti-Communist political opposition (on the occasion of the plebiscite organized in 1946 where the Communists appealed to the population to vote "three times yes") the camp of *drei mal nein* (three times no). Just like that, in German. After Khrushchev got reinstated as the first secretary of the Communist Party in the Ukraine, he said to a Jewish veteran who wondered why the destruction of Ukrainian Jewry was not properly commemorated, "Here is the Ukraine and it is not in our interest that the Ukrainians should associate the return of Soviet power with the return of the Jews."[54]

The tone of patriotic rhetoric deployed in immediate postwar years by Polish Communists replicated the message of right-wing nationalists in many important respects. Anti-German hysteria combined with mellow Pan-Slavism into a blend familiar to followers of Roman Dmowski. And the key message—calling for and promising "national unity" and invoking "national will"—was even more on target.

"Nation," in all its forms and linguistic variations, be it as a noun or as an adjective, was the most frequently enunciated word in public speeches and party documents of this period. A young Polish historian, Marcin Zaremba, gives an excellent analysis of this phenomenon in a recent study.[55] Integral verbal nationalism—organic metaphors of *Blut und Boden,* or rather of "blood and bones" (*z krwi i kości*), when sketching the purported lineage of the movement (as part and parcel of struggles for national liberation by Polish patriots of earlier centuries)—replaced class analysis and Marxist arguments of historical inevitability. The word "communism" was nowhere to be seen, frankly, to the discomfort of some old comrades. They also must have frowned at the spectacle of a seasoned party operative—comrade Tomasz to those who knew him from the organization—who now as Boleslaw Bierut identified himself as a man without party affiliation (*bezpartyjny*) and soon took an oath of office concluding with a formulaic "so help me God" to serve as the country's first president (chairman of the KRN, the National Council). The Polish Communist Party (Komunistyczna Partia Polski, or KPP), dissolved by the Comintern on Stalin's orders in 1938, was reconstituted after the Communists belatedly joined the anti-Nazi underground struggle, but as the Polish Workers' Party (Platne Pacholki Rosji, or PPR). It remained so named until the "unification congress," when it absorbed the Polish Socialist Party in December 1948 and reappeared under the name of the Polish United Workers' Party (Polska Zjednoczona Partia Robotnicza, or PZPR), again without the word "Communist" in its name. All these disguises notwithstanding, the public was not fooled, as a popular reading of the acronym PPR as "Platne Pachotki Rosji" (Russia's mercenary knaves) showed plainly.

But the Communists were not dissuaded. Knowing the corrosive power of persistence—repetition as cornerstone of successful propaganda—they went after the whole range of their political opponents' traditional vocabulary. At Stalin's insistence, a core of Communist activists, while being groomed to play leading roles in postwar Poland, banded together in the Soviet Union into an organization called the Association of Polish Patriots (Związek Patriotów Polskich, or ZPP). Wanda Wasilewska, an *éminence grise* of this association, was somewhat miffed initially.[56] The word "patriot," she pointed out to Stalin, has a "compromised" connotation to Polish Communists. To which he replied that "every word can be given a new meaning, and it is up to you what meaning it will be endowed with."[57]

In the realm where Soviet Communists established themselves in power, suffusing language with new meanings was the most effective mechanism of social control, next only to direct application of police terror. In this case—a pretty daring one even by the standards of the time—the term "Polish patriots" was proposed as a label designating an organization grouping individuals ready to serve as proxies of the Soviet power.

Behind this screen of "Polish patriotism," "national unity," "national will," "blood and bones," "raison d'état," "so help me God," and mellow Pan-Slavism, sovietization of Polish society was energetically pursued. To quote Jakub Berman, one of the most influential politburo members at the time, "The history of the workers' movement acquires blood and body (*nabiera krwi i ciala*) when we manage to place it in the wholeness of national history. It is time to tie together, to organically unify the history of our party and of the workers' movement with the history of the nation."[58] Given this tenor of Communist Party legitimization efforts, no wonder that it did not have much room (even if it had any will) to simultaneously champion, however construed, Jewish interests.

Thus, their benign neglect of the Holocaust of Polish Jewry and putting it aside with other unmentionables did not necessarily exemplify bad faith on the part of the new rulers but flowed naturally from the essence of leading ideology and practicalities of the moment. When Stalin's increasingly aggressive anti-Semitism is factored in, the implicit social contract between the Communist authorities and newly subjugated Polish society—that they would mutually benefit by considering the wartime fate of Polish Jews a nonissue and would encourage and facilitate the remainder of Polish Jewry's departure from the country—became a given. My sense is that this was an implicit "give" for the "take" of power which the Communists grabbed at the Soviet Union's and their own behest. And so, in the soon-to-be-opened Auschwitz museum dedicated to the commemoration of international antifascist struggle and martyrology, throughout the entire period of Communist rule in Poland, the word "Jew" could hardly be found at all.

The proof of the pudding is in the eating. And no matter how we look at it, one must recognize that in the brief span of five years following the end of the war—at the time of consolidation of the Communist rule in Poland and, if my argument stands, as a constitutive part of the process—Poland was rendered *judenrein* (free of Jews). The last cleansing touches were made during two subsequent waves of Jewish emigration both permitted and induced by the Communist authorities, in 1956–57 and in 1968–69. Thus, quite appropriately, under the stewardship of the man who had been accused of "nationalist deviation" in 1948 and came back to power in 1956 as a patriotic Communist, Władysław Gomulka, what had begun advertised proudly as the "national road to socialism" ended twenty years later, in 1968, *toute proportion gardée* (relatively speaking), in national socialism plain and simple.

Rather than bringing communism to Poland, as a facile historiography of this period maintains, after millennial presence in these lands, the Jews were finally driven out of Poland under the Communist regime. In the words of the Nobel prize–winning poet Czeslaw Milosz, Poland's Communist rulers fulfilled the dream of Polish nationalists by bringing into existence an ethnically pure state.

NOTES

Except where noted otherwise, all English translations in the text and notes are mine.

1. Maria Hochberg-Marianska, Noe Gruess, *Dzieci oskarzaja* (Kraków: Centralna Zydowska Komisja Historyczna w Polsce, 1947).

2. Perhaps the best-known episode of this sort can be found in Marcel Reich-Ranicki's memoirs, simply on account of their worldwide popularity. But the story should not be taken as an anecdote. It came as a shocking realization to survivors and brought fear together with tangible persecution into the lives of rescuers. "In conclusion of my story," writes Dr. Henryk Stecki, "I also want to mention that after I returned to Kraków, some two to three weeks following my departure from the village where I stayed last, it became known that I was a Jew. Already after this area got liberated I was threatened there with death, and the good, innocent (*Bogu ducha winni*) people who gave me shelter were threatened with flogging and having their house set on fire" (Zydowski Instytut Historyczny [hereafter ZIH], 301/445). Shraga Feivel Bielawski returned to his native village of Wegrow, near Warsaw, after the war and saw an acquaintance who helped his sister and kept some family valuables which allowed them to survive. "I was so excited to see him that I ran over to him, grabbed his hand and bent down to kiss it. Suddenly he shoved me away firmly, rejecting me. I looked up to see what had happened. I saw the Poles standing and looking at us. I understood. Pierkowski had to push me away because he was ashamed to let them see a Jew getting so close to him. . . . Even the people who had helped us were afraid to show us kindness in public" (Shraga Feivel Bielawski, *The Last Jew from Wegrow* [New York: Praeger, 1991], 147). A Jewish boy survived in a Catholic orphanage in Kraków, where both the priest in charge and his teacher knew that he was Jewish and covered up for him. The teacher took him to her house after the war but soon, writes Zygmunt Weinreb, "she had to give me away, because people started to make it difficult for her that she was keeping a Jew. But I still go to visit Mrs. Thielowa, and she always calls me Czesio, because that's how she is used to" (ZIH, 301/406). Regina Almowa's husband served as an officer in the Polish Army before the war. After an *Aktion* (action) in Przemysl, she found herself in desperate straits. "All acquaintances and good friends completely failed me," she wrote in her deposition before the Jewish Historical Commission after the war. "In the end I recalled the family of my husband's commanding officer and I was kept there for about ten days. The younger lady probably would have kept me longer, but her mother was very nervous, so I decided that I must leave their house. I will always keep a recollection of this woman, but I will not mention her name because under the present circumstances I would risk exposing her to contempt from her compatriots [*wspolziomkow*]. I find this all the time to be the case that people who saved the Jews do not want their fellow citizens to know about it" (ZIH, collection 301, deposition 681). Social ostracism toward ethnic Poles who helped Polish Jews during the war was a pervasive phenomenon in liberated Poland, in both urban and village environments, cutting across various social milieus.

3. Centralny Komitet Zydow w Polsce [hereafter CKZP], Wydzial Organizacyjny, file 304, folder 3. For full identification of the source, one needs to know the date of the document. If it appears in the text, I do not give it again in the footnotes.

4. Ibid.

5. Ibid.

6. Ibid.

7. State Archive in Kraków [hereafter SAK], Provincial Office (Urzad Wojewódzki hereafter UW]) 2, File 1073, Kraków.

8. Memo from the County Jewish Committee in Chrzanow to the Sociopolitical Department of the Cracow Voivodship, July 11, 1945, SAK, UW 2, File 1073.

9. CKZP, Wydzial Produktywizacji 303/XII/6, 25.IV.45.

10. CKZP, Wydzial Produktywizacji, 303/XII/18, VI–VII, 46.

11. Ewa Kozminska-Frejlak, "Polska jako ojczyzna Zydow—zydowskie strategie zadomowienia sie w powojennej Polsce (1944–1949)," *Kultura i Spoleczenstwo* 43, no. 1 (1999): 131.

12. SAK, UW 2, File 1073.

13. CKZP, Wydzial Organizacyjny, 304/3.

14. CKZP, Wydzial Organizacyjny 304/5, 2.V.45.

15. Ruth Gay, *Safe Among the Germans. Liberated Jews After World War II* (New Haven, CT: Yale University Press, 2002).

16. Heda Margolius Kovály, *Under a Cruel Star: A Life in Prague, 1941–1968* (New York: Penguin Books, 1986), 46–47.

17. Pawel Machcewicz and Krzysztof Persak, eds., *Wokol Jedwabnego,* 2 vols. (Warsaw: Instytut Pamieci Narodowej [Institute of National Remembrance], 2002), 2:305.

One could point out that a normative order of sorts regulated access to plundered Jewish property. The governing rule was simple: those who participated in the killings had a better claim than anybody else. Thus, when Helena Klimaszewska from the village of Goniadz went to nearby Radzilów to get an apartment for her in-laws—she knew there were vacancies there, after the Jews had been killed—she was rebuffed by a certain Feliks Godlewski (she told the story during a deposition at his trial after the war), who reproached the claimants for not having been there when people were needed to kill the Jews and only now showing up to claim apartments. "You could have killed ten Jews and you would have gotten a house," she quoted him as saying at the time. Her mother-in-law protested that the family had made a contribution on that day as her grandson, Jozef Ekstowicz, was the one who climbed onto the barn where the Jews were assembled and doused its roof with gasoline. It is not clear from the transcript how persuasive her protestations were for Godlewski and whether the women got the apartment they were seeking (see Machcewicz and Persak, *Wokol Jedwabnego,* 1:41, 246; 2:932, 954).

18. Bielawski, *Last Jew from Wegrow,* 72.

19. Yad Vashem, 03/3033–1636/255. The original of Chaja Finkels-ztajn's testimony was only partially translated by the IPN, and the segment re-counting their peregrinations after the Radziłów Jews had been killed has not been included in the volume. A similar exchange is recounted by Bielawski from the vicinity of Wegrow, where he was trying to find a hiding place at the house of a peasant with whom he used to do business: "He thought for a moment and replied, 'this is a time when everyone is paying attention to everyone else's business. If my neighbors or friends knew that I was hiding Jews, I would be in big trouble. They would think I had made much money from the Jews and would report me to the Germans'" (Bielawski, *Last Jew from Warsaw,* 72). Yet another conversation along the same lines was over-heard by a Jewish boy, Emanuel Kriegel, hiding in a peasant's house near Buczacz: "Our landlady was visited by a *banderist* [member of a Ukrainian nationalist organization], Turbota Michal, and one Pole, his helper, to see her daughter. The *banderist* boasted that he killed forty Jews in the forest, and he pried our landlady to confess that she keeps Jews at her place because she has money. And it is known that who has money must be keeping Jews. But our landlady did not confess" (ZIH, 301/196).

20. Irving Heymont, *Among the Survivors of the Holocaust, 1945: The Landsberg DP Camp Letters of Major Irving Heymont, United States Army* (Cincinnati: American Jewish Archives, 1982), 49–50.

21. Gay, *Safe Among the Germans,* 183.

22. The issue of Jewish flight from Poland as part of Brikha was intro-duced into Polish-language historiography by Natalia Aleksiun-Madrzak in a series of three articles published in 1996 in the *Biuletyn Zydowskieg Instytutu Historycznego.* She is preparing a translation of David Engel's monograph *Bein shihrur livrichah: Nitsdei ha-sho'ah be-Polin veha ma'avak al hanhagatam 1944–1946* (Tel Aviv: Am Oved, 1996) into Polish.

23. *Gazeta Wyborcza,* April 1, 2001.

24. See Pawel Machcewicz's introduction to Machcewicz and Persak, *Wokol Jedwabnego.*

25. For his extensive legal expertise on the Jedwabne trials, see Andrzej Rzeplinski, "Ten jest z ojczyzny mojej? Sprawy karne oskarzonych o wy-mordowanie Zydow w Jedwabnym w swietle zasady rzetelnego procesu," in Machcewicz and Persak, *Wokol Jedwabnego,* 1:353–459.

26. See especially Andrzej Zbikowski, "Pogromy i mordy ludnosci zydowskiej w Lomzynskim i na Bialstocczyznie latem 1941 roku w swietle relacji ocalalych Zydow i dokumentow sadowych," in Machcewicz and Persak, *Wokol Jedwabnego,* 1:159–271; and Jan J. Milewski, "Wybrane akta proce-

sow karnych z lat 1945–1958 w sprawach o udzial w zbrodni na ludnosci zydowskiej w Radzilowie," in Machcewicz and Persak, *Wokol Jedwabgnego,* 2:863–983.

27. Ian Kershaw, *Hitler, 1889–1936 Hubris* (New York: W.W. Norton and Co., 2000), chap. 13.

28. Hal Lehrman, *Russia's Europe* (New York: D. Appleton Century Co., 1947), 187.

29. Ibid.

30. See Antoni Dudek and Grzegorz Pytel, *Boleslaw Piasecki: Proba biografii politycznej* (London: Aneks, 1990), 156–62; and Robert Levy, *Ana Pauker: The Rise and Fall of a Jewish Communist* (Los Angeles: University of California Press, 2001), 75–77.

31. Jan T. Gross, *Neighbors: The Destruction of the Jewish Community in Jedwabne, Poland* (Princeton, NJ: Princeton University Press, 2001), 116. For a full text of Zygmunt Laudanski's petition, see Machcewicz and Persak, *Wokol Jedwabnego,* 2:607–9.

32. Hal Lehrman, "Hungary: Liberation's Bitter Fruit," *Commentary,* January 1946, 30.

33. "Sprawozdanie z powiatu bochenskiego," 21 August 1945, SAK, UW 2, File 91.

34. CKZP, Prezydium, 303/3.

35. Ida Gertsman, "Zajscia w Kielcach," *Biuletyn Zydowskiego Instytutu Historyznego,* no. 4 (1996): 23–24.

36. CKZP, Wydzial Organizacyjny, 304/35, 29.VI.46.

37. "Komisja Specjalna w Krakowie, Oświęcim," 27 January 1947, CKZP, Central Special Commission, Box 1–2.

38. SAK, Jewish Voivodship Committee, File 14, p. 87.

39. This is an estimate by the late Dr. Lucjan Dobroszycki.

40. See Gross, *Neighbors,* 129–31.

41. CKZP, Central Special Commission, Box 1–2, pp. 156–58.

42. "O stanie badan nad pogromem kieleckim: Dyskusja w Zydow-skim Instytucie Historycznym (12. III. 1996) z referatem wprowadzajacym prof. Krystyny Kersten," *Biuletyn Zydowskiego Instytutu Historycznego,* no. 4 (1996): 11.

43. Ibid.

44. Jerzy Kochanowski, ed., *Protokoly posiedzen Prezydium Krajowej Rady Narodowej, 1944–1947* (Warsaw: Wydawnictwo Sejmowe, 1995), 200.

45. Ibid., 302.

46. In Amos Elon, *The Pity of It All: A History of Jews in Germany, 1743–1933* (New York: Metropolitan Books, Henry Holt and Co., 2002), 346.

47. Personal communication.

48. "O stanie badan," 11.

49. CKZP, Wydzial Prawny, 303/XVI/408.

50. Memo, 6 November 1946, CKZP, Central Special Commission, Box 1–2, Folder 1, p. 114.

51. He ordered a statement distributed all over his diocese in which the following was put forth: "All statements about ritual murders are lies. Nobody from among the Christian population in Kielce, in Częstochowa, or anywhere else, has ever been harmed by Jews for ritual and religious purposes. We do not know of a single case of a Christian child that has been abducted by Jews. All news and stories spread on this topic are either deliberately invented by criminals or come from confused people who do not know any better, and they aim to provoke a crime. . . . We trust that responsible citizens of Częstochowa attached to principles of Christian morality will not follow criminal suggestions and will not debase themselves by raising their hands against a fellow-citizen only because he is of a different nationality and denomination" (*Gazeta Wyborcza,* March 3–4, 2001).

52. *Opinia,* no. 15, July 25, 1946.

53. *Kuznica,* no. 8 (1946).

54. Amir Weiner, *Making Sense of War: The Second World War and the Fate of the Bolshevik Revolution* (Princeton, NJ: Princeton University Press, 2001), 212.

55. Marcin Zaremba, *Komunizm, legitymizacja, nacjonalizm: Nacjonalistyczna legitymizacja wladzy komunistycznej w Polsce* (Warsaw: Instytut Sudiow Politycznych PAN, Wydawnictwo Trio, 2001), esp. chaps. 4 and 5.

56. A fascinating political biography of Wasilewska still remains to be written. She was the daughter of Leon Wasilewski, Pilsudski's close friend and interwar Poland's first minister of foreign affairs. She was a writer and an activist of the Polish Socialist Party in her own right, until she met Stalin during the 1939–41 Soviet occupation of eastern Poland and promptly gained his confidence and friendship. She was possibly the only woman who wielded political influence with the Soviet ruler. Wasilewska later married a prominent Communist Ukrainian Party activist and writer, Alexander Korneichuk, and remained in the Soviet Union after the war.

57. Zaremba, *Komunizm, legitymizacja, nacjonalizm,* 131

58. Berman's speech of September 15, 1946, quoted in Zaremba, 168.

II. I·D·E·O·L·O·G·Y

Thomas Pegelow

Linguistic Violence and Discursive Contestation Preceding the Holocaust

THE NAZI-LED COALITION GOVERNMENT BEGAN TO RESHAPE Germany's elites shortly after coming into existence in 1933. Brutal SA violence and a first wave of racial legislation targeted leftist and German Jewish members of the intellectual and functional elites in federal, state, and municipal administrations and forced many of them from office. Noticeably, paragraph 3 of the Law for the Restoration of the Professional Civil Service of April 7, 1933, which served as a model for numerous subsequent anti-Jewish decrees until 1935, singled out Germans with Jewish grandparents whom it constructed as of "non-Aryan origin."[1] The Nuremberg Racial Laws of September 15, 1935, replaced the April 1933 laws' category of "non-Aryanness" with the binary construct of "Jews" and "citizens of German and kindred blood." The first supplementary decree to the Reich Citizenship Law of November 14, 1935, established the "Jewish *Mischling*" as a legal category. The decree created—in the language of Nazi bureaucrats—a "third race," denoting descendants of one or two "full-Jewish" grandparents.[2] These laws formed, in Claudia Essner's apt interpretation, a "system" that underpinned the entire scope of Nazi anti-Jewish measures, including the dismissal of previously exempted German Jewish civil servants in late 1935.[3]

As a consequence, legal and political discourses as well as every-day language imposed the racialized categories of Jew and *Mischling* on people's subjecthood. In Nazi Germany, as Michael Burleigh has argued, "suffering was determined by categories."[4] On the one hand, language constituted a subject "within the possible circuit of recognition" and inside the "community of the German *Volk*."[5] On the other hand, language could also develop into linguistic violence by constructing a person outside of and excluded from social and national life. Such violence did not cause physical injuries like the truncheons of SA thugs. It rather inflicted conceptual injuries by aggressively imposing exclusionary categories and contributing to what Marion A. Kaplan has described as these people's "social death."[6] The Nazi constructs of Jew and *Mischling* denied individuals and religious communities the right to use their own identificatory categories and determine their sense of self. This linguistic violence by necessity preceded and accompanied the Nazis' physical onslaughts that continued throughout the 1930s and culminated in the November 1938 pogroms.

In the prewar period, while Nazi leaders called for the "stringent separation between Germans and Jews,"[7] Nazi laws and legal discourses continued to project the possibility of exceptions from anti-Jewish measures and even legal definitions of Jewishness. Scholars such as Jeremy Noakes, Beate Meyer, and more recently Bryan Mark Rigg have described the legal procedures, the workings of the Nazi bureaucracy as well as the petitioners' general strategies and limited prospects.[8] For all their crucial contributions, these historians have not systematically explored the shaping and constructive force of language and discourse itself, neither in particular exchanges between petitioners and state or party officials nor in the negotiation and renegotiation of these people's identities. Beate Meyer's insightful work on *Mischlinge,* for instance, only briefly acknowledges the use of language and exploitation of contradictions in Nazi legal categories.[9] Studies that explicitly focus on language during the Nazi era, such as Victor Klemperer's *Lingua tertii imperii* (*Language of the Third Reich,* or *LTI*), tend to overestimate the manipulative power of Nazi terminology and do not leave enough room for agency. Klemperer, a convert to Protestantism whom Nazi decrees constructed as a "full Jew," contends that nobody, not even German Jews, escaped committing "the same sin" of speaking and being corrupted by the *LTI.*[10]

This essay highlights how Germans with Jewish ancestors claimed their "Germanness" by engaging in practices which I describe as "discursive contestation." Within the constraints of discourses, these individuals often used conflicting languages to reformulate their own and their families' sense of self. They drew on patriotic parlance, discursive depictions of bodily difference, and polyphonic and contradictory notions of the dominant Nazi categories, without being able to fully control the outcome of their discursive interventions in a dictatorial regime that increasingly turned against them. Their practices unfolded along a continuum from partial support and conformity with Nazi discourses to measures of resistance to the concepts of the regime.

While my recently completed study focuses on German Jewish and gentile communities at large,[11] this essay restricts its analysis to engagements by Jewish converts to Christianity and so-called *Mischlinge* in the aftermath of the promulgation of the Nuremberg Racial Laws. At the time, the ongoing social ostracism and physical violence, loss of employment, and worries about their children's future prompted most converts and *Mischlinge* to step up activities to defend their place in German society. This essay specifically centers on those petitioners who sought an exemption from anti-Jewish measures according to paragraph 7 of the first supplementary decree to the Reich Citizenship Law and locates their practices in the institutional procedures and discourses. It also focuses on the applicants who dealt with the Reich Agency for Kinship Research (Reichsstelle für Sippenforschung, or RfS), which issued "decisions on descent" (*Abstammungsbescheide*) for many of these petitioners for exemptions.[12] Subordinated under the Reich Interior Ministry, the RfS by the mid-1930s was the sole administrative body to decide people's descent in cases of doubt, though its position remained embattled in the institutional chaos of the Nazi state.[13] Immediately following the decrees to the Nuremberg Laws, applications for exemptions reached the desks of Nazi bureaucrats in increasing numbers. The Interior Ministry alone received 295 petitions in late 1935 and 1,400 in the following year. The number of petitions sent to lower-level bureaucracies is no longer quantifiable, but there is evidence that it was much higher.[14] The same can be said about the Reich Agency for Kinship Research, since the authorities charged state and regional administrative bodies with handling cases that were not in doubt. In 1935, the RfS received 17,670 applications. In 1936, the number rose to 24,529.[15]

The applications by converts and their descendants, when compared to responses by the majority of German Jews who still vocally claimed their Germanness in the early phase of the regime, often took extreme forms and were hardly representative for all Germans of Jewish ancestry. Yet, their practices are particularly effective in revealing the increasingly desperate strategies of the most highly assimilated segment of this diverse population that the Nazis sought to exclude.

Their case sheds light on the constantly shifting and contested boundaries between Jewishness and Germanness that evolved—in Steven Aschheim's words—"co-constitutionally," that is, as "contextually and interactively constructed."[16]

The discursive interventions of converts and *Mischlinge* were shaped by Nazi decrees and the bureaucratic procedures they set in motion. Petitioners deliberately used the Nazi wording and rules to increase their chances for a desired response. They learned about these rules in the press, through instructional leaflets from the bureaucracies, from lawyers, and simply by word of mouth. On December 4, 1935, Hitler authorized the Interior Ministry to process "applications for parity of treatment" (*Gleichstellungsanträge*) with people "of German blood" (*Deutschblütigen*) according to paragraph 7 of the first supplementary decree to the Reich Citizenship Law. The ministry decreed that applications had to be submitted to the Bavarian and Prussian *Regierungspräsidenten* (district president) or, in the remaining states, to the *Land* (state) governments. These agencies had to determine if a case merited an exemption by considering "serious reasons from the point of view of the public at large—not only in the interest of the petitioner." Only then was the office supposed to inquire into their "personal, especially racial, spiritual, and character qualities, [their] participation in the World War and [their] political reliability." The agencies also had to request a statement from *Gau* party headquarters before transferring the files to the Interior Ministry in Berlin. The final decision on each applicant rested with Hitler himself.[17]

Looking back on the then recent activities of the Reich Agency for Kinship Research, the author of an RfS instructional leaflet noted in late 1938 that "Jewish *Mischlinge*" with a "Jewish" father and "German" mother did "not rarely" claim that they had not been the child of their legal father. "As a rule," the RfS official continued, "this is a mere assertion which is made in order to falsely produce proof of German blood [*Deutschblütigkeitsnachweis*]."[18] The RfS operated by its own sets of guidelines and distinct wordings that furnished the agency's employees with the language to use in composing their decisions on descent and confronted petitioners with excluding categories and procedural details. The RfS's work was primarily based on official documents such as the birth and marriage certificates of the examinees, their parents, and their grandparents.[19] Examinees could contest a decision by filing a "complaint about the ruling" (*Dienstaufsichtsbeschwerde*) with the

Reich Interior Ministry. The reopening of a case often led to a "genealogical and racial examination" (*Erb- und rassekundliche Untersuchung*) carried out at one of the designated anthropological institutes. These exams included the typing of the blood and comparative measurements of up to 130 body parts, including the hands, heads, and faces of the petitioners and their legal and supposed parents. If a parent was deceased or unavailable, these institutes often accepted the person's private family pictures.[20]

Genealogical certificates and racial examinations did not speak for themselves. Discourses restricted the meaning that examiners, RfS, and Interior Ministry officials could attribute to any anthropological observation and claim. Certificates, too, were not as readily available as Nazi officials might have initially assumed. Wilhelm Stuckart, state secretary at the Interior Ministry, claimed in a letter to the other Reich ministries on October 17, 1935, that on the basis of documents, "only 50 percent of all *Volksgenossen* (racial comrades) could completely prove their Aryan descent until 1800."[21] These numbers have to be seen in the context of the Interior Ministry's struggles with Nazi Party radicals for a less-inclusive definition of *Mischlinge* and the RfS's attempts to increase its significance and influence. Even if these figures were inflated, any lack of certificates increased the significance of language in the processes surrounding people's claims for Germanness, since it strengthened the weight of criteria that were discursively constructed and open to contestation.

Jewish converts to Christianity and individuals whom Nazi decrees labeled *Mischlinge* who applied for exemptions and RfS decisions on descent shared by far more dissimilarities than commonalities. With the exceptions of those *Mischlinge* who were part of organized Judaism and categorized as "designated Jews" (*Geltungsjuden*), these people mainly shared the commonality, as Aleksandar-Saša Vuletic aptly put it, that "they did not belong to the Jewish religious community."[22] Most of them showed a high degree of assimilation to German bourgeois values and lived in urban settings. A discernible number had also identified with the nationalist and even *völkisch* (racial) Germany prior to the rise of Nazism. The surviving records reveal that petitioners came from all social classes and professions but show an overrepresentation of members of the former intellectual and functional elites. Given their more intimate knowledge of legal discourses and connections to high-ranking officials in the ministerial bureaucracies, this "subgroup" was better positioned to clear the initial hurdles and thus left a longer paper trail.

Applicants for an exemption from Nazi racial laws or an RfS decision on descent relied on a variety of discursive strategies to challenge their gradual exclusion from the *Volksgemeinschaft* (racial community) and counter the conceptual injuries sustained from Nazi discourses. In line with the exemptions the Nazis had initially granted to veterans of the First World War, most petitioners adopted a patriotic language that highlighted their own and their relatives' military service for Germany during the past 130 years as a key component of their general patriotic public identity. In a letter to the Bavarian *Reichsstatthalter* (Reich governor) Ritter von Epp of December 7, 1935, the retired medical officer Dr. Franz Schulz stressed that it was his "entire pride to belong to the Infantry Regiment Leib since 1916 and participate in the struggles for Verdun."[23] The convert to Catholicism whom the Nuremberg Laws had redefined as a "full Jew" portrayed his application for an exemption as "safeguarding [his] honorary position" as an "old frontline soldier" at a time in which a new military law had "already deprived him of the honor to serve his *Volk* and fatherland." Schulz appealed to von Epp as his former commander to testify to his "love for the fatherland" and that he "fulfilled his duty devoting his entire strength on the battlefield." His call did not go unanswered. A few days later, von Epp's office informed Schulz that the *Reichsstatthalter* was willing to support his petition.[24]

The Stuttgart-based dentist Dr. Erwin Goldmann intensified this patriotic parlance by directly drawing on and even deliberately reifying Nazi jargon to stake out claims to Germanness. In a May 1937 letter to Winifred Wagner, Goldmann reiterated his "steadfast love and devotion to *Führer, Volk,* and fatherland." Goldmann evoked the authority of the Nazi leader and head of state by explicitly employing a Hitler quotation that celebrated the frontline soldier as the "honorary citizen of the nation." To exclude him along with his fellow "non-Aryan Christian" veterans from national life amounted, in the eyes of the Jewish convert to Protestantism whom Nazi decrees constructed as a "full Jew," to a "violation of the loyalty between war comrades." In addressing Richard Wagner's daughter-in-law, he sought to capitalize on Wagner's reputation to use her access to Hitler for interventions on behalf of members of the *völkisch* movement she considered "wronged" by Nazi policies.[25] While Goldmann succeeded—also with the help of advocates like Wagner—in making a case for the necessity of a racial examination, RfS officials did not read its results as meriting a change in his "racial status." Goldmann remained a "full Jew" and his children "*Mischlinge* of the first degree."[26]

Other petitioners engaged in different types of discursive contestation by exploiting the contradictions in the Nazi discourses' stereotypical depictions of "Jewish" bodily difference, such as large noses and black hair. These Nazi depictions continued to inform constructs used by anthropologists in their racial examinations on behalf of the Reich Agency for Kinship Research. In a letter to the Saxon Education Ministry of January 4, 1938, Felix Krueger, a recently retired psychology professor who had laid the foundation for structural psychology and the Leipzig school, contested the RfS's construct of his descent as "*Mischling* of the second degree." The sixty-three-year-old Krueger claimed that despite the documentary evidence, his mother's begetter was not his grandfather Sigmund Engel, a Jewish convert to Protestantism, but a gentile Polish merchant with whom Krueger's grandmother had an extramarital affair. Krueger claimed that he was "of purely Aryan, namely predominantly German, the rest Polish descent. We six siblings had all blond or light brown hair; we all are or were blue-eyed." Pointing out that the same was true for their parents, Krueger added, "the pictures submitted to the Reich Agency for Kinship Research upon its request should have proven this." Krueger reiterated anti-Semitic constructs of "Jewish" bodily difference that had become widespread in German culture and projected his own appearance against the Jewish Other. More than two years after this letter, a critically backlogged and understaffed RfS declared Krueger a person of "German or kindred blood." The revised decision explicitly pointed to the "outward appearance of the examinee and his mother."[27]

While a growing number of contestants evoked physical dissimilarities between themselves and a supposed parent, not all of them couched their claim in the blatant anti-Semitic language of the Nazi regime. In 1937, the twenty-four-year-old Helga Schlossberg applied for what she called a "declaration of Aryanness" (*Arischerklärung*). Supported by her unmarried mother, she questioned the identity of her documented begetter, a German Jewish manufacturer who had fled Germany to escape Nazi persecution. In letters to the Interior Ministry in the summer of 1938, Schlossberg stressed that "according to the opinion of Prof. Dr. Lunge," she had "no outward resemblance at all" to her supposed biological father. In fact, they could, Schlossberg paraphrased the doctors, "not find any Jewish features on me." She tried to construct a truth claim on her non-Jewish looks based on scientific discourses and the medical authorities. Yet Professor Lunge was only involved in typing her blood. In late 1938, a racial examination at Frankfurt University's Institute for Genetics and Racial Hygiene discerned similarities "in a few features" between Schlossberg and pictures of her contested father. The RfS affirmed her status as a *Mischling* of the first degree."[28]

While many examinees drew extensively on official Nazi language, it did not simply, as Victor Klemperer claimed, write and think for them.[29] Without being in control of the outcome of their discursive interventions in Nazi discourses, petitioners reiterated some Nazi categories which "improved" their status to escape their violent submission to others that excluded them from the community of Germans. They employed, in the words of one survivor, what most of them regarded as "foreign words, foreign categories." In his correspondence in 1937, Erwin Goldmann referred to his children as "half Aryans" to reaffirm their strong ties to Germanness. More recent interviews with his daughter suggest that this strategy had some impact—at least on the language of his offspring. When encountering fellow teenagers in the 1930s, Verena Groth recalled, "at some point I had to tell him or her, 'Listen, I'm half Aryan.'" Both father and daughter deliberately avoided using the much more exclusionary category "half Jew." Rudolf Petersen, a merchant from a long-established bourgeois family in Hamburg whose mother was the descendant of a German Jewish family of bankers, also talked of himself as a "half Aryan."[30]

Other petitioners brought more elaborate challenges against the dominant Nazi discourses and pushed the inherent contradictions in racialized categories further. Faced with the imminent removal from his Heidelberg University chair, Walter Jellinek sent a petition to the Chancellery of the Führer in November 1935. In his letter, Jellinek, one of the Weimar Republic's most prominent legal scholars, contested his construction as a "full Jew" with three "Jewish grandparents." He poignantly summarized the core point of his intervention in an intermediary report to the Stuttgart Education Ministry two months later: "In regard to his race, ISAK LÖB [his paternal great-grandfather; emphasis in the original], who matters as the father of ADOLF JELLINEK [his paternal grandfather], was *Aryan;* it is the rare, but clear case of an Aryan religious Jew [*arischer Religionsjude*]."[31]

Jellinek, a Protestant who had never belonged to a Jewish religious community, brought his legal expertise to bear in a direct challenge to paragraph 2, section 2 of the first decree of the Reich Citizenship Law. This decree turned a grandparent's belonging to a Jewish religious community into "legal evidence" (*Rechtsbeweis*) of her or his "full Jewishness."[32] Jellinek thus attempted to disrupt the very link between religion and race in Nazi constructs, playing off the inability of Nazi administrators and scholars to discern Jewishness on solely "racial" grounds. In September 1935, the head of the Racial Policy Office, Walter Groß, for example, had to admit that scientists did not expect to reach final results in their quest to determine a person's race without using other criteria such as religion. "The Nazi racial politics," he noted, nonetheless, "could not postpone important measures" until that time. Jellinek's contestations prompted the Interior Ministry and RfS to launch lengthy investigations. In February 1941, a letter from Frick's ministry finally rejected Jellinek's claims and reaffirmed his categorization as a "full Jew." The officials, however, left it open for him to produce more evidence and reopen the case.[33]

Though in less intricate ways, other RfS examinees such as Heinz Kardinal made use of the same strategy. The surviving fragments of his file indicate that the twenty-six-year-old Kardinal challenged the agency's decision on his descent in the spring of 1937 by portraying the "Sabbotniki" as a "Jewish sect" that had originally practiced Christianity and not Judaism. He cited the "racially" non-Jewish descent of members of this sect that encompassed his maternal grandparents to claim his own "Aryanness."[34] Jellinek and Kardinal's discursive contestations did not question the validity of the concept of a "racial Jew" (*Rassenjude*) but weakened its equation with categories such as "religious Jew" and further blurred the lines between Germanness and Jewishness. To question a key category of the Nazi state would have ended their cases, which were at the mercy of Nazi bureaucrats. Jellinek's correspondence with his brother Otto reveals the calculated nature of his intervention but also indicates that he, as Jellinek biographer Klaus Kempter argues, came to believe in some of these constructs.[35] Many more contesters, as postwar testimonies suggest, deliberately used Nazi categories in their correspondence with party and state agencies but sought to maintain a sense of self that was rooted in counterdiscourses and a non-*völkisch* understanding of German-ness.[36]

Christian Germans with Jewish ancestors encountered a renewed wave of linguistic violence after the Nuremberg Racial Laws, when Nazi discourses publicly imposed categories of "full Jews," *Mischlinge,* and *Geltungsjuden* on them. This process furthered their exclusion from the German society and culture with which most of them had strongly identified. In particular, people who belonged to the early twentieth-century intellectual and functional elites used the very Nazi discourses to contest these violent impositions. Many of them made use of exemption clauses in Nazi law or contacted the Reich Agency for Kinship Research. They specifically employed patriotic and militaristic parlance, drew on discursive images of physical difference, and sought to exploit the inherent contradictions in Nazi constructs and defini-tions. Given their lack of any significant political allies or influence in Nazi Germany, petitioners of Jewish ancestry could only rarely get past their marginalized location of speaking and writing, and so their interventions in Nazi parlance were riddled with problems. Most of these women and men failed in their attempts to disrupt their con-struction as non-German and to repeat the "injuries of speech without precisely reenacting them."[37] They paradoxically were in danger of reifying the very categories they sought to protest.

Yet, in particular contexts, including incomplete certificates, un-clear legal provisions, and elicited support by figures with high stand-ing in the Nazi regime, practices of discursive contestation helped petitioners escape the linguistic violence of Nazi categories. To even keep petition processes open and examinees' "racial status" in flux could aid often desperate converts or *Mischlinge* who had to deal with the progressive destruction of their material and social existence along with their shattered cultural and national identities. To speak the language of Nazi perpetrators did not automatically lead to a de-sired outcome, but it remained a key component of interventions that "raised" petitioners' "racial status." Even the most striking practices of conforming to Nazi discourses as shown by Erwin Goldmann did not secure the much-wanted goal of inclusion in the *Volksgemeinschaft.* Felix Krueger, by contrast, faced the initially reduced violence of being labeled a "*Mischling* of the second degree" and successfully used anti-Semitic images of physical difference. His career at Leipzig University nevertheless ended prematurely. Acts of contestation by other converts and so-called *Mischlinge* deliberately resisted concepts of the regime and moved toward the opposite end of the continuum. The discursive engagements of these individuals meanwhile were never complete and constantly revisited, in particular as the Nazis' seeming legalization approach to "the Jewish question" increasingly gave way to physical violence as the interwar period drew to a close. In the fall of 1941, the petitioners' practices fully turned into a matter of life and death, when the Nazi leadership began to implement its genocidal policies against Germans of Jewish and partially Jewish ancestry.

NOTES

I would like to express my gratitude to Konrad H. Jarausch, Christopher R. Browning, Doris L. Bergen, and Ann B. Kaplan for their invaluable suggestions. Research for this article was made possible by a dissertation fellowship from the Graduate School of the University of North Carolina at Chapel Hill and a research fellowship of the Miles Lerman Center for Jewish Resistance at the United States Holocaust Memorial Museum in Washington, DC.

1. See "Gesetz zur Wiederherstellung des Berufsbeamtentums vom 7. April 1933," *RGBl* 1 (1933): 175–77; and "Erste Verordnung zur Durchführung des Gesetzes zur Wiederherstellung des Berufsbeamtentums vom 11. April 1933," *RGBl* 1 (1933): 195.

2. "Erste Verordnung zum Reichsbürgergesetz vom 14. November 1935," *RGBl* 1 (1935): 1333–34; B. Lösener, "Erläuterungen und Bemerkungen zur Reichsbürgerrechtsverordnung," 31 October 1935, Institut für Zeitgeschichte (IfZ), Munich, F 71/2.

3. Cornelia Essner, "Der Mythos des 'Mischlings,'" in *Francia: Forschungen zur westeuropäischen Geschichte,* ed. Deutsches Historisches Institut Paris (Stuttgart: Thorbecke, 2000), 134.

4. Michael Burleigh, *The Third Reich: A New History* (New York: Hill and Wang, 2000), 18.

5. Judith Butler, *Excitable Speech: A Politics of the Performative* (New York: Routledge, 1997), 4–5.

6. Marion A. Kaplan, *Between Dignity and Despair* (New York: Oxford University Press, 1998), 5.

7. See N. N., "Deutschlands Ziel in der Judenfrage," *Völkischer Beobachter* (Berlin), November 16, 1938, 7.

8. Jeremy Noakes, "The Development of Nazi Policy Towards the German-Jewish 'Mischlinge,' 1933–1945," *Leo Baeck Institute Year Book* 34 (1989): 315–19; Beate Meyer, *"Jüdische Mischlinge"* (Hamburg: Doel-

ling und Galitz, 1999); Bryan Mark Rigg, *Hitler's Jewish Soldiers* (Lawrence: University Press of Kansas, 2002).

9. See Meyer, *"Jüdische Mischlinge,"* 159.

10. Victor Klemperer, *The Language of the Third Reich* (London: Athlone Press, 2000), 192, 190.

11. Thomas Pegelow, "Linguistic Violence: Language, Power and Separation in the Fate of Germans of Jewish Ancestry, 1928–1948" (Ph.D. diss., University of North Carolina, Chapel Hill, 2004).

12. The RfS was originally set up under the name of Sachverständiger für die Rasseforschung beim Reichsminister des Innern (Expert in Racial Research at the Reich Minister of the Interior) in 1933 in order to determine the "racial status" of civil servants. For an institutional study, see Diana Schulle, *Das Reichssippenamt* (Berlin: Logos, 2001).

13. See "RdErl. d. Reichs- und Preussischen Ministers des Innern to alle Landesregierungen," 26 October 1934, IV 5018/15.8., IfZ Munich, F 71/1; and "RdErl. d. Reichsministers des Innern," 25 June 1938, I e 38 II/382 5018 b, NA, RG 242, T-70, reel 14, frame 3517885.

14. See Bernhard Lösener, "Als Rassereferent im Reichsministerium des Innern," *Vierteljahrshefte für Zeitgeschichte* 9 (1961): 283; and Meyer, *"Jüdische Mischlinge,"* 157.

15. On the number of RfS cases, see the agency's report for the first half of 1936 in Bundesarchiv Berlin (BArch), R 1509/alt R 39/8.

16. Steven Aschheim, "German History and German Jewry," *Leo Baeck Institute Year Book* 43 (1998): 317–22.

17. See *"RdErl. d. Reichs- und Preussischen Ministers des Innern v. 4.12.1935 - I B 3 /416,"* *MbliV* 50 (1935): 1455–56. On the overall procedure, see also Noakes, "Development of Nazi Policy," 315–18.

18. See Reichsstelle für Sippenforschung [RfS], *Der erb- und rassenkundliche Abstammungsnachweis vor der Reichsstelle für Sippenforschung* (Berlin, 1938), 2, in BArch Berlin, R 1509/39, p. 1.

19. See Frhr. von Ulmenstein, *Der Abstammungsnachweis* (Berlin: Verlag für Standesamtswesen, 1936), 14, 69; and RfS, *Merkblatt X 104/35* (Berlin, 1935), in BArch Berlin, R 1509/17, p. 5.

20. Ulmenstein, *Der Abstammungsnachweis,* 61, 14; and RfS, *Der Erb- und rassenkundliche Abstammungsnachweis,* 1–3.

21. See "Reichs- und Preussischen Ministers des Innern to Reichs- und Preussischen Minister für Wissenschaft, Erziehung und Volksbildung," October 17, 1935, I B 3 /256 III, NA, RG 242, T-70, reel 13, frame 3517576.

22. Aleksandar-Saša Vuletic, *Christen jüdischer Herkunft im Dritten Reich* (Mainz: Philipp von Zabern, 1999), 14.

23. I used pseudonyms for people's names unless they were figures of public importance or their memoirs have been published. In conjunction

with the record number, they can be easily located in the specific archival collections.

24. Bayerisches Hauptstaatsarchiv (BayHStA), Munich, Reichsstatthalter Epp, Nr. 355/1.

25. See Erwin Goldmann to Winifred Wagner, May 21, 1937, Erwin Goldmann Collection, Archive of the Zentrum für Antisemitismusforschung, TU Berlin; and Brigitte Hamann, *Winifred Wagner oder Hitlers Bayreuth* (Munich: Piper Verlag, 2002), 261–69.

26. For the manuscript, see Erwin Goldmann Collection. On his encounter with the RfS, see Wolfgang Benz, *Patriot and Pariah* (Berlin: Metropol Verlag, 1997), 53.

27. United States Holocaust Memorial Museum (USHMM), Washington, DC, RG-14.011M, "Sächsiches Hauptstaatsarchiv in Dresden Records, 1897–1944," roll 20, pp. 212, 36.

28. See Helga Schlossberg to Hauptmann Steinkopf, Reichs- und Preussischen Ministerium des Innern, 13 June 1938, BArch Berlin, R 1501/5246, p. 80; and Schlossberg to Steinkopf, May 23, 1938, p. 77.

29. Klemperer, *Language of Third Reich,* 61.

30. See Vuletic, *Christen jüdischer Herkunft,* 29; Goldmann to Wagner; Verena Groth, interview by author; and Meyer, *"Jüdische Mischlinge,"* 218.

31. BArch Berlin, R 1509/91, pp. 38, 66.

32. See Cornelia Essner, "Die Alchemie des Rassenbegriffs und die 'Nürnberger Gesetze,'" *Jahrbuch für Antisemitismusforschung* 4 (1995): 212, 206.

33. See N. N., "Die Rassenpolitik des Nationalsozialismus," *Völkischer Beobachter* (Berlin), September 10, 1935, 2. On Jellinek, see BArch Berlin, R 1509/91, pp. 48–52.

34. See BArch, R 1509/49, pp. 25–26.

35. Otto Jellinek to Walter Jellinek, November 11, 1935, Bundesarchiv Koblenz, N 1242/9; and Klaus Kempter, *Die Jellineks 1820–1955* (Düsseldorf: Droste, 1998), 543.

36. See, for instance, Marie Sauer, "Eine 'privilegierte Misch-Ehe,' die keine war," in Ben Barkow, ed., *Testaments to the Holocaust* (Farmington Hills, MI: Gale microfilm, n.d.), series 1, sec. 2, reel 51.

37. Butler, *Excitable Speech,* 40–41.

Jürgen Matthäus

Anti-Semitism as an Offer: The Function of Ideological Indoctrination in the SS and Police Corps During the Holocaust

---

IN DEALING WITH QUESTIONS OF MOTIVATION, HISTORIANS STAND on shaky ground as we have to rely on dubious sources and quickly reach the limits of our profession. Before we can safely embark on the path toward explaining why the perpetrators did what they did, we need to have a road map with clear landmarks for orientation. Such a landmark is the ideological indoctrination of Himmler's police and SS apparatus—that part of the Nazi executive that comprised the majority of those directly involved in the murder of European Jewry. Despite its importance, the issue raises more questions than we can currently answer: How did indoctrination work in general and in its anti-Semitic component in particular? What were its aims and methods? Did it have an influence on the men subjected to it? According to conventional wisdom, indoctrination—or in Nazi German, *weltanschauliche Erziehung*—of the SS and police was shallow, vulgar, and boring, a variation of prevailing anti-Semitic propaganda slogans with little practical effect.[1] The persistence of this assessment is surprising in a number of ways. First, discarding ideological indoctrination as a factor relevant for the Holocaust is not the outcome of solid empirical research: to this day, the massive amount of available Nazi sources has not been thoroughly analyzed, nor have any efforts been made to collect relevant postwar statements by those actively or passively involved in *weltanschauliche Erziehung*. Second, while other key issues of Holocaust history have been reexamined over time—for example, the decision-making process, the importance of middle-ranking functional elites, and regional developments—the wave of historiographical diversification bypassed the issue of anti-Semitic indoctrination. Sixty years after the events, we seem to know infinitely more about the broad mechanics of the genocidal machinery than about the mind-set of those who operated it. This phenomenon is not only a result of the problems inherent in researching motivation, it is also a reflection of trends in scholarship—especially in Germany—that disregarded important parts of historical reality.[2]

The debate over "ordinary men" versus "ordinary Germans" clearly gave a boost to research into perpetrator motivation, yet it barely touched on the questions of how and to what effect Himmler's apparatus indoctrinated its men. The two approaches—one focusing on short-term situational factors, the other on long-term sociocultural ones—clashed head-on.[3] However, they both paid little attention— one less than the other—to what actually had happened between 1933 and the beginning of organized mass murder, again a rather astounding phenomenon if one considers that the mainstream of Holocaust research was and is concentrating on this very time period prior to the crossing of the threshold toward genocide. One of the insights historians have come to embrace in the last decade or so is the perception that the Final Solution was not an event triggered by a single decision from the top leadership but a process characterized by the complex interaction of various groups and strata in society. The discussion about the importance of ideology for the Holocaust was for a long time dominated by "Hitler's Weltanschauung," as if the Führer just had to press a button and his ideas would become reality. We know from the work of Ian Kershaw and others that many Germans were "working towards the Führer," be it in the Berlin bureaucracy or in the killing fields of Eastern Europe, and that a significant minority of Holocaust perpetrators were, in the words of Christopher Browning, "ideologically motivated men ready to kill Jews and other so-called enemies of the Reich from the start."[4] Yet we know very little about what caused this ideological motivation and about the role of anti-Semitic indoctrination for encouraging different groups of perpetrators to participate in the "Final Solution of the Jewish question." Far from presenting a final assessment on the subject, the following remarks are designed to outline the main functions of ideological indoctrination in the SS and police leadership for the killing process.[5]

After 1933 until the end of the Third Reich, the SS and police leadership continuously showed a high degree of interest in ideological indoctrination. After Hitler's coming to power, Himmler was convinced that *weltanschauliche Erziehung* was key to the coherence and effectiveness of his growing SS and police apparatus. Through his direct intervention as well as via specially formed training offices and other institutional means, Himmler wanted to make sure that indoctrination received a high priority in the daily activities of his men even under adverse circumstances. The SS and police leadership's continuous interest in ideological indoctrination was not simply the result of Hitler's well-known obsession with propaganda. Instead, *weltanschauliche Erziehung* fulfilled specific functions within Himmler's apparatus that varied over time. Initially, it was designed to blend together its heterogeneous parts and to prepare its members for the task of policing German society and ridding it of its enemies. This homogenizing aspect remained strong throughout, and over time it gained importance due to the expansion of the small SS elite corps into a huge empire of various organizational, functional, and ethnic groups.[6] In 1933, the SS had just several thousand members; at the end of the war Himmler commanded more than a million men (and several thousand women) in the ranks of the SS, police, and Waffen-SS, most of them in fighting units and most unable to meet the rigid prewar membership standards.[7] With the turning of the tide after Stalingrad, ideological indoctrination became more and more a substitute for the declining military might of the Reich. The "fanatical soldier" was to ensure that Germany would achieve the *Endsieg* (final victory)—an idea shared by the German military leadership.

Ideological indoctrination in the SS and police leadership received its manipulative value not through "brainwashing" or other coercive means, as claimed by many former participants after the war. Instead, it presented itself as a mix of direct and indirect methods that affected its participants over time in varying degrees. This approach resulted from the overall aim, which was less one of producing fixed, inflexible rules of behavior than one of producing a specific attitude, a posture, a mind-set; the German term used most frequently at the time to describe this concept is *Haltung*. The desired attitude was characterized by energetic ruthlessness, self-conscious determination, and the ability to adjust one's actions quickly to the respective situation. If one looks for personifications of this mind-set and what it meant in practical terms, we can find them in Himmler's regional representatives—the Higher SS and Police Leaders (Höhere SS- und Polizeiführer, or HSSPF)—and in the special units of the Security Police and SD—the Einsatzgruppen and their subunits—that operated in the heartland of the Holocaust, first in Poland and later in the Soviet Union.[8] The war in the East provided the opportunity to combine theory and practice: in summer 1941, at the beginning of Operation Barbarossa, the participants of a training course at the SS school in Fürstenberg were sent to the eastern front and distributed among the Einsatzgruppen. Unit commanders competed in taking the most drastic measures against those whom they regarded as "enemies of the Reich" and embarked on gigantic killing sprees that annihilated the members of entire Jewish communities. One of the young officers from the Fürstenberg training course, Joachim Hammann of Einsatzkommando 3, was responsible for murdering tens of thousands of Jews in Lithuania—a country that, despite its large prewar Jewish population, already in late 1941 was declared *judenrein,* or "free of Jews."[9]

Many more examples can be found in the careers of Security Police and SD officers that prove how ideology permeated their learning, teaching, and doing and how all three aspects formed a functional unity. Otto Hellwig, an old career police officer, became first head of the Security Police (Sicherheitspolizei, or Sipo) and SD school in Berlin-Charlottenburg, later unit commander in an Einsatzgruppe deployed in Poland and involved in the murder of Jews until he was appointed SS and Police Leader (SS- und Polizeiführer, SSPF) in the Ukrainian district of Zhytomyr.[10] Paul Zapp wrote a training manual on the Jewish question before he led an Einsatzkommando in the Soviet Union and became SSPF in Simferopol.[11] Georg Heuser, a member of the criminal police, had just completed his training when he was seconded to an Einsatzkommando in the occupied Soviet Union followed by his appointment as Gestapo chief in the Belorussian city of Minsk; after his retreat from Belorussia, he taught at a Sipo and SD school until he took over command of an Einsatzkommando to quash the Slovak uprising.[12] Siegfried Engel was in charge of a Reich Security Main Office department on *weltanschauliche Erziehung* before he was transferred to Italy; for his crimes there a German court convicted him in 2001 while his active involvement in ideological indoctrination, as in most other cases in which investigations against Himmler's training officers took place after the war, escaped legal scrutiny.[13]

To achieve and maintain the desired *Haltung,* formal training was to be supplemented by informal get-togethers, parties, and other social events. Vagueness and reliance on after-hours activities were partly the result of practical shortcomings (lack of proper teachers, tight schedules, other duties) that gained in importance over time. In addition, there was a definite lack of interest on the part of Himmler and his cronies to rule out options for future SS and police tasks depending on how the situation in Germany and beyond would develop. The more the borderlines of Nazism expanded, the more opportunities were opening up that before had not been anticipated as viable and realistic ways of dealing with the Jewish question. The concept of *Haltung* reflected the continuous, highly radicalizing actionism that was characteristic for the Third Reich's functional elites; in its integrated, almost holistic approach toward education, training, and personnel management, it remained an important element of continuity in the postwar period.[14]

Anti-Semitic issues were part and parcel of ideological indoctrination, yet overall—quantitatively speaking—they did not figure prominently in the training curricula of either SS or police. The institutional infrastructure needed to indoctrinate the SS and police apparatus was created between 1933 and the beginning of the war. Various offices within Himmler's apparatus further cultivated the ground that other state and party agencies—the Hitler Youth, schools, the SA, the Reich Labor Service, the army—had already broken. Simultaneously, the slogan that "the Jew has to go" became one of the underlying premises of Nazi policymaking commonly known and widely accepted throughout Germany. The workings of institutional hierarchies, peer adaptation, and organizational culture ensured that the urgency to address the Jewish question formed an integral part of the esprit de corps in Himmler's realm of influence even when it was not reiterated at each and every opportunity.[15] Socialized during the Third Reich and subjected to a constant barrage of anti-Semitic propaganda, those young men who joined the SS and police during the war not only knew the Final Solution as one of the abstract aims for the Nazi millennium but had witnessed its practical implementation in German public life since 1933.

Weltanschauliche Erziehung presented itself as a mixture of "positive" elements—idealized interpretations of German history and utopian dreams about racial excellence through proper breeding—and "negative" notions invoked to create what George Mosse called the counterimage to the Aryan ideal type.[16] If we are looking for pronounced expressions of anti-Semitism in the training material of Himmler's men, we can find them: already in the early phase of Nazi rule, guards in concentration camps referred to Jewish prisoners as "subhumans" and treated them accordingly. The need for radical measures against what was called *Weltfeind Nummer Eins* (world enemy number one) was stressed repeatedly in print media and highlighted by graphic imagery including propaganda photographs and movies. Articles in SS and police journals left no doubt that the war against the Soviet Union would "seal the fate of European and Near Asian Jewry" and offer a chance to get rid of a "world plague."[17] These and many similar *Stürmer*-like pronunciations seem to speak for themselves, especially if viewed through hindsight; however, the material—training manuals, journal articles, speeches, and slides—offers little more than standard Nazi platitudes: "the Jew" is presented as the archenemy, the wire-puller behind all other enemy groups (e.g., Communists, Freemasons, the churches). The first step—exclusion from German social and economic life—had been taken after 1933; in the long run, the Jewish question was to be resolved more comprehensively.

The understanding of the phrase "Final Solution" as used in the training literature as well as in speeches by Hitler and other top Nazis depended to a large degree on the interpretation by the recipient in a specific situation or setting, and this interpretation in turn was shaped by preconceived notions. Himmler and his top officers never relinquished their hope in the effects of ideological indoctrination; yet they did not envisage it as a blueprint for solving the Jewish question through the physical extermination of all Jewish men, women, and children—a course of action they decided on, for all we know, only after the beginning of Operation Barbarossa.[18] The anti-Semitic material produced by the relevant training offices in its random combination of prevailing prejudices, platitudes, and projections presented something for everyone. In most cases, a Final Solution in whatever shape or form was presented as a matter of course, a quasi-natural phenomenon like the fight against a disease that, as far as human involvement was concerned, had no agent or object, no victim or victimizer. Many of the few sources we have on the rationalizations presented by German perpetrators at the time of mass murder contain such phrases as "one generation has to see this through" or "it has to happen sooner or later anyway" even when it is obvious that these men were driven by hatred, greed, or other personal motives.[19]

From the beginning, the perception of the Jewish question in the minds of police and SS men was influenced not only by direct indoctrination but also by lessons derived from practical measures taken against Jews. The range of anti-Jewish activities involving Himmler's men was very broad: from enforcing laws and police regulations via arrests and assistance for Nazi activists to the use of physical violence including murder. Early precedents were set that influenced group behavior and mentality, as in the case of the concentration camps, where the targeted persecution of Jews started very early.[20] Before the German attack on the Soviet Union, important thresholds on the way toward the organized mass murder of "enemies of the Reich" were passed during Kristallnacht, the incorporation of Austria, and the war against Poland. The gradually increasing degree of radicalism used in dealing with Jews filtered only indirectly into the training material provided to police and SS men. Instead of clearly spelling out how Jews should be treated, it offered rationalizations for what was taking place on the killing fields and in the killers' minds. The working and effectiveness of this mechanism are reflected in private letters SS and policemen sent home to their families and friends: the most outrageous acts of violence committed, sometimes by the authors themselves, were presented as logical consequences of Hitler's abstract announcement that a world war would bring about the destruction of European Jewry.[21]

To state that anti-Semitic indoctrination was irrelevant because it did not directly call for the murder of the Jews ignores the key functional elements of *weltanschauliche Erziehung*. As with the Nazi system as a whole, the executive activities of Himmler's apparatus were dominated less by formal, unambiguous pronouncements than by general directives stipulating the desired aim while leaving open the methods to be adopted. The causal interrelation among hazy directives from the top, radical initiatives from below, and the subsequent radicalization of central guidelines goes a long way toward explaining the murderous events in the occupied parts of Eastern Europe;[22] ideological indoctrination was an integral element of this nexus. Instead of providing clear lessons, ideological training did different things to different people: for those eager—for whatever reason—to push on with the Final Solution, it offered an incentive to do so, and these people formed what Chris Browning calls the "crucial nucleus for the killing process" in Eastern Europe.[23] There can be no doubt that the process of mass murder rested on the personal responsibility of members of the SS, police, and other agencies; however, ideological indoctrination reinforced the killer's notion of acting not as an individual but as a part of a functional elite collectively responsible for reshaping "the East" by eliminating everyone who would endanger the German vision of Lebensraum. The administrative apparatus established by the Reich in the occupied territories with the SS and police as its core in conjunction with the brutalizing effect of their own actions ensured that Himmler's men could implement the most radical measures on a habitual basis.

The process character of the Holocaust and its mental mechanisms can be exemplified by a key document that shows how important the Berlin leadership deemed informal means of indoctrination to be for transforming mass murder into a matter of bureaucratic routine. Instead of removing his men, as often alleged,[24] from exposure to massive direct violence by looking for new killing techniques, Himmler opted for softening the psychological impact of mass murder on the executioners as part of *weltanschauliche Erziehung*. On December 12, 1941, at a time when—according to some historians—Hitler decided to kill all European Jews, Himmler issued a secret order to his SS and police leaders from the Führer's headquarters.[25]

> Our given task to guarantee security, quiet, and order in the regions entrusted upon us, especially behind the German front, demands from us that we eliminate without consideration every source of resistance and that we subject in the harshest form enemies of the German people to the just death sentence.
>
> It is the holy duty of higher officers and commanders to *personally* make sure that none of our men who have to fulfil this grave duty ever become brutalized or suffer damage in mind and character. This task will be fulfilled through strictest discipline in matters of official duties, through comradely get-togethers on the evening of a day which had brought such a heavy task. However, the comradely get-together should never end in abuse of alcohol. It should be an evening devoted to—according to the possibilities—sitting together and eating in the best German domestic form and on which music, lectures, and the taking of our men into the most pretty areas of German spiritual and mental life should fill the hours.[26]

In this context, it is noteworthy that Himmler did not even mention Jews and that he called for sober, almost solemn get-togethers. To be sure, as Klaus-Michael Mallmann has shown, many of the *Sieges-feiern* (victory parties) conducted directly after an anti-Jewish action turned into mindless drinking orgies that in some cases triggered further violence.[27] These "excesses," however, were less an aberration than they were the result of Himmler's determination to open safety valves for releasing the mental pressure working on his subordinates—a kind of psychological care firmly integrated into the SS and police apparatus. As can be seen from personnel records and other sources, the utterly fantastic aim of avoiding "brutalization"—or, as it is called in the German sources, *Verrohung*—of those directly involved in the murder of Jewish men, women, and children remained an important criterion for the assessment of the leadership abilities of an officer, often—as statements by former SS and policemen attest to—until well after the war. *Weltanschauliche Erziehung,* with its get-togethers, alcoholic excesses, speeches, lectures, and visits to theaters, concerts, and sports events, was to provide not only legitimization for but also an alternative program to the Final Solution as part of a milieu that involved almost all Germans in the occupied parts of Eastern Europe.[28]

There are a number of important issues yet to be addressed by future research, and one of them is the question of how ideological indoctrination of the SS and police compares in its development, means, and effects to manipulative efforts in Nazi Germany that targeted other groups—most important, the German army in its war of destruction in Eastern Europe—or German society as a whole. Also, we do not quite know which accepted sets of belief were taken for granted on joining the SS or police and how the intensity of indoctrination varied in the various branches of Himmler's empire. Obviously, there were differences among the SD, the SS proper, the police, and non-German auxiliaries. It would be too easy, however, to assume that the most pronounced expressions of Jew hatred can be found in the files of Himmler's hard-core elite: the security police and SD that manned the Einsatzgruppen and other killing squads. Available sources point to the fact that the training materials of the German Order Police were especially outspoken in their anti-Jewish rhetoric, and it will be important to find out to what extent that explains the key role the Order Police played in the Holocaust all over German-dominated Europe.[29]

To sum up, the effect of ideological indoctrination on the implementation of the Holocaust by members of the SS and police has to be seen in the context of Nazi policy as a whole as well as within the wider training framework with its emphasis on creating a specific state of mind (*Haltung*) rather than a distinct line of action. Anti-Semitic indoctrination worked not as an order or a preconceived blueprint for murder but as an offer that could be used to rationalize participation in various forms of anti-Jewish actions. Settings and circumstances mattered, yet their perception as in the case of "the East" depended to a large degree on stereotypes and prejudices transported and reinforced by the preceding ideological manipulation. Scholars have come to stress the importance of the split between unprecedented mass murder and the upholding of normalcy as a key phenomenon in the psyche of the perpetrators;[30] what has been overlooked so far, however, is that this split was as inherent in ideological indoctrination prior to and during the Holocaust as it was the result of mental numbing or postwar denial. The effects of this subtle, interactive manipulation can be seen in the ease with which genocide became daily routine and in the stubbornness with which the perpetrators, shielded by German society, after 1945 declined to take responsibility for their actions.

NOTES

1. For examples, see Jürgen Matthäus, "Ausbildungsziel Judenmord? Zum Stellenwert der 'weltanschaulichen Erziehung' von SS und Polizei im Rahmen der 'Endlösung,'" *Zeitschrift für Geschichtswissenschaft* 8 (1999): 680–81. The opinions presented in this article are those of the author and do not necessarily reflect the opinions of the United States Holocaust Memorial Museum.

2. For an overview of trends in perpetrator-oriented historiography, see Gerhard Paul, "Von Psychopathen, Technokraten des Terrors und 'ganz gewöhnlichen' Deutschen: Die Täter der Shoah im Spiegel der Forschung," in *Die Täter der Shoah: Fanatische Nationalsozialisten oder ganz normale Deutsche?* ed. Gerhard Paul (Göttingen, 2000), 13–90; Jürgen Matthäus, "Out of Focus: Historiography and the Perpetrators of the Holocaust," in *The Historiography of the Holocaust*, ed. Dan Stone (New York, 2004).

3. See Christopher R. Browning, *Ordinary Men: Reserve Police Battalion 101 and the Final Solution in Poland* (New York, 1992); and Daniel J. Goldhagen, *Hitler's Willing Executioners: Ordinary Germans and the Holocaust* (New York, 1996). What is usually referred to as the "Goldhagen debate" has produced its own body of literature; see Geoff Eley, ed., *The "Goldhagen Effect": History, Memory, Nazism; Facing the German Past* (Ann Arbor, 2000).

4. Christopher R. Browning, postscript to *Nazi Policy, Jewish Workers, German Killers* (Cambridge, 2000), 175; see also Ian Kershaw, *Hitler: 1936–1945; Nemesis* (London 2000); Peter Longerich, *Politik der Vernichtung: Eine Gesamtdarstellung der nationalsozialistischen Judenverfolgung* (Munich, 1998); Saul Friedländer, *Nazi Germany and the Jews,* vol. 1, *The Years of Persecution, 1933–1939* (New York, 1997).

5. See Jürgen Matthäus, Konrad Kwiet, Jürgen Förster, and Richard Breitman, eds. *Ausbildungsziel Judenmord? "Weltanschauliche Erziehung" von SS, Polizei und Waffen-SS im Rahmen der "Endlösung"* (Frankfurt am Main, 2003).

6. See the essay by Edward Westermann in this volume.

7. In 1944, the German Order Police comprised (excluding fire brigades and auxiliary policemen, but including reservists) about 300,000 men, the Waffen-SS roughly 900,000, and the Security Police and SD about 70,000; see Raul Hilberg, *Die Vernichtung der europäischen Juden* (Frankfurt, 1991), 211; Heinz Höhne, *Der Orden unter dem Totenkopf: Die Geschichte der SS* (Munich, 1984), 8.

8. See Ruth Bettina Birn, *Die Höheren SS- und Polizeiführer: Himmlers Vertreter im Reich und in den besetzten Gebieten* (Düsseldorf, 1986); Helmut Krausnick and Hans-Heinrich Wilhelm, *Die Truppe des Weltanschauungskrieges: Die Einsatzgruppen der Sicherheitspolizei und des SD 1938–1942* (Stuttgart, 1981).

9. Knut Stang, "Kollaboration und Völkermord: Das Rollkommando Hamann und die Vernichtung der litauischen Juden," in *Die Gestapo im Zweiten Weltkrieg: "Heimatfront" und besetztes Europa,* ed. Gerhard Paul and Klaus-Michael Mallmann (Darmstadt, 2000), 464–80. On the Holocaust in Lithuania, see Yitzhak Arad, *Ghetto in Flames: The Struggle and Destruction of the Jews in Vilna in the Holocaust* (New York, 1982).

10. Wendy Lower, *Nazi Colonial Dreams: German Policies and Ukrainian Society in Zhytomyr* (Ph.D. diss., American University, 1999).

11. Konrad Kwiet, "Erziehung zum Mord: Zwei Beispiele zur Kontinuität der deutschen 'Endlösung der Judenfrage,'" in *Geschichte und Emanzipation,* ed. Michael Grüttner, Rüdiger Hachtmann, and Heinz-Gerhard Haupt (Frankfurt, 1999), 435–57.

12. See Jürgen Matthäus, "Georg Heuser: Routinier des sicherheitspolizeilichen Osteinsatzes," in *Karrieren der Gewalt: Nationalsozialistische Täterbiographien,* ed. Klaus-Michael Mallmann and Gerhard Paul (Darmstadt, 2004).

13. Michael Wildt, *Generation des Unbedingten: Das Führungskorps des Reichssicherheitshauptamtes* (Hamburg, 2002), 742–44. On postwar investigation involving SS and police officers with a background in ideological indoctrination, see Konrad Kwiet, *Von Tätern zu Befehlsempfängern:*

Legendenbildung und Strafverfolgung nach 1945, in Matthäus, Kwiet, and Förster, *Ausbildungsziel,* 114–39.

14. For German schools, see Elke Nyssen, *Schule im Nationalsozialismus* (Heidelberg, 1979), 115–21; and Barbara Schneider, *Die Höhere Schule im Nationalsozialismus: Zur Ideologisierung von Bildung und Erziehung* (Cologne, 2000), 101–31. On the continuity of public relations from the Third Reich to the Federal Republic, see Peer Heinelt, "Der Führer und wir: Über die Gründerväter der bundesdeutschen Public Relations," *konkret* 9 (2002): 15–17; and Peer Heinelt, *"PR-Päpste": Die Kontinuierlichen Karrieren von Carl Hunthausen, Albert Oeckl, und Franz Ronneberger* (Berlin, 2003).

15. See Raul Hilberg, *Sources of Holocaust Research: An Analysis* (Chicago, 2001), 134–35.

16. See the chapter on anti-Semitism in George L. Mosse, *The Crisis of German Ideology: Intellectual Origins of the Third Reich* (New York, 1964).

17. "Judas Hoffnung—Judas Ende!" *Das Schwarze Korps,* October 23, 1941, 1–2; "Die Seuche der Völker: Zum 22.6.1941," *SS-Leitheft* 4a, o.D., pp.11–12, Bundesarchiv Berlin NSD 41/77 (my translation).

18. For the transition from persecution to mass murder, see Christopher R. Browning, "Beyond 'Intentionalism' and 'Functionalism': The Decision for the Final Solution Reconsidered," in *The Path to Genocide: Essays on Launching the Final Solution* (Cambridge, 1992), 88–101.

19. For the importance of material considerations as an integral element of the Nazi system, see Frank Bajohr, *Parvenüs und Profiteure: Korruption in der NS-Zeit* (Frankfurt am Main, 2001).

20. See Jürgen Matthäus, "Verfolgung, Ausbeutung, Vernichtung: Jüdische Häftlinge im System der Konzentrationslager," in *Jüdische Häftlinge im KZ Sachsenhausen,* ed. Günter Morsch and Susanne zur Nieden (Berlin, 2002).

21. For examples, see Christopher R. Browning, "German Killers: Behavior and Motivation in the Light of New Evidence," in Browning, *Nazi Policy,* 145–54; and Matthäus, Kwiet, and Förster, *Ausbildungsziel,* 69–75.

22. See Longerich, *Politik der Vernichtung.*

23. Browning, postscript to *Nazi Policy,* 175.

24. During Himmler's visit to the eastern front in summer 1941, most recently referred to by Hans Mommsen, *Auschwitz 17. Juli 1942* (Munich, 2002), 126–27.

25. See Christian Gerlach, "Die Wannsee-Konferenz, das Schicksal der deutschen Juden und Hitlers politische Grundsatzentscheidung, alle Juden Europas zu ermorden," in *Krieg, Ernährung, Völkermord: Forschungen zur deutschen Vernichtungspolitik im Zweiten Weltkrieg* (Hamburg, 1998), 85–166.

26. Secret SS order by Himmler, Dec. 12, 1941, translated from Wolf-

gang Benz, Konrad Kwiet, and Jürgen Matthäus, eds., *Einsatz im "Reichs-kommissariat Ostland": Dokumente zum Völkermord im Baltikum und in Weißrussland 1941–1944* (Berlin, 1998), 28 (emphases in the original); see also Hilberg, *Sources,* 115–16.

27. Klaus-Michael Mallmann, "'Mensch, ich feiere heut' den tausend-sten Genickschuß': Die Sicherheitspolizei und die Shoah in Westgalizien," in Paul, *Die Täter der Shoah,* 109–36.

28. For elements of this milieu created by Germans in occupied Eastern Europe, see ibid. and Klaus-Michael Mallmann, Volker Riess, and Wolfram Pyta, *Deutscher Osten 1939–1945: Der Weltanschauungskrieg in Photos und Texten* (Darmstadt, 2003).

29. See Omer Bartov, *The Eastern Front, 1941–45: German Troops and the Barbarization of Warfare* (New York, 1986); for the German Or-der Police, see Edward B. Westermann, "'Ordinary Men' or 'Ideological soldiers'? Police Battalion 310 in Russia, 1942," *German Studies Review* 21 (1998): 41–68; Edward B. Westermann, "Himmler's Uniformed Police on the Eastern Front: The Reich's Secret Soldiers, 1941–1942," *War in History* 3 (1996): 309–29.

30. On "doubling" as a psychological mechanism, see Robert Jay Lif-ton, *The Nazi Doctors: Medical Killing and the Psychology of Genocide* (New York, 1986), 417ff.

Edward B. Westermann

Ideology and Organizational Culture: Creating the Police Soldier

THE TRANSFORMATION OF THE POLICE INTO POLITICAL SOLDIERS AND instruments of genocide occurred in large part due to the efforts of Heinrich Himmler and Kurt Daluege to create an organizational culture within the Ordnungspolizei (Order Police) that married a "martial attitude" with Nazi racial ideology. The concept of organizational culture offers a useful framework for evaluating the institutional goals and standards established within the entire SS and police complex. In this essay, "organizational culture" refers to the "basic assumptions and beliefs that are shared by members of an organization, that operate unconsciously, and that define in a basic 'taken for granted' fashion an organization's view of itself and its environment."[1] In short, organizational culture sets the boundaries for accepted behavior, establishes institutional goals, and defines the standards of group membership. Contemporary research demonstrates the "key role" of leadership in defining the organizational culture of law enforcement agencies. One study described leadership as the "glue" holding all parts of the organization together through the propagation of a shared vision.[2]

Without a doubt, the Reich leader of the SS, Heinrich Himmler, and the chief of the Order Police, Kurt Daluege, shared a vision of the police and expended substantial effort in promulgating this vision among the members of the organization. In the prewar years, and especially as Hitler embarked upon his quest for an empire in the East, the Order Police battalions became a special target of Himmler's efforts and a ready instrument for the conduct of annihilation. Indeed, two dominant characteristics within the organizational culture of the police offer strong evidence for explaining the actions of the police battalions on the eastern front.

First, the militarization of the police constituted a central objective of the Order Police leadership from the initial National Socialist seizure of power until the ultimate collapse of Hitler's Thousand-Year Reich. The concept of militarization was not simply limited to the establishment of a hierarchical police organization with military capabilities but also encompassed a specific Weltanschauung that married the concept of military duty with absolute obedience and the vision of a "higher purpose." Second, after the unification of the Order Police under the command of Himmler in June 1936, the police leadership increasingly pursued efforts to inculcate the "police soldier" with National Socialist values in a process of *Verschmelzung* (merging) the police in a psychological and physical sense with the SS.

THE "POLITICAL SOLDIER"

The various German police forces under the Weimar Republic were strongly influenced by military standards and ideals. Indeed, the vast majority of the police personnel in the first years of the republic consisted of former professional soldiers or those who had served in the Great War. The Weimar police were in many respects caught between the current of a preexisting military identity and the tide of modernization that offered the hope for a professionalization of the police. While it is difficult to determine whether the Weimar police constituted a "quasi military or modern organization," it was certainly apparent that the military character of its members played a key role in shaping their own political views.[3] The nationalistic philosophy and the military ideals of the police made them susceptible to the "stab in the back" myth in which Germany's defeat in the war could be laid at the feet of profiteers, leftists, and Jews.[4] In turn this image of "treasonous" leftists and Jews helped shape the personal and political beliefs of many policemen throughout the interwar period.

THE NATIONAL SOCIALIST IDEAL

The majority of the Weimar police certainly were not closet Nazis merely waiting for Hitler to achieve power before revealing their true colors; however, the military experiences and political sympathies of the police made them a prime and attentive audience for the Nazi message after January 30, 1933. In fact, National Socialist leaders wasted little time in bringing their message to the police. On February 7, 1933, Hermann Göring, the new Prussian minister of the interior, spoke to officers and men of the Prussian Uniformed Police. Göring opened his speech by exclaiming, "Comrades! With special joy I greet you as the uniformed members of the police. For the most part, the honored field gray uniform of the German soldier unites us. Therefore we belong together."[5] For Göring, the shared honor of military service united these men with him and ultimately with the ambitions and the philosophy of the Nazi Party, including the use of the police in a "battle of extermination" (*Ausrottungskampf*) aimed at the Marxist "pestilence" within Germany.[6]

A decree of April 19, 1933, mandating the exchange of salutes between military and police members constituted one outward sign of the elevation of the status of the police and their symbolic union with the military.[7] However, National Socialist leaders did not limit their actions to symbolic gestures alone. Already on February 28, Göring issued a decree that members of the party and its sister organizations were to receive priority as applicants for the Order Police.[8] In June 1933, as chief of the Prussian police, Kurt Daluege composed a secret memorandum emphasizing the training and indoctrination of the Prussian police, Germany's largest police force, along a "military point of view." He also suggested an eight- to ten-week-long training course for some fifty SA and twenty-five SS men who were intended to take over leadership roles in the Prussian police at the rank of captain and above. According to Daluege, this initiative would "bestow the suitable expression of the close ties between the state instruments of power [the police] and the SA and SS."[9]

On April 28, 1934, Daluege prepared a press release for the German news service DNB entitled "The Unity of the SA with the Police." In this article, he observed that "as a national political necessity, the Prussian police in its entire organization" would be infused with "veteran and proven SA, SS, and Stahlhelm members." Daluege then went one step further by noting that "the politically schooled soldiers of the movement are the guarantors that the National Socialist ideology (*Ideenwelt*) will serve the general good of the Prussian police."[10]

Daluege's article was important in two respects. First, it demonstrated the speed by which the National Socialist leadership gained control over the police after the seizure of power and how quickly the Nazis were able to openly pursue their aims in shaping the police according to their ideal. Second, the large-scale infusion of the "political soldiers" of the movement from the SA, SS, and Stahlhelm helped reinforce both the military character and the political commitment of the Order Police to Hitler's government. In this respect, the incorporation of members from the party's paramilitary organizations served the twofold purpose of reinforcing the militarization of the police and strengthening the organization's identification with the political and racial views of National Socialism. Daluege matched his rhetoric with action, and by November 1934, some ten thousand members of the SA and SS had joined the ranks of the police and police administration in the state of Prussia alone.[11] In another initiative, Göring ordered the incorporation of the SA's 3,100-man Feldjägerkorps into the ranks of the Prussian uniformed police in April 1935.[12]

During the initial years of the consolidation of National Socialist power, Daluege continued to propound his vision of an Order Police force built upon martial values and commitment to the party. In a speech to commanders of the Order Police on April 25, 1935, he remarked that the introduction of the green police uniform stood as an outward manifestation of the new relationship between the people and the police. The adoption of a standardized military-style uniform for the police also served to emphasize the unity of the police corps as one corporate body. Daluege concluded his remarks by reminding his police commanders of the need for the police officer corps to remain at a high level of military proficiency.[13] One month later, in a scripted response to a question concerning the "new attitude" within the Order Police, Daluege identified the presence of a martial character within the police and remarked, "While the member of the German police corps is a civil servant, duty demands that he will, and must, always see himself as a soldier."[14]

In the initial phase of National Socialist rule, Daluege was not the only member of the political leadership emphasizing the soldierly character of the police. Reich Minister of the Interior Wilhelm Frick ended his preface to the 1936 edition of the police yearbook with the assertion that "honor, devotion to duty, soldierly bearing, and unity with the people are the highest virtues that must distinguish the German police."[15] Another author described the reemergence of "soldierdom" (*Soldatentum*) in the "new police" and noted that the source of the National Socialist policeman's authority was his "soldierly honor" (*Soldatenehre*). One visible symbol of the changed status of the police involved the elimination of the police baton, a hated symbol and reminder of the years of political street fighting, and the reintroduction of the sword for police officers and the bayonet for enlisted police ranks. Furthermore, policemen were allowed to wear military badges and decorations won during the Great War.[16] It would be a mistake to underestimate the significance of seemingly minor uniform changes; indeed, for the professional soldier or policeman, awards and decorations constitute badges of honor and play an important role in establishing the individual's identity and status within a hierarchical organization. The introduction of the standardized green uniform, swords, bayonets, and the authorization to wear military awards served as visible expressions of the Nazi vision for the policeman as a state soldier with the explicit expectation of support for the regime and National Socialist ideals.

HIMMLER TAKES COMMAND OF THE ORDER POLICE

On June 17, 1936, Hitler appointed Heinrich Himmler as the chief of the German Police in addition to his duties as the Reich leader of the SS. Hitler's selection of Himmler provided evidence of the Führer's desire to see the police merged with the "Party's soldiers," the SS, in both an organizational and a philosophical sense.[17] Himmler made his expectations for the police absolutely clear: "We are a land in the heart of Europe, surrounded by open borders, surrounded in a world that is becoming more and more bolshevized in which the Jew in his worst form increasingly takes control through the all destructive tyranny of Bolshevism. . . . We have to expect that this battle will be a battle of the generations, the primeval contest between men and subhumans [which] in its contemporary form is the battle of the Aryan peoples against Jewry and its organizational manifestation, Bolshevism."[18] Near the end of his speech, Himmler noted that he would need the loyalty and the commitment to duty of each individual within the "soldierly corps" (*soldatisches Korps*) of the police to achieve his vision.

Himmler's words not only presented his expectations of the police under his command but also created an organizational culture within the police in which anti-Semitism and anti-Bolshevism emerged as institutional norms. Clearly, not every policeman embraced the extreme implications of Himmler's rhetoric, but it is equally clear that his vision established an atmosphere promoting the development of a police mentalité that promoted the ideal of a soldierly corps locked in an apocalyptic battle with "Jewish Bolshevism." In addition, Himmler's remarks made it apparent that one of his objectives included the "merging" of the SS with the police, a goal he pursued through several initiatives in the following years. These measures included the authorization for SS personnel serving in the Order Police to wear the SS runes as well as the SS police sword.[19] In addition, Hitler awarded unit flags to the police in the "Blood Banner" ceremony during the Nuremberg Party rally in 1937, a ceremony intended to demonstrate the blood bond between the Nazi Party, the SS, and the police.[20]

The "Blood Banner" ceremony was largely symbolic. A more concrete example of the "merging" between the soldiers of the party (the SS) and the police occurred with the acceptance of commissioned graduates of SS officer candidate schools (*SS-Junkerschulen*) into the Order Police.[21] In a related measure, Himmler's absolute commitment to the ideological conversion of the police led him to transfer responsibility for the ideological training of the police to the SS Training Office in 1938.[22] By September 1938, Himmler appeared to be satisfied with his initial efforts, and he remarked on the "favorable progress" made in the recruitment of Order Policemen and the incorporation of "numerous" members of the police into the SS.[23] By 1941, Himmler's dual-track strategy—of on the one hand, introducing SS personnel into the police and, on the other hand, focusing on ideological indoctrination—appeared to be working. Thirty percent of all regular Order Police with officer rank belonged to the SS; 66 percent of all regular Order Police with officer rank held membership in the Nazi Party, with 20 percent of these officers recognized as "old fighters" (*alte Kämpfer*), members of the NSDAP prior to Hitler's appointment as Reich chancellor. In comparison, 7 percent of all reserve Order Policemen with officer rank belonged to the SS, and 67 percent of all reserve Order Policemen with officer rank held membership in the NSDAP, with 18 percent of these officers qualifying as "old fighters."[24]

THE HIGHER SS AND POLICE LEADERS

In a speech to Higher SS and Police Leaders on January 23, 1939, Daluege opened his remarks by asserting, "The Ordnungspolizei as the uniformed branch of the German Reich police displays today the image of a tightly organized soldierly police troop, soldierly in its organization and soldierly [and] National Socialist in its outward and innermost character."[25] Daluege's speech once again stressed the martial identity of the Order Police and explicitly tied the policeman's military values to those of the party. In this respect, Daluege was preaching to the choir as his audience, the Higher SS and Police Leaders (Höhere SS- und Polizeiführer, or HSSPF) of the Third Reich, consisted of a group of men who epitomized the martial and party ideal that he espoused.

Already on September 15, 1938, almost a year before the outbreak of war, Himmler ordered the establishment of HSSPF positions throughout the Reich "in order to finally ensure the union of the SS and police in the highest positions of command authority."[26] In one respect, the creation of the position of HSSPF represented the ultimate "merging" of the SS and the police.[27] Additionally, the position of HSSPF was suited perfectly for the coordination of wartime police and military duties, a not coincidental aim of the Reich leader of the SS. Indeed, after the outbreak of war, the HSSPF played a central role in the initiation and the coordination of National Socialist racial policies in the East.

A demographic profile of these men identified a number of similarities in their professional backgrounds. First, the majority of the HSSPF belonged to the "front generation," or men who had served in the German military in World War I.[28] In fact, the personal identity of these men was inextricably linked to their military experience and their own self-image as soldiers, and many continued to describe themselves as "soldiers" even after their demobilization at the end of the war.[29] However, the HSSPF were not merely "soldiers" shaped by their military experience, they were also the elite of the SS, "party soldiers" who received the task of shaping the police forces under their control in their own images and defining the organizational culture within their commands. The HSSPF not only established the parameters for the expected behavior of the policemen under their command, but they also created an environment that linked martial values with National Socialist racial ideology, and they decided which individuals merited advancement into leadership positions within the police corps. The ability to control promotion within the organization allowed the HSSPF to mold the police in their image and offered a powerful tool for inculcating and perpetuating their own political, military, and racial ideals.

THE ORDER POLICE AT WAR

During the Polish campaign, the Order Police battalions emerged as a capable instrument for military operations as well as the prosecution of racial policy. Daluege, like Himmler, also realized the important role played by the police battalions in Poland and recognized their utility as military formations for future campaigns. In a letter of March 7, 1940, Daluege wrote to Himmler requesting an immediate meeting to discuss "fundamental questions of the further employment of the Order Police in many new tasks."[30] Two weeks later, in a letter concerning replacements for the officer corps of the police battalions, Daluege ordered that priority be given to graduates of SS leadership schools, qualified policemen from the ranks, and finally officers from the Wehrmacht who had been demobilized due to war injuries, in that order. Furthermore, he directed that officers for the police training battalions should be selected solely on the basis of their military talents and only *after* the war would they be evaluated on their potential for police duties.[31] Hitler's creation of the SS Police Division and Daluege's comments both provide further evidence of the special status enjoyed by the police battalions in the wake of the Polish campaign. These initiatives also highlighted the Nazi Party and police leadership's continued efforts at both militarizing these forces and "merging" their identities with that of the SS.

Prior to the invasion of the Soviet Union, the police battalions serving in occupied Poland emerged as key prosecutors of "antipartisan" actions. From the perspective of the police leadership, the use of the battalions in antipartisan operations reflected the unique status of these units. On June 2, 1940, Himmler made this unique status explicit in a directive entitled "Guidelines for the Conduct of the Ideological Education of the Order Police during the War." Himmler's directive noted that a distinction needed to be made between the ideological instruction of the police battalions (*geschlossene Formationen*) and that of other branches of the police. The goal of the training for the men of the police battalions involved their education as "martial combatants" (*soldatische Kämpfer*). Furthermore, Himmler directed that the weekly ideological instruction of the police battalions focus on the goal of "shaping the political consciousness of the martial combat-ant."[32] Himmler's directive is important in two respects. On the one hand, he viewed these men not only as police soldiers but moreover as "political soldiers" whose police identities were inextricably tied to a martial character and the political aims of the National Socialist regime. On the other hand, the directive created a special status for the men of the police battalions, which, in turn, implied a special role for these units.

The opening of the campaign against the Soviet Union provided the police battalions with an opportunity to test the limits of their unique status. Of the nine police battalions placed directly at the disposal of the HSSPF during the invasion, seven were regular police battalions with numerical designations in the 300s. These "300-level" battalions consisted in large part of recruits from the twenty thousand men mobilized from the year groups 1909 through 1912 in October 1939, and from their ranks emerged units that would cut a bloody swath through the western Soviet Union in the opening stages of the campaign.[33] It is important to note that the vast majority of the police battalions' members came from these or younger year groups and were not overage reservists as found in Christopher Browning's study of PB 101. In fact, only twenty of the approximately one hundred police battalions established during the war were composed of overage reservists, and even in the case of these reserve battalions, the majority of the officers and senior enlisted men came from the ranks of career policemen.[34] Not surprisingly, these units having undergone exten-sive training under the command of older career police commanders proved to be ready-made instruments for the prosecution of racial policy on the eastern front.

The police battalions that entered the Soviet Union in the sum-mer of 1941 were led by officers and senior enlisted men whose back-grounds and training, as well as the organizational culture within the police, had prepared them for a war of extermination in the East. In fact, Himmler and Daluege brought this message to the police bat-talions themselves during visits to the eastern front in 1941 in which they tasked these formations with the final annihilation of Bolshe-vism.[35] In the initial six months of the German invasion, the Order Police battalions responded to Daluege's message by murdering tens of thousands of Jews, Bolsheviks, and Slavs, among others. In January 1942, Daluege once again provided an unambiguous message of his expectations for the members of the police battalions. He instructed the police battalions that the objective of combat on the eastern front was the development of an unreserved and firm "combat spirit" (*Kampfgeist*), and he stressed the primary object of the attack as the "ruthless annihilation of the enemy."[36]

CONCLUSION

In the end, the vast majority of the police battalions operating in the occupied Eastern territories proved to be not only capable but also willing instruments of annihilation. In a speech celebrating the tenth year of National Socialist rule in January 1943, Daluege praised Himmler for his success in creating a "police combat troop of the National Socialist movement." He continued, "For Adolf Hitler, this corps of the SS and the police represents his struggle for a greater Germany, Europe, and the world. Its task is the annihilation of the eternal enemies of all *völkisch* and racially conscious nations."[37] The actions of the Order Police formations on the eastern front provided the ultimate testament to Himmler's and Daluege's success in shaping the Order Police into political soldiers. In the end, it was not German culture but rather the organizational culture within the police that transformed civil servants with right-wing sympathies into "political soldiers of destruction."

NOTES

1. Edgar H. Schein, *Organizational Culture and Leadership* (San Francisco: Jossey-Bass, 1985), 6. For a more detailed discussion of this argument, see Edward B. Westermann, *Hitler's Police Battalions: Enforcing Racial War in the East* (Lawrence: University Press of Kansas, 2005).

2. Stephen J. Harrison, "Police Organizational Culture: Using Ingrained Values to Build Positive Organizational Improvement," *Public Administration and Management: An Interactive Journal* 3, no. 2 (1998).

3. Richard Bessel, "Militarisierung und Modernisierung: Polizeiliches Handeln in der Weimarer Republik," in *"Sicherheit" und "Wohlfahrt": Polizei, Gesellschaft und Herrschaft im 19. und 20. Jahrhundert,* ed. Alf Lüdtke (Frankfurt am Main: Suhrkamp, 1992), 324, 329, 343.

4. Bruce Campbell, *The SA Generals and the Rise of Nazism* (Lexington: University Press of Kentucky, 1998), 11.

5. Erich Gritzbach, ed., *Hermann Göring: Reden und Aufsätze* (Munich: Zentralverlag der NSDAP, 1939), 17.

6. *Vossische Zeitung* (Berlin), March 18, 1933. All English translations from German sources in this essay are mine.

7. *Völkischer Beobachter* (Berlin), April 20, 1933.

8. "RdErl d. MdI v. 28.2.1933, IIb II51b Nr. 6/33," February 28, 1933, T580, roll 97, National Archives and Records Administration (hereafter cited as NARA), College Park, MD.

9. "Der Preußische Minister des Innern, Sonderabteilung Daluege, Tgb. Nr. S.D. 2717. Ha. K.," 15 June 1933, T580, roll 220, file 61, NARA. Marked "Eigenhändig!" and "Streng Vertraulich!"

10. "Deutsches Nachrichtenbüro, Die Verbundenheit der SA mit der Polizei," April 28, 1934, T580, roll 220, file 61, NARA.

11. Hans Kehrl, *Jahrbuch der Deutschen Polizei, 1936* (Leipzig: Verlag von Breitkopf und Härtel, 1936), 32.

12. "Feldjägerabteilung IIIb, Tgb.-Nr. III/pers./5504/35 Dr. R./Stan., Betrifft: Eingliederung in die Schutzpolizei," 30 April 1935, T580, roll 96, NARA. See also "SA der NSDAP, Der Oberste SA-Führer, Führungsamt, F 2 Nr. 19239, Betrifft: Feldjägerkorps," May 23, 1935, T580, roll 96, NARA.

13. "Ansprache des Generalleutnants der Landespolizei Daluege and die Kommandeure der Schutzpolizei," April 25, 1935, T580, roll 216, file 3, NARA.

14. "Entwurf für das Zwiegespräch am Mikrophon," 8 May 1935, T580, roll 216, file 3, NARA.

15. Kehrl, *Jahrbuch,* n.p. This was the first volume in an annual series devoted to the police.

16. Ibid., 33.

17. Max Domarus, ed., *Hitler: Reden und Proklamationen, 1932–1945,* vol. 1 (Wiesbaden: R. Löwit, 1973), 881. Hitler admitted this desire in a directive dealing with the SS dated August 17, 1938.

18. Speech by Heinrich Himmler at the state ceremony marking his appointment as chief of the German Police, June 18, 1936, T580, roll 216, file 3, NARA.

19. "Der Führer, Berlin den 16. Januar 1937," January 16, 1937, T580, roll 219, file 57, NARA.

20. Robert L. Koehl, *The Black Corps: The Structure and Power Struggles of the Nazi S.S.* (Madison: University of Wisconsin Press, 1983), 48.

21. Bernd Wegner, *Hitlers politische Soldaten: Die Waffen-SS 1933–1945* (Paderborn: Ferdinand Schöningh, 1982), 142. In 1937, 40 percent, and in 1938, 32 percent of all *Junkerschulen* graduates entered the ranks of the Order

Police, indicating the importance placed by Himmler on the introduction of demonstrated "true believers" into the police officer corps.

22. Karl-Heinz Heller, *The Reshaping and Political Conditioning of the German Ordnungspolizei, 1933–1945: A Study of Techniques Used in the Nazi State to Conform Local Police Units to National Socialist Theory and Practice* (Ann Arbor, MI: University Microfilms, 1974), 101–2.

23. "Der Reichsführer S.S. und Chef der Deutschen Polizei im Reichsministerium des Innern, O-Kdo. P I (1) Nr. 208/38," September 22, 1938, T580, roll 95, NARA.

24. "Zahlenmäßige und statistische Unterlagen zur Besprechung der Befehlshaber und Inspekteure der Ord.-Polizei vom 1.-4. Februar 1942," February 1–4, 1942, T580, roll 96, NARA.

25. "Der Weg der Ordnungspolizei," January 23, 1939, T580, roll 216, file 5, NARA.

26. Ibid.

27. Richard Breitman, *The Architect of Genocide: Himmler and the Final Solution* (New York: Knopf, 1991), 36.

28. Ruth Bettina Birn, *Die Höheren SS- und Polizeiführer: Himmlers Vetreter im Reich und in der besetzten Gebieten* (Düsseldorf: Droste Verlag, 1986), 350–51.

29. Ibid., 352.

30. Kurt Daluege to Heinrich Himmler, March 7, 1940, T580, roll 219, file 59, NARA.

31. Kurt Daluege to Police General Adolph von Bomhard, March 21, 1940, T580, roll 221, file 63, NARA. On April 27, 1940, Daluege wrote a letter to von Bomhard reminding him that the selection of officers and senior noncommissioned officers for the training battalions was the "first priority." He also complained to von Bomhard that in two cases the candidates submitted for these positions had been found completely unsuitable and that he expected disciplinary measures to be taken against the officers who recommended these men for duty with the police training battalions. See Daluege to von Bomhard, April 27, 1940, T580, roll 219, file 59, NARA.

32. "Der Reichsführer S.S. und Chef der Deutschen Polizei im Reichsministerium des Innern, O-Kdo. WE (1) Nr. 104/1940, Betr.: Richtlinien für die Durchführung der weltanschaulichen Erziehung der Ordnungspolizei während der Kriegszeit," June 2, 1940, RG 15.011M, roll 11, file 155, Collection of the U.S. Holocaust Memorial Museum Archive (hereafter cited as USHMMA), Washington, DC.

33. Peter Longerich, *Politik der Vernichtung: Eine Gesamtdarstellung der nationalsozialistischen Judenverfolgung* (Munich: Piper, 1998), 307. Police battalions in this group include the notorious units 307, 309, 310, and 322. For a more detailed demographic breakdown of a 300-level battalion, see

Edward B. Westermann, "'Ordinary Men' or 'Ideological Soldiers'? Police Battalion 310 in Russia, 1942," *German Studies Review* 21 (February 1998): 41–68.

34. Longerich, *Politik der Vernichtung*, 306, 307, 662. Of the fifty-two reserve police battalions in existence at the beginning of 1941, thirty-one of these battalions came from the ranks of the twenty-six-thousand-man replacement force released to the police in October 1939. See Longerich's footnote 42. For example, in Reserve Police Battalion 61, ten of thirteen officers, or 76 percent, belonged to the SS, and nine of thirteen, or 69 percent, held party membership. See Stefan Klemp, *Freispruch für das "Mord-Battalion"* (Münster, 1998).

35. War diary entry of the Police Training Battalion–Vienna (PB 322), July 9, 1941, RG 48.004M *Military-Historical Institute, Prague,* roll 2, frame 200906, USHMMA.

36. Edward Westermann, "Himmler's Uniformed Police on the Eastern Front: The Reich's Secret Soldiers, 1941–1942," *War in History* 3 (1996): 326.

37. "Zum 10. Jahrestage der nationalsozialistischen Revolution, S.S. und Polizei im großdeutschen Freiheitskampfe," January 30, 1943, T580, roll 216, file 2, NARA.

James Waller

Becoming Evil: A Model of How Ordinary People Commit Genocide and Mass Killing

ACCORDING TO JEWISH-CHRISTIAN TRADITION, THE FIRST TIME THAT death appeared in the world, it was murder. Cain slew Abel. "Two men," says Elie Wiesel, "and one of them became a killer."[1] Through-out human history, social conflict is ubiquitous. Wars erupt naturally everywhere humans are present. Since the Napoleonic Wars, we have fought an average of six international wars and six civil wars per *de-cade.* An average of three high-fatality struggles have been in action somewhere in the world at any moment since 1900. The four decades after the end of World War II saw 150 wars and only 26 days of world peace—and that does not even include the innumerable internal wars and police actions. Buried in the midst of all of our progress in the twentieth century were well over a hundred million persons who met a violent death at the hands of their fellow human beings. That is more than five times the number from the nineteenth century and more than ten times the number from the eighteenth century.[2]

Anthropologist Michael Ghiglieri even contends that war vies with sex for the distinction of being the most significant process in human evolution. "Not only have wars shaped geopolitical boundaries and spread national ideologies," he writes, "but they also have carved the distributions of humanity's religions, cultures, diseases, technologies, and even genetic populations."[3]

There is no sign that we are on an ascendant trajectory out of the shadow of our work of de-creation. At the close of the twentieth century, a third of the world's 193 nations were embroiled in con-flict—nearly twice the cold war level. The bipolar cold war system has disintegrated into a system of "warm wars," with randomized conflicts popping up in all corners of an interdependent world. Retired Army Major Andy Messing Jr., executive director of the conservative-oriented National Defense Council Foundation, warns that the growing proliferation of weapons of mass destruction and an increasing world population only add to the danger. In his words, "It's going to be a very tough next 20 years."[4] Even more liberal-leaning voices recognize that present-day population growth, land resources, energy consumption, and per capita consumption cannot be sustained without leading to even more catastrophic human conflict.

The persistence of inhumanity in human affairs is incontrovertible. The greatest catastrophes occur when the distinctions between war and crime fade; when there is dissolution of the boundary between military and criminal conduct, between civility and barbarity; when political, social, or religious groups embrace mass killing and genocide as warfare. I am not speaking here of isolated executions but of wholesale slaughters. As collectives, we engage in acts of extraordinary evil, with apparent moral calm and intensity of supposed purpose, which could only be described as insane were they committed by an individual.

Aptly dubbed the "age of genocide," the twentieth century saw a massive scale of systematic and intentional mass murder coupled with an unprecedented efficiency of the mechanisms and techniques of mass destruction. On the historical heels of the physical and cultural genocide of American Indians during the nineteenth century, the twentieth century writhed from the near-complete annihilation of the Hereros by the Germans in Southwest Africa (now Namibia) in 1904; to the brutal assault of the Armenian population by the Turks between 1915 and 1923; to the implementation of a Soviet man-made famine in the Ukraine in 1932–33 that left several million peasants starving to death; to the extermination of two-thirds of Europe's Jews during the Holocaust of 1939–45; to the massacre of approximately half a million people in Indonesia during 1965–66; to mass killings and genocide in Bangladesh (1971), Burundi (1972), Cambodia (1975–79), East Timor (1975–79), and Rwanda (1994); and, finally, to the conflict that continues to plague the former Yugoslavia. All told, it is estimated that sixty million men, women, and children were victims of mass killing and genocide in the last century alone.[5]

There is one unassailable fact behind this ignoble litany of human conflict and suffering: political, social, or religious groups wanting to commit mass murder do. Though there may be other obstacles, they are never hindered by a lack of willing executioners. That is the one constant upon which they can count. They can always find individual human beings who will kill other human beings in large numbers and over an extended period of time. In short, people are the weapons by which genocide occurs. How are people enlisted to perpetrate such extraordinary evil?

Unlike many of the researchers in perpetrator behavior, I am not interested in the higher echelons of leadership that structured the ideology, policy, and initiatives behind a particular genocide or mass killing. Nor am I interested in the middle-echelon perpetrators, the faceless bureaucrats who made implementation of those initiatives possible. Rather, I am interested in the rank-and-file killers, the ordinary men and women at the bottom of the hierarchy who personally carried out the millions of executions. These people were so ordinary that, with few exceptions, they were readily absorbed into civil society after the killings and peacefully lived out their unremarkable lives—attesting to the unsettling reality that genocide overwhelms justice. One point stands clear: to understand the fundamental reality of mass murder, we need to shift our focus from impersonal institutions and abstract structures to the actors, the men and women who actually carried out the atrocities.

The goal of this essay is to offer a psychological explanation of how ordinary people commit extraordinary evil. It is an attempt to go beyond the minutiae of thick description ("who," "what," "when," and "where") and look at the bigger questions of explanation and understanding: to know a little less and understand a little more.

The essay is divided into three parts. First, I will advance my central argument that it is ordinary individuals, like you and me, who commit extraordinary evil. Second, I will outline an explanatory model of extraordinary human evil that considers the wide range of factors involved in the process of ordinary people committing extraordinary evil. Finally, I will conclude the paper with three suggestions of specific directions for future research.

ORDINARY ORIGINS OF EXTRAORDINARY HUMAN EVIL

The origins of extraordinary evil cannot be isolated in the extraordinary nature of the collective; the influence of an extraordinary ideology; psychopathology; or a common, homogeneous, extraordinary personality type.[6] Perpetrators of extraordinary evil are extraordinary only by what they have done, not by who they are. They cannot be identified, a priori, as having the personalities of killers. Most are not mentally impaired. Nor are they identified as sadists at home or in their social environment. Nor are they victims of an abusive background. They defy easy demographic categorization. Among them, we find educated and well-to-do people as well as simple and impoverished people. We find church-affiliated people as well as agnostics and atheists. We find people who are loving parents as well as people who have difficulty initiating and sustaining satisfying personal relationships. We find young people and old people. We find people who are not actively involved in the political or social groups responsible for institutionalizing the process of destruction as well as those who are. We find ordinary people who went to school, fought with siblings, celebrated birthdays, listened to music, and played with friends. In short, the majority of perpetrators of extraordinary evil are not distinguished by background, personality, or previous political affiliation or behavior as being men or women unusually likely or fit to be genocidal executioners.

We are then left with the most discomforting of all realities—ordinary, "normal" people committing acts of extraordinary evil. This reality is difficult to admit, to understand, to absorb. We would rather know Extraordinary Evil as an extrahuman capitalization. This reality is unsettling because it counters our general mental tendency to relate extraordinary acts to correspondingly extraordinary people. But we cannot evade this discomforting reality. We are forced to confront the ordinariness of most perpetrators of mass killing and genocide. Recognizing their ordinariness does not diminish the horror of their actions. It increases it.

Understanding that ordinary people commit extraordinary evil still begs an explanation. *How,* exactly, do ordinary people come to commit extraordinary evil? This question remains a matter of contentious debate within the academic community. There are, for instance, those who argue that extraordinary evil is done by ordinary individuals who have created or activated a second self to commit that evil. I call these "divided-self" theories of extraordinary human evil.

Most relevant here is the famous series of studies on obedience to authority conducted in the early 1960s by Stanley Milgram.[7] Milgram's experiments posted a simple but intriguing question: how far would ordinary Americans go in inflicting serious harm on a perfectly innocent stranger if they were told to do so by an authority figure? In his initial experiment, of a sample of average Americans, nearly two-thirds were willing to administer what they believed to be life-threatening shocks to an innocent victim, well after he lapsed into a perhaps unconscious silence, at the command of a single experimenter with no apparent means of enforcing his orders. These basic findings have been replicated at least forty times and have held, without regard to age, gender, or level of education of the subjects, in a range of obedience conditions that tested more than a thousand individuals at several universities.

How, and why, did the subjects so readily delegate their moral decision making, and behavior, to an authority? Milgram postulated a discontinuous, altered state—the "agentic" state—as responsible for the behavior of his subjects. The agentic state, activated by one's integration into a hierarchy, occurs when a person "sees himself as an agent for carrying out another person's wishes."[8] In the agentic state, one is in a state of openness to regulation by an authority; it is the opposite of the state of autonomy. It is a change in one's self-perception, a cognitive reorientation induced when a person occupies a subordinate position in a hierarchical system.

In the agentic state, inner conflict is reduced through the abrogation of personal responsibility. Unable to defy the authority of the experimenter in Milgram's study, subjects attributed all responsibility to him. In Milgram's words, "The most far-reaching consequence of the agentic shift is that a man feels responsible *to* the authority directing him but feels no responsibility *for* the content of the actions that the authority prescribes" (italics in original).[9] In the agentic state, Milgram argued, we are not governed by the operations of our own conscience; instead, our conscience has been momentarily switched off or given over to the "substitute" conscience of the authority.

Overtly adopting a divided-self approach, Milgram argues, "Moved into the agentic state, the person becomes something different from his former self, with new properties not easily traced to his usual personality."[10] It is a dichotomous and all-or-nothing proposition—we are in either one state or another at any given time. Milgram's notion of an "on-off" switch reflects the acutely abrupt nature of the agentic shift—a necessary conceptualization given that Milgram's subjects began and completed their task of administering what they regarded as life-threatening shocks to an innocent victim within the window of one laboratory hour.

Although logically compelling, the empirical evidence supporting the agentic shift is, in fact, weak or contradictory. Mantell and Panzarella, for instance, found that there was *no* relationship between the degree of obedience exhibited by subjects and the subjects' assignment of responsibility. In their research, there were both obedient and defiant subjects who accepted 100 percent of the responsibility, and there were those who accepted none at all. In Mantell and Panzarella's words, "Although the majority of subjects in a command situation like the baseline condition administer all of the shocks, they have not surrendered personal responsibility in becoming agents of the experimenter. Some have. But others continue to hold themselves responsible. A monolithic view of the obedient person as a purely passive agent who invariably relinquishes personal responsibility is a false view."[11]

Despite the lack of empirical evidence for "something different" from a former self in explaining Milgram's results, both scholars and laypersons have continued to hold on to the notion that there is a mystical shift from one self to another that enables a person to commit extraordinary evil. There is something emotionally compelling about the idea that extraordinary evil is committed by a "double" of some sorts—ourselves become not ourselves. Our fascination with the notion of a divided self, or two selves occupying the same person, is reflected in impressive mythological and literary roots. Throughout history, the divided self has appeared via the human imagination as a monster, a dragon, a white whale, an extraterrestrial, or a man or woman so evil that we cannot see ourselves in him or her.

We see this line of thinking yet again in the oft-cited work of Robert Jay Lifton. Drawing on extensive, face-to-face interviews with twenty-nine medical professionals involved at high levels in Nazi medicine, twelve former Nazi nonmedical professionals of some prominence (lawyers, judges, economists, teachers, architects, administrators, and party officials), and eighty former Auschwitz prisoners who had worked on medical blocks (more than half of them doctors), Lifton advances the explanatory concept of "doubling" to answer the question of how ordinary people come to commit extraordinary evil.[12] Doubling maintains that the doctors created a second dissociated self to do evil, one related to, but more or less autonomous from, the prior self. The two selves are encapsulated, walled off from one another to avoid internal conflict. The second self is a complete functioning self that has its own psychological framework (divided from the prior self) within which ordinary intellectual and moral standards are annulled.

While doubling may be an initial tool of adaptation to evildoing, it offers little in terms of an explanatory principle for understanding how ordinary people commit extraordinary evil.[13] Most social scientists today maintain a firm belief in the existence of a coherent, authentic, integrated self that is essential to normal psychological functioning. This self may have a fluid, evolving character that is in a continual process of becoming. Along the way, this self may play different roles in different settings—but it is one unitary self nonetheless. As Berel Lang puts it, "It is more plausible to infer a single moral agent—one that granted greater conviction to evil than to good—than two independent moral domains that were constantly being traversed."[14] There is no credible reason to believe that we *temporarily* become wholly different people, with different ways of thinking, feeling, and behaving, when we commit extraordinary evil.

In short, we need a new understanding of how ordinary individuals come to commit extraordinary human evil; a unified theory in which all of us, "normal human beings," must confront our universal potential for extraordinary evil.

EXPLANATORY MODEL OF EXTRAORDINARY HUMAN EVIL

I offer a theoretical model that considers the wide range of factors involved in the process that transforms ordinary people into perpetrators of extraordinary evil.[15] This four-component explanatory model—drawing on existing literature, eyewitness accounts of extraordinary evil by killers and victims of a wide range of genocides and mass killings in the twentieth century, and classic and contemporary research in social psychology—is not an invocation of a single broad-brush psychological state or *event* to explain extraordinary human evil. Rather, it is a detailed analysis of a *process* through which the perpetrators themselves—either in committing atrocities or in order to commit atrocities—are changed. The model (see facing page) specifically explicates the forces that shape our responses to authority. It does so by looking at who the perpetrators are (actor), the situational framework they are in (context of the action), and how they see the "other" (definition of the target).

Our Ancestral Shadow

Is there a basic inborn proclivity or tendency of human nature that limits, or enables, the possibility of cooperative, caring, nonviolent

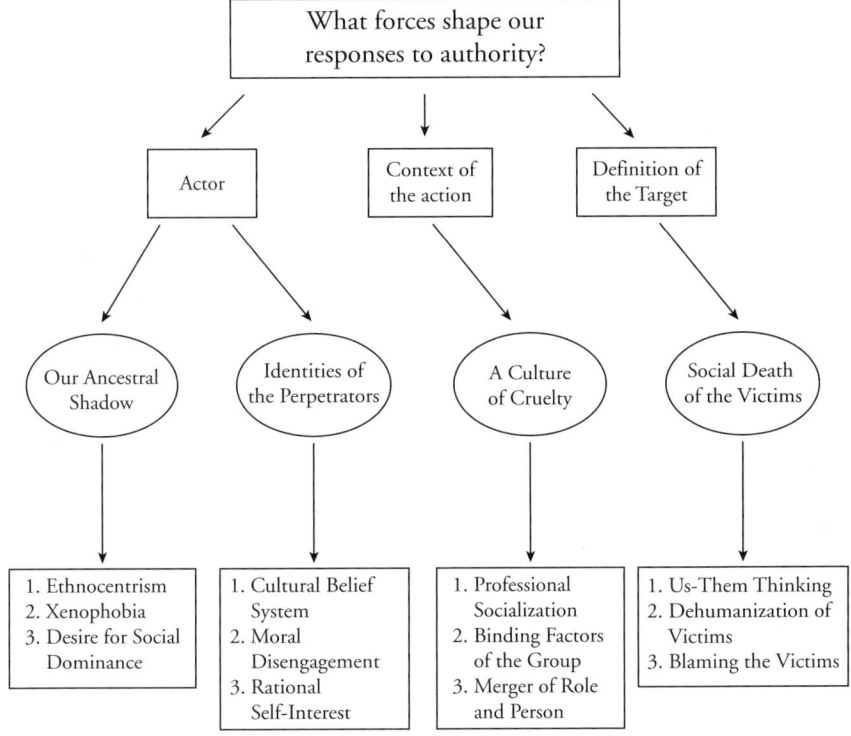

A Model of Extraordinary Human Evil

relations between social groups? The subfield of psychology that was most responsible for bringing us back to rethinking the issue of human nature is evolutionary psychology (EP). EP is a multidisciplinary approach within the Darwinian paradigm that seeks to apply theories of evolutionary biology in order to understand human psychology. The specific goal of EP is to discover and understand the design of the human mind in terms of Darwinian evolution. EP is really engineering in reverse. In forward engineering, we design a machine to do something. In reverse engineering, we figure out what a machine—in this case, the human mind—was designed to do. EP's central premise is that there is a universal, evolved psychological architecture that we all share by virtue of being humans—*a* universal human nature. It has reminded us that we are part of the natural world and, like other animals, we have our own particular psychological tendencies or instincts.[16]

I focus on three such tendencies of human nature that are particularly relevant in shaping our responses to authority. Studies worldwide show not only that these tendencies are universal in people but also that they start in infancy.

1. *Ethnocentrism,* the tendency to focus on one's own group as the "right" one.

2. *Xenophobia,* the tendency to fear outsiders or strangers. In some important ways, xenophobia complements ethnocentrism. There is no "us" without a corresponding "them" to oppose.

3. *The desire for social dominance.* Occasionally, our desire for social dominance has prosocial consequences as we realize that helping others creates friendships and coalitions that are useful in our struggle for power. At other times, however, our evolved desire for social dominance means that we have a predisposition to respond to certain kinds of situations aggressively (sometimes even violently) to get our way.

These are some of the powerful, innate, "animal" influences on human behavior that represent evolved social capacities lying at the core of human nature. They are the underlying, distant capacities that, in concert with other immediate and proximal influences, help us understand our capacity for our extraordinary evil to one another. In short, natural selection has left deep traces of design in our minds, and at least some of those designs leave us evolutionarily primed with the capacity to perpetrate extraordinary evil against each other.

Identities of the Perpetrators

Building on our universal human nature, we must also recognize that the *particular* dispositions and personalities of perpetrators also matter. There is certainly something about *who* the perpetrators are that must be taken into account in understanding how ordinary people commit extraordinary evil. What are the dispositional influences in responding to authority that are most relevant to understanding perpetrators of extraordinary evil?

In that vein, this component of the model explores the impact of three specific factors that shape the particular identities of the perpetrators.

1. *Cultural belief systems* about external, controlling influences on one's life; authority orientation; and ideological commitment.

2. *Moral disengagement* of the perpetrator from the victim—facilitated by the practices of moral justification, euphemistic labeling of evil actions, and exonerating comparisons.

3. One's *rational self-interest,* both professional and personal. These levels of rational self-interest can help explain both the initial willingness of perpetrators to participate in extraordinary evil as well as the enormous vested interest that promotes their sustained involvement.

We must recognize that these dispositional influences are by no means confined to extraordinary circumstances. From early on in our lives, these influences operate in everyday situations in which we routinely do things that bring us gains at the sake of costs to others.

A Culture of Cruelty

Perpetrators create, and are created by, an immediate social context—a culture of cruelty—that helps them initiate, sustain, and cope with their extraordinary evil. Such a culture (by "culture," I am not referring to the macro level of societies but rather to the micro level of groups within societies) makes each perpetrator believe that all men are capable of doing what he does. There are three momentum-inducing features of a culture of cruelty that are most relevant to understanding how ordinary people commit extraordinary evil.

1. The role of *professional socialization,* often institutionalized in military and paramilitary organizations and built on escalating commitments, ritual conduct, and the repression of conscience.

2. The *binding factors of the group* that cement one's adherence to the group and its activities—including diffusion of responsibility, deindividuation, and conformity to peer pressure.

3. The *merger of role and person* that helps us understand how evildoing organizations change the people within them. As we work our way into a culture of cruelty, the culture of cruelty also works its way into us.

The huge predominance of extraordinary evil committed in the world is, in some sense, a societal product in which a complex and sustained series of social forces enables ordinary people to commit extraordinary evil. In that process, the perpetrators are themselves fundamentally changed and become capable of autonomously and knowledgeably committing extraordinary evil.

Social Death of the Victims

This brings us to the fourth, and final, component of our explanatory model of how ordinary people commit extraordinary evil: perpetrators' definition of the target of their atrocities, or who the victims have been made out to be in the eyes of the perpetrators. Often, the common ground between perpetrators and victims in a mass killing or genocide is obliterated by social and legal sanctions. It is the development of moral sanctions, or exclusions, however, that results in the social death of the victims. There are three mechanisms central to understanding the social death of the victims, or the legitimization of the "other" as the enemy, in cases of mass killing and genocide.

1. *Us-them thinking* as the basis for how we so quickly and easily form groups, differentiate our group from others, favor those in our own group, and even swiftly mobilize to aggress against those in another group.

2. The various processes involved in the *dehumanization of victims* (for example, the use of language, actions, and propaganda that define the victims as less than human).

3. *Blaming the victims,* a legitimization of the victim as the enemy and, thus, deserving of their victimization.

The social death of victims may come after the extraordinary evil, or it may lead to it. Most times, it makes sense to argue that the social death of victims precedes their physical death. At times, though, one could argue that the social death of victims is a *consequence* of their physical death. In such cases, the social death of victims—as a justification mechanism—comes quickly after the killings begin.

DIRECTIONS FOR FUTURE RESEARCH

In my research, I have found that the fascination of the question of how ordinary people commit extraordinary evil pales in comparison to the frustration of incomplete, inadequate, and incoherent explanations that dot the academic landscape. To be sure, some good work has been done. To be equally sure, though, many of the explanatory efforts have emphasized the particular instead of the whole—uninterpreted fact instead of fundamental principle. This model is an attempt to synthesize and systematize the diversity of explanations into one coherent whole. At this point, I envision three specific directions for future research.

1. *Scholars in genocide studies now need to take the model and test its applicability to a broader range of cases of perpetrator behavior.*
The opening of archives through Eastern Europe; the emergence of primary source materials from Cambodia, Rwanda, and the former Yugoslavia; and the cultivation of oral collections from victims and perpetrators of extraordinary evil around the world continue to yield even more documentation against which this model can be compared. Is the model a valid and reliable fit for the diversity of perpetrator behavior across human history? Is it sensitive to the vast array of cultural differences that characterize perpetrators of mass killing and genocide throughout the world?

As just one particularly intriguing example, we need to determine the specific applicability of the model to female perpetrators of mass killing and genocide. Most analyses of women in military or paramilitary actions have emphasized their complicity in supporting husbands, sons, and brothers; working in factories making weapons of destruction; or standing silently by as witnesses to the atrocities committed in their lands or on foreign shores. Contemporary research, however, reveals an increasing and extensive documentation of females involved in extraordinary evil—either in defined military roles or as bureaucratic or brutal genocidal killers.

2. *We need to clarify the relative importance of each of the components in the model.*
Which components are more central, or more psychologically primary, than others? Which are more important, which are less important, and which are relatively trivial? Recognizing that the components of the model are not, in reality, as easily separable as they appear on paper, where are the discernible areas of overlap that may be clarified to sharpen the model's explanatory capability?

Do certain pieces of the model correlate more to the initial willingness of ordinary people to commit extraordinary evil while other pieces correlate more to perpetrators' sustained involvement in extraordinary evil? Which components act jointly, and which are unlikely, by themselves, to lead ordinary people to commit extraordinary evil? What, if anything, do we lose by reducing the complex phenomenon of extraordinary evil to discrete, component elements?

3. *Future research needs to discover what practical applications the model has for inhibiting ordinary people from committing extraordinary evil.*

The lesson that ordinary people commit extraordinary evil should not be compartmentalized only as "bad news"—a disturbing, unsettling, disquieting truth about the human condition. The lesson does contain potentially "good news" as well: the commission of extraordinary evil is no longer a mystery. By understanding how ordinary people commit extraordinary evil, we gain insight into how such evil can be lessened. When we understand the ordinariness of extraordinary evil, we will be less surprised by evil, less likely to be unwitting contributors to evil, and better equipped to forestall evil. It is important to understand the conditions under which we can be transformed into killing machines. The more we know, and the more open we are to seeing ourselves as we are, the better we can control ourselves. If we can understand more accurately how ordinary people come to commit extraordinary evil, there is at least a faint glimmer of hope that we all may, ultimately, be delivered from extraordinary evil.

NOTES

1. Quoted in Lance Morrow, "Evil," *Time,* June 10, 1991, 52.
2. William Eckhardt, "War-Related Deaths Since 3000 BC," *Bulletin of Peace Proposals,* December 1991; and Ruth Leger Sivard, *World Military and Social Expenditures* (Leesburg, VA, 1986).
3. Michael P. Ghiglieri, *The Dark Side of Man: Tracing the Origins of Male Violence* (Reading, MA: Perseus Books, 1999), 162.
4. "Third of Nations Mired in Conflict," Associated Press Report, December 30, 1999.
5. Roger W. Smith, "Human Destructiveness and Politics: The Twentieth Century as an Age of Genocide," in *Genocide and the Modern Age: Etiology and Case Studies of Mass Death,* ed. Isidor Wallimann and Michael N. Dobkowski (Syracuse, NY: Syracuse University Press, 2000), 21.
6. For a complete critique of the work of those who argue that the

origins of extraordinary human evil lie not in ordinary individuals but in extraordinary groups, ideologies, psychopathologies, or personalities, see James Waller, *Becoming Evil: How Ordinary People Commit Genocide and Mass Killing* (New York: Oxford University Press, 2002).

7. Stanley Milgram, *Obedience to Authority: An Experimental View* (New York: Harper and Row, 1974). Also see Waller, *Becoming Evil*, 102–11.

8. Milgram, *Obedience to Authority*, 133.

9. Ibid., 145–46.

10. Ibid., 143.

11. David Mark Mantell and R. Panzarella, "Obedience and Responsibility," *British Journal of Social and Clinical Psychology* 15 (1976): 242.

12. Robert Jay Lifton, *The Nazi Doctors: Medical Killing and the Psychology of Genocide* (New York: Basic Books, 1986).

13. See Waller, *Becoming Evil*, 116–23, for a more detailed critique.

14. Berel Lang, *Act and Idea in the Nazi Genocide* (Chicago: University of Chicago Press, 1990), 53.

15. For more detail, see chapters 5–8 in Waller, *Becoming Evil*.

16. For an accessible introduction to evolutionary psychology, see Leda Cosmides and John Tooby, *Evolutionary Psychology: A Primer* (1997), http://www.psych.ucsb.edu/research/cep/primer.html.

III. G·E·N·D·E·R A·N·D S·E·X·U·A·L V·I·O·L·E·N·C·E

Patricia Szobar

The Prosecution of Jewish-Gentile Sex in the Race Defilement Trials

AS A TOPIC OF HISTORICAL INVESTIGATION, THE QUESTION OF SEXUAL violence in the Holocaust might be divided into two overarching categories. The first category comprises the forms of sexual violence that accompanied and arguably were integral to the National Socialist regime's exterminatory project and program of imperialistic expansion. It includes, for example, the rapes committed by German soldiers in the occupied territories, forced prostitution in the camps, the brutal and often deadly treatment of forced laborers accused of violating prohibitions on sexual contact with Germans within the boundaries of the Reich, and finally the sexualized dehumanization of Jewish and other victims within the Holocaust itself. The second overarching category includes the sexual violence that accompanied the National Socialist project of racial hygiene, including reproductive violence such as forced abortion and forced sterilization as well as the persecution of sexual minorities, such as homosexuals, who constituted an apparent threat to the National Socialist social and sexual order.

At first glance, the race defilement proceedings in the Third Reich do not fit neatly into this admittedly crude typology, particularly given that the vast majority of these forbidden relationships were consensual, in striking contradiction to the forms of sexual violence I mentioned a moment ago. In what follows, however, I shall argue that the concept of sexual violence does, in fact, help us understand some of the more crucial meanings and effects of the Nazi regime's enforcement of its blood purity laws. In the first half of this essay, I shall focus on the way that Germans, both Jewish and gentile, experienced the Nuremberg Laws and their enforcement as a violation of the most private and intimate spheres of daily life. In the second half, I shall attempt a preliminary analysis of the rhetorical and representational violence contained within the highly sexualized language that permeated the persecution of Jewish-gentile relationships in the Third Reich.

As is well known, concerns about Jewish-gentile intermarriage and miscegenation with "non-Aryan" races had been a central ideological obsession among National Socialists from the start. Following the seizure of power, such propagandizing against the mingling of races was transformed from obsession to policy, and mixed couples immediately noticed a marked change in local atmosphere. Particularly in smaller towns, disapproving local gossip and speculation flourished. On many occasions, popular disapproval spilled over into direct harassment and violence in *Aktionen,* or "actions," that typically were orchestrated by Nazi rowdies and members of the SA. In one representative incident in Wiesbaden in 1933, a crowd of "twenty to thirty persons," headed by local SA members, cornered two Jewish men and their Aryan girlfriends on the street. The young women were slapped and pushed to the ground, resulting in what the report called "scrapes and bruises." The two Jewish men were forced to carry signs announcing their "shame" while being paraded through town to the accompaniment of a jeering crowd.[1] In similar incidents that took place across Germany, it was often the Aryan woman who was compelled to wear a sign announcing her crime and "parade her shame" in public squares in town. Within this atmosphere of gossip, harassment, and outright violence, mixed couples increasingly became fearful of appearing together in public, and some did, in fact, succumb to the pressure to end their relationships.

More than two years after the seizure of power, in September 1935, the regime announced the Law for the Protection of German Blood and Honor, which forbade "mixed marriages" and extramarital relationships between "full Jews" and persons of "German or related blood."[2] This escalation from popular and officially condoned harassment to legal prohibition and sanction came as a tragic blow for many mixed couples. Certainly, some of the relationships that were investigated and charged were casual romantic affairs or brief sexual encounters. But for many young mixed couples, the Nuremberg Laws dashed hopes of marriage, and many memoirs from the period record instances of young couples committing suicide following the passage of the Nuremberg Laws. In other cases, the new blood purity laws criminalized relationships of long standing, and many couples who had cohabited for years and raised children together found themselves suddenly confronted by a police investigator at their door. In spite of their well-founded fear of discovery and punishment, many mixed couples attempted to continue their relationship in secret. When couples did elect to end their relationship, it was a decision often made at the cost of great anguish.

Ultimately, over the course of the next decade, many thousands of Jewish and gentile Germans were investigated for violations of the Nuremberg Laws, and nearly three thousand Jewish and gentile men were eventually brought to trial for the crime of race defilement. Even though women could not be formally charged with race defilement under the law, Jewish women were often held as witnesses in protective custody for the course of the investigation and trial, and sometimes for many months thereafter. For Jewish men convicted of race defilement, sentences initially ranged from three months to a year of jail. Soon, however, sentences for Jewish men became increasingly severe, ranging from a year to four years of penal servitude. Many Jewish men who had served sentences for race defilement were subsequently turned directly over to the Gestapo for transfer to a concentration camp. Within the camps, the stigma of race defilement appeared to elicit particularly sadistic treatment of Jewish men, who were singled out for special forms of torture and death. In Munich, for example, records from postwar trials of Nazi criminals recount the existence of *Prügelkommandos* (beating squads) in the camps who took enormous and regular pleasure in beating and torturing Jewish men convicted of race defilement. Likewise, Raul Hilberg relates that Jewish race defilers in camps such as Sachsenhausen were subjected to special forms of torture, including suffocation in a broom closet and being hosed with cold water.[3]

By contrast, Aryan men who were convicted of race defilement generally received shorter sentences and were more likely to serve jail time rather than be sentenced to penal servitude. Upon release, however, Aryan men often found themselves virtual outcasts, stripped of their rights of citizenship and unable to find employment. Aryan women charged as witnesses often spent weeks, even months, in protective custody; many lost their jobs, reputations, and standing in the community, and custody of their children. For both Aryan and

Jewish men and women, therefore, the Nuremberg Laws were a cruel violation of their right to form romantic and life partnerships with the person of their choice. An investigation or a conviction on a charge of race defilement, in turn, could have fateful, even fatal, consequences for the accused.

In addition to the violence that accompanied the enforcement of the blood purity laws on a daily, practical level, the rhetoric of race defilement was permeated with aggressive, sexualized symbolism and imagery. In particular, legal representations of Jewish men and women accused of violations of the blood purity laws were imbued with derogatory and highly emotive sexualized images. Jewish men were portrayed as deviant by definition; they were called the "seducers of maidens" who displayed "unbridled appetites," "unnatural inclinations," and "perverse desires." Jewish male sexuality was represented as animalistic and base, yet possessed of a calculated, "shameless and criminal" desire to defile Aryan womanhood. Jewish men were repeatedly accused of wishing to molest any Aryan girl or woman under their employ, which served to further buttress the rationale for prohibiting the employment of Aryan domestic help in Jewish households. Time and again, the courts heaped abuse on Jewish men, who "in typical Jewish fashion" tried to exploit Aryan women "for their own sexual gratification." Such sexual hysteria, in turn, was extremely effective in fomenting anti-Semitic discrimination and widespread public and police harassment of Jewish men. In Berlin, for example, hysteria surrounding the supposed pornographic exploitation of "German women" by Jews was exploited to drive Jewish gynecologists out of professional practice, while elsewhere Jewish medical students were forbidden from conducting gynecologic examinations on Aryan female patients. Thus, as Robert Jay Lifton has suggested, a form of "sexual anti-Semitism" was potently added to existing economic and political persecution as an effective means to stigmatize and socially marginalize Jewish men.[4]

Jewish women were characterized in similar fashion as promiscuous, morally corrupt, and sexually predatory, and they were often accused of concealing their Jewish identity from the hapless Aryan man. A 1937 verdict described the Jewish woman summoned as a witness in a race defilement case in typically derogatory terms: "The witness is a sexually predatory, morally depraved Jewess. With her unrestrained sexual drives and her brazen behavior she held the two accused men in thrall."[5] In depicting Jewish women as sexually aggressive and corrupt, legal rhetoric effectively denied Jewish women the esteem rhetorically accorded Aryan femininity. Both Jewish men and women were depicted as sexual predators intent on spreading disease and degeneracy throughout the population, thus rhetorically legitimizing their exclusion from the body politic.

The language used to depict Aryan masculinity and femininity is, not surprisingly, relatively restrained in comparison to the contemptuous language to describe Jewish men and women. On the one hand, judicial rhetoric depicted Aryan masculinity as naturally dominant and oriented toward sexual gratification, characterizing Aryan men's relationships with Jewish women as understandable, though unfortunate, lapses in judgment. Yet at the same time, sexual relations with a "Jewess" were regarded as a uniquely dishonorable act, a besmirching of the honor of the *Volk* that violated the most fundamental duty of the citizen of "German blood." To mitigate the image of the sexually errant and undisciplined Aryan man, legal discourse often attempted to highlight potentially extenuating or mitigating circumstances. Often it was suggested that the Aryan man had been seduced, and many magistrates characterized Aryan male defendants as "weak-willed," "in need of leadership," and "highly susceptible to outside influence." Other judicial verdicts suggested diminished capacity even in cases where the defendant had been found legally responsible for his acts. Often the courts described the Aryan defendant as "not particularly intelligent," "mentally backward," or possessed of a "moderate-grade mental deficiency," which served to explain his diminished capacity and inability to exercise sexual restraint.[6]

Aryan women summoned as witnesses in race defilement proceedings were also subject to severe scrutiny and judgment. Although legal rhetoric often pointed to the Aryan woman's sexual inexperience as the cause of her seduction, Aryan women were simultaneously depicted as undisciplined, stubborn, frivolous, and always potentially available and corruptible. This negative portrayal of Aryan femininity was echoed in popular representations of Aryan women as well. For example, denouncers and witnesses often employed harsh and highly sexualized language to characterize the behavior and comportment of Aryan womanhood. In a typical instance, an anonymous denouncer to the Gestapo wrote a postcard fulminating about the "offensive indecency" of the many "bitches" and "whores" who consorted with

Jewish men.[7] In the most vituperative denunciations, the often highly misogynistic language clearly drew upon images of the sexually loose woman, now colored by the additional accusation of racial as well as sexual infidelity.

Such aggressively sexualized rhetoric and representations, in fact, permeated the entire course of investigation and enforcement. In the process of a race defilement investigation, one of the central tasks of the police and prosecution was compiling and reconstructing the evidence for the illegal sexual relationship. In order to obtain sufficient evidence for conviction, defendants and witnesses were interrogated repeatedly until they offered an account of the alleged sexual encounter that convinced in its abundance of detail. Interrogators questioned defendants and female witnesses on the most precise and intimate facts, probing for information on the maneuvers of seduction, the couple's state of arousal, where and how they touched, what clothing they wore and what clothing they removed, the positions of their body, and whether "gratification" was achieved. Police and judicial interrogations also devoted a great deal of attention to whether intercourse had taken place "in a normal fashion" or whether what were termed "perversions" were involved. Investigators asked specific and direct questions regarding any sexual acts outside of "normal" coitus. When the couple did engage in "perversions," the investigative and court records described the acts in explicit detail.

Although the first decree governing the implementation of the Nuremberg Laws stated that only sexual intercourse was punishable under the law, in practice local courts gradually began to expand the definition of "sexual intercourse" in their rulings. This practice was ultimately ratified by a decision of the Reich Supreme Court, which asserted that any behavior that could serve to "gratify the desires of at least one of the partners" was sexual and fell under the scope of the racial purity laws.[8] Though local courts welcomed the high court decision as a precedent-setting advance, in practice the need to determine whether an act was designed to achieve sexual "gratification" had an unintended effect as local police officials began to pursue with remarkable thoroughness whether the "sexual desires" of one or both partners had in fact been gratified.

Many of the details elicited with such vigor in the course of interrogations seemed virtually irrelevant to the assessment of guilt and to the sentencing process. For example, during the course of interrogations, investigators routinely inquired whether intercourse had taken place "with protection" or "without protection," a detail that never served as a mitigating or exacerbating factor in sentencing despite the avowed intent of the Nuremberg Laws to "prevent the birth of mixed-race offspring." Such relentless attention to detail on the part of Gestapo and judicial interrogators can partially be accounted for by a standard of proof that necessitated painstaking documentation of the crime. However, the sheer repetition of the sexual details elicited during the course of the investigation is striking and cannot entirely be accounted for by the practical necessities of the legal process. Sexual details were repeated in the police investigative records, in court records before the investigating magistrate, in summary form for the final verdict, and in written reports to an overwhelming number of other legal, health, social welfare, educational, and medical authorities.

Even as such explicit questioning was legitimized as a rational necessity, it was clear to some Nazi contemporaries that this probing for sexual detail on the part of investigators was animated by an underlying form of male fantasy. Indeed, the excessive zeal with which police and judicial investigators questioned women about details of their sexual encounters evoked concern at the highest official levels. In August 1942, the Reich Ministry of Justice issued a directive stating that official questioning of female witnesses should be aimed only at determining whether a sexual encounter had taken place. More explicit inquiries about the nature of the sexual encounter should not be pursued; to persist in such inquiries "would raise the question of a peculiar 'inner or mental attitude'" on the part of the interrogator.[9] Despite such official cautions, police and judicial interrogators continued to display a "will to knowledge" and an obsessive attention to sexual detail that went far beyond the standards of legal proof. Whether or not it was an intended effect, by subjecting men and women accused of race defilement to such relentless questioning and exposure of intimate detail, this sexualized process of enforcement served to dehumanize and objectify its victims and break the personal and political identity of the accused. Perhaps, as Dagmar Herzog and Elizabeth Heinemann have both recently suggested, such a potent mingling of power and desire within legal discourse can only be explained by a theoretical framework that combines psychoanalytic with Foucaultian insights and approaches to recognize the importance of unconscious fantasies to the operation of violent, fascist technologies of dominance and control.[10]

Since race defilement proceedings were, at least in part, open to the public, many of these sexual details circulated in local gossip. Press reports were also fairly explicit, at least in the early years following the Nuremberg Laws. Later, however, it became official policy not to publish the names of the Aryan female partners of Jewish race defilers, and the press was instructed to avoid repeating the more scurrilous sexual details and to dampen the sensationalistic tone of their accounts. Despite their efforts, local officials continued to worry that the public commotion was having a dangerously "exciting" effect, particularly on local schoolchildren who avidly followed accounts of trials in newspapers and the luridly sensationalistic *Der Stürmer.*

It was the Nuremberg Laws that arguably penetrated most deeply into the private and intimate spheres of social and family relations, fatefully separating Jewish from non-Jewish Germans. Unlike many other anti-Semitic laws, whose discriminatory effects were experienced with near exclusivity by the Jewish population, the blood purity laws drew Jews and non-Jews alike into the enforcement process. As historians such as Marion Kaplan have noted, the mere existence of the Nuremberg Laws was enough to intimidate Jews and cause many Germans to withdraw from Jewish friends and from family members in "mixed" relationships and marriages.[11] Though the avowed aim of the Nuremberg Laws was to quash all interracial sexuality, legal discourse paradoxically narrated the proliferation of illegal and "deviant" sexual encounters.

Paradoxically, in recounting and reiterating sexually explicit testimony, both official propaganda and legal rhetoric suggested the rampant sexualization of daily life. As a form of sexual spectacle, the race defilement trials in turn became all the more effective in inciting a form of community surveillance based on the sexual policing of women and Jews. By authorizing voyeurism and prurient fantasies, this aggressively explicit imagery and rhetoric helped enable the co-opting of citizens into a network of sexualized surveillance and self-policing. Given the very short lifetime of the Third Reich, such modes of enforcement could only function successfully by resting upon older, existing patterns of explanation and control, most prominently the sexual monitoring of women and racial "others." In critical ways, therefore, Nazi discourses and practices of racial enforcement establish a line of explanatory continuity to a regime that is often regarded as the very antithesis of a modern, democratic society.

NOTES

A longer version of this essay originally appeared as an article in *Journal of the History of Sexuality* 11, no. 1/2 (2002): 131–63.

1. Hessisches Hauptsstaatsarchiv (hereafter cited as HHStA) 483/5008.

2. The Nuremberg Laws also included a new Reich Citizenship Law.

3. Raul Hilberg, *Perpetrators, Victims, Bystanders: The Jewish Catastrophe, 1933–1945* (New York, 1992). Turning Jewish men and women directly over to the concentration camp after being released from protective custody or penal servitude became official policy in 1942.

4. Robert Jay Lifton, *The Nazi Doctors: Medical Killing and the Psychology of Genocide* (New York, 1986), 10. Regarding the persecution of Jewish gynecologists and medical students, see Saul Friedländer, *Nazi Germany and the Jews*, vol. 1, *The Years of Persecution, 1933–1939* (New York, 1997), 159–61; and Michael Burleigh and Wolfgang Wippermann, *The Racial State: Germany, 1933–1945* (Cambridge, 1991), 78. Borrowing from the title of Klaus Theweleit's study, Friedländer terms the prurience and explicitness of sexual anti-Semitism a projection of National Socialist "male fantasies."

5. Verdict quoted in Hans Robinsohn, *Justiz als Politische Verfolgung: Die Rechtsprechung in "Rassenschandefällen" beim Landgericht Hamburg* (Stuttgart, 1977), 67; see also HHStA 461/16892. Curiously, however, legal discourse devoted less attention to interrogating Jewish femininity and female sexuality than might be supposed, given a seeming likelihood that Jewish women would figure centrally as exotic, liminal creatures within the fascistic sexual imagination. This silence about the Jewish female body and sexuality is replicated in the scholarly literature. Burleigh and Wippermann, for example, devote little attention to Jewish women in their section on the "purification" of Jewish influence from the body of the nation. Likewise, Sander Gilman's studies of discourses of Jewish sexuality focus on representations of Jewish men and masculinity. Burleigh and Wippermann, *Racial State*, 77–112; Sander Gilman, *Difference and Pathology* (Ithaca, NY, 1985); Sander Gilman, *The Jew's Body* (New York, 1991).

6. See, for example, HHStA 461/16143; HHStA 461/16677; HHStA 461/17795; HHStA 461/16679. Aryan masculinity remains as yet to be explained fully in the historical scholarship. In Burleigh and Wippermann's insightful and pathbreaking chapter on men in the Third Reich, for example, class ultimately largely stands for and subsumes Aryan masculinity per se (*Racial State*, 267–302).

7. HHStA 461/15666.

8. Martin Tarrab-Maslaton, *Rechtliche Strukturen der Diskriminierung der Juden im Dritten Reich* (Berlin, 1993), 84.

9. Bundesarchiv Potsdam R22/845.

10. See Dagmar Herzog, "Hubris and Hypocrisy, Incitement and Disavowal: Sexuality and German Fascism," *Journal of the History of Sexuality* 11, no. 1/2 (2002): 3–21, esp. 4; and Elizabeth D. Heineman, "Sexuality and Nazism: The Doubly Unspeakable?" *Journal of the History of Sexuality* 11, no. 1/2 (2002): 22–66.

11. Marion Kaplan, *Between Dignity and Despair. Jewish Life in Nazi Germany* (New York, 1998), 46; 78–81.

Christa Schikorra

Forced Prostitution in the Nazi Concentration Camps

PROSTITUTION UNDER THE NAZI REGIME WAS HIGHLY REGULATED AND subject to state control. Both health and welfare authorities and the criminal police registered and monitored alleged prostitutes as a preventive measure with the avowed aim of protecting the "*Volk* community" and creating a perfect "Aryan race." Young girls and women who engaged in what the Nazi authorities regarded as errant sexual behavior could come to official attention as suspected prostitutes and be classified as "asocial" or "mentally deficient." Violations of a bewilderingly large number of regulations could result in punishments ranging from jail or prison sentences to incarceration in a concentration camp.[1] In addition to the regulated and supervised prostitution in urban brothels, Nazi authorities also established a network of brothels for the Wehrmacht in the occupied nations, organized brothel visits for foreign forced laborers, and established the so-called special constructions (*Sonderbauten*) in the concentration camps.[2] Even though these were all forms of state-regulated sexuality, the various brothel systems and facilities had little in common. This essay examines the brothel system in the concentration camps, focusing on the experiences of inmates of the Ravensbrück women's concentration camp who were compelled to engage in what, according to the logic of the Nazi concentration camp system, was termed as "forced labor" in the camp brothels.

I begin with a survey of the issue of forced prostitution at Ravensbrück as a form of slave labor within the camps, with reference to historical accounts and documents. This brief analysis will also include a summary of the construction of the categories of the "deficient" and the "asocial."

The topic of forced prostitution in the concentration camp brothels touches on many taboos and assumptions that are closely linked to structures of prejudice. Both survivor testimony and historical scholarship often fail to acknowledge work in a camp brothel as slave labor. Here the assumption that prisoners volunteered to work in brothel commandos plays a key role. The women who worked in the brothel commandos were generally referred to as prostitutes. Thus their status as prisoners and as victims was disguised or made to disappear behind a label that was taken to typify the woman herself, rather than the reality of her forced labor.

When the first camp brothels were established in early 1942, female prisoners in Ravensbrück were selected and "prepared" for the work. As the largest women's concentration camp in the Reich, Ravensbrück played a key role in the "provision" of prisoners for brothel commandos.[3] At first, women were "recruited" for the brothels with the promise of release after six months. According to survivor testimony, a significant number of prisoners who wore the black triangle volunteered; it was generally assumed that these women had worked as prostitutes prior to their incarceration.[4] According to some accounts, prisoners from the punishment blocks also were selected for the brothel commando. A few accounts of women who were forced into prostitution have been recorded.[5] However, most testimony comes not from the forced prostitutes themselves but from political prisoners. Their accounts document both their outrage at the establishment of the brothels as well as their attempt to dissociate themselves from the work done there.[6] Lily Unden stressed that no women from Luxembourg worked in the brothels: "Fourteen days after my arrival at Ravensbrück, a female prison guard, dressed for the occasion in very elegant civilian clothing, came to inform the prisoners in the arrival block of the existence of this enterprise. It was a particularly lucrative enterprise for the concentration camp administration, which kept the largest portion of the takings. Volunteers were recruited regularly and it was mostly the promise of much better living conditions that captured the attention of interested elements. Since there were a number of professional prostitutes among us, there were always a few who took it upon themselves to do this degrading task. But no women from Luxembourg were among them."[7]

Even the prisoners repeatedly emphasize that brothel labor was not accorded the same status as other forms of slave labor. In her testimony, Wanda Kiedrzynska described the "recruitment" of Polish women: "When the commandant called all the Polish women together and had the block elder inform them that they could register to work in the brothel, it evoked general outrage and protest. Two Polish women who had answered the appeal had their hair cut off by two others who were sent to the punishment block."[8] The moral outrage over this "offer" from the SS gave rise to a national solidarity that, despite the threat of punishment, saw to it that no Polish women accepted this work.

Although the work was supposedly voluntary, it must be noted that under camp conditions, every "work opportunity" proffered by the SS had a compulsory quality. Some women may have registered for the commando in full knowledge of the work that would be expected of them. But the hope of better living conditions was an equally important incentive. Indeed, such considerations played a role for all of the "good" commandos in which camp inmates hoped to enlist, not just the brothel commando.[9] Thus, while a few women did volunteer for work in the brothel commando, often because of the promise of release, many others were selected against their will by the SS.

The concentration camp brothels were established following an order issued by Heinrich Himmler during an inspection of the Mauthausen concentration camp.[10] Their establishment was justified by the argument that male prisoners needed incentive to work. In spring 1943, Oswald Pohl, head of the SS Central Office of Economic Administration (*Wirtschaftverwaltungshauptamt*), issued a regulation governing brothel visits by inmates who were considered either ethnic Germans (*Reichsdeutsch*) or, at a minimum, "Aryan." Brothel visits by male inmates were included under the system of officially regulated privileges. On May 15, 1943, the Regulation on the Granting of Privileges to Prisoners, also called the Decree on Bonuses, took effect. Incentives would be granted for special work performance, including (1) improved imprisonment conditions, (2) extra rations, (3) cash bonuses, (4) purchase of tobacco, and (5) visits to a brothel.[11]

The brothels were also employed for forcible "tests of renunciation" of male prisoners who were convicted of homosexuality under Paragraph 175 of the criminal code and incarcerated in concentration camps.[12] In this forcible sexual interaction, punishment and proof of heterosexuality were joined, and both the men and the women were victimized.

Following the construction of the first brothel in Mauthausen in summer 1942, additional barracks were built in other camps. Brothel barracks, which were referred to as the "special constructions," were typically sited at the camp perimeter. Most brothel barracks were fenced in, and the women who worked there were not permitted to leave the area. The barracks also contained a waiting room and a few smaller rooms, a doctor's office, and basic sanitary facilities. At first, the brothel commandos were supervised by female SS guards from Ravensbrück. In late 1943, following an order from the SS Central Office of Economic Administration, the guards were replaced by prisoners. According to the confidential circular, "In place of guards, older female prisoners are to be employed in the special constructions. At Ravensbrück . . . there are a number of experienced female prisoners available who have already managed brothels."[13]

Several survivor interviews describe the living and work conditions in the brothel commandos. Frau B., born in 1924 in Halle, was first incarcerated in a Gestapo work camp for "refusal to work" and later deported to Ravensbrück in December 1943. Her testimony recalls how she came to work in the brothel commando: "One day in spring 1945 during roll call, several numbers were called, and mine was one of them. We were told that we were supposed to go to a—what was it called? Not a brothel, but a special commando. We were told to report to the orderly's room. In the orderly's room we were told: wait. We weren't told why we were supposed to go there. Then we were sent to the infirmary. There we were examined, we were swabbed. Then we had to go to the camp commandant and remove all our clothing. We were inspected, just like a meat inspection. Then they said, 'yes, fine, bring them away.' We were about eight women, six or eight women, those of us who were selected."[14]

Frau W., born in 1918 in Gustrow, was deported to Ravensbrück on December 15, 1939. According to her testimony, the pretext for her arrest by the Gestapo was her acquaintance with a restaurant owner who was classified as a "half-Jew." In summer 1943, she was selected for the brothel by the camp commandant Max Koegel, the senior guard Johanna Langefeld, the camp physician Dr. Gerhard Schiedlausky, and several other SS men whose names she did not know. In a detailed account, Frau W. described her arrival in Buchenwald and her work there:

> After a long journey, I saw a large gate and a great, long camp road, just like at Ravensbrück. Aha, just as I thought, another concentration camp. . . . There was an extra block, a barrack, just like the barracks everywhere. The truck stopped. Doors opened, prisoners out. The block was enclosed by a great wooden wall about seven feet high all the way around. Between the block and the wooden wall was a distance of about six feet. That's where we were put. . . . The two female guards then told us: We were now in a prisoner brothel, we would be well-cared for, we would be given proper food and drink, and as long as we submitted then nothing would happen to us. . . . At first I had extreme water retention. And the Hauptsturmführer Gust said, "We'll get you back into shape." I received food from the SS kitchen, all those weeks, and they really did manage to get me back on my feet. That is why I didn't have to the first three weeks. The others had to start right away. When I was well again and had to get to work, I didn't want to do it anymore, and I kept thinking about how I could quit. I didn't, though, and the first time I had to take a prisoner, I defended myself. I told him that I had a pair of nail scissors and that I was going to stab him. That if he touched me he wouldn't leave in one piece. . . . Our clothing consisted of a white pleated skirt, small panties, and a bra. Every evening we had to let eight men mount us in the space of two hours. It worked as follows: they came in, went to the doctor's office for an injection, and then got their room number, that is, the prisoner, took care of business there, in, up, down, out, and back again, then they got another injection and left. We had a bathroom with a bidet and toilet. So we weren't lacking in cleanliness.[15]

Frau W. also testified regarding the conditions in the prisoner brothels: "We didn't have to work when we had our periods. Once a prisoner became pregnant. Her child was taken away three times in a row to the station, so not just once, but three times. Then she left. We weren't given any birth control. We were also monitored, and nothing unusual was permitted. Only the normal way—into the room, onto the woman, off the woman, out of the room, fifteen minutes in all. The doors opened into the hall, and they had peepholes for the SS."[16]

Frau D., born in Hamburg in 1921, succinctly described her forced prostitution in the SS brothel in Buchenwald: "It was completely impersonal, we felt like robots. No one paid us the slightest attention, we were the lowest of the low. We were only good for this. There was no conversation, no small talk, not even the weather was mentioned. Everything was mechanical and indifferent. After a while, we began to get undressed and go through the motions automatically. They finished their business and left."[17]

When women in the brothel commandos became pregnant or contracted sexually transmitted diseases, they were returned to Ravensbrück. Pregnant inmates often were subjected to abortions, and many women died as a result of the operations. According to Antonia Bruha, an inmate who worked in the infirmary, "They returned to the camp, often infected with syphilis or gonorrhea. When they had syphilis, for example, they were given injections and were subjected to various experiments to find cures, or they didn't receive any medical treatment and were simply left to die."[18] According to the testimony of Erika Buchmann, a block elder in the punishment block, "Most of them returned to detention or the punishment block and if they had a venereal disease or were pregnant, to the extermination transport."[19]

When forced prostitutes returned to Ravensbrück after work in the brothels, they were often "wrecks," humiliated and physically broken. The initial promise of the SS that brothel workers would be released from imprisonment after six months proved to be a ruse. Instead, brothel workers were exchanged for new women after six months and returned to their former camp. Himmler's directive that only prostitutes should be selected for work in brothel commandos was ignored. Presumably the number of women who volunteered for brothel labor declined following the initial reports of the women who returned from the brothels. Women who were forced to work as prostitutes with the promise of release were not, in fact, released from incarceration. Indeed, many of these women died as a result of their work from disease, abortions, and violence.

Because of the fragmentary condition of the files, there are only limited data regarding the number and the length of service of Ravensbrück inmates who worked in brothels at other concentration camps. Following Mauthausen and Gusen, the next brothels were established at Auschwitz (June 30, 1943), Buchenwald (July 15, 1943), Flossenbürg (March 25, 1944), Neuengamme (spring 1944), Dachau (May 1944), Mittelbau-Dora (late summer 1944), and Sachsenhausen

(August 8, 1944).[20] Each brothel commando included approximately ten to fifteen women. After a six-month stay, the inmates were replaced and returned to Ravensbrück. It is estimated that more than five hundred Ravensbrück inmates worked as prostitutes in brothel commandos.

Women who were detailed to work in the brothel commandos were available for such work because they had already been deemed "inferior" within the framework of racial hygiene. What is important to note in this respect is that it was the women's supposed "asocial" nature that legitimized the claim of "racial inferiority" and, even more crucially, the regime's claim upon these women's bodies. In the brothels of the male camps, the bodies of these women were forcibly exploited in order to increase male work capacity.

When these women are remembered as "prostitutes" rather than as prisoners who worked in forced prostitution, this characterization reinforces the original stigma presumed by the construct of "the asocial," which accepted as a given that women who worked in these commandos had been prostitutes prior to their incarceration or that they had been classified as "asocial" as a result of "promiscuous behavior."[21] What remains elided is that forced prostitution within the concentration camp entailed a dual relationship of violence. As Elizabeth D. Heineman stresses, "Understanding this type of prostitution as an exchange between men and the state is a profound insight into the 'rationalized' uses of male sexuality—and its costs to women."[22]

The "special construction" commandos in the various concentration camps are rarely mentioned in research on forced labor in the camps.[23] In introducing the topics of female sexuality as well as violence against women as a legitimate focus of inquiry, historians of women have made it possible to examine a variety of sexual taboos as well as forms of female subjugation. Thus, in the late 1980s, survivors began to be interviewed about previously taboo topics, including forced prostitution in the camps. In contemporary exhibitions of concentration camp sites in Germany, the existence of brothels within the camp complex and the issue of forced prostitution in the camps are beginning to receive mention within the larger presentation of camp history. In addition, several memorials have now included aspects of the problem of forced prostitution in their newest exhibition designs.[24]

For many years, women who worked as forced prostitutes have fought for recognition as victims of Nazism, yet forced prostitution has yet to be accorded official status as a crime of the Nazi state. This lack of recognition is the result not only of traditional and contemporary stigmatization of prostitution but also of a refusal to acknowledge the existence of sexual violence against women. The fact that survivors often did not inform the authorities of their work in a camp brothel and rarely spoke of their experiences demonstrates the burden and the fear of discrimination the survivors continue to face today. The persistence of traditional notions is apparent not only in how female sexuality is treated by contemporary society but also by the fact that women who were stigmatized as "asocials" continue to be marginalized. The assumption that the women were themselves to blame for their fate has served to deny their claim to recognition and rehabilitation.

NOTES

This essay was translated from the German by Patricia Szobar.

1. Julia Roos, "Backlash Against Prostitutes' Rights: Origins and Dynamics of Nazi Prostitution Policies," in *Journal of the History of Sexuality* 11, no. 1/2 (2002): 67–94; Annette F. Timm, "The Ambivalent Outsider: Prostitution, Promiscuity and VD Control in Nazi Berlin," in *Social Outsiders in Nazi Germany,* ed. Robert Gellately and Nathan Stoltzfus (Princeton, 2001), 192–211. Regarding prostitutes classified as "asocials," see Christa Schikorra, *Kontinuitäten der Ausgrenzung: "Asoziale" Häftlinge des Frauen-Konzentrationslagers Ravensbrück* (Berlin, 2001).

2. Insa Meinen, *Wehrmacht und Prostitution während des Zweiten Weltkrieges im besetzten Frankreich* (Bremen, 2002); Franz Seidler, *Prostitution, Homosexualität, Selbstverstümmelung: Probleme der deutschen Sanitätsführung 1939–1945* (Neckargemünd, 1977). Regarding the forced prostitution of Korean women in the Pacific theater, see Mira Choi and Regina Mühlhäuser, *"Wir wissen, daß es die Wahrheit ist . . ." Gewalt gegen Frauen im Krieg: Zwangsprostitution koreanischer Frauen 1936–1945* (Berlin, 1996); and also the articles in the journal *Josei Senso Jinken* [*Women/War/Human Rights*] 2 (1999), edited by Ogoshi Aiko.

3. Christa Paul, *Zwangsprostitution: Staatlich errichtete Bordelle im Nationalsozialismus* (Berlin, 1994); Christa Schulz, "Weibliche Häftlinge aus Ravensbrück in Bordellen der Männer-Konzentrationslager," in *Frauen in Konzentrationslagern: Bergen-Belsen, Ravensbrück,* ed. Claus Füllberg-Stolberg, Martina Jung, Renate Riebe, and Martina Scheitenberger (Bremen, 1994), 135–46.

4. Along with other "asocials" and the Sinti and Romanys, prostitutes in the camps were forced to wear the black triangle.

5. Testimony has been recorded of four Ravensbrück survivors who worked in camp brothels. See "Bordell in deutschen Konzentrationslagern," in *K(r)ampfader: Kasseler Frauenzeitung,* vol. 1, Reinhild Kassig and Christa Paul, (1991): 26–31; Paul, *Zwangsprostitution,* 45–57; Peter Heigl, "Zwangsprostitution im KZ Lagerbordell Flossenbürg," in *Geschichte quer* 6 (1998): 44–45; *Das große Schweigen,* produced and directed by Maren Niemeyer and Caroline von der Tann, television film, 30 min., Ostdeutscher Rundfunk (ORB), 1995.

6. See Jack G. Morrison, *Ravensbrück: Everyday Life in a Women's Concentration Camp 1939–1945* (Princeton, NJ, 2000), 201–4. Morrison includes a descriptive section along with memoir accounts from political prisoners, but unfortunately his account lacks a critical perspective.

7. Mahn- und Gedenkstätte Ravensbrück Archiv, Vol. 28, Report 490 of L. Unden, 1956, p. 29.

8. Wanda Kiedrzynska, *Ravensbrück kobiecy obóz koncentracyjny* (Warsaw, 1961). An unpublished manuscript in German translation is located at the Mahn und Gedenkstätte Ravensbrück Library. See manuscript, esp. 29.

9. "Good" commandos included indoor work assignments, assignments under elders or *Kapos* known to be more tolerant, and assignments where prisoners had access to resources such as food, clothing, information, or social contacts.

10. Affidavit of Dr. Schiedlausky from August 8, 1945, and March 4, 1947, Nuremberg documents NO-508 and 2332. Schiedlausky was the camp physician at Mauthausen. On June 11, 1942, the first women from Ravensbrück were transferred to the prisoner brothel in Mauthausen. See Andreas Baumgartner, *Die vergessenen Frauen von Mauthausen: Die weiblichen Häftlinge des Konzentrationslagers Mauthausen und ihre Geschichte* (Vienna, 1997). See especially the section titled "Die ersten Häftlingsfrauen: Zwangsprostituierte," 93–102.

11. Nuremberg document NO-400.

12. Günter Grau, "Die Verfolgung und 'Ausmerzung' Homosexueller zwischen 1933 und 1945: Folgen des rassehygienischen Konzepts der Reproduktionssicherung," in *Medizin unterm Hakenkreuz,* ed. Achim Thom and Genadij I. Caregovodcev (Leipzig, 1989), 91–110; Heinz Heger, *Die Männer mit dem Rosa Winkel: Der Bericht eines Homosexuellen über seine KZ-Haft von 1939–1945* (Hamburg, 1972); KZ-Gedenkstätte Neuengamme, ed., *Beiträge zur Geschichte der national-sozialistischen Verfolgung in Norddeutschland,* vol. 5, *Verfolgung Homosexueller im Nationalsozialismus* (Bremen: Edition Temmen, 1999).

13. Confidential circular of November 20, 1943, from the SS WVHA, Amtsgruppe D to the camp commandants, Institut für Zeitgeschichte, Munich, Fa 506/12.

14. Testimony of Frau B. in Paul, *Zwangsprostitution,* 45.

15. Testimony of Frau W. in Paul, *Zwangsprostitution,* 52–54.

16. Ibid.

17. Testimony of Frau D. in Paul, *Zwangsprostitution,* 109.

18. See the testimony of Antonia Bruha in *"Ich geb Dir einen Mantel, daß Du ihn noch in Freiheit tragen kannst": Widerstehen im KZ; Österreichische Frauen erzählen,* ed. Karin Berger, Elisabeth Holzinger, Lotte Podgornik, and Lisbeth N. Trallori (Vienna, 1987), 149–50.

19. Erika Buchmann, *Frauen im Konzentrationslager* (Berlin, 1959), 86. See also the report about the nineteen-year-old Polish woman who was killed after becoming pregnant during her forced labor as a prostitute in the Sachsenhausen camp brothel. Christl Wickert, "Tabu Lagerbordell: Vom Umgang mit der Zwangsprostitution nach 1945," in *Gedächtnis und Geschlecht: Deutungsmuster in Darstellungen des nationalsozialistischen Genozids,* ed. Insa Eschebach, Sigrid Jacobeit, and Silke Wenk (Frankfurt am Main, 2002), 41–58, esp. 50.

20. Inmates of Auschwitz-Birkenau's women's camp worked in the main camp of the Auschwitz complex. See Hermann Langbein, *Menschen in Auschwitz* (Vienna, 1987), 455; and Primo Levi, *Ist das ein Mensch? Erinnerungen an Auschwitz* (Frankfurt am Main, 1979), 31.

21. Schikorra, *Kontinuitäten der Ausgrensung,* 230–34.

22. Elizabeth D. Heineman, "Sexuality and Nazism: The Doubly Unspeakable?" in *Journal of the History of Sexuality* 11, no. 1/2 (2002): 22–66, quotation at 54.

23. Wolfgang Sofsky mentions camp brothels only in the context of increased work incentives for the male camp prisoners. According to Sofsky, the brothel system was as important as tobacco within the system of bonuses. In his section on work in the camps, however, Sofsky fails to mention slave labor in the camp brothels. See Wolfgang Sofsky, *Die Ordnung des Terrors: Das Konzentrationslager* (Frankfurt am Main, 1993), esp. 197. See also Ulrich Herbert, Karin Orth, and Christoph Dieckmann, eds., *Die nationalsozialistischen Konzentrationslager: Entwicklung und Struktur,* 2 vols. (Göttingen, 1998). In this work on the development and structure of the National Socialist concentration camp system, no mention is made of the subject of forced prostitution in the brothels.

24. Wickert, "Tabu Lagerbordell," 55–56.

Doris L. Bergen

Sexual Violence in the Holocaust: Unique and Typical?

SEXUAL VIOLENCE IS EVIDENT IN MANY ACCOUNTS OF THE HOLOCAUST. Consider the following examples. During the war, a Jewish girl was hidden with a Christian family—in Poland in this case, but it might have been elsewhere. Those people saved her life at great risk to themselves; at the same time, male members of the family abused her sexually.[1] In the summer of 1944, as German soldiers forced Hungarian Jews onto transports to Auschwitz, they conducted a crude vaginal search on a teenage girl, who later described the violation in her memoir.[2] Another memoir, by a Polish Jewish woman, recounts the shame of forced nakedness before leering male guards and officials upon her arrival at Auschwitz.[3] A man tells how a Jewish woman he knew ended up in a camp brothel; after the war, she concealed that part of her past.[4] Sexual abuse of hidden children and adults; dismemberment, assaults, and threats of assaults on sex organs; rape and sexual slavery: all appear, sometimes starkly, more often obscured and disguised, in memoirs and testimony from those targeted for assault as well as in perpetrators' records.[5]

The question for those who study and teach about the Holocaust is what to do with such information. There are, it seems, at least four options. We can overlook sexual violence as part of warfare wherever and whenever it occurs and therefore unworthy of much thought. Or we can refuse to discuss sexual violence because it is inappropriate, disturbing, and offensive. Alternately, we can sensationalize it, as often occurs in popular culture, where the Holocaust and violent sex are frequently intertwined.[6] Or, most difficult of all, we can confront and try to understand it.[7]

In this essay, I suggest some ways to analyze sexual violence in the Holocaust. In doing so, I demonstrate some of the kinds of evidence available and explore how sexual violence functioned in this particular system of mass death. Sexual violence in the Holocaust, I argue, was both typical of other genocides and wars and unique. It was typical in the acts themselves—rape, mutilation, violation of taboos, dismemberment—but unique in the patterns it followed and the meaning given to those acts by a particular ideology, that is, by National Socialist ideas of "race and space," by the Nazi quest to realize a hierarchy based on "race" and "blood" and to expand the German empire through conquest and domination.

Nazi ideology, I demonstrate, did not constitute a barrier to violence of a sexual nature, as some commentators have argued.[8] Instead, ideology shaped the forms that sexual violence took: it helped determine what the authorities permitted, encouraged, and rewarded; it influenced what those "on the ground" could even imagine as possible; it decided what would be recorded, in the sense that disobedience would be concealed or punished. Nazi ideology determined what kinds of violence furthered the goals of the Third Reich. It continues to influence what kinds of acts and violations fit into definitions of the Holocaust and thereby get admitted as relevant into discussions like this one.

THE NEED FOR A BROAD APPROACH

I have three suggestions for the study of sexual violence in the Holocaust, all of them about breadth. Most appropriate, I propose, are a broad definition of sexual violence; an approach that considers both men and women; and a concept that can encompass a wide range of target groups. If we cast a wide net, we will ensure the most productive discussion possible.

Defining Sexual Violence

By a broad definition, I mean that we need to understand sexual violence as including more than rape. The enormous interest in mass rape that emerged in the 1990s with the wars in Croatia and Bosnia-Herzegovina was crucial in acknowledging sexually violated women as victims of war crimes and opening up discussion of issues long considered unspeakable. At the same time, those events influenced the discourse about other cases of expulsion and genocide and generated a sense that if there was no organized, mass rape, there was no sexual violence.[9] Indeed, popular and academic commentators frequently contrasted the sexual brutality of the wars in the lands of the former Yugoslavia with the supposed orderliness of Nazi genocide against the Jews.[10] Likewise, studies of sex slaves used by the Japanese in World War II, the so-called comfort women, produced certain expectations, which, although important in grasping that set of events, could cause those reflecting on German history to miss important points by defining them out of existence.[11]

Sexual violence in Nazi-dominated Europe did not include organized mass rape on the scale of the wars in Croatia and Bosnia, nor did it involve as extensive a system of sexual slavery as the Japanese imposed in the Pacific. Nevertheless, the Nazis too used sexual violence against their victims. A few examples follow. In 1940, General Johannes Blaskowitz assembled some candid descriptions of German crimes in conquered Poland. Troubled by the demoralizing effect on the troops, he prepared a list of twenty-nine of the most egregious offenses. A number of those were sexual in nature. One incident he described is particularly instructive, because it indicates the scope of sexual violence and the varied forms it could take. It is a terse account:

> On 18 February 1940 in Petrikau, two sentries . . . abducted the Jewess Machmanowic (age eighteen) and the Jewess Santowska (age seventeen) at gunpoint from their parents' homes. The soldiers took the girls to the Polish cemetery; there they raped one of them. The other was having her period at the time. The men told her to come back in a few days and promised her five zlotys.[12]

Only one of the women was raped, but would anyone claim that only one experienced sexual violence?

The Blaskowitz memorandum described another incident in more detail. Blaskowitz had not witnessed it himself but had been told about it by two Germans stationed in Poland. In mid-January 1940, those two men watched while a German police officer forced two Poles, a twenty-two-year-old woman and a man, to dig their own graves, in preparation for execution. The man was accused of having shot someone, and the woman had supposedly hidden cartridges in her bosom. A crowd of people gathered, and some ventured to say that the woman appeared harmless. The police officer responded that she was "worse than the man," and moreover he was curious, "whether she was even wearing underpants." He would soon find out, he announced, "because she still has to be interrogated by me." The German police officer then beat the two Poles with a shovel, first the man, then the woman. He also whipped the woman in the face with his leather glove. She fell down, her legs spread apart, and her skirt rode up. Onlookers could see that her undergarments were soaked with blood. The police officer yelled, "Now she is on the rag, so there won't be any fucking." Later it turned out that there had been a case of mistaken identity, and the woman was not executed. But she still had to bury the Polish man.[13]

In this case too, sexual violence seems incontrovertible, yet no rape occurred. Instead, the German policeman used sexual remarks and sexualized parts of the body to torment the Poles and demonstrate his absolute power over them. By focusing the attention of the crowd to parts of the body understood as sexual and forcing public violation of taboos, he expressed total contempt for his victims and encouraged the same disgust on the part of his audience.

Including Men

The account of the policeman's abuse in Poland reminds us of a second area in which the study of sexual violence in the Holocaust needs a broad approach: it needs to include men. Sexual violence, when it is discussed, tends to be relegated to the subfield of women's history, as if it were something that happens to women—not something done to them—and as if only women could be its victims. Such assumptions distort our perspective and can lead to the kind of sentimentalizing or even glorifying of oppression that Joan Ringelheim decries in her articles on women and the Holocaust.[14] Considering men allows us to analyze the indirect as well as direct ways that men too became targets of sexual violence. It also opens up the question of how sexual violence affected its perpetrators, who were usually, though not always, men.[15]

Even when men were not the primary targets of sexual violence, they often suffered its secondary effects. For example, men suffered destruction of their dignity through the kind of emasculation the Polish man experienced at the hands of the German policeman. Related cases, involving undressing at killing sites and camps as well as assaults and threatened assaults on mothers, sisters, daughters, and neighbors, likely created similar feelings in victimized men, both those forced to bare their own bodies to their enemies and those made to witness the dishonor of women under their protection. Often guarded on sexual topics, heterosexual men's accounts nevertheless offer glimpses of their sexual vulnerability.[16]

Men targeted by the Nazis also experienced sexual violence in direct ways, for example, in attacks on their genitals. In the fall of 1939, bands of ethnic German thugs rampaged through Poland, killing thousands of civilians, most of them Jews or members of elites. Rape but also dismemberment and castration were common in orgies of violence in which the attackers sometimes brandished buckets of testicles they had cut off their victims.[17] Later in the war, German treatment of Soviet prisoners of war and captured partisans repeated such acts of violation and intimidation.

We know somewhat more about sexualized attacks on homosexual men, both because of the conventions and preoccupations of Nazi record keepers and because of the existence of at least a small number of eyewitness accounts from victims. The memoir recorded in Heinz Heger's *The Men with the Pink Triangle* provides vivid—almost unbearable—descriptions of sexual abuse of gay men. In one incident, at a concentration camp in Germany, guards tortured a man imprisoned for homosexual activity. Their attack focused on his groin: whips, boiling water, ice, and electric shocks were all means of their terror.[18] Research by John Fout, Geoffrey Giles, and others has further increased awareness of persecution—including sexual abuse—of homosexual men in the Third Reich.[19]

The impact of sexual violence on its perpetrators is less well understood. No one has followed the lead of Klaus Theweleit, who ventured into the quagmire of brutal sexual fantasies and murderous deeds of the Freikorps men in the years immediately after World War I, to write a comparable study of killers in World War II.[20] So far one can only speculate as to the effect that atrocities of a sexual nature had on the men who made them happen. Were these perpetrators titillated? Drawn together in a blood pact? Repulsed? Reinforced in the belief in their own superiority? The following incident suggests all of those possibilities.

In late summer 1942, according to the testimony of a Wehrmacht soldier, an SS division murdered approximately three hundred people, most of them Jews, in a village near Cholm. The SS forced Jewish men to dig a trench and then machine-gunned the assembled Jews into it. Those who survived the shooting they buried alive. The killers grabbed children by the legs and smashed their heads against walls. They used their trucks to chase down anyone who escaped, shooting them "like rabbits." The soldier's account of this orgy of violence included one explicitly sexualized scene, a kind of stylized gang rape:

> A young girl had hidden on the rafter of a barn. When some SS men discovered her, one of them climbed up behind her, while the others arranged themselves under the beam in a circle with their bayonets outstretched. The girl was then jabbed with his bayonet until she was forced to jump down. She was literally skewered. When I asked the responsible SS lieutenant . . . why this terrible act was carried out, he answered: "We threw the Jews out of Germany, and now we need to destroy them here, too."[21]

Other soldiers reported that they saw their comrades rape and murder Soviet women; shoot young girls who had been forced laborers for their own units; and denude, dismember, and defile the bodies of Soviet nurses they had already killed. The men who did these deeds could hardly remain unchanged by their own brutality, any more than those who observed them could feel nothing. A member of a German armored division who described the murdered nurses may have shaped his response to fit the expectations (and vocabulary) of his Soviet interrogators, but it seems unlikely that he invented the cruel details:

> These vicious deeds, these shameful acts of our German "bearers of culture" are surely unique in the world and in history. In cruelty they can hardly be outdone. I want to also add the shameful words that the bearers of culture heaped on the dead women's bodies. (You! Don't you have any charms? No, they are already cold. Well then, light a fire down there, and the thing will become nice and warm.) In this way these bearers of culture belabored and mocked the naked, dead, female corpses. Such deeds can not be reproduced in words.[22]

Considering Various Target Groups Together

Nazi sexual violence affected men as well as women in all of the groups targeted for attack: Jews, people deemed "handicapped," Romanys,

Poles, Soviet POWs, Communists, homosexuals, Jehovah's Witnesses, Afro-Germans. Examples are myriad. Nazi doctors classified as a "life unworthy of living" one inmate from a mental hospital whose "defects" included frequent masturbation and homosexual activity.[23] Romany and Sinti survivors of Auschwitz have described the humiliation that Gypsy women experienced when Nazi guards forced them to be naked in front of their own children. Sterilization is another terrible infringement of Gypsy taboos. Many Sinti women in Germany felt shamed into silence and unable to demand restitution after the war. In one case, when a woman did so, the doctor assigned to examine her turned out to be the same man who had sterilized her.[24] Eyewitness Wanda Poltawska and others have detailed the brutal "experiments" conducted on the sexual organs of Polish women in the women's concentration camp of Ravensbrück.[25] It is crucial to consider various target groups of Nazi assault together, not to set up destructive competitions in suffering but to understand how sexual violence in the Holocaust was shaped by and reinforced the National Socialist hierarchy of "blood."

Sex, sexual prohibitions, and sexual violence served to mark divisions between groups and thereby reify Nazi distinctions. To analyze these interlocking processes, we need to examine various target groups in relation to one another. Already in 1935, the Nuremberg Laws criminalized sex between people defined as "Jews" and those classified as "Aryans."[26] During the war, regulations forbade members of the German military and the SS from intimate relations with Polish, Ukrainian, and other Slavic women. Criteria related to sex, sexual activity, and reproduction were also central to the Nazi project of defining *Volksdeutschen*—ethnic Germans—for the purpose of privileging those deemed bearers of "German blood" over their Slavic, Jewish, or other neighbors. Two factors were critical in such classifications: Who would—and should—serve in the Wehrmacht? And who should have sex with whom, whether within marriage or outside of it? Even these supposedly positive distinctions involved sexual invasiveness and often violence.

For example, SS inspectors assessed the racial potential of the fetuses of pregnant slave laborers in Germany. If the fetus was ruled "desirable," the woman was required to carry the pregnancy to term and submit the child for "Germanization"; if it was found "undesirable," she was forced to abort. Inspectors based their decisions on the appearance of the woman and the man who had impregnated her and on political and ideological factors such as whether either of the parents expressed affection for Adolf Hitler or had a reputation for disobedience to the Reich. Files of the SS Race and Settlement Office's Wiesbaden branch contain the records of one inspector for early 1945. His report for January 1945 praised the "cleanliness and diligence" of a young female candidate for Germanization from the Banat and evaluated the racial potential of several fetuses.[27]

We can see also how sexual violence served to reinforce the Nazi racial hierarchy if we examine regulations for brothels. The Reich Ministry of the Interior's memorandum of October 1942 regarding sexually transmitted diseases is instructive. "For the protection of German blood," the circular began, "bordellos shall be established for the alien workers laboring in the territories of the Reich. They are to be staffed by prostitutes from the respective ethnic groups. General planning is in the hands of the Reich Criminal Police Office." All prostitutes, whether German or "alien," were to be examined regularly for sexually transmitted diseases, but foreign prostitutes were to be kept as isolated as possible in the so-called B Barracks, that is, the Bordello-Barracks.[28] Both explicitly and implicitly the memo indicated that sexual relations between so-called Aryans and aliens could not be prevented altogether.

A circular from Military Supreme Command dated January 27, 1943, described measures to be taken against venereal diseases in brothels intended for German soldiers. It forbade uncontrolled prostitution and called instead for establishment of brothels under military supervision. All of the women working there were to receive a number and a control card so that any sexually transmitted diseases could be traced back to individual prostitutes. Doctors would examine each woman twice a week. Almost at the end of the instructions one sentence linked this exploitation of women directly back to the Nazi racial hierarchy: "Jewesses are to be excluded."[29]

That order implies an admission that Jewish women had not always been excluded from forced labor in Nazi brothels. Other sources likewise suggest that at least in certain times and places, the prohibition against sexual relations between people defined as Jews and those classified as Aryans was ignored or defied. In his diaries from the Vilna Ghetto, Herman Kruk mentions Jewish women who were snatched off the streets and forced into Wehrmacht bordellos. Two such entries, from late 1942, noted that Jewish women had been arrested and charged with *Rassenschande* (race defilement) for having intimate relations with German soldiers.[30] Both through comparable experiences and by their divergence, the fates of different victims of Nazism were interconnected.

FUNCTIONS OF SEXUAL VIOLENCE

In the Nazi system, sexual violence reinforced dominant hierarchies. The particular functions varied, depending on one's placement in the hierarchy at a given moment. For those cases where Germans had crossed the line from persecution to attempted total destruction, sexual violence served to dehumanize the victims and thereby maximize the distance between killers and their prey. Against people targeted for enslavement, sexual violence served to intimidate and demean in order to facilitate conquest and subjugation. For the perpetrators, sexual violence also functioned as the flip side of "normal" sex; that is, sexual violence by contrast increased the value of sanctioned sexual relations between members of the so-called master race, intimacy that helped restore a sense of physical, emotional, and social well-being to men whose sense of themselves must have been shaken by the atrocities they had committed.

Dehumanization of the Targets of Annihilation

In January 1943, Jewish women were officially and explicitly excluded from brothels serving the Wehrmacht. Were they then spared the terrors of sexual violence? The answer, as we have already seen, is no. Doubtless many unsanctioned acts of rape occurred; but given that Aryan men could be punished for sexual relations with women from groups labeled "undesirable," they had extra incentive to destroy evidence of their transgressions by killing their victims. Meanwhile, if rape of Jewish women by men deemed Aryan was forbidden, other forms of sexual violence were permitted and even encouraged by the authorities.

In her memoir *Five Chimneys,* the Hungarian Jewish survivor Olga Lengyel describes the following scene: Sometime in 1942 or 1943, a group of guards at a Nazi killing center developed a particular form of amusement for themselves. They forced a Jewish woman to undress her daughter and then watch while trained dogs violated the girl.[31] Those men engaged in sexual violence but did not risk a reprimand for contravening any laws.

What could be the function of such atrocity? Above all it seems to have been dehumanization, that is, to destroy the dignity and claim to humanity of those targeted for destruction in order to make the perpetrators' job easier. It is notable in this case that the primary victims were a woman and a child; their dehumanization might have been particularly important to killers who still bore some vestiges of chivalry that might inhibit violence toward women and children.

This dynamic—the use of horrific, taboo-breaking sexual violence, often involving coerced participation on the part of the victims themselves—is evident in many cases of genocide and mass expulsion, especially where neighbors attack neighbors. One can see similar patterns of what Daniel Goldhagen calls "excess cruelty"—that is, kinds of torture that would be unnecessary and even counterproductive in some cold, industrial form of killing[32]—in eyewitness accounts from Jedwabne in 1941, or Croatia, Bosnia, or Rwanda in the 1990s.[33] Such violence, in my assessment, serves not merely as an expression of deep hatreds (as Goldhagen contends) but rather has the practical function of helping the killers distance themselves from their victims, people they often know well, if not personally, then at least as a group.

Sexual violence seems to be a particularly effective form of dehumanization, because sexual activities and sexual organs are so closely associated with individual and group honor. As Marianne Hirsch has pointed out, Nazi dehumanization of Jews included—and often focused on—"desexualization," that is, on efforts to destroy women's sense of themselves as women and men's sense of themselves as men.[34] Thus the kind of humiliating acts upon arrival in the camps that so many women survivors describe—the nakedness, the searches, and shaving—were not just about practical exigencies or providing some kind of thrill for male guards, although they may have begun for those reasons; they were one more means of removing prisoners from their torturers' sphere of "normal" treatment of women and fellow human beings.

What of the other groups of people targeted by the Nazis for total destruction? Did sexual violence accompany the murder of those deemed handicapped? I have seen little evidence that it did—although no doubt there were individual incidents. Perhaps in this case the killers already felt assured—by eugenicist thinking, by Nazi ideology, even by the institutionalization of those slated for murder—that their victims fell outside the realm of people deserving consideration as fellow human beings. In other words, the perpetrators may have recognized few ties of common humanity to those victims they categorized as "lives unworthy of living" and hence have needed no extra means to destroy a dignity or claim to personhood that they never recognized in the first place.[35]

More research is also needed to determine whether Romany women shared the experiences of Jewish women as members of a group slated for total destruction. What might be expected is that in this case too, sexual violence took many forms: rape sometimes, although not systematically because of ideological constraints and formal prohibitions, but more often murderous, sexualized violence—dismemberment, humiliation, forced violation of taboos.

Nazi ideology emphasized the barriers between members of the so-called Aryan master race and the targets of genocide: people deemed handicapped, Gypsies, and above all, Jews. They were marked for annihilation; that goal in turn shaped the patterns of sexual assault. If the "Final Solution" was murder, then it became counterproductive to encourage sexual interaction or forced pregnancy. Instead, Nazi leaders and propagandists worked to discourage German killers and their henchmen from considering women from the groups marked for destruction as objects of sexual desire. Nazi ideology and practice constructed taboos around such women, so that the idea of intercourse with them, at least by the time mass killing had become official policy, might seem comparable to having sex with animals or corpses.[36] Here a terrible paradox seems to have come into play: rape is something one only does to fellow human beings. In cases of people marked for annihilation, sexual violence had other functions, namely, to destroy any claims to personhood and its associated rights.

Demeaning and Destroying Communities

For those target groups on the other side of the Nazis' genocidal divide, sexual violence served a related but different function. Sexual violence against Slavic people, for example, or against Jews early in the war, served above all to demean people as members of a community, to destroy ties among them and break their spirits. In these contexts, we do find cases of rape—many of them, including explicit orders to send Polish women caught "fraternizing" with so-called Aryan men to brothels as punishment. For example, a 1940 memorandum from *Reichsstatthalter* Arthur Greiser in Wartheland stipulated that "Polish female persons who engage in sexual relations with members of the German Volk can be sent to a brothel."[37]

In the mid-1990s I spent some time in Bydgoszcz, known to Germans in the Nazi era as Bromberg. One of the first sites pointed out to me was a handsome building that, according to local residents, had housed the SS brothel. There, it was said, young Polish women were held in sexual slavery until they were killed or sent to concentration camps.[38] Nazi law criminalized sexual relations between people categorized as "Poles" and those classified as "Germans"—including *Volksdeutsche*—as it did sex between Aryans and Jews. In January 1940, the Press Information Service of the Reich Propaganda Ministry even issued a directive to German newspapers urging them to do everything to express the "instinctive revulsion of the German people against everything which is Polish" and to "transform this instinctive revulsion into a lasting revulsion."[39] And yet in this case, Nazi Germans accepted sexual interaction—even required it—and used it to humiliate and demoralize populations to be expelled and crushed but needed in the meantime as slaves.

An example of Nazi notions about sex as a tool against the Poles comes from the files of the German special court (*Sondergericht*) in Bromberg/Bydgoszcz. In 1940 the court heard a case of incest involving a fifteen-year-old Polish girl and her father. The man, a basketmaker, was unable to support his family, who lived in a poorhouse. According to the judgment, when his wife died three years earlier, she had instructed her oldest daughter to "take her place" in the father's bed. Three German judges signed the decision "in the name of the German people." It conveyed the extent to which these men shared prejudices central to National Socialism and used their positions to further key aspects of that ideology.

Although the incest allegedly had been carried on for several years, the sentences handed out were relatively light: a year for the daughter, two for her father. As the judgment explained, those decisions had nothing to do with clemency: "The accused are . . . morally deformed people who do not show the slightest understanding of the disgusting nature of their action," the judges wrote. Such moral deficiency, they claimed, was typical of Poles. Polish law too had forbidden sexual relations between relatives, they conceded. But, they continued,

> it is nevertheless known to the court that in certain areas of the former Polish state's territory, sexual intercourse between father and daughter was completely common and was not viewed as immoral by the Polish population. The German people has an interest in ensuring that among the members of the Volk pure relations reign. But we are not interested to the same extent about whether such things occur among the Polish population in ways that are not visible to the outside world.[40]

Why not let them ruin their bloodlines, the judgment implied; they were supposedly inferior in any case and slated for nothing better than enslavement.

With sexual violence against the Slavs, a paradox or push-pull dynamic is apparent. On the one hand, for the Nazi German victors, sex served as an assertion of power over conquered people and as punishment for women deemed inferior or criminal.[41] At the same time, however, sexual relations—even coercive, brutal sex—opened a door to fraternization. As a result, Nazi enforcers swung back and forth between punishing sex between those classified as Germans and those deemed Poles and condoning or even encouraging it. For example, a German SS man was arrested in October 1940 for sneaking into a deportation center to spend the night with a Polish woman who was being forcibly resettled. His superiors chastised but then released him.[42] The files say nothing about the woman's treatment.

Given the nature of the topic and the millions of deaths, it is impossible to get reliable statistics about wartime rape and sexual violence of other kinds. Still, it seems reasonable to conclude that rape by Germans was more common among women from those groups targeted for enslavement—above all, Slavs—than among those slated for total destruction. Racial taboos toward Slavic women were less absolute and less zealously enforced than toward Jews, and later in the war, the physical condition of at least some members of the group may have been more conducive to their being viewed as objects of sexual interest.

But even in the case of Slavic women, the Germans did not follow an official policy of mass rape. Nazi authorities worried about fraternization and continually tried to reduce the possibility of sexual relations with the enemy. Here another bitter irony becomes apparent. Rape and sexual violence were forms of degradation, but they could also serve as reminders of the common humanity of victims and perpetrators, and in some cases they could even arouse sympathy for the victims. Hence the Nazi regime's simultaneous encouragement of abuse and assault of conquered peoples—including sexual violence—and its crackdowns on sexual relations, even when they were coercive and brutal, between Germans and their enemies.[43]

Sex as Normalizer

The third function of sex and the Holocaust that I want to discuss here is not specifically about sexual violence but about another aspect of the issue, and that is the sanctioned, "healthy" sex lives of the perpetrators. Thanks to Claudia Koonz, Gudrun Schwarz, and others, we now know something about the ways that women enabled deadly acts.[44] Through their presence—and their sexual intimacy—wives of perpetrators helped their husbands normalize and civilize their deeds and restore themselves as functioning people.

Teresa Stangl, wife of Franz Stangl, commandant of Sobibor and then Treblinka, described her experiences to the journalist Gitta Sereny. Each time Mrs. Stangl was confronted with information about her husband's involvement in mass murder, she responded by refusing—or becoming unable—to have sexual relations with him. "I couldn't be near him," she reported delicately. Each time, however, it seems that Mrs. Stangl overcame her inhibitions, because later, when even more explicit evidence was forced to her attention, she would again react with revulsion to intimacy with her husband.[45]

Here we see yet another irony. Rape and other kinds of sexual violence were forms of degradation, but they could also serve as reminders of the common humanity of perpetrators and victims. In the interest of preventing dangerous sexual relations, German authorities from Heinrich Himmler down encouraged women to visit their men at the killing fields and even take up residence at death camps. Other Aryan women were also made available to the perpetrators, as members of female SS units, communications experts, camp guards, secretaries, and clerks. Contact, including sexual relations, with these "desirable" women not only led to possible reproduction and decreased the men's temptation to seek sexual release in prohibited relationships; it also perpetuated among the men a feeling that they remained decent people who could still love and be loved.[46] Male perpetrators' need to reinforce a sense of their own humanity existed in tandem with—indeed, depended upon—a drive to dehumanize or demean the objects of their brutality. In this equation, sex became both a means to destroy the other and a way to help perpetrators forget their own participation in those acts of destruction, to revive and renew themselves, to preserve a sense of their own vitality and decency.

CONCLUSIONS

When we open up our perspective—with a broader definition of sexual violence, a more inclusive category of people to be considered, and an understanding of the fates of different target groups as intertwined—we find that the crimes of the Holocaust were steeped in sex. Was sexual violence in the Holocaust unique? No: we can see it functioning in similar ways elsewhere, for example, over the course of the twentieth century, in cases from Belgium to Bosnia, from Nanjing to Bangladesh, Cambodia, and Rwanda. Was it typical? Not completely: as examination of its functions indicates, it took specific forms linked to National Socialist ideology and practice.

One puzzle remains in the consideration of uniqueness and typicality, and that involves sex itself. Is sex unique? Does sexual violence function in ways that have no parallels? Again, I can only venture a yes and a no. Yes, because sex is a particularly powerful tool, surrounded as it is by taboos and intensity. It raises interpretive difficulties for scholars that are not typical of other areas of inquiry. The invasive nature of research on sexual issues poses serious challenges. I think, for example, of the son of one Jewish woman who survived the Holocaust. He always suspected that his mother was raped during the war but never dared to ask her.[47]

Reticence in the sources is echoed—or magnified—in the scholarship, and even those accounts that do speak out often meet with embarrassed silence. Scholars continue to argue over whether or not the brothels at Auschwitz and elsewhere included Jewish women or whether rape of Jewish women by Aryan men occurred on a scale that could be deemed statistically significant.[48] There is also the issue of pain: the historian of the Holocaust Yehuda Bauer once told me that many of his graduate students began dissertations on gender and the

Holocaust, but almost none of them managed to stay with those top-ics. Those students, most of them women, found they had to switch to other areas of research, to matters they did not feel in such acute, excruciating ways on their own bodies.[49] In the face of so much suf-fering, moreover, the usual scholarly tools—footnotes, organizational frameworks, chronological analyses—can seem inadequate and even pathetic. Definitive answers are hard if not impossible to find. Who can blame anyone for turning their attention elsewhere?

And yet, sex is not completely without parallels. Other cultural and social phenomena shared some of the roles of sexual violence in the Holocaust. Religion too sometimes served to dehumanize and demean victims as well as to restore perpetrators' sense that they were still decent human beings.[50] Music functioned in similar paradoxical ways, as torturers forced their prey to sing humiliating songs, mocked them, and then retired with string quartets and pianos to soothe their troubled spirits.[51] Even dancing appears in many accounts of geno-cidal acts (not only in the Holocaust), as perpetrators demanded that their victims dance to their deaths. These similarities might prove fruitful for comparative studies and even offer tools to help uncover the meanings of sexual violence in genocidal contexts. The many dif-ficulties, however, mean the challenge of analyzing sexual violence in the Holocaust will probably remain for a long time.

NOTES

I would like to thank Diane Caplin, John K. Roth, and Carol Rittner, R.S.M., for comments on a version of this essay that I presented at the Uni-versity of Ulster, Magee College, Derry. Thanks as well to the Institute for Scholarship in the Liberal Arts at the University of Notre Dame for funding my travel to Northern Ireland. Students in my classes on Fascism, Gender, and War at the University of Tuzla and European Women in the Twentieth Century at Notre Dame helped clarify my thinking on topics addressed here. Research in Germany and Poland was funded by the Max Planck Institute for History in Göttingen and the Graduate School of the University of Notre Dame. Members of the European History writing group—Martin Beisswenger, Laura Crago, Raully Donahue, Gary Hamburg, Semion Ly-andres, Daniel Mattern, Mark McCarthy, Catherine Schlegel, and Nicole Thompson—provided feedback on a draft, as did Elizabeth Heineman. Dagmar Herzog's help has been crucial. All English translations from original German sources are mine unless credited otherwise.

1. See the documentary film *Diamonds in the Snow,* directed by Mira Reym Binford, 16mm and VHS (1994; Norddeutscher Rundfunk/Westdeutscher Rundfunk, Fritz Bauer Institut, FBW002822). For an account of threatened sexual abuse, see Nelly S. Toll, *Behind the Secret Window: A Memoir of a Hidden Childhood During World War Two* (New York: Dial Books, 1983); esp. 89–90, 147–48.

2. Aranka Siegal, *Upon the Head of the Goat* (New York: Puffin Books, 1981), 213.

3. Sara Nomberg-Przytyk, *Auschwitz: True Tales from a Grotesque Land,* trans. Roslyn Hirsch (Chapel Hill: University of North Carolina Press, 1985), esp. 13–16.

4. Bernd Gotfryd, *Anton the Dove Fancier and Other Tales of the Holocaust* (New York: Pocket Books, 1990).

5. Descriptions of sexual vulnerability of victims appear in many eyewitness accounts; see, for example, Etty Hillesum, *An Interrupted Life: The Diaries of Etty Hillesum, 1941–1943* (New York: Pantheon, 1983); Charlotte Delbo, *None of Us Will Return,* vol. 1, *Auschwitz and After,* trans. Rosette C. Lamont (New Haven, CT: Yale University Press, 1992); Fania Fenelon, *Playing for Time,* trans. Marcelle Routier (New York: Berkley, 1979); Adina Blady Szwajger, *I Remember Nothing More,* trans. Tasja Darowska and Danusia Stok (New York: Simon and Schuster, 1988); Liana Millu, *Smoke over Birkenau,* trans. Lynne Sharon Schwartz (Philadelphia: Jewish Publication Society, 1991); Alicia Appleman-Jurman, *Alicia: My Story* (New York: Bantam, 1988); Isabella Leitner, *Fragments of Isabella: A Memoir of Auschwitz,* ed. Irving A. Leitner (New York: Thomas Y. Crowell, 1978); and Gerda Weissman Klein, *All But My Life* (New York: Noonday, 1990). See also excerpts in John K. Roth and Carol Rittner, *Different Voices: Women and the Holocaust* (New York: Paragon, 1993).

6. On sensationalization, see Joan Smith, "Holocaust Girls," in *Misogynies: Reflections on Myths and Malice* (New York: Fawcett Columbine, 1992), 125–38. Smith singles out William Styron, *Sophie's Choice* (New York: Random House, 1979); the movie version of *Sophie's Choice,* directed by Alan J. Pakula, DVD (1982; Santa Monica, CA: Live Entertainment, Artisan Home Entertainment, 1999); and D. M. Thomas, *The White Hotel* (New York: Penguin, 1981), esp. 249–50, as pornographic embodiments of sex and death. One might also add the Italian film *Il portiere di notte* [*The Night Porter*], directed by Liliana Cavani, videocassette (1974; Los Angeles: Embassy Home Entertainment, 1984). Elizabeth D. Heineman discusses eroticization of the Holocaust in "Sexuality and Nazism: The Doubly Unspeakable?" *Journal of the History of Sexuality* 11, nos. 1–2 (2002): 22–66, esp. 54–65.

7. Efforts have been made to address sexuality and the Holocaust at

Lessons and Legacies conferences. Two papers presented in 1996 (Marion Kaplan, "Gender: A Crucial Tool in Holocaust Research"; and Atina Grossmann, "Trauma, Memory, and Motherhood: Germans and Jewish Displaced Persons in Post-Nazi Germany, 1945–1949") appear in Larry V. Thompson, ed., *Lessons and Legacies,* vol. 4, *Reflections on Religion, Justice, Sexuality, and Genocide* (Evanston, IL: Northwestern University Press), 163–70, 171–211. See also introduction and articles in Dagmar Herzog, ed., *Sexuality and German Fascism* (New York: Berghahn Books, 2004); Omer Bartov, "Kitsch and Sadism in Ka-Tzetnik's Other Planet: Israeli Youth Imagine the Holocaust," *Jewish Social Studies* 3, no. 2 (1997): 42–76; Geoffrey J. Giles, "'The Most Unkindest Cut of All': Castration, Homosexuality, and Nazi Justice," *Journal of Contemporary History* (January 1992): 41–61; Sara R. Horowitz, *Voicing the Void: Muteness and Memory in Holocaust Fiction* (Albany: State University of New York Press, 1997); Susannah Heschel, "Feminist Theory and the Perpetrators" (paper presented at Lessons and Legacies Conference, Northwestern University, Evanston, IL, 2000); Ann Taylor Allen, "The Holocaust and the Modernization of Gender: A Historiographical Essay," *Central European History* 30, no. 3 (1997): 349–64; and Judith Magyar Isaacson, *Seed of Sara: Memories of a Survivor* (Urbana: University of Illinois Press, 1998), esp. 44, 61.

8. For example, Roger Smith, in a paper presented at the Scholars' Conference on the Holocaust and the Churches, Minneapolis, March 1996. This paper on rape and genocide argued that the Holocaust was atypical of twentieth-century genocides because it did not involve mass rape.

9. See Alexandra Stiglmayer, *Mass Rape: The War Against Women in Bosnia-Herzegovina* (Lincoln: University of Nebraska Press, 1994).

10. For example, remarks made by Vittorio Hösle in response to a presentation by Norman Naimark at the University of Notre Dame in March 2001, especially Hösle's description of the Nazis as more "modern" than their genocidal counterparts elsewhere because of their supposed restraint from sexual violence against their victims.

11. See Toshiyuki Tanaka, *Hidden Horrors: Japanese War Crimes in World War II* (Boulder, CO: Westview Press, 1996).

12. Attachment to report from the Senior Commander, Eastern Division (Oberbefehlshaber Ost), Headquarters Castle Spala, 6 February 1940, in Bundesarchiv-Militärarchiv Freiburg (hereafter cited as BA-MA Freiburg), RH 53–23/23, p. 28 in file.

13. Ibid., pp. 23–26.

14. Joan Ringelheim, "Women and the Holocaust: A Reconsideration of Research," *Signs* 10 (1985): 741–61; revised and expanded version in Roth and Rittner, *Different Voices,* 363–418; also Joan Ringelheim, "Thoughts About Women and the Holocaust," in *Thinking the Unthinkable: Mean-*

ings of the Holocaust, ed. Roger Gottlieb (New York: Paulist Press, 1990), 141–49.

15. On charges that Nazi women perpetrated sexual crimes, see Alexandra Przyrembel, "Transfixed by an Image: Ilse Koch, the 'Kommandeuse of Buchenwald,'" *German History* 19, no. 3 (2001): 369–99; on images of German women camp guards as sexually deviant, Insa Eschebach, "Interpreting Female Perpetrators: Ravensbrück Guards in the Courts of East Germany, 1946–1955," in *Lessons and Legacies,* vol. 5, *The Holocaust and Justice,* ed. Ronald Smelser (Evanston, IL: Northwestern University Press, 2002), 255–67.

16. For example, Alexander Donat, *The Holocaust Kingdom* (New York: Holocaust Library, 1978); Thaddeus Stabholz, *Seven Hells,* trans. Jacques Grunblatt and Hilda R. Grunblatt (New York: Holocaust Library, n.d.); Jack Pomerantz and Lyric Wallwork Winik, *Run East: Flight from the Holocaust* (Urbana: University of Illinois Press, 1997); and Henry Friedman, *I'm No Hero: Journeys of a Holocaust Survivor* (Seattle: University of Washington Press, 1999).

17. Christian Jansen and Arno Weckbecker, *Der "Volksdeutsche Selbstschutz" in Polen 1939/40* (Munich: R. Oldenbourg, 1992).

18. Heinz Heger, *The Men with the Pink Triangle,* trans. David Fernback (Boston: Alyson Publications, 1980).

19. John C. Fout, "Background Presentation" (paper presented at United States Holocaust Memorial Museum Colloquium on Persecution of Homosexuals in the Third Reich, Washington, DC, April 2000); Geoffrey J. Giles, "The Institutionalization of Homosexual Panic in the Third Reich," in *Social Outsiders in Nazi Germany,* ed. Robert Gellately and Nathan Stoltzfus (Princeton, NJ: Princeton University Press, 2001), 233–55; Günter Grau, *Homosexualität in der NS-Zeit: Dokumente einer Diskriminierung und Verfolgung* (Frankfurt: Fischertaschenbuch Verlag, 1993).

20. Klaus Theweleit, *Male Fantasies,* 2 vols., trans. Stephen Conway, Erica Carter, and Chris Turner (Minneapolis: University of Minnesota Press, 1987).

21. Christian Farber, quoted in Hannes Heer, ed., *"Stets zu erschiessen sind Frauen, die in der Roten Armee dienen": Geständnisse deutscher Kriegsgefangener über ihren Einsatz an der Ostfront* (Hamburg: Hamburger Edition, 1995), 29–30.

22. Hans Prudhoff, quoted in Heer, *"Stets zu erschiessen,"* 80–81. In the same collection, see also quotations from Herbert Büttner, 37; Karl Blayel, 52; and Albert Niederwieser, 78–79.

23. See document 768, excerpt from the medical record of a patient transferred to the killing center at Meseritz, in Jeremy Noakes and Geof-

frey Pridham, *Nazism: A History in Documents and Eyewitness Accounts, 1919–1945,* 2 vols. (New York: Schocken, 1988).

24. Conversations with Gabrielle Tyrnauer; transcripts of her tapes with Sinti survivors, in special collections at Bailey-Howe Library, University of Vermont, Burlington, VT.

25. See Germaine Tillion, *Ravensbrück,* trans. Gerald Satterwhite (Garden City, NY: Doubleday, 1975); also Wanda Poltawska, *Und ich fürchte meine Träume* (Abensberg, 1994). Regarding experiments in Auschwitz, see Olga Lengyel, *Five Chimneys* (New York: Howard Fertig, 1983).

26. "Law for the Protection of German Blood and Honor," September 15, 1935, excerpted as doc. 403 in Noakes and Pridham, *Nazism,* 2:535. On charges of racial dishonor in Germany, see Patricia Szobar, "Telling Sexual Stories in the Nazi Courts of Law: Race Defilement in Germany, 1933 to 1945," *Journal of the History of Sexuality* 11, nos. 1–2 (2002): 131–63.

27. SS-Oberscharführer Reinhold Ratzeburg, "Dienstreisebericht 2/45," Wiesbaden, 28 January 1945, Hessisches Hauptstaatsarchiv Wiesbaden, 483/7360, pp. 1–2.

28. Circular, Reichsminister des Innern to Reichsstatthalter in den Reichsgauen (Landesregierungen), Regierungspräsidenten, Polizeipräsidenten in Berlin, Gesundheitsämter, "Betr.: Bekämpfung der Geschlechtskrankheiten. Ärztliche Betreuung der fremdvölkischen Prostituierten," Berlin, 24 October 1942, pp. 1–2, Archiwum Panstwowe in Poznan (hereafter cited as AP Poznan)/299 (Reichsstatthalter)/2161 (Bekämpfung der Geschlechtskrankheiten 1942–1943).

29. Oberkommando der Wehrmacht, signed i.A. Dr. Handloser, to various, including OKH/S In; OKM/AMA/G; Reichsführer SS; Wehrmachtbefehlshaber, Berlin, 27 January 1943, in various places, pp. 4–5, in AP Poznan/299/2161, pp. 23–24.

30. Herman Kruk, *The Last Days of the Jerusalem of Lithuania: Chronicles from the Vilna Ghetto and the Camps, 1939–44,* ed. Benjamin Harshav, trans. Barbara Harshav (New Haven, CT: Yale University Press, 2002), 266, 366, 372.

31. Lengyel, *Five Chimneys,* 185.

32. On "excess cruelty," see Daniel Jonah Goldhagen, *Hitler's Willing Executioners: Ordinary Germans and the Holocaust* (New York: Alfred A. Knopf, 1996), 17, 452–53.

33. See Jan T. Gross, *Neighbors: The Destruction of the Jewish Community in Jedwabne, Poland* (Princeton, NJ: Princeton University Press, 2001), esp. 56–65. On Bosnia, see Ed Vulliamy, *Seasons in Hell: Understanding Bosnia's War* (New York: St. Martin's Press, 1994), esp. 195–201; on Rwanda, see Philip Gourevitch, *We Wish to Inform You That Tomorrow We Will Be Killed*

with Our Families: Stories from Rwanda (New York: Farrar Straus and Giroux, 1998), esp. 110–31. Also useful is Norman M. Naimark, *Fires of Hatred: Ethnic Cleansing in Twentieth-Century Europe* (Cambridge, MA: Harvard University Press, 2001).

34. Marianne Hirsch, "Surviving Images: Holocaust Photographs and the Work of Postmemory," in *Visual Culture and the Holocaust,* ed. Barbie Zelizer (New Brunswick, NJ: Rutgers University Press, 2001).

35. Some illustrations of the mentality of the T-4 killers appear in Noakes and Pridham, *Nazism,* 2: chap. 36. See also Henry Friedlander, *The Origins of Nazi Genocide: From Euthanasia to the Final Solution* (Chapel Hill: University of North Carolina Press, 1995).

36. Propaganda films comparing Jews to rats, such as the notorious *Der Ewige Jude* (*The Eternal Jew*), and bus tours through the ghettos, during which Germans could see the "subhuman" existence of the Jews, served to create an image of Jewish women as beneath sexual interest. See document 786, report by Polish government-in-exile regarding Warsaw, May 1942, in Noakes and Pridham, *Nazism,* 2:1069; also Yizhak Ahren, Stig Hornshøj-Møller, and Christoph B. Melchers, *"Der Ewige Jude": Wie Goebbels hetzte* (Aachen: Alano Verlag, 1990).

37. Reichsstatthalter, signed Greiser, to Höheren SS- und Polizeiführer beim Reichsstatthalter in Posen, Posen, 25 September 1940, "Betrifft Umgang der deutschen Bevölkerung des Reichsgaues Wartheland mit Polen," p. 2, United States Holocaust Memorial Museum Archive (hereafter cited as USHMMA) RG-15.029M.

38. Note also the film *Women in Prison,* directed by Geza Radvanyi, videocassette (1951), shot on location in women's detention centers in northern Italy after World War II. A subplot involves a Polish woman who spent the war in the East as a sex slave for the Germans.

39. See doc. 652 in Noakes and Pridham, *Nazism,* 2:934.

40. Judgment, signed Raasch and two others, "Wegen Blutschande," pp. 2–3, Archiwum Panstwowe w Bydgoszczy (State Archive of Bydgoszcz; hereafter cited as AP Bydgoszcz) 80/248, pp. 25–26.

41. See Christl Wickert, "'Das grosse Schweigen': Zwangsprostitution im Dritten Reich," in *Werkstatt Geschichte* 13 (1996): 90–95; Christa Paul, *Zwangsprostitution: Staatlich errichtete Bordelle im Nationalsozialismus* (Berlin: Edition Hentrich, 1994); and Christa Schikorra, "Prostitution weiblicher KZ-Haftlinge als Zwangsarbeit: Zur Situation 'asozialer' Häftlinge im Frauen-KZ Ravensbrück," *Dachauer Hefte* 16:112–24.

42. "Bericht über die Evakuierungsaktion im Kreise Kulm," signed SS Oberscharführer, Thorn, 3 October 1940, AP Bydgoszcz 97/16, p. 91.

43. The fear that sexual relations would lead to fraternization was evi-

dent in Germany's occupied territories in the West as well as the East. See Insa Meinen, *Wehrmacht und Prostitution während des Zweiten Weltkriegs im besetzten Frankreich* (Bremen: Edition Temmen, 2002).

44. Claudia Koonz, *Mothers in the Fatherland: Women, the Family and Nazi Politics* (London: Jonathan Cape, 1987); Gudrun Schwarz, *Eine Frau an seiner Seite: Ehefrauen in der "SS-Sippengemeinschaft"* (Berlin: Aufbau Taschenbuch, 2001). Also of interest: Rudolf Hoess, *Commandant of Auschwitz: The Autobiography of Rudolf Hoess,* trans. Constance FitzGibbon (London: Pan Books, 1974); and Alison Owings, *Frauen* (New Brunswick, NJ: Rutgers University Press, 1993).

45. Gitta Sereny, *Into That Darkness: An Examination of Conscience* (New York: Vintage Books, 1983), esp. 131–33, 154–55, 355–62. Goldhagen shows wives visiting their husbands at mass killing sites; so do Browning and Hoess. Goldhagen, *Hitler's Willing Executioners;* Christopher Browning, *Ordinary Men: Reserve Police Battalion 101 and the Final Solution in Poland* (New York: HarperCollins, 1992), 92–93; Hoess, *Commandant of Auschwitz.*

46. See Gaby Zipfel, "Wie führen Frauen Krieg?" in *Vernichtungskrieg. Verbrechen der Wehrmacht, 1941–1944,* ed. Hannes Heer and Klaus Naumann (Hamburg: Hamburger Edition HIS, 1995), 460–74.

47. See account in Helen Epstein, *Children of the Holocaust: Conversations with Sons and Daughters of Survivors* (New York: Penguin, 1988), 227.

48. For example, review of *Auschwitz,* by Deborah Dwork and Robert Jan van Pelt, in *Pro Memoria Information Bulletin, Auschwitz-Birkenau State Museum* 5–6 (January 1997); also comments by Yehuda Bauer made from the audience at Scholars' Conference on the Holocaust and the Churches, Minneapolis, March 1996; comments by Judith Isaacson at Lessons and Legacies IV Conference, Notre Dame University, South Bend, IN, November 1997; and debate between Omer Bartov and Henry Friedlander at symposium on Outsiders in Nazi Europe, Madrid, December 1998.

49. Conversation with Yehuda Bauer, University of Vermont, Burlington, October 1993.

50. On Christianity as a means to soothe the consciences of perpetrators, see Doris L. Bergen, "Between God and Hitler: German Military Chaplains and the Crimes of the Third Reich," in *In God's Name: Genocide and Religion in the Twentieth Century,* ed. Omer Bartov and Phyllis Mack (New York: Berghahn Books, 2001), 123–34.

51. See Doris L. Bergen, "Music and the Holocaust," in *The Holocaust: Introductory Essays,* ed. Wolfgang Mieder and David Scrase (Burlington, VT: UVM Center for Holocaust Studies, 1996), 133–47.

Rochelle G. Saidel

The Jewish Victims of Ravensbrück Camp

THE NAZIS' LARGEST CONCENTRATION CAMP FOR WOMEN, RAVENS-brück was located about fifty miles from Berlin. Although there were Jewish women imprisoned there for nearly the entire six years of the camp's existence, Ravensbrück has not generally been studied as part of the Final Solution. However, an estimated twenty thousand to twenty-five thousand Jewish women, or about 20 percent of the total of the camp's population, were inmates at some time during the period from May 1939 to April 1945. Thousands of Jewish women were murdered there or sent from there to be murdered elsewhere. Based on interviews with survivors, visits to the Ravensbrück memorial, and archival research, this study integrates the experiences of the camp's Jewish female prisoners into its history.

By including the stories of Jewish victims in the history of the camp, this research contributes to correcting misperceptions in the memorialization of Ravensbrück that have existed on both sides of the Iron Curtain. For most of its years under the jurisdiction of the Soviet Union and then the German Democratic Republic (GDR), the Ravensbrück memorial site did not mention that there were Jewish prisoners. Just as the portrayals of victims at the camp memorial left out the Jewish women, Ravensbrück has generally been left out of Jewish memorialization of the Holocaust in the United States. Today this situation has changed, more in Germany than in the United States. This research on the Jewish victims, a minority in Ravensbrück, contributes to rectifying the fact that these victims have often been overlooked in scholarship and memorialization in the United States.

In this essay, I briefly summarize the camp's background and then present a chronology of the groups of Jewish women who were at the camp during almost all of its history, recounting the stories of some of the individuals. Finally, I offer a brief gendered analysis of women's experiences and a discussion of the politics of memorializing the camp's Jewish victims.

BACKGROUND ON HOW RAVENSBRÜCK CHANGED

While it is not my task here to provide detailed background on Ravensbrück, it is necessary to point out how the camp degenerated. Ravensbrück cannot be described in a monolithic way because, like all concentration camps, it changed for the worse over time. Those who arrived at various times during the camp's six years of existence found extremely dissimilar situations. It was drastically different at the end of World War II than it was intended to be when it was inaugurated in the spring of 1939. As the camp's population grew to more than ten times the originally planned number of women, the living conditions and treatment rapidly deteriorated.

Because of the changes in the situation at the camp during its six years of existence and the destruction of many records by the Nazis as the Soviet Army approached, it is difficult to present a complete and accurate picture. This is particularly true regarding the fate of the Jewish victims because thousands of them arrived during the camp's chaotic last months and often were not even accounted for. Furthermore, early Jewish prisoners were either murdered or transferred to death camps by the fall of 1942. It is unusual to find a Jewish survivor who arrived before 1943 or even during that year.

Between May 1939 and June 1944, 43,000 women were brought to Ravensbrück. The deportation to Ravensbrück of women from prisons and camps in Poland, Austria, France, Belgium, Holland, Norway, Yugoslavia, and other occupied countries caused the number of inmates to rise dramatically from 1943 onward. Camp records account for about 10,000 new arrivals in 1943, and in 1944 more than 70,000 inmate numbers were given out.[1] Other reasons for the increased population of the camp included the beginning of evacuations from Majdanek and Auschwitz in 1944, the deportation of 12,000 non-Jewish women and children from Warsaw after the Warsaw uprising in August 1944, the mass transports of Hungarian Jewish women in the fall of 1944, and the evacuees sent on a death march from Auschwitz in January 1945. By the last weeks of the camp's operation, there were 1,100 women in each barrack, a building which had been designed for about 250. Every straw sack in the three-tiered bunk beds held two, three, or more women. There was a plague of lice and danger of disease from the water.

Of the about 132,000 women who were in the camp at some time between 1939 and 1945, approximately 20 percent were Jewish.[2] An estimated 100,000 to 117,000 of the total population of prisoners did not survive. It is not possible here to do more than outline the chronology of the groups of Jewish women who arrived and mention an individual or two from each group as examples. Obviously, this approach is somewhat of a generalization, as there was a tremendous amount of coming and going at the camp and there were no neatly defined chronological groups. Furthermore, it is important to bear in mind that individual survivors can report only on their own specific and limited familiarity with the totality of the camp, so their accounts are not always the same.

JEWISH WOMEN IN RAVENSBRÜCK

Spring 1939 to Fall 1942

Jewish women were in the camp from the earliest days. It has generally been accepted that the first transport consisted of 867 women who arrived in May 1939, mostly German antifascists, either Social Democrats or Communists, some coincidentally Jewish. They arrived from Lichtenburg in Saxony, a fortress that had been used as a women's camp from March 1938 until May 1939.[3] Before that (from October 1933 until March 1938), the first women's camp was located in a workhouse in Moringen, near Hannover, but women were generally incarcerated in prisons during the early years. The Ravensbrück camp ledger for May 21, 1939, lists 974 women prisoners in the camp, 137 of them Jewish. Of this group, one woman's long trip to the camp passed through Moscow and Rio de Janeiro.

Olga Benário Prestes was born on February 12, 1908, to Eugenie and Leo Benário, a Jewish upper-middle-class Munich family. She joined the Communist youth organization in Munich at age fifteen and left home to carry out her revolutionary activities. She was imprisoned for the first time at the age of eighteen in 1926, and two years later she fled to Moscow. She was named as a member of the Presidium of the Communist Youth International and in 1934 was chosen by the Comintern to accompany Brazilian Communist leader Luís Carlos Prestes to Brazil to help him in his revolutionary activities there. When his November 1935 revolution failed, she was captured and imprisoned in Rio de Janeiro. In the meantime, she and Prestes had fallen in love, and she was pregnant. At the time of the Prestes revolution, Brazilian President Getúlio Vargas had a friendly relationship with the Hitler regime. To retaliate against Luís Carlos Prestes, in September 1936 Vargas sent Olga back to Nazi Germany under armed guard. Upon her arrival in Berlin in October, she was brought to the prison for women on Barnimstrasse, and her daughter, Anita, was born there on November 27. At the age of fourteen months, the baby was miraculously rescued by Prestes's mother.

Olga was transferred to Lichtenburg in February 1938 and then sent on the first transport from Lichtenburg to Ravensbrück in the spring of 1939. A great heroine in both camps, she was assigned as a *Blockälteste* (block elder), in charge of an unruly group of women whom she organized and taught the necessity of personal hygiene. Olga carried out many acts that raised the women's spirits and worked to better their conditions, despite her own suffering. She even made a small secret atlas to teach other prisoners about geography and the war, and this amazingly detailed atlas survives today in the Ravensbrück archives. She also collaborated on a clandestine newspaper and helped organize extra rations of bread and margarine for women in the infirmary.

In addition to her other work assignments, she was a slave laborer for the Siemens electric company at Ravensbrück. In January 1940, along with seventy-nine other women, Olga was sent to the prison bunker and remained there for thirty days. She had been among the prisoners kept for "security reasons" in closed barracks when *Reichsführer* Heinrich Himmler visited the camp. She was whipped and almost on the verge of death, but when she was released she had to immediately return to forced labor at the Siemens factory.[4]

Olga, at age thirty-four, was among those Jewish political prisoners gassed at Bernburg in the winter and early spring of 1942. Her murder was part of the Nazis' organized extermination called "14f13." The first selections in Ravensbrück began in December 1941 and January 1942, and those women selected were predominantly Jewish. Beginning in February 1942, they were sent to the Bernburg mental asylum, where they were killed in the gas chamber. An estimated fifteen hundred to sixteen hundred female prisoners were taken there.[5]

Because of this "14f13" project, the only exception to the camp's growth was between February and April 1942.[6] There was also a transport of 1,000 Jewish women to Auschwitz on March 26, 1942. Another 522 Jewish women were sent to Auschwitz on October 6, 1942. These actions were part of Himmler's command to make camps in the territories within the German Reich *judenrein* (free of Jews) and send Jewish inmates to Auschwitz and Majdanek. While there were Jewish prisoners in the camp from its first days, I know of only one who was there during its first three years and survived. Herta Soswinski, an Austrian Jewish political prisoner, arrived on January 14, 1942, and was sent to Auschwitz in October 1942.[7] Although there may have been some exceptions, Jewish women who were in Ravensbrück before 1942 were murdered at the camp or sent to Auschwitz-Birkenau or another camp by the fall of that year.

Fall 1942 Through 1943

However, soon afterward, Jewish women began to arrive at Ravensbrück again, and they continued to do so until its last days. While there may be others who arrived earlier, the earliest arrival I know of after the operation of October 6, 1942, is Sali Solomon Daugherty, a Dutch Jew who now lives in Jaffa, Israel. She was born in Amsterdam on March 21, 1933, to a Dutch mother, Rosetta Wertheim Solomon, and a Romanian father, Marco Solomon. Sali came to Ravensbrück by way of Westerbork, in either late November or early December 1942, along with her mother and aunt. This arrival was less than two months after Ravensbrück had supposedly been purged of Jews, and it demonstrates that there were Jewish women in the camp for nearly the entire six years of its existence. Furthermore, it is possible and even probable that there were other Jewish women at the camp, even during the time between the October transport to Auschwitz and Sali's arrival. In addition to women who arrived as known Jews, there were Jewish women at the camp whose "racial" background was unknown to the Nazis. They had been arrested with false papers as non-Jews, for example, for resistance activities.[8] Sali was eight when she arrived, and she remained in the camp until she was rescued and taken to Sweden by the Red Cross in April 1945. Although she does not have many clear specific memories of her time at the camp, some things began coming back to her as we spoke. "The screaming and the hitting people—I remember that I saw all this," she said. "And people that were hit until they died on the ground."[9]

Stella Kugelman Nikiforova was only four years old when she entered the camp with her mother.[10] Stella was born in 1939 in Antwerp, the only child of Luis Gustavo Kugelman Griez, a Spanish Jew from Barcelona, and Rosa Klionski, a British Jew from London. They met while they were studying in Belgium, where they fell in love and married; Stella was born there. I met her quite by accident in Brazil and interviewed her with the help of a translator.

Not only were Stella's parents Jewish but they were also members of the resistance in Antwerp after the Nazi occupation of Belgium on May 10, 1940. They were arrested in 1943, along with sixty families that had been carrying out acts of sabotage. Even though little Stella was only four years old, her documents stated that she was a political prisoner, and, along with her mother, she had to wear a red triangle in the camp. This preschool "political prisoner" even had a number: 25,622. She said she was dark and looked Spanish and was taught to say in German at the camp, "I am Spanish." She was told never to tell anyone she was Jewish.[11]

Her mother died of tuberculosis within three months of their arrival at the camp, and Stella was then cared for by a series of substitute mothers. The women hid her where the Nazis were afraid to enter, the barrack that housed women with tuberculosis or typhus. Stella was at Ravensbrück until its evacuation. Her most vivid memories of camp life are of the last few days of April 1945, when she was six years old. She was with the Russian women prisoners in the chaos of the forced march, and a prisoner of war who was a doctor in the Soviet Army kidnapped Stella and another child. She returned to the Soviet Union with these two children in order to be "rehabilitated" as a heroic rescuer of children, rather than risking the possibility of being accused of treason for divulging secrets as a prisoner of war. After clearing her own name with the authorities, the woman placed Stella in a cruel orphanage in an isolated area about five hundred kilometers south of Moscow.

Stella had always thought that her father might be alive, and after her 1957 release from the orphanage at age eighteen, she started looking for him. He had immigrated to São Paulo, Brazil, remarried there, and started a new life. When Stella visited her father for the first time in 1963, she was a twenty-four-year-old woman and they had no language in common. Stella felt uncomfortable with her father's new wife and constrained by the unfamiliar language, climate, and culture. After six months she went back to the Soviet Union. When I met her in 1994, she had returned briefly to São Paulo to take care of legal matters after her father's death. She lives in Saint Petersburg.

1944

Most of the survivors I know of who arrived in 1944 were from Hungary, caught in the Nazis' last major roundup of Jews in the summer and fall of that year. One other woman who told me her story was arrested posing as a Christian in the aftermath of the general Warsaw uprising, and yet another was turned in by a neighbor in Bratislava. In a series of seemingly arbitrary transfers that must have been traumatizing, by the beginning of 1945 all but one of these women had been sent on to another camp. Although I have quite a few rich testimonies from women who arrived in Ravensbrück in 1944, I have space here to briefly summarize only one case as an example.

Margaret Wohl Guiness (known as Margo) arrived in Ravensbrück in August 1944 and in November was transported to Dortmund and then to Bergen-Belsen.[12] She was arrested in Budapest, where she and her older sister, Bozena, had been living in a pension and posing as Christians. The daughters of Theodor Wohl and Anne Ritter Wohl, they had fled there from Kosice, Czechoslovakia, after the Nazi takeover. Then fourteen years old, Margo had the false identity papers of seventeen-year-old Maria Karolchik.

One day when the sisters returned to their room in June 1944, the Gestapo was waiting for them, and they were arrested on suspicion of espionage. They were also suspected of being Jewish. After imprisonment and interrogations, in August the sisters were deported to Auschwitz, where Margo continued to claim she was seventeen. The next day, along with about one thousand other women, they were selected for transfer to Ravensbrück. It had never been proven that the sisters were Jewish, and she remembers that most of the women in their cattle car transport were non-Jews.

At Ravensbrück the sisters were not designated as Jewish. Margo worked in the Siemens factory. She said that in November, Dr. Karl Gebhardt selected her for a "medical" experiment, but she and her sister managed to get on a transport to another camp, Dortmund. After bombs destroyed the factory roof in Dortmund, they were evacuated to Bergen-Belsen. Margo was then ill with typhus for six weeks. She and her sister were taken to Sweden by the Red Cross, and Margo describes as "the saddest loss" and "the darkest area of my life" the fact that her sister was so ill that she died there.

Many women were sent on to satellite camps, but the conditions in Ravensbrück continued to deteriorate, with many more women in each block than had originally been planned. Thousands of women did not even have part of a bunk and were lying on the floor without so much as a blanket. Already insufficient rations became more and more meager as time went on. When five hundred or more Jewish women arrived from Hungary in fall 1944, a big tent with a straw floor was erected. The women lay in their own dirt in the freezing cold and died in masses. Some two thousand Hungarian Jewish women arrived at the camp between November 19 and November 28. The tent, erected between Blocks 24 and 26 in the middle of the camp, "housed" Hungarian Jews as well as women evacuated from Auschwitz, and up to three thousand women were left there to perish with virtually no water, food, or blankets.[13]

1945

Most Jewish women who survived Ravensbrück entered the camp in late January or early February 1945, after the evacuation of Auschwitz. They reached the camp in extremely bad shape, after surviving against all odds in their former camp and during a murderous death march, and then riding in open railroad cars in subzero weather. Arriving toward the end of Ravensbrück's operations, when conditions were at their worst, most stayed only a short time before moving on to one of the camp's satellites. Because of these circumstances, some of these women have limited or almost no memories of their experiences at Ravensbrück. However, others have vivid recollections that contribute to an understanding of the camp's last chaotic months.

In survivor registries and testimony archives in the United States, Israel, and Europe, most of the Jewish women who list Ravensbrück as one of the camps they endured are those who arrived with this group. Therefore, among the women who agreed to be interviewed or share unpublished memoirs with me, the majority arrived from Auschwitz-Birkenau or one of its satellites in late January or early February 1945.

The number of Jewish women who arrived from Auschwitz is unknown, but it is in the thousands. For example, Lidia Rosenfeld Vago, who lives in Petach Tikvah, Israel, has kept track of the survivors from her group at the *Werkunion,* the ammunition factory at Auschwitz. She told me that thousands of Jewish women were sent from Auschwitz to Ravensbrück. She believes that all of the eleven hundred women who were slave laborers at the *Werkunion* with her were sent on the death march toward Ravensbrück. Many of them did not survive the trip.[14]

Lidia was born on November 4, 1924, to Dr. Endre Rosenfeld and Dr. Jolan Harnik in Gheorgheni, a small town in the Carpathian Mountains.[15] Lidia, her mother, and her sister Anikó arrived in Auschwitz on June 10, 1944, and her mother was sent immediately to the gas chamber. She and her sister were there for seven months, working in the *Werkunion* ammunition factory until the massive evacuation on January 18, 1945. Upon arrival in Ravensbrück, Lidia and her sister were first sent to the infamous tent, which was often a death sentence. "We were among the last to be jostled in, and several hundred other newcomers spent the rest of the night on the frozen snow outside," she said. After the registration process, Lidia and her sister were sent to a block with tiered bunks. Lidia and Anikó were sent to work stuffing straw mattresses. They were sent on to Neustadt-Glewe, a satellite camp, on February 16, and were liberated from there on May 2, 1945.

On April 30, 1945, the Soviet Army reached Ravensbrück and found only 3,000 desperately weak, sick, and dying prisoners. At least 7,500 to 8,000 women, hundreds of them Jewish, had been evacuated by the Red Cross to Switzerland and Sweden during the final month of the camp's existence. Another 15,000 women prisoners had been driven out on April 28 and, under Nazi guard, had embarked on a death march toward the northwest. The SS had intended to dynamite the camp and murder the remaining 3,000 women, but some brave men from the nearby men's camp destroyed the explosives.

A BRIEF CONSIDERATION OF GENDER

The experiences of Jewish female victims of Ravensbrück add to our ability to study the roles that gender and physiology played during the Holocaust. Gender—the social, political, and economic aspects of

differences between men and women—refers to the hierarchy of relationships between men and women in traditionally patriarchal society.
Jewish women had to confront certain questions both as Jews and as
women. Every survivor's story is distinct, but women's experiences were
generally in some ways different from those of men in the context of the
universal suffering of all victims of the Holocaust. Learning about the
experiences of Jewish women in a women's camp can help us to better
understand these distinctions. On the one hand, there were positive
aspects related to gender that enabled women to better struggle against
the subhuman conditions of degradation, deprivation, terror, and even
death at Ravensbrück. For example, homemaking and nurturing skills
were "women's work," and women's familiarity with these roles equipped
them to form surrogate families, care for each other, and perform the
hygienic and housekeeping routines that helped them sustain life.

On the other hand, gender-associated qualities caused some of
the women to suffer. For example, because of the social relations
between women and men, girls were brought up to be modest, and
many women were traumatized when forced to parade naked before
men and even other women. Women were also taught to be submis-
sive and "the weaker sex," and they had to overcome this ingrained
self-image in order to stay alive. Obviously, other variables, such as the
socioeconomic, political, and national backgrounds of the women,
also played a role.

As for physiological differences between men and women, both
common sense and survivor testimonies point to women's vulnerabilities. Pregnancy could be punishable by death, or at least by forced
abortion. There are many testimonies about women prisoners in various camps helping other women miscarry or abort in order to save
the life of the mother. Likewise, there are stories of prisoners who
killed their own newborn infants because there was no hope for the
babies and their presence could cause suffering or death to others.
Menstruation was another vulnerability for women in Ravensbrück
and other concentration camps. Testimonies about the inability to
menstruate and anxiety about later being able to conceive are quite
common. Several women, however, told me of the embarrassment of
continuing to menstruate or having a final period after arrival in a
concentration camp.[16]

The women's fear of rape and sexual abuse combined gender and
physiological vulnerabilities. The racial laws enacted in Germany in

1935, which made it illegal for "Aryans" to have sexual relations with Jews, should have protected Jewish women against rape and forced prostitution. However, there is evidence in historical accounts and testimonies that these laws were often broken. Most women survivors do not talk about their own sexual exploitation, but some of them tell stories of their comrades' suffering. The question of gender during the Holocaust only began to be explored about twenty years ago, and its significance has not yet been resolved.[17]

THE POLITICS OF MEMORIALIZING RAVENSBRÜCK'S JEWISH VICTIMS

As I was shocked to learn on my first visit to Ravensbrück in 1980, Jewish women were nowhere to be seen in the collective memorialization of victims at the camp memorial for most of the time that it was under the jurisdiction of the GDR. However, today the professional staff of the camp memorial and other researchers are seriously involved with including the history of Jewish victims. It is not difficult to comprehend the reason that Jewish victims were previously left out or why they are now included. The way we memorialize any event is colored by who is doing the remembering and for what purposes.

From the end of World War II until the dismantling of the Soviet bloc, the three major concentration camp sites in the GDR—Ravensbrück, Buchenwald, and Sachsenhausen—were conceptualized as Communist shrines. The Ravensbrück memorial site was first under the jurisdiction of the Soviet Union and in 1959 became a national *Mahn- und Gedenkstätte,* or memorial site, of the GDR. The memorial site highlighted the histories of the Communist heroines, especially German Communists, who had been imprisoned in the camp and did not mention that Jewish women were among the victims (even though the Nazis had singled them out as Jews).

Perhaps this highlighting of communism and Communists at the camp memorial was one reason that the camp was virtually unknown for decades in the United States, even after Holocaust memorialization became a powerful force in the Jewish community. In the last years of the GDR's existence, a small exhibit was put in place to commemorate the Jewish victims, as well as a Jewish memorial. This is an important historical fact that needs to be emphasized because it is often assumed that there was no change in this regard until after unification.[18]

When I next returned to Ravensbrück in March 1994, the site was in a state of transition from its GDR days to a new Western approach. Even though the Berlin Wall had fallen in November 1989, the last Soviet soldiers who had been stationed on Ravensbrück's grounds since the end of World War II did not leave until the summer of 1993. The entire former concentration camp then came under the jurisdiction of the Stiftung Brandenburgische Gedenkstätten (the State of Brandenburg Memorials Foundation). In 1994, the small Jewish memorial room (conceived under the GDR) was closed because it was being moved to a larger space and being redone for the forthcoming 1995 fiftieth anniversary ceremonies. Although I could not see the Jewish exhibit, I was fortunate to see the Ravensbrück memorial in its transitional state in 1994, while it was still a muddy and untidy vast wasteland.

By the time I returned for the ceremonies marking the fiftieth anniversary of liberation in April 1995, the site had been "gentrified." The camp memorial's texts and exhibits had also been changed to reflect the camp's figurative "relocation" to the West. The Communist interpretation of what had happened during the Third Reich had been revised to conform to the new post-Soviet political reality. A new presentation about the Jewish victims of the camp (including Jewish Communists) was then prominent among the exhibits in the prison cells of the punishment bunker. In striking contrast to the many years when Jewish victims were left out of the camp's story, the camp officials arranged a special meeting with the delegation of Israeli survivors to ask them how they would like to see the memorial evolve.

By my next visit in June 2001, the landscape of the memorial had been expanded and changed. The empty area that had held the Soviet troops was coated with black slag, and markers indicated sites of barracks and other buildings that they had razed. One of the former SS houses at the camp entrance was being readied as a conference center, especially for educational programs for youth groups. Including Jewish victims in memorialization at the camp was accepted without question.

The case of how Jewish women's experiences in Ravensbrück have been neglected in memorialization in both the German Democratic Republic and the United States (for different reasons) demonstrates that ideological considerations influence who and what is memorialized or emphasized in history. Regarding women's experiences, much research is still needed on gender and how and why women and men faced adversity in different ways. And regarding Jewish victims, we still have to ensure that their stories are appropriately included in all of the places where they were victimized. The experiences of Jewish women in Ravensbrück are distinctively Jewish and gendered, but they are also applicable to a much broader understanding of prejudice and genocide.

NOTES

This essay is based on the author's recent book, Rochelle G. Saidel, *The Jewish Women of Ravensbrück Concentration Camp* (Madison: University of Wisconsin Press, 2004).

1. Fragments of arrival lists and inmate numbers from January 1 to December 31, 1943, numbers 15918 to 25891; 1944 arrival lists at Ravensbrück Memorial Archive.

2. The estimated statistic used at the Ravensbrück memorial site in 1995 was that 10 percent of the population was Jewish, which was much too low. By 2000 this estimate was revised to about 15 percent, but the actual number was most likely even higher. In a 1995 interview at her home outside of Paris, the president of the French Amicale de Ravensbrück, survivor Dr. Marie-José Chombart de Lauwe, said that many women passed through the camp on the way to Auschwitz or other camps and were never included in the count of those interned. Many of these women who were taken to other camps were Jews. There will never be specific numbers for any of the groups of women at the camp because the Nazis burned many records in the crematorium before fleeing.

3. It is difficult to pin down statistical information about Ravensbrück, and even the date of the first transport of women to the camp has been contested. Although most accounts state that the first transport arrived by train from Lichtenburg in the spring of 1939, the earliest remaining *Zugangsliste* (arrival list) in the Ravensbrück Archive is dated November 11, 1938. I have never seen an explanation for this early list, dated when the camp's construction was just beginning. According to Erika Buchmann, *Die Frauen von Ravensbrück* [*The Women of Ravensbrück*] (Berlin: GDR, 1959), 28, the first women's transport arrived at the Fürstenberg train station on March 23, 1939.

4. For more information, see Jutta von Freyberg and Ursula Krause-Schmitt, *Moringen–Lichtenburg–Ravensbrück: Lesebuch zur Ausstellung* (Frankfurt: Verlag für Akademische Schriften, 1997), 133.

5. For more information, see Bernhard Strebel, "Ravensbrück: Das

zentrale Frauenkonzentrationslager," in *Die nationalsozialistischen Konzentrationslager: Entwicklung und Struktur,* ed. Herbert Ulrich, Karin Orth, and Christoph Dieckmann (Göttingen: Wallstein Verlag, 1998), esp. 235.

6. The 14f13 project was part of a euthanasia program known as T4 (as its address was Tiergartenstrasse 4, Berlin). The program was designed for adults who were mentally or physically "unacceptable" by Nazi racial standards and were murdered at one of four euthanasia centers, including Bernburg. See Saidel, *Jewish Women of Ravensbrück,* chap. 3, for more details about Jewish women from Ravensbrück who were murdered at Bernburg.

7. See Herta Soswinski, "Why We Have to Tell About It," in *Auschwitz: The Nazi Civilization,* ed. Lore Shelley (Lanham, MD: University Press of America, 1992), 125–44.

8. I have interviewed several such women, whose stories are told in Saidel, *Jewish Women of Ravensbrück.*

9. Sali Solomon Daugherty, interview by Rochelle G. Saidel, December 28, 2000, Jerusalem, in the author's possession.

10. Stella Kugelman Nikiforova, interview by Rochelle G. Saidel, November 2, 1994, São Paulo, Brazil (in Russian, with Dr. Alla Millstein Gonçalves as interpreter), in the author's possession.

11. Evidently the Nazis did not identify Stella's mother as a Jew when she was arrested, or she and Stella would have been forced to wear a yellow triangle along with the red one.

12. Margaret (Margo) Guiness, interview by Rochelle G. Saidel, March 13, 1998, Long Beach, CA, in the author's possession.

13. The SS listed a total of 46,070 women in Ravensbrück and its satellites on January 15, 1945. See Strebel, "Ravensbrück: Das zentrale Frauenkonzentrationslager," 225–27.

14. Lidia Vago, interview by Rochelle G. Saidel, April 22, 1995, traveling from Berlin to Ravensbrück, in the author's possession.

15. Ibid. For more information on Vago's experiences during the Holocaust, especially in Auschwitz, see Lidia Rosenfeld Vago, "One Year in the Black Hole of Our Planet Earth: A Personal Narrative," in *Women in the Holocaust,* ed. Dalia Ofer and Lenore J. Weitzman (New Haven, CT: Yale University Press, 1998), 273–84.

16. Vago, interview by Rochelle G. Saidel, April 22, 1995.

17. The first public event on the question is recorded in Esther Katz and Joan Ringelheim, eds., *Proceedings of the Conference of Women Surviving the Holocaust* (New York: Institute for Research in History, 1983). More recent analytical studies include Dalia Ofer and Lenore J. Weitzman, eds., *Women in the Holocaust* (New Haven, CT: Yale University Press, 1998); Nechama Tec, *Resilience and Courage: Women, Men and the Holocaust* (New Haven, CT: Yale University Press, 2003); and Elizabeth Baer and Myrna Goldenberg,

eds., *Experience and Expression: Women, the Nazis, and the Holocaust* (Detroit: Wayne State University Press, 2003).

18. I had pressed for inclusion of Jewish victims as Jews beginning in 1980 and kept up a correspondence with my contact in the GDR, Werner Händler. The head of the Sachsenhausen survivor committee, he informed me in 1988 that such an endeavor was under way in Ravensbrück. He had discussed this endeavor with GDR officials, for example, in a letter dated July 25, 1985: Werner Händler to General Hermann Axen, Member of the Politburo, Archive of Brandenburg Memorials Foundation/Ravensbrück Memorial, Document number RAI/3–5 VI 1007.

IV. C·O·L·L·A·B·O·R·A·T·I·O·N
A·N·D   T·H·E
E·A·S·T·E·R·N   F·R·O·N·T

Martin Dean

Schutzmannschaften in Ukraine and Belarus: Profiles of Local Police Collaborators

Serafinowicz makes a good impression, he is a pleasant and easy-going type, has a somewhat sly character possessing a slightly shifty eye, but could not be described as anything approaching a brutal type. Obviously because of his strong physical development and his ability to adopt an authoritative manner, he made a considerable impression on the German occupying forces in Poland and these qualities account for his liking for the promotion he received while serving [them].

THIS WAS THE ASSESSMENT MADE BY COLONEL A. P. SCOTLAND, AN experienced British war crimes investigator, who interrogated Semion Serafinowicz, the former head of the police in the Belorussian town of Mir, shortly after the war.[1] Serafinowicz had been denounced by some of his former Polish Army colleagues in London, but at this time no eyewitness to his activities came forward. The case against him was dropped in 1948 following his dishonorable discharge from the Polish forces and only resurfaced again in the 1990s. Colonel Scotland's report is interesting in its attempt to characterize Serafinowicz on the basis of a brief interview. While Scotland clearly underestimated Serafinowicz's capacity to commit violent crimes, assuming mistakenly that the responsibility for such crimes lay solely with the Gestapo, the evidence of numerous other witnesses, who observed Serafinowicz on a daily basis, confirms much of Colonel Scotland's assessment of his personality and ambition.

What kind of men served the Germans as local police collaborators in the *Schutzmannschaften*? This question can perhaps best be answered on the basis of a few detailed individual case studies that quickly reveal the admixture of personalities, motives, and experiences among these men. I choose to use the police term "profiling," often used when looking for serial killers, as there may be certain common types and attributes that can be discerned. At the same time, the sample analyzed here is certainly not large enough to provide the basis for firm conclusions. And as in any police investigation, it would be a mistake to rule anything out; there is always the exception that proves the rule. Rather, these brief sketches are intended to give a face to some of the men described more anonymously in my book *Collaboration in the Holocaust*. In particular, the surprisingly rich nature of the sources, including detailed testimonies collected from scores of witnesses in certain major investigations as well as much contemporary and postwar documentation provide considerable insights into the actions, personalities, and motives of individual policemen.

There are nevertheless certain limitations to these investigative sources. As Chris Browning has noted with his large sample of witnesses from the Starachowicze Jewish forced labor camps, postwar criminal investigations can tell you a great deal about a few specific perpetrators, whose behavior is the focus of intense questioning. Yet the great bulk of the perpetrators (in Browning's case, mostly Germans) remain faceless. Similarly with the local police, there are a few names, usually the most senior and active policemen, who are mentioned by many witnesses, while the remainder remain (in Browning's words) "nondescript."[2] Thus we are not dealing with a representative sample but rather the analysis of a minority that rose to positions of power or who came to attention on account of their brutality. Nonetheless, in many ways these men set the tone for the activities and identity of the group.

The archival trail is surprisingly rich. For Serafinowicz, unfortunately neither his personal documentation of service with the Germans nor his postwar KGB file—usually containing witness statements of local inhabitants questioned just after the war—has been uncovered. But this key documentation is available for many other collaborators. Nonetheless, Serafinowicz is mentioned in several contemporary German reports, and there is documentation of his service with the Thirtieth Waffen-SS Division, the Free Polish (or Anders Army), and also interviews conducted by the British immigration authorities. This latter documentation led to my tracing his presence in Britain in 1993, while investigating several of his subordinates in the Mir police.[3]

Other records on him include statements in postwar Soviet, Polish, and German investigations; survivor testimonies; and even the documents of Soviet partisan units. In addition, Scotland Yard detectives interviewed several hundred witnesses in Mir and around the world, many of whom recalled Serafinowicz in some detail. In particular, more than twenty former policemen spoke about their service under Serafinowicz in Mir and other units. Only small snippets from this mass of documentation can be reviewed in this essay.

Serafinowicz was born in 1910 of Belorussian parents and performed military service in the Polish Army during the 1930s.[4] Just before the war, he was a measurer at a local mill, where he worked together with Jews fairly amicably on an everyday basis.[5] He came from a poor family and had a son from a previous liaison. Relatives of his Polish wife were deported during the Soviet occupation, and he was himself arrested but released shortly afterward. Under the Germans he made a rapid career ascent, soon being appointed as head of the police in the smaller nearby town of Turzec before taking up his position as head of the *rayon* (or district) police in Mir in October 1941. He nominated his friend and colleague from the mill, Piotr Galecki, as his successor in charge of the Turzec police.

The local police in Mir under Serafinowicz's command participated in a number of murderous actions against the Jews and other local inhabitants. Just a few examples will be cited here that provide specific insights into Serafinowicz's character. For instance, at the end of October 1941, the Germans and local police selected more than fifty Jews in Turzec and escorted them to a grave site near the Jewish cemetery. A Jewish eyewitness, Yehuda Gesik, who dug the graves, saw

> 55 Jews approaching, accompanied by policemen. . . . Serafinowicz started the shooting when the first victim was his former friend Chanan Chaimowicz. In 1940 Chaimowicz was the manager of the mill and Serafinowicz was the main miller. They used to play cards together and arrange parties. The shooters stood about 10 meters away from the first group and all of them shot at the same time. The victims fell into the grave.[6]

A couple of weeks later during the mass slaughter of some fifteen hundred Jews in and around Mir, the daughter of the Polish schoolteacher, Regina Bedynska, left her house during the afternoon to get some water from the well opposite. As she approached the well, she saw four Jewish adults and a child walking toward the fields along a side street. At the same time, Serafinowicz and three policemen were standing in the main street armed with rifles. One of the policemen alerted his boss by touching his elbow. Serafinowicz turned around, aimed, and fired at the Jews who were trying to escape. The shot hit a Jewish woman, who fell down on top of her child. The child crawled out from under the woman, shouting, "Mother, get up, Mother, get up." However, the woman did not move.[7]

During the period that the surviving Jews were living inside the Mir castle ghetto in the summer of 1942, Serafinowicz set a trap to try to catch Jews who were looking to buy weapons.[8] He even ordered Oswald Rufeisen to render only a partial translation from the informant to the German gendarmerie commander Reinhold Hein, so he could claim the credit for uncovering the Jewish resistance group.[9] He was also allegedly involved in preparing the graves for the second Mir massacre that took place on August 13, 1942, following a mass escape of some two hundred Jews with the help of the Jewish spy in the police, Oswald Rufeisen.[10] Rufeisen, who acted as Serafinowicz's translator to the Germans, described Serafinowicz's key role as the immediate contact between Hein and the local population.[11]

As someone who lived in Serafinowicz's house for several months and worked with him closely every day, Rufeisen's statements provide a uniquely detailed insight into Serafinowicz's character. Rufeisen described Serafinowicz as being not especially anti-Semitic; rather, his obedience resulted from a belief the Germans would remain victorious and an expectation of corresponding promotion and rewards. Serafinowicz also had a hatred of the Bolsheviks arising from his personal experiences.[12]

Serafinowicz's calculating and pragmatic approach to collaboration with the Germans can also be seen in his conduct of partisan warfare. He sometimes used specific antipartisan actions for settling his own personal scores.[13] He protected local peasants he knew to be sympathetic to the Germans from the threat of indiscriminate German reprisals. At the same time, the local police under his command participated in a number of brutal reprisal actions against the non-Jewish local population, including the murder of the families of suspected partisans. A conservative estimate of the number of non-Jews killed by the police in the Mir *rayon* during the German occupation lies in the order of four hundred people, many of them women and children.[14]

Serafinowicz was also not averse to using directly brutal methods himself at times. Some survivors recall him whipping Jews in early 1942, apparently when drunk.[15] In another incident, together with other policemen, he engaged in beating and abusing a Jew named Azrel before Azrel was shot. Serafinowicz became especially angry when a large sum of money was found hidden in Azrel's boots. He reportedly shouted, "Where have you got all that money from, when even I, the Head of the Police don't have that much!"[16] Serafinowicz was promoted and decorated by the Germans, and they transferred him to Baranowicze in 1943 to command an antipartisan hunting platoon (*Jagdzug*) of some one hundred men. There is no doubt that he was ambitious and took pleasure in outward demonstrations of his importance. One survivor has described him as being very dressy, like an officer: "He wore a black uniform with stripes, indicating his rank. He had beautiful fine knee high leather boots with spurs and sometimes he wore a leather jacket that further distinguished him from the ordinary policemen. He also had a very beautiful belt with silver toned trim, a holster hung off the belt and in it was a pistol."[17] One of the German gendarmes who served in Baranowicze still recalled Serafinowicz clearly fifty years later, on account of his striking *Schimmel* (white horse).[18]

Aharon Harkavy, a Jew who worked with Serafinowicz before the war, says that at that time he "became especially friendly with him . . . because he was always smiling and pleasantly mannered. We had a Jew with us named Kaminiecki a man of high education as an economist, and he always warned us that although we liked Serafinowicz . . . he was a very dangerous character. He somehow had a gut feeling about Serafinowicz."[19]

It is in accordance with Serafinowicz's opportunistic nature that he subsequently deserted from the Germans in November 1944 and, unlike many of his former police colleagues, had a relatively successful postwar career in London as a builder. He did not have to face his accusers, including Oswald Rufeisen, in court in London until 1996. By then he was only a shadow of his former self. After lengthy preparations, including a full-scale pretrial hearing of the evidence, his actual trial was stayed for health reasons before it even started. He died just a few months later.

The other man charged with war crimes in Great Britain, Andrei Sawoniuk, is more immediately recognizable as one of Colonel Scotland's "brutal types." He was a Ukrainian, brought up in a very poor family in Domachevo, near Brest-Litovsk, where the town's three thousand Jews made up some 75 percent of the local population. He lived in a small wooden house with his mother, brother, and grandmother. They all slept in the same room. Before the war he used to earn some money doing odd jobs for the Jews, such as lighting their fires on Shabbat and tending their livestock. There was no male parent in his household, and his mother died of cancer prior to 1939.[20]

Sawoniuk joined the local police soon after the arrival of the Germans in the summer of 1941. Although he had only just turned twenty, he quickly rose to a position of power as one of the leading police deputies on account of the high turnover in the police leadership, his knowledge of some German, having spoken Yiddish with his Jewish neighbors before the war, and especially his willingness to carry out German orders.[21]

What were Sawoniuk's motives in serving in the local police? According to a conversation overheard by a Jewish survivor, Sawoniuk replied to a relative who warned him about service in the police that he was not too worried about a possible German defeat, stating that "in the meantime I'll try to do what I want—to have a good life, to kill, to drink and to take what I can."[22] Sawoniuk undoubtedly nurtured a strong resentment against the Jews arising from his former position of servility toward them. But many local people have vivid recollections of him, recounting his unrestrained brutality throughout the occupation toward Jews and non-Jews alike.

One of the most important documents for assessing Sawoniuk's behavior during the occupation is a KGB investigative file of some two hundred pages, mostly compiled shortly after the war. Numerous local witnesses recall seeing Sawoniuk beating Jews and other prisoners. Many comment that he was promoted within the police due to his loyalty to the Germans. There are also a number of allegations that he personally shot specific individuals or groups of victims, both Jews and non-Jews. Not atypical is the comment of one witness that word got around that "he was a most bloodthirsty person and that many people died at his hands." According to one of his former police comrades, Sawoniuk was the "most active policeman in all the repressive measures . . . [who] went to the executions of his own accord."[23]

These Soviet interrogations are not the most reliable source material, containing some inaccuracies, but scores of interviews conducted by Scotland Yard detectives produced many similar descriptions, including several persons who claimed to have seen Sawoniuk shoot people. Sawoniuk was tried and convicted by a British jury at the Old Bailey in 1999 on two counts of murder. One witness saw him shoot two Jewish men and a Jewish woman who had been captured shortly after the liquidation of the ghetto, and another man witnessed him shooting a larger group of Jewish women at about the same time. Others described him beating Jews and Soviet prisoners of war on the way to a notorious execution site. Shots were heard shortly afterward. Most conclude that he was eager to demonstrate his loyalty to the Germans through his brutality in order to earn promotion and other rewards. The Germans were clearly relieved to find such people to do their "dirty work" for them.[24]

As a young man with a chip on his shoulder, Sawoniuk combined anti-Semitism born from personal animosity with a similar greed and ambition to be found in Serafinowicz. The main difference was that Sawoniuk possessed no slyness or personal charm. He merely relished the power of life and death he held over others and the reign of naked terror he inspired. By comparison, even the names of the German commandants have faded from the memories of the local inhabitants, while the fear Sawoniuk inspired has not been forgotten.

In his book *Neighbors,* Jan T. Gross puts forward the hypothesis that many of those who participated in the murder and plunder of the Jews in the Polish town of Jedwabne may also have collaborated with the Soviets, both before and after the German occupation.[25] While this thesis is not without some foundation in terms of behavioral patterns, it appears to have been only a limited phenomenon with regard to the Ukrainian and Belorussian *Schutzmannschaften.* Both the Germans and the Soviets made considerable efforts to identify and punish those connected to the previous power structure, and only a few men appear to have held significant positions in the police under both regimes.

For example, one policeman in the Nieswiez *rayon* of Belarus, Piotr Sergeyev, who had previously served in the local NKVD (the Soviet predecessor to the KGB) and came originally from Russia, was recruited into the Nazi local police in the fall of 1941. Sergeyev was tried by the Soviets after the war, and his interrogations surprisingly include admissions of complicity in German crimes. For instance, he admitted participating in the shooting of the Jews in the town of Snov and taking Jewish property. In subsequent appeals he complained vigorously about his treatment, claiming that many of his admissions were false, having been made under duress, and that in fact he had tried to save Jews and also remained in contact with the partisans. At the same time, he did admit a certain degree of collaboration in German crimes, characterizing himself as an "accidental perpetrator" caught in the wrong place at the wrong time. In his appeal letters Sergeyev also stressed his lack of education and tough upbringing, arguing that he was only a small fry (literally, a "criminal insect") compared with the real criminals who had stayed in the West. There may be some truth in his version of events, as he was one of only a few former policemen who, having escaped to Germany in 1945, heeded Soviet appeals to return home and was then prosecuted despite assurances that no retribution would take place. A more revealing insight into his character may be found, however, in the reported comment of his wife, who complained to a neighbor after one of the actions that "again my blockhead has come [home] all [covered] in blood."[26]

In preparing this essay, I found unexpected corroboration for some of my findings in the work of colleagues conducting similar research. At a recent symposium on the Holocaust in Lithuania at the U.S. Holocaust Memorial Museum, Michael MacQueen of the U.S. Office of Special Investigations (OSI) gave an eerily similar presentation about the character and motivation of Lithuanian perpetrators, based on his own impressive array of case studies.[27] As MacQueen came independently to conclusions almost identical to my own, here I will respond briefly to his analysis.[28]

MacQueen identified six basic motivations or types for Lithuanian perpetrators, referring to the work of Alfonsas Eidintas:[29]

1. *Revenge,* by those who had suffered at the hands of the Soviets.

2. *Careerists,* who sought personal advancement under the new regime.

3. *Turncoats,* who attempted to expiate service to the Soviets by enthusiastic loyalty to their new masters.

4. *Greedy individuals,* seeking to gain booty.

5. *Anti-Semites,* who had baited the Jews before the war and participated in anti-Jewish violence under the Nazis.

6. So-called *accidental perpetrators,* who just happened to be recruited and went with the flow.

To this list should perhaps be added both the sadistic types and those who lusted for power, two groups which relished the opportunities that opened up with service in the local police. My main comment on this analysis would be to stress, as the detailed examples demonstrate, that usually a combination of several of these motivations played a role within each individual. This contention clearly undermines those interpretations that overstress one explanation to the exclusion of all others—because the various motivations were often inextricably linked.

Largely missing from this list is the more common defense heard from German trials of "obedience to authority"—clearly this defense was not a very good argument toward the Soviet authorities that condemned all collaboration with the enemy. Punishments could be stiff in the local police—but despite rampant disobedience in many respects, I have not seen examples of *Schutzmänner* refusing to shoot Jews. Rather, there are examples of policemen taking bribes from Jews smuggling food into the ghetto, or very occasionally allowing Jews to escape.[30] Authority was not confronted but sometimes undermined from within.

The question of anti-Semitism deserves some attention, as it is a complex one that can be easily misunderstood. Some local policemen were known as notorious anti-Semites who beat up local Jews. These men were particularly active in the killing actions. Anti-Semitism in prewar Poland consisted of economic, nationalist, religious, and political elements, with alleged Jewish sympathy for the Soviets and supposed complicity in Soviet crimes after 1939 giving it a powerful boost. Yet it lacked the dehumanizing racial basis that was at the core of the Nazi philosophy. For the local police, it was more a matter of personal animosity for political or economic reasons.

There was some attempt by the Nazis to provide political education to the local police forces serving them. Such education included a considerable amount of vitriolic racist anti-Jewish propaganda, stressing the "Judeo-Bolshevik menace to Europe." However, the detailed guidelines were only issued from Berlin in the late summer of 1942, reaching the local posts several weeks later.[31] By that time, most of the ghettos had already been liquidated. Since many policemen were barely literate and the propaganda message probably lost some of its impact in translation, generally more practical motives than ideological indoctrination must be sought for local police behavior.

By comparison to Lithuania, where the Holocaust unfolded rapidly in 1941, the later liquidation of the many remaining ghettos in Belarus and Ukraine in 1942 and 1943 saw the more systematic involvement of much of the local police, probably some twenty-five thousand men.[32] They were often tasked with murdering Jews found hiding in the emptied ghettos and forests in the wake of the main actions, as documented in the Sawoniuk case. By 1942 the Jews were forewarned by the previous wave of Einsatzgruppen killings in 1941 and took more effective countermeasures by hiding in bunkers or openly resisting, such that the active participation of the local police became essential to completing the task.

MacQueen also stressed the increased brutality and gruesome intimacy of the killings in Lithuanian villages, where the perpetrators often knew their victims personally. In the impoverished rural communities, the role of personal enrichment, corruption, and plunder was considerable. The multitude of ethnic conflicts played out by the local police in Nazi-dominated Ukraine and Belarus are in some ways more reminiscent of the recent struggles for property and ethnic cleansing in the former Yugoslavia.

In one respect I will disagree with MacQueen's contention that it is impossible to generalize about the perpetrators. While he is right that people from all backgrounds and walks of life ended up in the killing squads, nonetheless the statistical analysis of a large sample of perpetrators does permit some cautious conclusions. In particular, the foot soldiers of the *Schutzmannschaft* consisted almost entirely of local farmers and peasants (some 75 percent), most with only four years of school. The noncommissioned officers included a few craftsmen and low-level professionals, such as Serafinowicz, recruited mainly for communications and leadership skills.[33] The active core was driven particularly by self-made careerists, the dynamic force of any society, who were particularly susceptible to the new opportunities and the disorientation of society's moral compass created by Nazi rule. There was also a smattering of Poles among the main perpetrators (about 10 percent), as the Germans were sometimes forced to rely on the pre-

1939 administrative class, despite their great suspicion and repression of the Polish "intelligentsia."[34] Nearly all of the active perpetrators were recruited voluntarily up to the summer of 1942. Thereafter forms of compulsion were used to expand the *Schutzmannschaft* to more than two hundred thousand men, employed primarily in anti-partisan warfare.

Local Belorussians, Ukrainians, and even some Poles collaborated with the Germans for a number of reasons and did not always have identical interests with the occupiers. This account, based mainly on oral testimonies from local inhabitants, has naturally underplayed the German role in directing events but also reflects the view as seen from below. It is important to stress that the Holocaust would not have taken place without the Nazi occupation, but nevertheless, local police volunteers played a key role in its implementation. It is not possible to understand fully their motives, which remain locked inside their own, often self-distorted memories. But the examination of their lives and actions serves to remind us that real people, and not stereotypes, carried out these atrocities.

What lasting impressions are left by these glances into the abyss of human behavior? This was not a depersonalized Holocaust using machinery and distance to conceal its brutality. Here many of the perpetrators of the Holocaust personally knew the victims and had lived together with them previously as schoolmates, coworkers, and neighbors. Thus local economic and personal relations did play some role in the implementation of German plans, with collaborators enjoying a degree of free agency, especially in view of the shortage of German personnel and their limited knowledge of local conditions.

Returning to Colonel Scotland's mistaken assessment of Serafino-wicz, two lessons come to mind. First, it is important to judge men not by their words or fair-seeming appearance but by their deeds. Second, it took the opening of the former Soviet archives and much detailed research to reveal the true story of local collaborators that remained concealed from Colonel Scotland, who let his man go. The legacy of the many layers of war crimes investigations is a surprisingly rich historical record. The collaborators themselves are now of interest only to history and historians. But with the gradual opening of the KGB archives, a more detailed if still murky picture of these characters can be drawn.

NOTES

1. War Crimes Unit (WCU) of London Metropolitan Police, Home Office, IND File S66787, Semion Serafinowicz, Report of Lt. Col. Scotland to Major Thompson, April 20, 1947. See also A. P. Scotland, *The London Cage* (London: Evans Bros., 1957), regarding his interrogation of leading German Army officers during the war.

2. Christopher R. Browning, "The Factory and Slave Labor Camps in Starachowice, Poland: Survivors' Testimonies" in Center for Advanced Holocaust Studies (ed.), *Forced and Slave Labor in Nazi-Dominated Europe: Symposium Presentations* (Washington, DC: Center for Advanced Holocaust Studies, United States Holocaust Memorial Museum, 2004), 63–76.

3. On the background to the British war crimes legislation that came into force in 1991, see David Cesarani, *Justice Delayed* (London: William Heinemann, 1992); and David Cesarani, *War Crimes: Report of the War Crimes Inquiry* (London: Her Majesty's Stationery Office, 1989).

4. WCU, Michael Breslin, April 26, 1993.

5. Dorking Committal Proceedings, testimony of Josef Harkavy, March 25, 1996 (hereafter cited as Dorking, with name of subject and date of testimony). Harkavy even mentioned that most of the Jews who worked with Serafinowicz liked him very much at the time.

6. Yehuda Gesik, *The Turec Jewish Community, 1900–1944* (Tel Aviv: privately printed, 1958).

7. Dorking, Regina Bedynska, February 28, 1996.

8. Dorking, Oswald Rufeisen, February 23, 1996.

9. Nechama Tec, *In the Lion's Den: The Life of Oswald Rufeisen* (Oxford: Oxford University Press, 1993), 128–29.

10. Bundesarchiv-Ludwigsburg, B 162, 2 AR-Z 16/67 vol. 6, pp. 1146–55 E.F., 13 March 1969.

11. WCU, Oswald Rufeisen, May 6, 1993.

12. Dorking, Oswald Rufeisen, February 21–28, 1996. On the unique value of Rufeisen as a witness, see Christopher R. Browning, *Nazi Policy, Jewish Workers, German Killers* (Cambridge: Cambridge University Press, 2000), 155. Browning also served as an expert historical witness for the Crown Prosecution Service in both the Serafinowicz and Sawoniuk prosecutions.

13. WCU D1768; see also WCU, D3589; and Dorking, Valentina A. Keda, March 18, 1996. See also WCU, Olga N. Stankevich, August 12, 1992: "Serafinowicz noticed two men in our group against whom he had some personal grudge."

14. Martin Dean, *Collaboration in the Holocaust: Crimes of the Local Police in Belorussia and Ukraine, 1941–44* (London: Macmillan; New York:

St. Martin's Press, published in association with the United States Holocaust Memorial Museum, 2000), 131.

15. WCU, Elsbieta Marcwinska, May 1994; David Wengier, May 1994; Cila Zakheim, April 1993.

16. WCU, statement of Georgy Ivanovich Kot, September 1993. See also the statement of Nikolay Nikolayevich Chenyavsky, December 11, 1968, from the Polish trial of Michal Bachruszyn, Institute for National Remembrance, Warsaw (Instytut Pamieci Narodowej), SW Ksz 72–74, describing the same incident.

17. WCU, Lev Abramovsky, April 28, 1993.

18. WCU, Ernst Strauch, July 1994.

19. WCU, Aharon Harkavy, December 5, 1991.

20. A fairly accurate characterization of Sawoniuk can be found in post-trial press reports; see Sue Clough, "Poor Boy Who Became a Nazi Killer," *Daily Telegraph,* April 2, 1999.

21. Ibid.

22. Committal proceedings against Andrei Sawoniuk at the Old Bailey, testimony of Ben-Zion Blustein, 1998.

23. KGB Brest, Search File for Andrei A. Savanyuk (English translation, WCU IND File D9965). Sawoniuk was initially not traced in the UK due to the discrepancies between the Russian and Polish spellings of his name. I tracked down the correct spelling in the former Stasi Archives in Berlin after the fall of the Berlin wall.

24. Committal proceedings against Sawoniuk; Clough, "Poor Boy Who Became a Nazi Killer." I was unable to attend the trial in 1999, as I had already taken up my current appointment with the United States Holocaust Memorial Museum once historical research on the case had been completed.

25. Jan T. Gross, *Nachbarn: Der Mord an den Juden von Jedwabne* (Munich: C. H. Beck), 109–18. [*Neighbors: The Destruction of the Jewish Community in Jedwabne, Poland* (Princeton, NJ: Princeton University Press, 2001), 152–67]. Alfonsas Eidintas in his recent work on Lithuania refers to this phenomenon as "expiation"—as those who were implicated in the crimes of the previous regime sought to cover their traces by enthusiastic collaboration with the new masters.

26. KGB Minsk, Court Record in the Case of Piotr Sergeyev[-Korolev], October 28–29, 1949, and subsequent appeal letters.

27. On the initial background to the OSI, see, for example, Allan A. Ryan, *Quiet Neighbors: Prosecuting Nazi War Criminals in America* (San Diego: Harcourt Brace Jovanovich, 1984).

28. Michael MacQueen, "Lithuanian Collaboration in the 'Final Solution'" (paper presented at U.S. Holocaust Memorial Museum Center for

Advanced Holocaust Studies Panel Discussion on Lithuania and the Holocaust, Washington, DC, October 28, 2002). For my own previous analysis of perpetrator motivation among collaborators, see Dean, *Collaboration,* 75–77, 161–67.

29. Alfonsas Eidintas, *Zydai, lietuviai ir holokaustas* (Vilnius: Vaga, 2002).

30. On bribing local policemen, see, for example, Michael Diment, *The Lone Survivor: A Diary of the Lukacze Ghetto and Svyniukhy, Ukraine* (New York: Holocaust Library, 1991), 124–40.

31. See State Archive for the Zhitomir Oblast, 1182–1–17, 128–31 Order of *Befehlshaber der Ordnungspolizei* von Bomhard on the training of the *Schutzmannschaft,* August 1942.

32. Dean, *Collaboration,* 162.

33. Ibid., 74–75.

34. On the participation of Poles in the *Schutzmannschaft,* see Martin Dean, "Die Armija Krajowa und die Beteiligung von Polen bei der einheimischen Hilfspolizei in den von den Deutschen besetzten ostpolnischen Gebieten," in *Die polnische Heimatarmee: Geschichte und Mythos der Armia Krajowa seit dem Zweiten Weltkrieg,* ed. Bernhard Chiari (Munich: Oldenbourg, 2003).

Rebecca Golbert

"Neighbors" and the Ukrainian Jewish Experience of the Holocaust

JAN T. GROSS'S BOOK *NEIGHBORS: THE DESTRUCTION OF THE JEWISH Community in Jedwabne, Poland* (2001) documents, through postwar Jewish testimonies, the massacre of Jews in the town of Jedwabne by their neighbors in the summer of 1941. It has generated intense public debate in Poland in the aftermath of its publication among the descendants, in broad terms, of the very neighbors who carried out or witnessed such spontaneous (and German-incited) massacres against Jews at the beginning of the war. The Jedwabne debate concerns contested sites of the memory of interethnic conflict rather than sites of contemporary conflict in and of themselves. It is in this sense that Poland remains a landscape riddled with violent conflict and its ghosts even in the absence of Jews and other minorities around whom such conflicts were centered.

The primary goal of this essay is to contribute a comparative, ethnographic perspective to the discussion of neighbors, or collaborators, during the Holocaust and the changing ability of postwar and post-Communist societies in Eastern Europe to come to terms with issues of wartime complicity in the massacre of their Jewish populations. As such, my insights are drawn from an examination of Holocaust discourse and practice in postwar and post-Communist Ukraine. As an anthropologist, I use methods that differ from those of the historian. In contrast to David Engel, who complains that the discussions of *Neighbors* have transferred from the historical events themselves to the contemporary debates about those events,[1] my own work explores contemporary meanings and constructions of the past—through personal and collective memories and testimonies, memorial sites and spaces, and commemorative ceremonies. Stories of social and ethnic relations and conflict both during and after the Holocaust are woven into Jewish discourses and practices and emerge as the focus of survivor testimonies, community dynamics and tensions, memorial projects, and local financial transactions between Jews and Ukrainians to preserve Holocaust sites and Jewish cemeteries.

Holocaust historians may take issue with an anthropological approach to the Holocaust for several reasons. Most important, its reliance on contemporary Jewish and non-Jewish sources raises significant questions about faulty testimony and historical inaccuracies (these complaints have been raised by Robert Jan Van Pelt and Piotr Wróbel in various public forums). How can Jewish survivors and Ukrainian witnesses be expected to remember events sixty years after their occurrence? Indeed, conflicting narrative sequences, distortions of time and place, confusions of dates and people do arise in contemporary survivor and witness testimonies. The use of such testimonies in establishing a historical chronology of events in German- and Romanian-occupied Ukraine may prove highly problematic. Moreover, contemporary visits to Holocaust sites may shed little light on the historical events that took place there.[2] Contemporary uses and abuses of Holocaust memorial spaces determine the meanings that derive from those sites both for individuals and for collectives. Those meanings, changing over time, may be shaped by the state, by distinct social groups, or by sculptors, architects, or leaders in a range of forms—in the construction of monuments, in the enactment of commemorative ceremonies, or in deliberate attempts to rid sites of their history by transforming them, building over them, erasing and reconstituting the places of memory. Do we really expect to reconstruct the history of the Holocaust through the study of Holocaust memorials, Holocaust commemorations, and the like?

As we learn from scholars ensconced in the study of cultural history and memory,[3] the Holocaust and other historical moments of trauma must also be examined in terms of postmemory, that is, through the lens of later experiences occurring under differing social and political circumstances, a lens that reshapes earlier experiences in light of a constantly changing present. With the distance of time, certain details of events do recede, and yet, others become more prominent and more central to debates about the past and its continued meaning. As Antze and Lambek write, "The meaning of any past event may change as the larger, continuing story lengthens and grows in complexity. As readers we are continuously reexploring the significance of earlier episodes of the story in light of what transpires later."[4] As such, contemporary Holocaust testimonies shed light on postwar policies and responses to the Holocaust, not only on the wartime events themselves. So too in the current period of post-Communist and post-Soviet transition, the testimonies of survivors and witnesses reflect a renewed urgency to engage with the past, in part in an effort to gain cultural recognition and ethnic visibility in the present. What aspects of the past are given priority in present-day testimonies and why?

And yet, it is not only for their contribution to post-Holocaust memory that present-day testimonies should be engaged. A historian's reliance on the documentation of the oppressors raises its own significant questions of reliability and distortion. While such archival documentation may shed light on the decision-making processes involved in the administration of camps and ghettos, even on the names of perpetrators and collaborators involved in the actions and activities of the occupation, only Jewish and other victim sources can evoke the experience of occupation, deportation, internment, death, and survival. In the absence of wartime diaries and memoirs written shortly after the war, contemporary testimonies of survivors and witnesses offer significant insights into the wartime (and also postwar) landscape of social and ethnic relations and violence, dynamics of power and dependency, survival strategies, everyday experiences and interactions, and perceptions of one another—as Jew, Ukrainian, German, Romanian, man, woman, child. Collaboration and betrayal are significant themes within these post-Soviet narratives of the Holocaust, reflecting a preoccupation with concerns that were largely silenced in the Soviet aftermath of the war.

REGIONAL DYNAMIC OF THE HOLOCAUST IN UKRAINE

The regional focus of my study of the Holocaust in Ukraine also shapes my perspective on collaboration and Ukrainian-Jewish wartime relations. My research examines memories of the Holocaust in Transnistria, the Romanian zone of occupation of Ukraine. It looks, in particular, at Holocaust sites in Vinnytsya Province, a territory divided by the German and Romanian occupations along the natural boundary of the southern Bug River (this river border was the site of much movement back and forth, both forced and clandestine, of prisoners and occupiers, not to mention partisans and ordinary bystanders). Both Ukrainian Jews and Romanian Jews—the latter deported from Bukovina, Bessarabia, and sometimes from Romania proper—were interned in the camps and ghettos of Transnistria, including the Romanian camp Pechora. While Vinnytsya Province was firmly incorporated into post-revolutionary Soviet Ukraine, Bukovina and Bessarabia were annexed by the Soviet Union from Romania in 1940.[5] During the course of my fieldwork in Ukraine, I interviewed survivors of Transnistria who continue to reside in the Vinnytsya region and in Bukovina.

Knowledge of the regional and geopolitical dynamic before, during, and after the German/Romanian occupation of Ukraine is important for several reasons. Most significantly, Ukrainian (and Moldovan and Polish) collaboration was most virulent in the western borderland territories annexed by the Soviet Union during 1939 and 1940 and reoccupied by the German and Romanian forces in the summer of 1941. The shifting politics of the borderland sparked ethnic conflict, suspicion, and betrayal. The "political" element of resentment and revenge fomented among the local non-Jewish populations in retaliation for "Soviet collaboration" (the welcoming of the Soviet forces in 1939 and 1940) among the local Jews—whether or not this legitimating argument of political anti-Jewish violence (asserted in the postwar period by Poles, Moldovans, and Ukrainians) holds any merit—was not such a significant force in the heartland of Soviet Ukraine in 1941.[6] By 1941 in central Ukraine, Jews and Ukrainians shared similar socioeconomic conditions and political outlooks, studying in the same schools, working in the same government-owned factories, striving toward a shared Soviet future. In contrast, the politics of the eastern Polish borderlands (the western borderlands of the Soviet Union) defined the climate of 1941 Polish-Jewish relations in Jedwabne.

In addition to prewar geopolitics, the wartime conditions of brutality, fear, and avarice created by the occupying forces made an impact on the vigor of Ukrainian collaboration and also on the degree of clandestine aid afforded to Jews by the local population. According to survivor and witness testimonies, local collaboration appeared to be more varied in the Romanian zone of occupation than in the German zone. So too Jews and Ukrainians suggest having feared their Romanian occupiers less than they feared the German forces across the Bug River. In this climate, the local repercussions for sheltering, feeding, or exchanging goods with Jews may have been slightly more tolerable. In general, the regional specificities of Transnistria embodied in survivor and witness testimonies allow a subtle reexamination of the reified categories of victim, perpetrator, and bystander. Although contemporary sources do not in any way question the brutal dynamics of power distinguishing and reinforcing these wartime categories, they nonetheless suggest that in Romanian-occupied Ukraine, people (Jews and Ukrainians) did indeed, at times, move across the conceptual and physical borders contained by the categories of victim, prisoner, rescuer, black marketer, shelter giver, betrayer, and perpetrator.

POSTWAR DYNAMIC IN UKRAINE

In addition to the regional dynamic of the wartime period, postwar conditions in Ukraine differed (and continue to differ) significantly from those in Poland. Most notably, the concept of "neighbors" has had continuing social and not only historical relevance, as Ukrainians and Jews have continued to live side by side in many Ukrainian towns and cities. While debates about collaboration and indifference during the Holocaust have been far less polarized than in Poland, that is also because little to no public forum for such debate existed during the Soviet period. In the immediate postwar period, the reintegration of survivors alongside bystanders and perpetrators into a society economically and morally bankrupt by the war and silent about the crimes of the Holocaust left many intimate questions of the Holocaust unresolved and, at times, festering. Countermemories and narratives, preserved in the privacy of the home and among family and friends, struggled to survive against public amnesia but rarely broached the thorny issues of wartime social and ethnic relations and betrayals. Silence about the Holocaust in general and about collaboration in particular appears to have been in large part a Soviet strategy to repress ethnic difference in wartime memory[7] but also, in response, a Jewish strategy of accommodation to postwar realities.

The Soviet Extraordinary State Commission, established during the war (1942–45) and charged with recording depositions from survivors and witnesses about wartime atrocities and their perpetrators in those territories liberated by Soviet forces, did lead to war crimes trials in the immediate postwar period. However, these trials were largely political in nature, more concerned with asserting the ideological triumph over Nazism that came with convicting collaborators than in revealing details about the crimes these collaborators had committed.[8] Sometimes survivors testified at these trials. Still, the majority of perpetrators were not convicted in the Soviet courts. Many fled with the retreating Romanian and German armies, were shot in retribution during the liberation of ghettos and camps, or were conscripted by the Red Army into penalized battalions to perish at the front. Still others were simply left to reintegrate into their communities or to resettle in other towns and villages where local inhabitants did not know their past. In response to the 1960 Eichmann trial in Israel and corresponding war crimes trials in Germany, the Soviet Union also held some later trials in the 1960s and 1970s.[9]

Of even greater concern to survivor communities in Ukraine was the postwar reintegration of those Jews who "did not behave well" in the camps and ghettos. Although a handful of Jews who had occupied positions of power in the Jewish administration of camps and ghettos were tried in the postwar period, the large majority were not. Without the option of the Jewish "honor" courts that Gabriel Finder describes for Poland,[10] Jews preferred not to accuse their fellow Jews in Soviet regional courts. Outside the legal system, social mechanisms in the Jewish communities worked to ostracize Jewish *polizei* and sometimes their children. Nonetheless, living among these "Jewish perpetrators" often brought out deep, lasting resentments that continue to this day, rekindled in the context of German pensions to Holocaust survivors administered by the Claims Conference, that do not distinguish among "good" and "bad" survivors. Indeed, the local politics of Holocaust memory in Ukraine often focus in on this level of intra-Jewish relations during and after the war (as will be discussed subsequently).

SOVIET PUBLIC DEBATES

The hushed postwar climate limited transmission of Holocaust memories to a tight network of family and friends. When political conditions permitted, survivors and their children would make pilgrimages to mass graves to hold private commemorative ceremonies for their loved ones. More rarely, individuals would build memorials at those sites without official permission. These were largely clandestine acts outside the public eye of the state. It was not until the 1960s that a more public debate emerged in the Soviet media, centered around the need to recognize and memorialize Jewish suffering at Babi Yar.[11] This debate among intellectuals—punctuated by the 1961 publication of Yevgeny Yevtushenko's poem "Babi Yar," Dmitry Shostakovich's Thirteenth Symphony setting the poem to music, Anatoly Kuznetsov's 1966 novel *Babi Yar,* and Ivan Dzyuba's remarks at a spontaneous commemoration in 1966 at the Babi Yar site—sought to wrest Jewish memory from the hands of the Soviet authorities, to reclaim it from oblivion.[12] While the Soviet debate on the Holocaust held certain parallels with those in the Polish press meticulously documented by Michael Steinlauf,[13] it was comparatively short-lived. When a memorial was finally built at Babi Yar in 1976, it failed to mention the plight of the Jews and was dedicated instead to "citizens of Kiev and prisoners of war."

The story of Babi Yar was repeated for many other Holocaust sites. The thrust of counter-Jewish memories during the Soviet period was the simple recognition of Holocaust sites as places of Jewish historical memory. Far from tackling the sensitive theme of Ukrainian collaboration, Soviet intellectuals and Jewish activists sought acknowledgment of the martyrdom of Soviet Jewry at Babi Yar and at other locations. Instead, at those locations where memorials were built with the support of the state, they were dedicated to "peaceful Soviet citizens" or "victims of fascism"; other sites remained unmarked or were built over in an effort to erase any trace of memory. Here the Soviet story parallels the Polish story of Communist internationalism—the conflation of Ukrainian, Russian, Jewish (and Polish) memory as the suffering of one Soviet (or Polish) people.[14]

Ukrainian scholarly attempts to address the Holocaust also occurred outside the Soviet Union, beginning in the 1980s. Émigré scholars succeeded in shifting the debate away from its Soviet ideological framework by recognizing the significance of the Holocaust; however, they simultaneously trivialized the Holocaust by asserting the relative suffering of Ukrainians during the war and arguing that collaboration was strictly an individual phenomenon, not a widespread practice.[15] Similar arguments have clearly been made in the Polish case.[16] The language of comparable suffering (filtered back into Ukraine through the Ukrainian diaspora) now dominates scholarship in postindependence Ukraine. Following in the tradition of the Soviet Jewish periodical *Sovietish haimland,*[17] more recent Ukrainian Jewish scholarship has also taken a more apologetic and conciliatory tack, emphasizing the efforts of Righteous Gentiles, the empathy of ordinary Ukrainians, and the respective tragedies of Jews and Ukrainians.[18] A gap thus remains between Western historiography, documenting widespread collaboration in the Holocaust in Ukraine,[19] and Ukrainian scholarship on the Holocaust, with its emphasis on individual culpability and comparative suffering. Martin Dean's book documenting the extensiveness of collaboration among the local police (*Schutzmannschaft*) in Belarus and Ukraine, like the texts of Shmuel Spector and John and Carol Garrard, firmly debunks the dominant arguments of Ukrainian scholars. However, these works do not have an audience in Ukraine; evidence of widespread collaboration has not yet been confronted either at a scholarly or a societal level. Moreover, one drawback of these works is that they do not examine the unevenness of Ukrainian collaboration (mentioned earlier) and along with it the diverse relationships and circumstances of neighbors from one region to another.

POST-SOVIET TRANSITION

In post-Soviet Ukraine, official and societal awareness of the Holocaust has increased significantly. In place of the clandestine commemorations held at Babi Yar and other Holocaust sites throughout the Soviet period, annual commemorations attended by government officials, Ukrainian intellectuals, Jewish leaders, and foreign dignitaries give solemn recognition to the suffering of Jews at Babi Yar and in the Holocaust more generally. Particularly large-scale commemorations were held on the occasions of the fiftieth and sixtieth anniversaries of the Babi Yar massacre (September 29, 1991, and September 29, 2001). Media coverage of these events has partially shaped popular knowledge of the Holocaust in Ukraine. Yet, despite the widening recognition of the Holocaust symbolized in such public commemorations of Babi Yar, the issue of Ukrainian collaboration has not been broached at this public level. The desire to overlook this complex and sensitive issue was most apparent in the media coverage of the sixtieth anniversary, which occurred a few weeks after the September 11 terrorist attacks in the United States. In a blatant example of historical and cultural relativism, the mainstream television broadcasting station 1 + 1 hosted a special program in which it invited members of the Jewish and Ukrainian intelligentsia, religious and lay leaders, foreign diplomats, even Ukrainian nationalists, to consider the legacy of Babi Yar by drawing comparisons to modern-day terrorism. The media squandered an ideal moment to reexamine, with some element of historical complexity, the significance of the Holocaust for postindependence Ukraine and for Ukrainian-Jewish (and other majority-minority) relations. This co-optation and simplification of the Holocaust by the Ukrainian media can be seen as an extension of the language of comparable suffering dominating scholarship in postindependence Ukraine, a reflection of the broader post-Soviet preoccupation with establishing unproblematized historical narratives to define the collective experience.[20]

In the post-Soviet transitional space of Ukraine, Jews and Ukrainians have embarked on parallel and intersecting quests of historical inquiry in an effort to remember and memorialize—and in so doing to ascribe meaning to the past and to the present. Among Jews, such collective memorial discourses and practices (including monument building) remain largely accommodational, attempting to inscribe the Jewish Diaspora experience on the local Ukrainian landscape while at the same time remaining sensitive to Ukrainian concerns and the limitations of inclusiveness. In contrast to Holocaust discourse in Poland, such strategies of Holocaust remembrance and commemoration seek not to polarize Ukrainian society at large but to engage Ukrainians in a nonconfrontational dialogue about the Jewish experience and Ukrainian-Jewish relations. The need to accommodate the sensitivities of neighbors thus infiltrates daily Jewish practices and shapes local interpretations of the past.

POST-SOVIET MEMORY DISCOURSES

Within this general post-Soviet climate of renewed historical inquiry and yet accommodation, Holocaust survivors give priority to narratives of Ukrainian-Jewish and intra-Jewish relations in their accounts of the Romanian occupation. The question of social distance (during and after the war) as a distinctive force in the shaping of postmemory emerges in this narrative context. The disproportionate weight given to intra-Jewish conflict and deception may reflect the close proximity of Jews in the camps and ghettos and in postwar communities, providing numerous occasions for tensions and resentments to build. In contrast to Jews and sometimes Ukrainians, Romanians and Germans emerge in these survivor testimonies as faceless forces of oppression, bearing no shape or distinct identity, the result of a clever social distancing that instituted Jews and Ukrainians as intermediary enforcers of the German and Romanian occupation system.

Testimonies among Pechora survivors offer a mixed picture of Ukrainian-Jewish relations during the war.[21] While survivors blame local Ukrainians who rose to power under Romanian occupation for ensuring their deportation from their hometowns (Tulchin, Bratslav, Trostianets, Shpikov) to the village and camp of Pechora, and while they remember with bitterness those Ukrainian camp guards renowned for their brutality, they also credit Ukrainian villagers (in Pechora and the surrounding villages) with their survival. This dominant narrative asserts that prisoners could not have survived this camp of starvation if villagers had not provided lifesaving support in the form of food, temporary shelter and hiding, and, most commonly, barter exchanges at the walled perimeter of the camp.[22] Ukrainian villagers would come to the gates of the camp, sometimes throwing potatoes or beets over the wall, more often trading flour or potatoes for some clothing or other remaining belongings among the prisoners. So too children would flee the camp at night in search of food to bring back to their families who stayed behind. The possibility of betrayal always loomed large, and indeed certain villages were distinguished among survivors by the rumored generosity or cruelty of their inhabitants. Nonetheless, children frequently fled to the outskirts of Pechora and to other villages, begging among Ukrainian peasants for scraps of potato peel, bread, and flour to bring back to the camp. These children would sometimes spend the night on the *pechka,* the old Russian stoves, with alcoves on top large enough for a child-size body. Elderly Ukrainian peasants from Pechora and nearby villages confirm such memories with their own. Similarly, Jews fleeing Pechora for the Mogilev or Bershad' ghetto recall finding a night's shelter in a Ukrainian home on the outskirts of a town or village en route. Despite the fear on both sides, these clandestine interactions appear to have been widespread in the Romanian zone of occupation of Ukraine.

Bessarabian and Bukovinan Jews, deported to Transnistria and ultimately to Pechora, recall very different stories of survival in the border territories. They contrast the Ukrainian peasants they met along their deportation route after crossing the Dniestr River (the border between Bessarabia and Ukraine) to the Moldovans they encountered before crossing into Ukraine.

In Bessarabia and Bukovina, as in Galicia and Volhynia, whole communities of Jews were wiped out by local collaborators in the first days of the war; these enthusiastic collaborators often did not even wait for their German or Romanian counterparts to arrive. According to several accounts, Moldovans along the deportation route paid Romanian soldiers to shoot Jews for their belongings.[23] In contrast, Ukrainians reached out to them with food as they passed.[24] Still, as compared to the Ukrainian Jews, the Romanian Jews may have benefited less from the aid of the local Ukrainian population in Transnistria due to greater linguistic, cultural, and social barriers and unfamiliarity with the local landscape and lifestyle.[25]

These same barriers created tensions and conflicts between Ukrainian and Romanian Jews interned together in the camps and ghettos of Transnistria.[26] Testimonies of survivors from the Mogilev-Podolsk ghetto and Pechora camp reveal layers of social and cultural misunderstanding and suspicion that culminate in accusations of greed, betrayal, and, ultimately, collaboration. In the Mogilev ghetto, Ukrainian Jews, though the local proprietors at the start of the war, were poor and Sovietized, their community infrastructure already dismantled. The deportees from Bessarabia and Bukovina, though already disoriented by successive displacements, brought with them distinct entrepreneurial skills, community organizational skills, the language(s) of the oppressor (Romanian, German), and, in some cases, valuables exceeding those possessed by local Jews;[27] these assets cast for the deportees a wider net of survival resources in the ghetto (including access to work in the Turnatoria, a metal factory revived by Romanian Jews, providing some economic security and protection from further deportation).[28] When the decree came from the Transnistria government in the summer and fall of 1942 to deport three thousand Jews to the death camp Pechora, the Jewish ghetto administration, consisting predominantly of Romanian Jews, ensured that poorer Mogilev Jews were deported first and in greater number; Romanian Jews were sent later.[29] Moreover, when Mogilev Jews fled Pechora and returned to their homes in the Mogilev ghetto, they discovered that Romanian Jews had become the new proprietors, often forbidding them from crossing the threshold, even betraying them to the authorities so that they would be deported to Pechora again. Many Mogilev Jews believe that no Romanian Jews were deported to Pechora, all having successfully bribed the local Romanian authorities to send Mogilev Jews in their place. This narrative of deep mistrust and betrayal continues to dominate the testimonies of Mogilev survivors today. Bukovinan and Bessarabian Jews, on the other hand, look back at the tensions with Ukrainian Jews from an altogether different perspective. Despite their own testimonies of victimhood, they express greater pity for the "provincial" Ukrainian Jews, who lacked the social, cultural, and economic resources of their more "cosmopolitan," non-Sovietized coreligionists.[30]

Ukrainian Jews narrate their own internal conflicts as well. As mentioned earlier, deep resentments festered in the postwar period over the social reintegration of Jewish "perpetrators"—including former camp and ghetto administrators, gravediggers, and *polizei*. However, postwar tensions have also raged in these small Jewish communities over other forms of wartime betrayal as well, particularly with regard to camp versus ghetto.[31] While the Ukrainian wartime landscape captured in the testimonies of Transnistria survivors appears more fluid, more forgiving of clandestine movements of people and goods, than that of the German occupation, distinct differences in degrees of brutality and the inevitability of death did exist between camp and ghetto conditions, between the Pechora camp and the Romanian ghettos.[32] Local Jews describe desperate attempts to flee the Pechora camp, only to encounter a poor reception among Jews in the ghettos of Bershad', Shargarod, Dzhurin, Tomashpol', and Tulchin (whence many Pechora survivors had been deported).[33] Ghetto Jews either feared official repercussions for the acceptance of unregistered Jews into the ghetto or sought to preserve their scarce resources of food and space among themselves. Many camp survivors were turned away from the ghettos with no option but to return to Pechora.[34] Those returning to Mogilev, as noted before, were at times betrayed to the Ukrainian and Romanian authorities and forcefully redeported. Romanian Jews fleeing Pechora may, at times, have tapped stronger networks of relatives and friends in the ghettos and received a more cordial reception; dispersed across Transnistria, Romanian Jews were also involved in the Jewish administration of most ghettos. Ukrainian Jews express a powerful sense of betrayal from their fellow Jews in "relatively" better wartime conditions; their testimonies contrast the stingy behavior of Jews in the ghettos to the generous behavior of Ukrainian peasants who fed and sheltered camp Jews during their flight. The play of social distance in the meaning and experience of betrayal is significant in such survivor discourses.

These intra-Jewish conflicts, tensions, and resentments among local Jews and between Romanian and Ukrainian Jews are highly complex and multifaceted, influenced by diverse prewar economic and political orientations; social and cultural misunderstandings; differing cultures of leadership, social organization, and mutual aid; and, of course, the ugly side of human nature in general under conditions of brutality and oppression and unequal structures of power. In Jewish communities such as Tulchin, camp and ghetto Jews silently faced off in the postwar period; today, Pechora survivors complain bitterly about the equal compensation (through Claims Conference pension funds) of their differing wartime suffering allotted by the German government.

POST-SOVIET MEMORIAL PROJECTS

In conclusion, I want to turn to the memorial projects of contemporary survivor communities, which seek to solidify in stone the meanings and interpretations of the past described in this essay. Jewish communities remaining in the small towns of central Ukraine burdened by the imprint of the Holocaust are preoccupied with memorializing their Holocaust experiences. These communities are small and disproportionately elderly; as Holocaust survivors, many of their members receive German pension funds to supplement their measly Ukrainian pensions. While some of these funds go to the cost of medicine and health care, food, apartment renovations, and support of children and grandchildren struggling in the post-Soviet economy (those children who have not emigrated to Israel, Germany, or the United States), survivors also donate funds to the creation of memorials—the archiving of their collective experience in photographs, documents, maps, stone monuments, and cemetery restorations. For the building of memorials at mass graves and camp and ghetto entrances, these communities also rely on the support of their compatriots who have emigrated and continue to send "communal remittances" home. They in turn send photographs and videocassettes of the monument unveiling ceremonies, keeping the extended diaspora community informed of important commemorative events and projects (to which transnational funds have been applied) in the hometown.

The impulse to memorialize certainly did not begin with the collapse of communism. As noted earlier, state-sponsored and clandestine memorials were built across Ukraine during the Soviet period; however, the memory embodied in these stone structures was often deliberately distorted to convey confusion about the location, numbers, and faces of victims. A reexamination of the Holocaust in Ukraine was sparked by the greater openness of the glasnost period and the renewed historical interest in society at large but also by the emerging possibility of German compensation afforded to Jews in Central and Eastern Europe (the Claims Conference–administered program, begun only in the 1990s, is called the Central and Eastern European Fund, or CEEF). Strict eligibility requirements for CEEF sent survivors (and community leaders) to regional archives in search of ghetto and camp registration lists. In the absence of documentation (or in the case of the arbitrary refusal of archives to produce such documents), many survivors sued in court for recognition of their wartime experience as *uzniki,* or prisoners of the camps and ghettos, basing their claims on the eyewitness testimonies of fellow survivors. This individual and communal process of documentation occurring among survivors in almost every Ukrainian town generated parallel processes of collective remembrance and memorialization (and the creation of survivor associations), albeit influenced by the rigors of conformity imposed from outside experts (i.e., the Claims Conference).[35]

The memorial projects of Jewish communities in the Vinnytsya Province seek mainly to rehabilitate and mark sites long forgotten or erased. Even so, the politics of memory play out in the process. In the early 1990s, Tulchin Jews unveiled a plaque on the wall next to the front entrance of the former Pechora camp, now a sanatorium (having reverted to its prewar function). The plaque is dedicated to the "thousands of Jews" who perished there (actually the initial plaque was inscribed to the "thousands of citizens" and was changed several years later). Several monuments adorn the Jewish cemetery and the woods on the outskirts of the village of Pechora, each dedicated by different individuals and communities. In this sense, Holocaust representation is often deeply particularized and fractured.[36] The Tulchin and Mogilev communities each have separate memorials to their victims of Pechora and even hold separate commemorative ceremonies at the site each year. Continuing the legacy of Soviet representations of the war, many communities also seek to recognize Righteous Gentiles (and their children), making them honorary community members for the purposes of receiving humanitarian aid packages from outside donors. The Jews of Mogilev-Podolsk established two memorials in the center of town on Stavisky Street (the border and main entrance to the ghetto), one to the victims of the Mogilev ghetto (unveiled in 1992), the other (unveiled more recently in April 2002) to Righteous Gentiles, many of whom are listed on the back of the monument.

Thus, the memorial work of survivor associations in the Vinnytsya Province is not preoccupied with bringing to light issues of local collaboration. On the contrary, survivors seek the participation of the local Ukrainian community in the memorialization and commemoration process, particularly in locations where no survivors remain to care for the memorial sites. In Pechora, for example, where no Jews live today, the ongoing maintenance of the mass grave sites in the cemetery and in the woods is the sole responsibility of the Ukrainian village council, with financial support from survivor communities nearby. Local Jews seek to fulfill the Jewish commandment to remember and memorialize the dead; however, they realize that when they and their children are no longer around (due to the old age and infirmity of survivors and the high emigration rates of their children), it will be up to Ukrainians to preserve and remember these local sites of Jewish suffering in small towns and villages throughout Ukraine.

CONCLUSIONS

In contrast to Poland, a substantial Jewish population remains in Ukraine. While its numbers are dwindling in the small towns bearing the legacy of the Holocaust—its children preferring internal migration to the larger Ukrainian cities or external migration to Israel, the United States, and Germany—the national Jewish community remains a force in Ukraine concerned with recognition of its unique past and its role in a postindependence Ukraine. Even small communities such as those at the center of my study of the Vinnytsya Province remain movers and shakers in their small towns, particularly when projects concern sites of Jewish memory and Holocaust memorialization. Still, precisely because of the Jewish stake in a Ukrainian future, Ukrainian Jews take a more diplomatic approach to the thorny issue of collaboration and Ukrainian-Jewish wartime relations. While they force Ukrainians to grapple with the Holocaust on a daily basis through public discourses and distinctive elements of visual culture, at all levels of Ukrainian society, from the capital to the village, Ukrainian Jews also continue to accommodate Ukrainian sensitivities to accusations of collaboration, considering that the collective conscience is not yet ready to come to terms with the darker side of Ukrainian wartime history.

What impact a book of the nature of *Neighbors* would have on contemporary Ukrainian society and Ukrainian-Jewish relations, particularly if written in Ukrainian or Russian by a well-respected "insider," can only be cause for speculation. Whatever the means of sparking public debate, when Ukrainian society does begin seriously to address the sensitive issue of collaboration, it will need to look honestly at the delicate social balance of innocence and guilt, heroism and complicity, generosity and cruelty. It will need to document the unevenness of collaboration from the border territories to the Ukrainian heartland and to examine the differing local conditions of and responses to occupation in the German and Romanian zones. So too Ukrainian society and its institutions will have to take a hard look at the repossession of Jewish property during and after the war, at postwar silences and the failure of the social and legal systems to redress human injustices (through criminal trials, restituted properties, and other appropriate actions) or to facilitate a collective process of healing through public memory and discourse. While some observers may attempt to blame the former Soviet system for these failures, Ukrainians and Jews will need to reexamine their wartime and postwar relationships as neighbors and come to terms with their contemporary significance. What I hope I have demonstrated here is that discussions of the Holocaust and wartime interethnic relations are not only about the past and "getting it right." They are also in a significant way about present-day social relations and identity politics, about the place of Jews (and their memory) in the postwar and post-Communist societies of Eastern Europe and their struggles for recognition and acceptance from the larger societies of which they are (or once were) a living, breathing part.

NOTES

1. Engel made this comment during the Lessons and Legacies roundtable on Polish-Jewish relations (November 1, 2002), from which my own essay emerges.

2. James E. Young, *The Texture of Memory: Holocaust Memorials and Meaning* (New Haven, CT: Yale University Press, 1993), 119.

3. For example, Pierre Nora, "Between Memory and History: Les Lieux de Memoire," *Representations* 26 (1989): 7–25; Natalie Zemon Davis and Randolph Starn, "Introduction," *Representations* 26 (1989): 1–6; Young, *Texture of Memory;* Paul Antze and Michael Lambek, "Introduction: Forecasting Memory," in *Tense Past: Cultural Essays in Trauma and Memory* (New York: Routledge, 1996), xi–xxxviii; Michael Steinlauf, *Bondage to the Dead: Poland and the Memory of the Holocaust* (Syracuse, NY: Syracuse University Press, 1997).

4. Antze and Lambek, "Introduction: Forecasting Memory," xix.

5. Before 1919, Bukovina had been the easternmost frontier of the Austro-Hungarian Empire; Bessarabia had been on the western frontier of the Russian Empire. In 1939 and 1940, the Soviet Union also annexed portions of eastern Poland and incorporated them into western Ukraine and Belarus.

6. In sharp contrast to the civil war period of 1917–20, during which the Judeo-Bolshevik myth served as a significant mobilizing force of anti-Jewish violence among Ukrainian forces and Ukrainian peasants. See Henry Abramson, *A Prayer for the Government: Ukrainians and Jews in Revolutionary Times (1917–1920)* (Cambridge, MA: Harvard Ukrainian Research Institute, 1999).

7. Zvi Gitelman, "Soviet Reactions to the Holocaust, 1945–1991," in *The Holocaust in the Soviet Union: Studies and Sources on the Destruction of the Jews in the Nazi-Occupied Territories of the USSR, 1941–1945,* ed. Lucjan Dobroszycki and Jeffrey S. Gurock (Armonk, NY: M. E. Sharpe, 1993), 3–28; William Korey, "A Monument Over Babi Yar?" in Dobroszcki and Gurock, *Holocaust in Soviet Union,* 61–76.

8. These trials thus revealed little about the local dynamics of occupation, including local participation in the wartime administration and in the destruction of Jewish communities. In fact, in the Extraordinary Commission Reports, overseen by NKVD officials, descriptions of the deportation, internment, and execution of local Jewish communities often omitted any mention of Jews, preferring instead the ambiguity of phrases such as "innocent [or peaceful] Soviet citizens." In these trials, perpetrators were handed out quick sentences ranging from ten to twenty-five years or more, rarely execution. The documentary film *Krasnodar: The Trial of Krasnodar, 1943,* directed by Irmgard and Bengt von zur Mühlen (Waltham, MA: National Center for Jewish Film, 1990), examines archival footage of one of the earliest Soviet war crimes trials, conducted before the completion of the war. Alexander Prusin, who examines the court proceedings of Soviet war crimes trials from 1945 and 1946, argues that despite their political propagandistic nature, these documents reveal valuable information about the Holocaust on

Soviet territory. See Alexander Prusin, "'Fascist Criminals to the Gallows!' The Holocaust and Soviet War Crimes Trials, December 1945–February 1946," *Holocaust and Genocide Studies* 17, no. 1 (Spring 2003): 1–30.

9. See Benjamin Pinkus, *The Soviet Government and the Jews 1948–1967: A Documented Study* (Cambridge, MA: Cambridge University Press and Israeli Academy of Sciences and Humanities, 1984).

10. Gabriel Finder, *Revenge and Reconciliation* (forthcoming book).

11. The site in Kiev at which more than fifty thousand Jews perished (more than thirty-three thousand in the initial massacres on September 29 and 30, 1941, and more in subsequent roundups) became symbolic of the Holocaust in Ukraine and in the Soviet Union more generally. By 1943, more than one hundred thousand people—including Jews, Gypsies, Ukrainian and Russian civilians, and Soviet prisoners of war of all nationalities—had been executed at Babi Yar. See Shmuel Spector, "Tragedia v Babyem Yaru," in *Babi Yar: k Pyatidesyatiletiyu Tragedii 29, 30 Septyabrya 1941 Goda,* ed. S. Spector and M. Kipnis (Jerusalem: Isdatel'stvo Biblioteka Aliya, 1991); Shmuel Spector, "The Holocaust of Ukrainian Jews," in *Bitter Legacy: Confronting the Holocaust in the USSR,* ed. Zvi Gitelman (Bloomington: Indiana University Press, 1997).

12. Korey, "Monument Over Babi Yar."

13. Steinlauf, *Bondage to the Dead.*

14. See Young, *Texture of Memory;* Steinlauf, *Bondage to the Dead,* 70.

15. See, for example, Bohdan Krawchenko, *Social Change and National Consciousness in Twentieth-Century Ukraine* (Edmonton: Canadian Institute of Ukrainian Studies, 1985); Ivan L. Rudnytsky, *Essays in Modern Ukrainian History* (Edmonton: Canadian Institute of Ukrainian Studies, 1987).

16. See Young, *Texture of Memory;* Steinlauf, *Bondage to the Dead;* Gross, *Neighbors.*

17. See Gitelman, "Soviet Reactions," 13–14.

18. M. I. Koval, "The Nazi Genocide of the Jews and the Ukrainian Population, 1941–1944," in Gitelman, *Bitter Legacy,* 51–60; see also publications of the Institute of Judaic Studies, Kiev.

19. Spector, "Holocaust of Ukrainian Jews"; Shmuel Spector, *The Holocaust of Volhynian Jews 1941–1944* (Jerusalem: Yad Vashem and Federation of Volhynian Jews, 1990); John and Carol Garrard, *The Bones of Berdichev: The Life and Fate of Vasily Grossman* (New York: Free Press, 1996); Martin Dean, *Collaboration in the Holocaust: Crimes of the Local Police in Belorussia and Ukraine, 1941–44* (London: Macmillan, 1999).

20. Ukrainian scholars such as Yaroslav Hrytsak, who have attempted to examine this sensitive period more honestly, suggest that they have faced significant domestic opposition, particularly in western Ukraine (Hrytsak

made this comment during his course The Making of Modern Ukraine at the Harvard Ukrainian Summer Institute in 2000).

21. The testimonies described here in general terms derive from field research in the Vinnytsya Province and in the Chernivtsi Province in the fall of 2002 and the spring of 2003. Research consisted of taped interviews with Jewish survivors and Ukrainian witnesses but also of informal conversations and participant observation in several survivor communities over the course of four months of fieldwork.

22. Literally no food or water was provided by the camp administration to the prisoners of Pechora.

23. See similar descriptions of "clothing packages" and robbing of corpses in Radu Ioanid, *The Holocaust in Romania: The Destruction of Jews and Gypsies Under the Antonescu Regime, 1940–1944* (Chicago: Ivan R. Dee, 2000), 142–66. Ioanid still places greatest emphasis on the brutality of the Romanian soldiers and gendarmes escorting the deportees.

24. Here it must be clarified that the Ukrainians encountered by Romanian Jews along the deportation route, after crossing the Dniestr River, were Sovietized Ukrainians in Vinnytsya Province, not those of the disputed borderland territories. See also Felicia Carmelly, *Shattered! 50 Years of Silence: History and Voices of the Tragedy in Romania and Transnistria* (Scarborough, ON: Abbeyfield Publishers, 1997), 116–17.

25. See Dalia Ofer, "The Holocaust in Transnistria: A Special Case of Genocide," in Dobroszycki and Gurock, *Holocaust in Soviet Union,* 134.

26. Romanian and Ukrainian Jews communicated with one another in Yiddish. Younger Ukrainian Jews, however, already educated in the Soviet system, did not always possess a fluent command of spoken Yiddish and were often illiterate.

27. See Ofer, "Holocaust in Transnistria," 134–35.

28. Siegfried Jagendorf, *Jagendorf's Foundry: Memoir of the Romanian Holocaust 1941–1944,* ed. Aron Hirt-Manheimer (New York: HarperCollins, 1991).

29. See Matatias Carp, *Cartea Neagra: Fapte si Documente Suferintele Evreilor din Romania, 1940–1944* (Bucharest: Societatea Nationala de Editura si Arte Grafice "Dacia Traiana," 1947), 285; Jagendorf, *Jagendorf's Foundry,* 100–1.

30. It should be noted that most historical accounts and memoirs of Transnistria have been written from the perspective of Romanian Jews. These include Carp, *Cartea Neagra;* Julius Fisher, *Transnistria: The Forgotten Cemetery* (New York: T. Yoseloff, 1969); Jean Ancel, ed., *Documents Concerning the Fate of Romanian Jewry During the Holocaust* (Jerusalem: Beate Klarsfeld Foundation, 1986); Avigdor Shachan, *Bekfor Halohat: Ghetaot Transnistria*

[*Burning Ice: The Ghettos of Transnistria*] (Tel Aviv: Beit Lohamei Haghetaot, 1988); Jagendorf, *Jagendorf's Foundry;* Ofer, "Holocaust in Transnistria"; Carmelly, *Shattered!;* Ioanid, *Holocaust in Romania.*

31. Discourses of comparative suffering abound in survivor testimonies, particularly regarding distinctions between the camp and ghetto experience and between the German and Romanian occupations. These discursive tensions raise sensitive questions concerning the categorization of Holocaust experience by survivors, historians, the German government and Claims Conference, and others. A more detailed discussion of real and perceived differences between and among German and Romanian ghettos and camps is beyond the scope of this essay. It should be noted, however, that in the narratives of Transnistria survivors, a ghetto signifies confinement to a set of houses along a street or a few streets; a camp signifies confinement to a building or buildings (or in some cases stables or barns), fully displaced from amenities of home, house, or town.

32. Other camps existing in the territory of Transnistria included Skazinets, Vapniarka (the subject of a work in progress by Marianne Hirsch and Leo Spitzer), Golta (the subject of a work in progress by Dennis Deletant), Bogdanovka, and Domanovka. Vapniarka and Golta were political camps for those (predominantly Romanian Jews) accused of Communist activities.

33. Tulchin Jews express particular resentment because their own relatives and friends, who, as specialists, were allowed to remain in the ghetto after the massive deportations to Pechora, turned them away without food or shelter.

34. Survivor testimonies suggest that the borders of these ghettos became more porous by 1943; thus, several Pechora survivors with whom I spoke spent their last months in Bershad', Tomashpol', Dzhurin, or Mogilev.

35. See Antze and Lambek, "Introduction: Forecasting Memory," xxiv.

36. See also Young, *Texture of Memory.*

Harvey Asher

The Holocaust and the USSR

BETWEEN SEVEN HUNDRED THOUSAND AND THREE MILLION JEWS WERE killed in the Nazi-occupied territories of the Soviet Union, most likely closer to the latter.[1] Within the original (prewar) Soviet borders, the Nazis saw a particular urgency in rapidly exterminating the Jews, whom they declared to be the mainstay of the Bolshevik regime. Most of the Jewish victims were machine-gunned in areas near the towns in which they had been rounded up, and sometimes they were killed in public before local spectators. The greatest number of executions of Soviet Jews started June 22, 1941, with the launching of Operation Barbarossa, and lasted through the winter of 1941–42. The numbers declined from the beginning of the winter of 1942–43, when the tide of the war turned following the Red Army's victory at Stalingrad, until Nazi removal from Soviet territory in 1944, although Jews continued to be murdered both at Auschwitz and on forced marches while the German army retreated.

The earliest accounts of the Holocaust in the Soviet Union suggest that Jewish fatalities might have been far fewer had Soviet authorities acknowledged that in the Soviet Union the Nazis were waging a war against the Jews and shared that information with its Jewish citizens. Unaware of their "special place" in the Nazi killing machine, thousands of Jews who might have fled instead unnecessarily fell into the hands of their executioners. The Soviets depicted the plight of its Jews as only one part of the broader Nazi plan to murder indiscriminately Soviet civilians from all nationalities: Russians, Ukrainians, Belorussians, Kazakhs, and so on. (Technically speaking, Jews in the Soviet Union were not considered a nationality, although the word "Jew" appeared on their internal passports.) Until the Gorbachev era, Soviet literature on the extermination of the Jews refused to use the word "Holocaust," which denotes uniquely Jewish aspects of the Nazi Final Solution, substituting instead the more inclusive Russian words *unichtozhenie* (annihilation) and *katastrofa* (catastrophe).

Some explanations for the Bolsheviks' deemphasis of the Jewishness of the Holocaust stress the Communists' linkage to Russia's centuries-long history of official and popular anti-Semitism, marked by pogroms, the Pale of Settlement, education quotas, the circulation (if not creation) of the Protocols of the Elders of Zion, forced assimilation, the Black Hundreds, and mass slaughter of Jews during the civil war, to name but a few of its manifestations. Presumably, Stalin shared this hostility toward the Jews because he, too, was an anti-Semite, and employed his position as *vozhd'* (leader) to compel both the party and the masses to pursue hostile policies toward the Jews both *during* the Holocaust as well as *after* the Great Patriotic War ended. For example, he refused to allow the publication of the *Black Book,* which contained graphic accounts by victims, on-the-spot observers, and perpetrators of the atrocities committed only against the Jews by German invaders throughout the occupied regions of the Soviet Union between 1941 and 1945.[2] He also quashed the Jewish Anti-Fascist Committee, which initially worked to gain Jewish support abroad for the Soviet war effort, and had most of its members murdered. Perhaps most menacingly, he launched the so-called Doctor's Plot, which some consider to have been the opening salvo for Stalin's plan to deport all Soviet Jews to Birobidzhan and other parts of Siberia.[3]

Yet there is a problem with prioritizing Stalin's anti-Semitism, for he was not a simple anti-Semite, nor was his hostility toward the Jews racially based.[4] Moreover, Stalin's personal feelings about the Jews were held in check by the Bolshevik history of defining themselves as protectors of the weak and oppressed, fighters against the enemies of social justice and national equality, at least until 1949, when a more Russocentric anti-Semitism moved to center stage. For another, Stalin appointed Jewish party secretaries such as Lev Mekhlis and Gregory Kannev.[5] And while he punished his daughter Svetlana's Jewish lover, screenwriter Alexei Kaplev, and avoided his Jewish son-in-law, Gregory Morozov, and the couple's son, Joseph, Stalin did not insist that Svetlana give up her Jewish paramours. Right up until his death, Stalin continued awarding prizes to Jewish writers and musicians. And, though the reasons are complex, the Soviet Union was the first country to recognize the state of Israel. Stalin's anti-Semitism was also held in check by the international components of Communist ideology, whose message of universal brotherhood and equality served as barriers against openly promoting anti-Semitism. Recent scholarship suggests that contingency and pragmatism were more important than Stalin's personal views in the reluctance of the Soviets to treat the Holocaust as specific to Jews.[6] The twenty-million-plus non-Jewish fatalities in the Soviet Union made the contrast between Jewish and non-Jewish deaths seem less sharp than in Western countries.[7] Additionally, Bolshevik ideology had a propensity to view *all* civilian murders as a consequence of racist fascism, seen as a degenerate form of capitalism. Marxism also influenced the Communist Party's unwillingness to define the Jews as members of a nation, as it called for the assimilation of Soviet Jews into the general population.[8] The decision to hide from the Soviet people and the Red Army what was happening to Jews in the camps was also based on the need to conceal the huge numbers of Soviet prisoners of war, a result, in large part, of Stalin's faulty military strategy. The captured soldiers, who had panicked and surrendered in droves in the early phases of the conflict, had been depicted to the public as courageous martyrs who continued to fight for the motherland with their last breath. In actuality, these prisoners had passively succumbed to execution, or died from hunger, cold, or slave labor, which led Stalin to avoid highlighting all aspects of the death camp horrors.[9] Finally, and most important, to show a special sensitivity toward Jews risked diminishing the all-Union effort and experience of the war to strengthen the legitimacy of the party. To "give" the war to the Jews threatened forfeiting the current plan to sustain the morale of the Soviet armed forces by portraying the conflict as one fought to assure the survival of the motherland from the Nazi evils being perpetrated against all the Soviet people.

Historians Ilya Altman and Claudio Sergio Ingerflom not only challenge the notion that the Soviet press remained silent on the Holocaust but also suggest that Soviet conduct included many examples of help rendered to the Jews during their ordeal and that, all in all, the Soviet record was not that much worse than the records of its wartime allies.[10] They trace the shifting attitudes and behavior of the Soviet regime toward the Jews through four time frames. The first runs from Hitler's ascension to power in 1933 until the Molotov-Ribbentrop pact of August 1939. A key politburo decision in September 1935 stopped the flow of Jewish refugees from Germany by requiring of them unreasonable monetary minimums, forced Soviet citizenship, proletarian origins, and compulsory physical labor under the supervision of the NKVD (the secret police; A, 229). Offers by Jewish organizations to help financially were rejected. Irrespective of these harsh restrictions, stories about the Nazi persecutions appeared fairly regularly in the Soviet press and on radio broadcasts. On occasions when the nationality of the Jewish victims was not mentioned specifically in the accounts, the listing of names allowed inferences to be drawn as to their origins. It is true, however, that the Jewish victims were often cited last on the list, or designated as "other," and even when acknowledging crimes specifically committed against Jews, the deaths of women and children were cited separately, giving the impression that they were not Jewish. On the other hand, between November 11, 1938, and the end of June 1939, the party organ *Pravda* published thirty-nine reports, articles, and commentaries about the attacks on Jews under German rule. Reports also appeared in the Yiddish press. Even during the twenty-two months of the Molotov-Ribbentrop pact, when the Soviet media usually refrained from covering Jewish atrocities, many Jews had information on the subject, and, as detailed later in this essay, stories about German atrocities against the Jews reappeared in the Soviet press almost immediately after the Germans invaded the Soviet Union. Lack of information, then, does not appear decisive for those Jews who chose not to flee the Nazi invaders. The key variable was the time that elapsed between the beginning of the invasion and the actual Nazi occupation of a particular territory.[11]

From the September 28, 1939, annexations of eastern Poland and the northern Caucasuses permitted by the Molotov-Ribbentrop agreement until the June 1941 German invasion, the Soviet Union acquired some two million additional Jews. Initially the Germans did not show great zeal in preventing Polish Jews in their occupation zone from fleeing to Soviet territory. However, most of those who tried to do so were driven back by border guards and the Soviet Army. Of the refugees that the Soviets *accepted,* even providing transportation for them (including those from Vilna), when the final disposition of the Polish territories took place, the NKVD sent back the politically and socially suspect, the aged, and the infirm. The other refugees (not just Jews) had the choice of going to work in gulags of the north and east or being deported back to the German zone; most eventually fled their workplaces, despite strict Soviet laws to the contrary, as they became economically and ideologically disillusioned. Those who stayed *became Soviet citizens.* To offer Jews citizenship was exceptional at a time when most countries refused to grant Jewish refugees even temporary residence permits (A, 232–33). Most refugees had hesitated to take up the Soviet offer because they preferred not to close off other more attractive havens, did not want to lose their Polish citizenship and leave loved ones behind, or hoped to leave the USSR if that became a later option. As the national identity among these Polish Jews was quite strong and their culture different from that of their Soviet Jewish brethren (they had their own political parties, spoke Yiddish, were more urban, etc.), they were not inclined to assimilate. Quite a few of them returned to German-occupied Poland where, of course, they were killed. Amazingly, some 250,000 Jews from the German-annexed territories fled to the interior or were inadvertently saved from Nazi annihilation when deported to Siberia or Central Asia. Israeli historian Dov Levin believes that the deportations were "the denouement of a lengthy series of Soviet attempts to solve the refugee problem in a constructive and humane fashion, at least in Soviet terms of the time."[12] In this strange if not bizarre way, the Soviet authorities ended up saving some thousands of Jews from the Nazi juggernaut.

Many scholars have remarked that after the signing of the August 1939 pact, Soviet official propaganda pretty much halted comments about Nazi persecution of the Jews. But was it this silence that explains the unwillingness of the Jews to evacuate the Nazi-occupied territory for the east? The data suggest that this was not the main reason for nonflight. Those caught in the Nazi net knew of the persecution of Jews in the Third Reich, but the violent outbursts there had not yet been systematic, certainly not exterminatory. By the time the Nazi invasion came and the large-scale killing began, it was too late. Also lulling the Jews were memories of the benevolent German occupation of 1918, when German authorities put an end to pogroms in the Russian areas they occupied. That earlier memory translated into the belief among some Jews that life would be better under the Germans than it was under the Soviets. That the Jews who lived inside the frontiers of 1939 (Smolensk, Kalinin, etc.) had only several weeks to decide whether to stay or leave before German troops arrived at the end of August and the beginning of September contributed to these Jews' hesitation to make a final decision.

If the Jews in the German zone did not flee, it was not completely due to lack of information but because they could not, especially in the midst of a frantic situation, believe or comprehend what was happening. (In that disbelief they were far from alone.) Furthermore, evacuation to the Soviet Union was far from a happy choice. It meant grueling work, lack of mobility, losing a chance for an evacuation permit, and giving up their material goods and their apartments to wander in the midst of winter. The Soviet reality was hardly the promised land in the eyes of the numerous inhabitants of the occupied region. Its depressed economy, prohibition of political activity, compulsory work on the Sabbath, closing down of Jewish community organizations and press—plus the "normal" discrimination against the Jews—weighed heavily on the decision not to accept the Soviet offer (A, 243).

As for the Jews of Soviet-occupied eastern Poland, they had good reason to regard the Red Army as liberators, given the Nazi noose hanging over their heads. For them, the Soviets were the lesser of two evils, "better Stalin than Hitler." In the first few weeks of the Red Army's presence, Jews understandably tended to interpret things in the most favorable light, overlooking some of the liabilities. After all, the Communist Party's official policy was to crack down on anti-Semitism, punish vandals, and execute some who killed Jews, while dispelling rumors of Jewish misdeeds and slanders against Christians. Consequently Jews paid less attention to concomitant party attacks on so-called Jewish chauvinism, so-called counterrevolutionary parties like the Bund, Jewish bourgeois nationalism, and so on.[13] While the Jews looked favorably on the Soviet occupation, the indigenous populations regarded the Soviet soldiers as invaders, and the contrary Jewish response augmented their already unfavorable image among their neighbors.

After November 1, 1940, the Soviet frontier was sealed, though it remained porous along the border, and Russian border guards in a hit-or-miss fashion let some refugees in and pushed others back. Soviet policy now was to crack down on the flow of Jews to their areas of control. By May 1940, local Soviet presses began to run articles referring to the refugees as "shirkers" and "black marketers"; they were rounded up and shifted to the interior. Georgi Alexandrov, head of agitprop, criticized Jewish predominance in several cultural establishments, referring to them as "national nihilists" and "destroyers of Russian cultural values," anticipating the party line of the late 1940s.[14]

In 1940, the German Office for the Emigration of the Jews in Berlin and Vienna, headed by Reinhard Heydrich and Heinrich Himmler, respectively, proposed shipping to the Soviet Union about 350,000 Jews from Germany, Austria, and Czechoslovakia, plus an additional 1,800,000 living in Reich-annexed territory, including the General Government zone set up in Poland, a clear indication that in 1940 the Nazis did not yet envisage a Final Solution. The Soviet refusal to accept these Jews, although they were aware of their tragic plight in Poland, perhaps led the Germans to search for other ways to get rid of them (A, 235–36). Officially, Soviet rejection of the offer was based on the fear that such an influx would lead to being infiltrated by a fifth column. Paradoxically, after tortuous diplomacy, a small number of these Jews who had made it to Vladivostok were allowed to receive "Sugihara visas," allowing them passage to safe sanctuaries, mostly to Kobe, Japan (A, 240).

The German invasion of the Soviet Union led to the occupation of the Ukraine, Belorussia, the Baltic republics, the north Caucasuses, and a large area of European Russia with a prewar population of eighty-five million. From the first days of the German invasion of the USSR, Sovinform (Soviet Information Bureau) dispensed information on the air and in the press about the persecutions of the Jews; the first communication on June 26 announced the pogrom at Bialystok. The head of the party in Belorussia, Panteleimon Ponamarenko, told Stalin that "the Jews terrorized by Hitler fled like beasts instead of fighting" (A, 245). He indicated that Nazi propaganda used the words "Yid" and "Communist" synonymously but that the Belorussian population rejected this type of propaganda.

On the other hand, Ponamarenko did not mention that the German occupation military authorities sponsored between two hundred and four hundred local periodicals and newspapers in regions that fell under their jurisdiction, whose reportage depicted the Jews as the main enemy. These reports led to neighbors closing their doors to Jews, and not just out of fear, for the same people helped non-Jewish war prisoners, an action also punishable by the death penalty. In his report of August 19, Ponamarenko no longer accused the Jews of fleeing but described fragmentarily the particular massacres and brutalities committed by the Nazis throughout Belorussia, reaffirming that Nazi propaganda did not win over the republic's population. More significantly, the Soviet republic NKVD branches gathered information on the deaths of Jewish prisoners of war and the Jewish population, which

Stalin read, confirming once more that the Soviet general secretary knew exactly what was happening to the Jews. In late August 1941, a number of leading Soviet Jewish luminaries spoke of the Nazi plans to exterminate the entire Jewish people and other "inferior" peoples, joining other media groups that appealed to the Soviet population to fight actively against the Nazi occupiers. This information helped more than 54 percent of people living in prepartitioned Poland to escape to the east by year's end, one-fourth of them Jews (A, 248). Large numbers of Moscow and Leningrad Jews were also evacuated.

However, in the recently annexed territory of the USSR, now under attack by the Nazis, the Red Army and border guards stopped all those who did not have an official evacuation document. For this reason, thousands of people (many of them Jews) fell into Nazi hands. No official order to provide help or raise the quota limitations was given. Whether the lack of help was due to Nazi anti-Jewish propaganda, whose effectiveness frightened the Kremlin, or to the Communist Party being a prisoner of its international creed of refusing to distinguish among victims by nationality, the bottom line is that in the early days following the German invasion of the USSR, a more generous Soviet policy could have saved thousands of lives.

In a November 7, 1941, speech, Stalin for the first and *last* time specifically mentioned Jews among a host of other Nazi victims. In this speech one already finds the thesis that the Nazi invasion brought suffering and death to *all* the Soviet people (A, 250), a theme subsequently reiterated in several addresses by Foreign Minister Vyacheslav Molotov. The overriding leitmotif of Stalin's communications and speeches on the Holocaust from 1942 through 1945 was that the Nazis sought to annihilate equally all the Slavic people. Yet despite Stalin's subsequent silence, on December 20, 1941, the state newspaper *Izvestiia* published a special communiqué on the extermination of Soviet Jews, based on an NKVD synthesis of information from what turned out to be a nonexistent official organization. Regardless of its suspect origins, the report indicates the Kremlin knew of the systematic extermination of Soviet Jews that began immediately after a place was occupied, how they were rounded up and transferred to the camps, and the brutal ways in which they were killed, especially the children. Death tolls for specific massacres were provided, not always accurately (A, 253–54). The report stressed death figures and did not appeal for action, perhaps out of fear that the German occupiers would have responded to such an exhortation by killing the non-Jewish population.

After the victory at Stalingrad, while Soviet leaders reduced official communiqués to a minimum, there does not seem to be an all-encompassing written or oral order imposing a blackout (A, 260). However, in a February 1944 memo, Georgi Alexandrov, with the approval of higher-ups, substituted the phrase "peaceful Soviet citizens" to label all Soviet subjects who had been annihilated by the Nazis. Not surprisingly, the Jews were to be treated as part of this larger category, not as special victims (A, 261). Other reports were "corrected" by higher military authorities so that the final document that went to the State Committee for Defense (headed by Stalin) deleted references to the Jews (A, 262). The alterations probably indicated that the military leaders at the front understood the new party line. Still, the excisions seem to have been done less to obscure the origins of the victims than to deny them separate status, for the final text did list the names of those killed, making it fairly easy to recognize their Jewish origins.

During the war years, Stalin did not initiate any anti-Semitic edicts or actions, suggesting that likely anti-Semitism per se was not the primary reason for the usual official silence on the particulars of the destruction of Soviet Jewry. Moreover, neither he nor any other member of the Kremlin leadership ever denied that huge numbers of Jews were being killed under horrible circumstances. The Kremlin attitude toward the Jews was subsumed to emphasizing the traditions of the Russian army and Russian patriotism as the best means to combat Nazi propaganda while maintaining the morale of population and army. Nothing was to be gained by highlighting the Jewish situation, for by the time the fortunes of the Soviet Army improved, most of Soviet Jewry had already perished, and dispensing information about their slaughter retrospectively would be of little military or propaganda value to the regime. To single out the plight of the Jews might prove counterproductive, as it risked encouraging analogies between the Nazi deportations of the Jews and Soviet transfers of entire nationality groups, such as the Chechens and Volga Germans (A, 270). Kremlin leaders also wished to avoid giving credibility to propaganda claims that the Nazis only wished to deal with Jews and Communists, especially in areas where the Soviet leadership needed to mobilize the population against the invaders, regions where anti-Semitism seemed to be on the increase in the second phase of the war (A, 273). After the war, the reasons for reducing the visibility of the Jews in the story of the Great Patriotic War included changing policy toward the new East Germany; the desire to avoid offending Soviet nationality groups, some of whose members had served as Nazi collaborators (usually referred to as "police" in sources like the *Black Book*); and reaction to the developing cold war by an anticosmopolitan campaign conspicuously directed against the Jews.

It should be clear by now that not all Communist Party decisions ignored or exacerbated the plight of the Soviet Union's Jewish inhabitants during the Holocaust and that what transpired was more complicated than Stalin simply acting out an endemic anti-Semitism by issuing a spate of anti-Jewish orders. At the same time, it is also true that much of what the Soviets did or did not do had a negative impact on Jewish survival. Arad observes, "Neither from the Soviet state or Party was there a single appeal to underground organizations or local population to help Soviet Jews."[15] A more generous refugee policy could have saved thousands of additional Jewish lives, as would acceptance that whatever the horrors perpetrated on countless numbers of innocent Soviet citizens by the Nazis, the situation of Soviet Jews was peculiar: only they were singled out for total extermination, down to every last man, woman, and child. While official and popular anti-Semitism does not appear to be the crucial variable, assuredly, the lengthy Russian culture of anti-Semitism meaningfully limited how the Jewish question was conceptualized, and it seriously influenced what the Soviet government and Communist Party would or would not do for its Jews during the Holocaust.

Whether the Soviet Union could have done more for its Jews during the Holocaust has been connected to the related subjects of the bombing and liberation of Auschwitz. In a recent article—characterized by fine detective work, given the source limitations on the subject—Jeffrey Herf shows that from the spring of 1944 to early fall 1945, if not before, the Red Air Force had the capability of bombing the death factories, Auschwitz in particular; by June 1943, Red Air Force tactical units were clearly closer to the target than American bombers were.[16] However, as this article makes clear, given its erratic and inconsistent responses to the Holocaust on its *own territory*, the failure of the Soviet regime to act comes as no suprise. Indeed there is not a single piece of evidence to indicate the Soviets ever considered bombing Auschwitz (A, 275).

The liberation of Auschwitz by the Russians shows that rescuing its prisoners—both Jews and Russians—never engaged the Soviet leadership's attention. (Stalin even refused to bargain for the release of his POW son, who subsequently perished in the camps.) General Vassili Petrenko, one of the liberators of the camp, indicates complete surprise at the horrors he encountered at Auschwitz, illustrating that the Red Army brass remained in the dark about conditions there. Neither he nor any of the other army commanders ever received a precise order to liberate the camp, as either a primary or secondary goal of the Vistula-Oder operation (P, 120). He tells of hearing from a colleague that when shown the plan drawn up by General Ivan Konev, head of the operation, Stalin simply pointed to the map of the region and said "for the gold" (P, 121), from which the officer presenting the plan drew the conclusion that priority was to be given to measures for preserving Silesia's industrial potential, not the prisoners of its infamous camp.

The January 17 directives received by the commanders of the first Ukrainian front (the troops engaged in the Vistula siege) from Stavka (General Headquarters) called for the offensive to take over the Oder River no later than January 30, liberating the cities along the front, while establishing a reinforced position on its west bank (P, 122).[17] The main military objective remained to liberate cities all along the front.

Preparing to cross the river and consolidate their position there would have taken at least three to four more days, the time estimated for getting the German defenders to pull out of the fighting zone (P, 124). If the Soviet troops had followed Stalin's plan to the letter, they would not have been able to take the industrial sector of Silesia and surrounding camps before February 2 or 3, and when the army units finally did get to occupy Auschwitz, they would have found only a mass of ruins, smoldering furnaces, and not a single living prisoner.

Fortunately, General Konev did not blindly follow the January 17 directive to the letter but carried it out flexibly based on his strategic knowledge, war experience, and an analysis of the battlefield situation. He took the initiative of avoiding a frontal assault, going around the German fortifications with tank units before linking up with other army units to attack from the north, the east, and the south, forcing the defending Hitlerites to flee to open terrain and destroying them there. His decision to adjust the battle plan for seizing the coal region of

Dabrowa (in Russian, Dombrovskii) and nearby Silesian cities proved decisive (P, 125–26). Hence the directive from Stavka was carried out before the January 30 deadline, allowing Auschwitz to be liberated on January 27, saving 7,000 prisoners from certain death (only 4,880 remained alive a month later).

The real question would not seem why Auschwitz wasn't bombed by the Russians or, for that matter, the Americans and British. Given that the political leadership of the three countries proclaimed that the fastest way to end the Nazi genocide was to defeat them on the battlefield as quickly as possible, what sense did an Auschwitz "diversion" make? More generally, given the long history of major powers' reluctance and aversion toward acting to stop genocides—Armenia, Cambodia, Rwanda—why would the Nazi Holocaust, against a group with little political capital, call for a more dramatic intervention?[18] Just as the Holocaust cannot be studied in isolation from the German past and the internal dynamics of the führer state, crucial for understanding the limitations of how the Soviets responded to the Holocaust is some familiarity with how the Soviet system worked—or, better, didn't work. Stalin's Russia was not a place in which humanism and compassion for individuals and groups was conspicuous. Soviet heavy-handedness and brutality were dispensed ecumenically to all subject nationalities, not just the Jews. Entire nationalities—Kalmucks, Crimean Tatars, Balkars, Meshketian Turks, Ingush—were ripped from their homelands and deported to remote regions of the country, condemned as collectively guilty of real and imagined offenses against the motherland. Entire classes, such as the kulaks during collectivization, were eliminated. Countless millions disappeared into the endless depths of the gulag, never to be heard from again. Millions more were victimized by the purges, in which the daily party assault against the population at large was extended to its own ranks. And millions of POWs and displaced people, often forced to return to the USSR against their will, knew full well the horrors awaiting them.

The Soviet experience, from the collectivization and the five-year plans of the 1920s until Stalin's death in March 1953, might be described as Stalin's war against his people, all of whom were considered potential enemies. As *Washington Post* journalist Anne Appelbaum puts it, "The population of the gulag and the population of the rest of the USSR shared many things besides suffering . . . the same slovenly working practices, the same criminally stupid bureaucracy, the same corruption, and the same sullen disregard for human life."[19] From the perspective of its congenital and pervasive dehumanizing treatment of *all* of its people, Soviet treatment of the Jews during the Holocaust was worse than some groups, better than others.

In today's Russia and the newly independent states, glasnost has allowed for reappraisals of the Holocaust, indicated by the spate of recent publications using the word "Holocaust" in the title.[20] Largely due to the efforts of Ilya Altman, director of Moscow's Holocaust Foundation, established in 1991, there have been conferences and symposia in Moscow and abroad attended by both international and CIS (Commonwealth of Independent States) scholars. The foundation has published more than one hundred articles on Holocaust-centered topics, worked with Yad Vashem, and recently came out with a ten-book series, the Russian Library of the Holocaust. Besides its scholarly presentations on the treatment of the Holocaust in the Soviet Union and in the post-Soviet situation, foundation goals include coming up with educational strategies for promoting the study of the Holocaust in the curricula of Russian secondary schools and institutions of higher learning.

Progress notwithstanding, it remains difficult to get Holocaust memorials built. After the war, the known sites where the massacre of tens of thousands of Jews happened were left unmarked. In no city except Minsk was there any memorial with a Yiddish inscription explicitly evoking the Holocaust. Local authorities interdicted all Jewish symbols in monuments and changed those that had been erected here and there. Even the laconic phrase "to the Jewish victims of the Holocaust," which appeared on a monument in Belorussia, was deemed unacceptable; seven individuals who proposed a memorial in Odessa were sent to the camps; the Jewish Museum in Vilnius was shut.[21]

It was only in 1991 that a national day to commemorate the victims of Babi Yar took place; even today it is not a site much visited or, for that matter, even known to many Ukrainians.[22] While other memorials followed where monuments allowed for the Star of David and Hebrew inscriptions, the results were far from ideal. The effort to add a Holocaust commemoration to the war memorial complex at Pokhlonnaya Gora in Moscow resulted in a structure that made reference to the Jews look like an afterthought.[23] The anniversary of the liberation of Auschwitz is still not a national holiday in Russia; however, since 1995 it has been celebrated in Moscow at the initiative of the Center for Research and Education on the Holocaust, which since 1992 has also organized a Day of Remembrance.

Despite the important efforts of Altman and his colleagues, it remains likely that as memories of the Great Patriotic War continue to recede in intensity from public memory—Russian war veterans complain about their current shabby treatment in the new Russian state—the willingness of the population to reengage the subject of the Russian Holocaust is unlikely. Young Russians are more concerned with immediate problems of adjusting to life in the new Russia than with preserving or resurrecting divisive memories. Moreover, the Jewish population throughout Russia and the Commonwealth of Independent States has pragmatic reasons not to raise questions of victimization, namely, the risk of raising the ire of their non-Jewish neighbors. As more Jews continue to leave Russia and the CIS states, it is unlikely that those who remain will have the clout or desire to devote their energies to the subject of the Holocaust in the former Soviet Union.[24]

NOTES

1. For the complex calculations, see Harvey Asher, "The Soviet Union, the Holocaust, and Auschwitz," *Kritika: Explorations in Russian and Eurasian History* 4, no. 4 (Fall 2003): 887–88 n.1. The author agrees with the estimate of between 2.75 million and 2.90 million cited in Yitzhak Arad, "Katastrofa sovetskogo evreistva," *Unichtozhenie evreev SSSR v gody nemskoi (1941–1944): Sbornik dokumentov i materialov* (Jerusalem: Yad Vashem, 1992), 5.

2. For details, see Harvey Asher, "The *Black Book* and the Holocaust," *Journal of Genocide Research* 1, no. 3 (1999): 401–16.

3. See Arno Lustiger, *Stalin and the Jews: The Complete History of State-Sponsored Terrorism of the Jews Under Stalin* (New York: Enigma Books, 2003), 255. Lustiger is less certain than Leonid Liuks about Stalin's murderous intentions; see Leonid Liuks, "Evreeiski vopros v politike Stalina," *Voprosy istorii*, no. 7 (1999): 56.

4. Adam Ulam, *Stalin: The Man and His Era* (Boston: Beacon Press, 1973), esp. 678–84.

5. Robert Conquest, "Stalin and the Jews," *New York Review of Books* 42, no. 12 (July 16, 1996): 48.

6. Zvi Gitelman, "Soviet Reactions to the Holocaust," in *The Holocaust in the Soviet Union: Studies and Sources on the Destruction of the Jews in the Nazi Occupied Territories of the USSR, 1941–1945,* ed. Lucjan Dobroszycki and Jeffrey Gurock (Armonk, NY: M. E. Sharpe, 1993), 16–18. Also see Lukasz Hirzowitz, "The Holocaust in the Soviet Mirror," in Dobroszycki and Gurock, *Holocaust in Soviet Union,* 207–13.

7. John Garrard, "Russia and the Soviet Union," in *The Holocaust Encyclopedia,* ed. Walter Laqueur (New Haven, CT: Yale University Press, 2001), 590.

8. Zvi Gitelman, "Politics and the Historiography of the Holocaust in the Soviet Union," in *Bitter Legacy: Confronting the Holocaust in the Soviet Union,* ed. Zvi Gitelman (Bloomington: Indiana University Press, 1997), 18.

9. Vassili Petrenko, *Avant et Après Auschwitz* (Paris: Flammarion, 2002), 133–36. The book is a translation of the Russian edition published by the Russian Library of the Holocaust, *Do i posle Osventsima: Uznikam natsistkikh lagere ismerti i voinam-osvoboditeliam posviashchaetsia* (Moscow, Fond Kholokosta, 2000). Quotations are from the French edition, modified here and there by substituting the Russian word or phrase as needed; English translations are mine (hereafter cited in text as P, followed by page numbers).

10. Ilya Altman and Claudio Segio Ingerflom, "Le Kremlin et L'Holocauste (1933–2001)," in Vassili Petrenko, *Avant et Après Auschwitz,* 217–81 (hereafter cited in text as A, followed by page numbers).

11. Mordecai Altshuler, "Escape and Evacuation at the Time of the Nazi Invasion: Politics and Realities," in Dobroszycki and Gurock, *Holocaust in the Soviet Union,* 85–90.

12. Dov Levin, *The Lesser of Two Evils: East European Jewry Under Soviet Rule, 1939–1941* (Philadelphia: Jewish Publication Society, 1995), 197.

13. Ibid., 61–62.

14. Ilya Altman, "The Holocaust and the Press in the Occupied Territories," in *Ten' Kholokosta,* ed. Ilya Altman (Moscow: Russian Holocaust Library, 1998), 265.

15. Arad, "Katastrofa sovetskogo evreistva," 23.

16. Jeffrey Herf, "The Nazi Extermination Camps and the Ally to the East: Could the Red Army and Air Force Have Stopped or Slowed the Final Solution?" *Kritika* 4, no. 4 (Fall 2003): 913–30. An abbreviated version of Herf's article appears in the present volume.

17. For the reluctance of the latter, see Asher, "Soviet Union," 893–96.

18. For the dismal track record of the international community in halting genocide, see Samantha Power, *A Problem from Hell: America and the Age of Genocide* (New York: Basic Books, 2002).

19. Anne Appelbaum, *Gulag: A History* (New York: Doubleday, 2003), xxviii.

20. For example, Mikhail Gefter, *Ekho Kholokosta i russkii evreiskii vopros* (Moscow: Nauchno-prosvettel'nyi tsentr Kholokost, 1995); Stephane Brukhfeld and Paul Levine, *Peredaite ob etom detiam Vashim: Istoriia Kholokosta v Evrope, 1933–1945* (Moscow: Tekst, 2000); and Mariia Altman, *Otritsanie Kholokosta: Istoriia I sovremennye tendentsii* (Moscow: Rossiiskaia biblioteka Kholokosta, 2001), to name but a few.

21. Ilya Altman, "Teaching the Holocaust in Russia," http://www.Yadvashem.org.il/download/education/conference/Altman/pdf.

22. See Nina Tumarkin, "Story of a War Memorial," in *World War 2 and the Soviet People: Select Papers from the Fourth World Congress for Soviet and East European Studies,* ed. John and Carol Garrard (New York: St. Martin's Press, 1993), 126–46, for the controversy surrounding the location and representation of the memorial.

23. For an excellent, brief account of the contemporary Holocaust scene in Russia, see Catherine Merridale, *Night of Stone: Death and Memory in Twentieth-Century Russia* (New York: Viking, 2000), 316–18.

24. Currently there are approximately 600,000 Jews residing in the former Soviet Union, nearly 1,000,000 fewer than the nearly 1,450,000 enumerated in the Soviet census of January 1989. See Zvi Gitelman, *A Century of Ambivalence: The Jews of Russia and the Soviet Union, 1881 to the Present* (Bloomington: Indiana University Press, 2001), 217–18.

Jeffrey Herf

The Nazi Extermination Camps and the Ally to the East: Could the Red Army and Air Force Have Stopped or Slowed the Final Solution?

IN HER NOW-STANDARD WORK ON THE HISTORY OF THE HOLOCAUST, the Israeli historian Leni Yahil asked why official recognition of the on-going mass murder did not lead to rescue and cessation of the killings. "Why," she asked, "were the Nazis able to continue the implementation of the final solution of the problem of European Jewry until the end of the war almost without impediment"?[1] During the war and then in the scholarly and public discourse about it afterward in Britain and the United States, the phrase "the Allies" came to be understood to mean only the Western two-thirds of the anti-Hitler coalition. The debate about what the Allies could and could not have done to stop or hinder the murder of the Jews also remained a solely "Anglo-American" discussion.[2] Hence it has neglected the Soviet Union, the wartime ally with the largest military forces on land and in the air which were in closest geographic proximity to the Nazi extermination camps and killing fields. Leading historians of the Soviet military in World War II or of the Holocaust have not addressed the issue of what the Soviet armed forces could and could not have done to stop the Holocaust.[3] This gap, which has only become more glaring in light of recent scholarly developments, needs to be closed.

First, historians of German policy and strategy had made a powerful case that the history of the Second World War and that of the Holocaust must be understood in close connection with one another.[4] Second, historians in the United States, Great Britain, and Germany have drawn our attention to the vast significance of the eastern front for the course and outcome of the war as a whole. In so doing, they have displaced previous and provincial Anglo-American narratives.[5] This deepened focus, both on the intersection of the war and the Holocaust and on the eastern front, impels us to ask the same questions regarding "Auschwitz and the Allies" of the Soviet military that have been addressed to the policies of the United States and Britain. Third, research of the past two decades has made apparent that the Allies, in particular the intelligence services of Britain and the United States, were more well informed about many details of the Holocaust than was previously thought.

On December 17, 1942, a Joint Allied Declaration was published in the name of eleven Allied governments and exile regimes that asserted that the German authorities were now carrying out Hitler's oft-repeated intention to exterminate the Jews of Europe, were transporting Jews from all territories under their control to Eastern Europe, and would be held to account by the Allies.[6] On December 18, 1942, the same declaration was published in Moscow in *Pravda*. More recently, Amir Weiner reiterates that despite Communist discourse that obscured the specific nature of Jewish suffering, "as early as October 1941 the murder of the Jews throughout Europe and the Soviet Union was publicly exposed."[7] Indeed, due to geographic proximity and the extensive intelligence networks of the Communist movement behind German lines, it seems reasonable to assume that the Soviet government was considerably better informed about the murder of the Jews than were its Western allies.[8] The research remains to be done on what the Soviet intelligence agencies and military leadership knew about the existence and location of the six main extermination camps (or to what extent information about the murder of the Jews was shared by the governments of the Soviet Union, Britain, and the United States). The leading work on the Soviet war available in English, John Erickson's *Stalin's War with Germany,* superbly documents the enormous scope of the battles on the eastern front. Yet it has nothing to say about the Soviet military response to the Holocaust.[9] Erickson reminds us of how enormous the Soviet military became. Soviet industry produced "78,000 tanks and 16,000 self-propelled guns, 108,028 combat aircraft, 12 million rifles and carbines, 6 million sub-machine guns, almost 98,000 field guns and 110,000 lorries. By these demonstrations, whatever the scale of measurement, the decisive role in defeating the 'Fascist Bloc' was played by the Soviet Union."[10] By July 1944, as

Gerhard Weinberg put it, "the Red Air Force controlled the skies over most of the [eastern] front."[11]

Ironically, it was Martin Gilbert, whose *Auschwitz and the Allies* (1981) used the Westerncentric Anglo-American meaning of the term "allies," who implicitly challenged these same limitations in his subsequent works *The Macmillan Atlas of the Holocaust* (1982) and *The Second World War: A Complete History* (1989). Each included maps which, perhaps for the first time, visually integrated the geography of the eastern front with the location of the death camps, thereby connecting the war in the East in space and time to chronology of the Holocaust.[12] In the remainder of this essay, I will combine geography and military capabilities, Gilbert's maps and data on the Soviet Air Force in particular, to pose anew the issue of what the Soviet military might have been able to do to stop or hinder the mass murders then in progress.

It would have been difficult for the Red Army or Air Force to stop or hinder the Holocaust in the period extending from June 21, 1941, to the Battle of Stalingrad in winter 1942–43. The military disaster visited upon Soviet forces, the loss of vast amounts of territory in the western Soviet Union, and the intact strength of both the Wehrmacht and the Luftwaffe all would appear to preclude significant Soviet military operations behind German lines. By December 1941, the German armies were holding a line from north to south which at its center was only thirty miles west of Moscow, and the Soviet Union was fighting desperately to avoid defeat. Eleven months later, in November 1942, the German front lines were still about two hundred miles west of Moscow. By July 1943, five months after the Soviet victory at Stalingrad, the Red Army had pushed the Germans back to a point about three hundred miles west of Moscow.

As Gilbert's map "Deportation, Massacre and Revolt, July 1943," indicates, in the two years from June 1941 to July 1943, the eastern front, and hence the Soviet Air Force, was no closer than 700 miles to the extermination centers at Chelmno and Sobibor, 750 miles to Belzec and Majdanek (not shown on his map but just south of Sobibor), 850 miles to Treblinka, and approximately 950 miles to Auschwitz-Birkenau.[13] However, following its victory in the enormous tank battle at Kursk in July 1943, the armed forces of the Soviet Union drove the Germans into retreat in fall 1943, and the front moved over 400 miles to the west. As a result, by December 1943, the front was now 250 miles from Chelmno and Sobibor, 300 miles from Belzec and Majdanek, 400 miles from Treblinka, and 500 miles from Auschwitz-Birkenau.[14]

According to recent scholarship, somewhat more than three million of the six million Jews murdered in the Holocaust lost their lives in Chelmno, Sobibor, Treblinka, Belzec, Majdanek, and Auschwitz-Birkenau, the six stationary killing centers in German-occupied Poland established by the Nazis between 1941 and mid-1942.[15] Scholarship of recent years has also drawn our attention to the fact that the Nazis murdered somewhat fewer than three million Jews with special forces, such as the SS Einsatzgruppen and Order Police, using machine guns, mobile gas vans, or starvation and disease in ghettos.[16] Most of these murders behind the German front took place from 1941 to 1943. They were carried out by battalion-size units of armed men and thus could only be stopped by armies on the ground. The only way to stop this kind of killing was to have armed forces reconquer the territories Germany occupied and win the war. Hence the debate about what the Allies could and should have done to stop the Holocaust concerns the possibility of destroying the extermination camps, rather than on attacking the mobile, harder-to-find special-unit murders. The death camps were stationary facilities vulnerable to attack from the air.

Judith Tydor Baumel, the associate editor of the recently published *Holocaust Encyclopedia,* presents the following data regarding the number of Jews killed and the time and location of their murders in the six major death factories: Majdanek, October 1941 through 1943, 235,000; Chelmno, December 1941 to April 1943, 150,000 to 300,000; Belzec, March 1942 to November 1942, 600,000; Sobibor, May 1942 to October 1943, 200,000 to 250,000; Treblinka, July 1942 to fall 1943, 750,000 to 800,000; and Auschwitz-Birkenau, spring 1942 to January 1945, 1 million to 1.5 million persons, 90 percent of them Jews.[17] These figures underscore two points. First, they illustrate the breathtaking speed of the Holocaust. By late fall 1943, the Nazis had murdered 2 million to 2.5 million Jews in the six death factories, five of which had completed their work and were closed, leaving only Auschwitz-Birkenau, whose gassing and crematorium facilities went into full operation in spring 1942, still in operation. The German armies on the eastern front were on the offensive until January 1943. The Luftwaffe had control of the skies behind the front lines for a longer period than that. The front lines did not begin to move west significantly until summer and fall 1943. These military facts suggest that even if Stalin had been willing to devote resources to destroying the extermination centers, there was little his military forces could have done so far behind German front lines between 1941 and 1943. The research remains to be done concerning such an issue. The facts of distance, the momentum of the war, and the remaining strength of the German military all suggest that the chances for doing so were slim, yet, as we will see, not nonexistent.

In January 1944 and throughout the spring, the eastern front began to move west as the Germans retreated in order to build up forces in the West to face the expected Anglo-American invasion in France. On January 27, 1944, the Red Army finally broke the 880-day siege of Leningrad. In February 1944, the Germans were in retreat on every sector of the eastern front. By late March, the front was fifty miles from eastern Galicia.[18] In April 1944, the Crimean offensive drove the Germans out of the last Soviet territory still under their control. The massive Belorussian offensive, Operation Bagration of June through August 1944 in the center of the eastern front, drove the Germans out of Minsk, Vilnius, Bialystok, and Lublin; left the Red Army on the outskirts of Warsaw; and, as John Erickson put it, "broke the back" of the Wehrmacht.[19] Majdanek was liberated in July 1944, and the former and no longer functioning death camps at Chelmno, Belzec, and Sobibor were now in Soviet hands. In September 1944, the Soviet journalist Vasily Grossman, arriving with the Red Army at the death camp at Treblinka, wrote vivid reports of the enormity of the crime.[20]

So, the question of what the Soviet military could have done to stop or hinder the killing of Europe's Jews by the spring of 1944 becomes a narrower one: What could the Soviet Air Force and the Red Army do to destroy the gas chambers, crematoriums, and rail lines leading to the one remaining death camp, Auschwitz-Birkenau, from spring 1944 to January 1945? In particular, would it have been possible to prevent the mass murder of the half million Hungarian Jews who were deported by rail to Auschwitz-Birkenau from April to November 1944?[21] As Gilbert's map "Distant Deportations, June 1944," indicates, in June 1944, while deportations of Hungarian Jews to Auschwitz-Birkenau were in progress, the eastern front was about 220 miles from the death camp.[22] By early August 1944, as the gas chambers and crematoriums worked at a furious pace, the front was now about 100 miles from Auschwitz.[23] American and British aircraft bombed factories near Auschwitz. Did the Soviet Air Force think of doing likewise?

The growth of Soviet air power in World War II suggests that if Stalin had been interested in using his military to destroy the death factories, he had formidable tools at his disposal to do so. The Soviet Air Force was massive. By mid-1943 it had gained air superiority over much of the eastern front (though not yet over occupied Poland), an accomplishment that one of its historians calls "one of the most remarkable turnabouts of World War II."[24] During the war, the Soviets produced a staggering number of aircraft—125,655 in all. The production figures by year were as follows: 9,770 in 1941; 25,436 in 1942; 34,884 in 1943; 40,241 in 1944; and 15,317 in 1945 up to May 10. Of these, according to the Soviet official history, 54,000 were fighters designed to attack other planes, 35,000 Shturmoviks intended to support ground forces, and 16,000 bombers.[25] Soviet strategists focused on integration of air and ground forces, or "combined arms operations" rather than the long-range "strategic" bombing characteristic of American and British bomber offensives.[26] The Soviet air arsenal also included several capable medium-range bombers. Beginning in 1940 and continuing to the end of the war, 11,427 models of the Pe-2, with a range of 746 miles and top speed of 336 miles per hour, were built. Beginning in 1943, the Soviets produced 2,527 units of the Tu-2 (Tupelev-2) with a top speed of 340 miles per hour and a range of 1,305 miles. Reflecting its focus on the combined arms operations, the single most produced plane was the Il-2 (Ilyushin-2); 36,163 models were built of this ground-attack aircraft which played a decisive role in the air over the great land battles of the eastern front, such as the Belorussian campaign.[27] During the final stages of the war, the Soviet air forces also included 862 American B-25 and 2,908 British A-20 Havoc medium-range bombers.

The official history of the Soviet Air Force bristles with indignation at Western efforts to minimize its contribution to the defeat of Nazi Germany: "What really caused the German defeat? Bourgeois falsifiers of World War II history attempt by any means at their disposal to minimize the role of the Soviet Air Force in the defeat of the Luftwaffe" by stressing the importance of Anglo-American bombing raids. "However, historical documents and facts overthrow these unfounded assertions. Before 1943, when the Fascist Luftwaffe was still strong and the battle for the control of the air was still in question, the American and English air forces had flown almost no raids against air targets in Germany." Moreover, the opening of the second front in 1944 had "no real influence on the struggle of our air force with Fascist air power." In 1944, Germany increased aircraft production from 24,365 to 40,482 planes. Hence, the Soviet historians argued that the loss of control of the air which the Germans suffered in 1943 was not due to Anglo-American bombing of German aircraft plants but to "the defeat of its best squadrons on the Soviet-German front." In the first half of 1944, partly due to an expansion by 3,000 planes, the Soviet Air Force "had nearly a fourfold advantage" over the Luftwaffe in the skies over the eastern front, making it possible for "the Soviet Air Force to complete its assignment of defeating the Fascist air forces without Anglo-American help."[28]

Even if we assume that this special pleading had more to do with Marxist-Leninist polemics than with a balanced analysis of the interaction of how both the Western Allies and the Soviet Union destroyed German air power, the power and activity of the Soviet Air Force was impressive. Between 1941 and 1945, it flew 3,124,000 sorties in which it dropped 30,450,000 bombs totaling 660,000 tons. Its pilots destroyed 57,000 German aircraft and 77,000 planes including those of Germany's allies. This figure was 2.5 times greater than Germany suffered on all other fronts. "Therefore," the official Soviet historians continue, "the Luftwaffe was defeated basically on the Soviet-German front."[29] They write that the Soviet Air Force gained "mastery of the air . . . in the summer of 1943." Specifically, in July 1943, "after the battle for Kursk, when the Luftwaffe lost about 3,700 aircraft in one and a half months control of the air completely and irrevocably passed into our hands along the entire Soviet-German front."[30] The official history adds that "in addition to our operations in support of troops, the air force struck systematically at administrative and political centers and military targets deep in the enemy's rear, and also against rail transportation and the enemy's strategic reserves."[31] Such "strategic bombing" amounted to only 5.4 percent of all Soviet Air Force sorties. However, given the huge total numbers of sorties flown, this meant that between 1941 and 1945, the official history records 168,000 missions as strategic bombing.[32]

These 168,000 strategic bombing missions included strikes

at administrative-political and military-industrial targets, harbors, naval bases, railroads, reserves and other targets deep in the enemy's rear. . . . As early as June and July of 1941, long-range bombers of the Supreme Command, together with aircraft from the Black Sea and Baltic Fleets, struck at targets in the oil fields in Rumania and the Western Ukraine, and also attacked military and industrial targets in Konigsberg and Danzig. Beginning on August 8, 1941, our bombers made several attacks on the capital of Fascist Germany, Berlin. Later in the war, especially in its third period, our attacks against the war industries and administrative centers increased. In a number of cases, they became major air operations. . . . Our operations against targets deep in the rear caused the enemy material losses, and forced the German command to shift considerable forces and antiaircraft equipment deep to the rear, thereby weakening defenses along the front.[33]

So if the Soviet air forces were able to conduct operations such as those just described as early as 1941, could some of the 168,000 strategic bombing sorties have included attacks on the six extermination camps while they were in operation even in the first two years of the war on the eastern front? If the Soviet Air Force was able to penetrate German defenses and deliver bombs far behind enemy lines on the aforementioned missions, could it also have done so in attacks on death camps? Was the issue ever raised? The research remains to be done.

The official history draws attention to another aspect of the air war that could be relevant for the Allies and the Final Solution, namely, assistance to armed partisan units fighting behind enemy lines. Indeed, it proudly notes that for "the first time in military history," aircraft were used to support partisans in the enemy rear. The official history refers to 109,000 sorties into the enemy's rear, including 13,000 that included landing on airfields and landing strips held by partisan units, which delivered 17,000 tons of ammunition, guns, food, radio transmitters, and medicine. Eighty-three thousand men were removed from partisan units and returned by air. According to the official history, "The evacuation of badly wounded and sick men from the enemy's rear saved the lives of tens of thousands of brave patriots."[34] If the Soviet Air Force was able "for the first time in military history" to use aircraft to aid partisan units, did it also have the capability to aid partisan units who would have attacked the death camps while they were operating to hinder or stop the Final Solution?

Finally, the official history points to another relevant dimension of the air war: aerial reconnaissance. Eleven percent of all sorties flown during the war were reconnaissance missions over and behind enemy lines. The proportion of photographic (as opposed to visual) observation increased from 10 percent in 1941 to 87 percent in 1945. During the war, 6,500,000 square kilometers (2,500,000 square miles) were photographed.[35] What, if anything, did the Soviet Air Force reconnaissance missions reveal regarding the Final Solution? Were these photographs analyzed at the time by Soviet intelligence agencies?

In light of the military capabilities of the Soviet Air Force, it is clear that from late 1943 to early 1945, and especially from spring 1944 to January 1945, the case for the possibility of effective Soviet aerial bombardment of the death factories becomes a more powerful one. The Soviet armed forces' Belorussian campaign, launched on June 22, 1944, destroyed the Wehrmacht's Army Group Center, liberated the last vestiges of German-occupied Soviet territory, paved the way for the invasion of Poland, and brought the Red Army to within a hundred miles of the Hungarian border. The Soviet Air Force joined the battle with 5,683 aircraft linked to five armies and one thousand bombers.[36] Vasily Grossman reported on the Belorussian campaign from Bobryusk, a heavily fortified German position protecting Army Group Center along the Berezina River above the Pripet Marshes.[37]

Von Hardesty, a historian of Soviet air power, summarizes the impact of Soviet air power between June 22 and July 4, 1944, as follows. "By July 4, the Soviet Belorussian offensive had achieved its objectives: Army Group Center ceased to exist as a military entity. The German High Command had lost nearly 300,000 men in less than two weeks. As a component in this dramatic victory, the V.S. had flown 55,011 sorties from June 22 to July 4, an average of 4,500 sorties per day. Over Belorussia, Soviet tactical air might flew into combat on an unprecedented scale, giving the V.S. absolute air superiority during the entire offensive."[38] Moreover, the Soviet Air Force in this campaign for the first time made skillful use of longer-range medium-range bombers: the LL-4, B-25 Mitchell, A-20 Havoc, Li-2. This vast air power over Bobryusk was unleashed against the Wehrmacht with devastating results in a massive battle that took place five hundred miles from Auschwitz.

The power of the Red Army and Air Force led to massive death and destruction of the German armed forces. About 52 percent of all German battlefield deaths took place on the eastern front. Moreover, a large portion of the 23 percent of the German soldiers who died in the final battles in Germany in the spring of 1945 died fighting the Red Army.[39] Rüdiger Overmans's findings concern time as well as location of death. According to Overmans, 34 percent of all German military deaths took place in 1944. Of the 1,802,000 German soldiers who died that year, 68 percent, or 1,232,946 soldiers, died on the eastern front (compared to 14 percent or 244,891 on the western front). This figure was 45 percent of all German battlefield deaths in the war. In August 1944 alone, 277,465 German soldiers died on the eastern front, meaning that on average, 8,950 German soldiers were dying at the hands of the Red Army and Air Force every day that month.[40] These figures are partly a consequence of Soviet control of the air. As the Red Army and Air Force were inflicting such losses on the German armed forces, would it have been possible to use a fraction of that air power to destroy Auschwitz-Birkenau before 500,000 Hungarian Jews were murdered there? The Soviet Air Force had aircraft with range long enough to reach the camp.

The evidence presented here suggests that if Stalin had had the political will to do so, he had the military capabilities at his disposal to have tried to save some of the Jews of Hungary. Perhaps even earlier interventions from the air might have been possible. Or, he could have invited the Americans and British with their longer-range bombers to help in the task. As Vasily Grossman reported, there was no shortage of pilots, Jews and non-Jews, in the Soviet Air Force willing and able to undertake such dangerous missions over German held territory.

Geography and military capability meant that the Soviet Union was in a better position to militarily intervene to stop or slow the Final Solution than were the Western Allies. Doing so would have required making an addition to the war's aims—something Stalin, whose own anti-Semitism burst into full bloom in the postwar period, was not interested in doing.[41] Yet it appears that probably by late spring 1943, if not earlier, and certainly by early spring 1944, the Soviet Union had a huge number of aircraft with the range to strike the death camps. Important questions about the chronology and geography of the war on the eastern front and the Holocaust remain to be addressed. This essay is an effort to encourage an overdue examination of questions which Martin Gilbert's maps of the 1980s raised but to which we still do not have good answers.

NOTES

A longer version of this essay appears in Jeffrey Herf, "The Nazi Extermination Camps and the Ally to the East: Could the Red Army and Air Force Have Stopped or Slowed the Final Solution?" *Kritika* 4, no. 4 (Fall 2003): 913–30. I would like to thank the editors of *Kritika* for their comments and permission to reprint material from this essay.

1. Leni Yahil, *The Holocaust: The Fate of European Jewry* (New York: Oxford University Press, 1990), 404.

2. See first Martin Gilbert, *Auschwitz and the Allies* (New York: Holt, Rinehart and Winston, 1981), but also the use of the term "Allies" in Robert Rozett's excellent "Bibliographical Essay" which concludes the *Holocaust Encyclopedia:* Robert Rozett, "Bibliographical Essay," in *The Holocaust Encyclopedia,* ed. Walter Laqueur (New Haven, CT: Yale University Press, 2001), 730–31. See also Michael J. Neufeld and Michael Berenbaum, eds., *The Bombing of Auschwitz: Should the Allies Have Attempted It?* (New York: St. Martin's Press, 2000); Richard Levy, "The Bombing of Auschwitz: A Critical Analysis," *Holocaust and Genocide Studies* 10, no. 3 (1996): 267–98; Robert Herzstein, "Is It Time to Stop Asking Why the West Failed to Save More Jews?" *Holocaust and Genocide Studies* 12, no. 2 (Fall 1998): 326–38.

3. On the Soviet war effort, see John Erickson, *Stalin's War with Germany: The Road to Stalingrad* (London: Weidenfeld and Nicolson, 1975; New Haven, CT: Yale University Press, 1999); and John Erickson, *Stalin's War with Germany: The Road to Berlin* (London: Weidenfeld and Nicolson, 1983; New Haven, CT: Yale University Press, 1999). Citations are to the 1999 editions. Amir Weiner's *Making Sense of War: The Second World War and the Bolshevik Revolution* (Princeton, NJ: Princeton University Press, 2001) does address the issue of the Holocaust in the context of the war, though not in regard to the Soviet military response. The now-standard single-volume history of the Holocaust, Yahil's *The Holocaust: The Fate of European Jewry,* discusses the Soviet Union in regard to possibilities of rescue and partisan warfare but, again, not with reference to the possibilities of action by the Red Army and Air Force.

4. See Christopher Browning, *Nazi Policy, Jewish Workers, German Killers* (New York: Cambridge University Press, 2000); Christopher Browning, *The Path to Genocide* (New York: Cambridge University Press, 1992); Christopher Browning, *Fateful Months: Essays on the Emergence of the Final Solution* (New York: Cambridge University Press, 1985); Omer Bartov, *Hitler's Army: Soldiers, Nazis and War in the Third Reich* (New York: Oxford University Press, 1991); Richard Breitman, *The Architect of Genocide: Himmler and the Final Solution* (New York: Knopf, 1991); and Gerhard Weinberg,

A World at Arms: A Global History of World War II (New York: Cambridge University Press, 1994).

5. See Weinberg, *World at Arms;* as well as Horst Boog, Jürgen Förster, and Joachim Hoffmann, eds., *Germany and the Second World War,* vol. 4, *The Attack on the Soviet Union* (Oxford: Clarendon Press, 1998); Richard Overy, *Why the Allies Won* (New York: Norton, 1995); and Omer Bartov, *The Eastern Front 1941–1945: German Troops and the Barbarization of Warfare,* 2nd ed. (New York: Palgrave, 2000).

6. Richard Breitman, *Official Secrets: What the Nazis Planned, What the British and Americans Knew* (New York: Hill and Wang, 1998), 153–54.

7. Weiner, *Making Sense of War,* 209.

8. On radio broadcasts and press reports of 1942 and 1943 by the Jewish Anti-Fascist Committee and also by the Freies Deutschland in Moscow that referred to the mass murder of the Jews, see Jeffrey Herf, *Divided Memory: The Nazi Past in the Two Germanys* (Cambridge, MA: Harvard University Press, 1997), 22–25.

9. Erickson, *Stalin's War with Germany: Road to Stalingrad;* Erickson, *Stalin's War with Germany: Road to Berlin.*

10. Erickson, *Stalin's War with Germany: Road to Berlin,* ix.

11. Weinberg, *World at Arms,* 708, 751, 780–81.

12. Gilbert, *Auschwitz and the Allies;* Martin Gilbert, *The Macmillan Atlas of the Holocaust* (New York: Macmillan, 1982); Martin Gilbert, *The Second World War: A Complete History* (New York: Henry Holt, 1989).

13. See Map 1, "Deportation, Massacre and Revolt, July 1943," in Gilbert, *Macmillan Atlas,* 162. For maps on the distance between the death camps and the front in 1942 and 1943, see pp. 119, 133, 154, 160.

14. See "Behind the Lines in the East, winter 1942–1943," and "The Eastern Front and the Red Army Advance, July–August 1943," in Gilbert, *Second World War,* 362, 454; and "Deportations, Massacre and Revolt, October 1943," in Gilbert, *Macmillan Atlas,* 173.

15. Judith Tydor Baumel, "Extermination Camps," in Laqueur, *Holocaust Encyclopedia,* 174.

16. On the Einsatzgruppen, see Leni Yahil, "The Final Solution: The First Stage; Einsatzgruppen," in Yahil, *Holocaust,* 253–87. See also Christopher Browning, *Ordinary Men: Reserve Police Battalion 101 and the Final Solution in Poland* (New York: HarperCollins, 1992). On what the Western allies knew about the actions of the Order Police, see Breitman, *Official Secrets,* 27–68.

17. Baumel, "Extermination Camps," 174–79. Also see Yahil, *Holocaust,* 356–62.

18. Gilbert, *Second World War,* 485–520; Erickson, *Stalin's War with Germany: Road to Berlin,* 137–91.

19. Erickson, *Stalin's War with Germany: Road to Berlin,* 199–247.

20. On Grossman, see Francois Furet, *The Passing of an Illusion: The Communist Idea in the Twentieth Century* (Chicago: University of Chicago Press, 1995), 468–77. For Grossman's wartime essays, see Vasily Grossman, *Années de Guerre* (Paris: B. Arthaud, 1945).

21. Asher Cohen, "Hungary," in Laqueur, *Holocaust Encyclopedia,* 314–21.

22. Map 2, "Distant Deportations, June 1944," in Gilbert, *Macmillan Atlas,* 194.

23. See "Deportations from Central Hungary, 15 May–8 July 1944," and "Deportations from Ruthenia and Northern Transylvania, 15 May–8 July 1944," maps in Gilbert, *Macmillan Atlas,* 196–97.

24. Von Hardesty, *Red Phoenix: The Rise of the Soviet Air Force, 1941–1945* (Washington, DC: Smithsonian Institution Press, 1982), 222.

25. Ibid., 252.

26. Overy, *Why the Allies Won,* 212–14.

27. Hardesty, *Red Phoenix,* 250–51.

28. Ministry of Defense of the USSR, *The Soviet Air Force in World War II: The Official History Originally Published by the Ministry of Defense of the USSR,* ed. Ray Wagner, trans. Leland Fetzer (New York: Doubleday, 1973), 382–83.

29. Ibid., 380.

30. Ibid., 381.

31. Ibid., 379.

32. Ibid., 385.

33. Ibid., 385–86.

34. Ibid., 386.

35. Ibid., 385.

36. Ibid., 189.

37. Vasily Grossman, *With the Red Army in Poland and Byelorussia* (London: Hutchinson, 1945), 10. Also cited by Hardesty, *Red Phoenix,* 194. In his dispatch (later included in his book *With the Red Army in Poland and Byelorussia*), Grossman described the scene of the thirty-two hundred sorties flown that day: "The sky was tumult . . . with the rhythmic roaring of the dive bombers, the hard, metallic voices of the attack planes, the piercing whine of Yakelov fighters. Fields and meadows were splashed with the darting outlines of hundreds of planes."

38. Hardesty, *Red Phoenix,* 195.

39. Rüdiger Overmans, *Deusche militärische Verluste im Zweiten Weltkrieg* (Munich: Oldenbourg, 2000), 265.

40. Ibid., 278–79.

41. On Stalin's postwar anti-Semitism, see Joshua Rubenstein and

Vladimir P. Naumov, eds., *Stalin's Secret Pogrom: The Postwar Inquisition of the Jewish Anti-Fascist Committee* (New Haven, CT: Yale University Press, 2001); Arno Lustiger, *Rotbuch: Stalin und die Juden* (Berlin: Aufbau Verlag, 1998); Arkady Vaksberg, *Stalin Against the Jews* (New York: Random House, 1994). See also Vasily Grossman, *Life and Fate* (1980; New York: Harper and Row, 1985).

V. D·I·M·E·N·S·I·O·N·S
O·F M·E·M·O·R·Y

Michael Thad Allen

How Technology Caused the Holocaust: Martin Heidegger, West German Industrialists, and the Death of Being

ONE POWERFUL INTERPRETATION OF THE HOLOCAUST—INAUGURATED, as far as I can determine, first by Martin Heidegger immediately after the war—condemns science and technology. To summarize briefly, the epistemological habits of highly advanced technological societies are supposed to shunt contemplation away from morality, culture, or what is sacred toward what Heidegger labeled "enframing," or the *Gestell*. To adopt the philosopher's somewhat arcane and very personalized vocabulary, an "enframing" mind reduces the world, in its multiplicity and wonder, to no more or less than is needed as input and output for industry and science. Nature, including human nature, becomes what Heidegger labeled "standing reserve." The Holocaust supposedly came to pass because an "enframing" mentality led the managers of Auschwitz to approach humanity itself as raw material, as no more than a resource. Once the sanctity of Being had been discounted and profaned, catastrophe quickly resulted.

This reasoning does offer the immediate advantage of a comparative perspective. If a technocratic-managerial calculus caused the Holocaust, monitory lessons might be drawn not just for Germany but for any advanced industrial society. Auschwitz, in other words, was not unique and could recur in any technological nation. It was Heidegger's expressed aim to encourage such comparisons, equating as he did the totalitarianism of Hitler's Germany with the United States and the Soviet Union. "Agriculture is today," he inveighed in 1949, "a motorized food industry, in essence the same as the manufacture of corpses in gas chambers and extermination camps, the same as the blockade and starvation of countries, the same as the manufacture of hydrogen bombs."[1] Though this citation is well known, its intended audience is not. Heidegger first linked the Holocaust to modern technology before elite businessmen in Bremen, the very elites responsible for manufacture and commerce—in other words, the very community responsible for the "enframing mentality" of modern industry which his essay blamed directly for the gas chambers was sitting before him. This was no unconscious miscalculation, for he repeated this lecture no less than twice to similar audiences, only months later at an elite spa resort in Baden-Baden, the Bühler Höhe; and then, in the fall of 1953, at a special symposium on The Arts in the Age of Technology at the Technical University of Munich. He first published a greatly compressed version of this lecture as one of his single most influential essays, "Die Frage nach der Technik" ("The Question Concerning Technology"), in 1954.[2] Thus, before its publication, Heidegger had rehearsed "The Question Concerning Technology" several times before very similar crowds, namely, the very people most responsible for the reconstruction of West Germany as a modern technological nation after the war. But these were the selfsame managers who had been no less active during rearmament in the mid-1930s or Albert Speer's industrial "miracle" in the time of total war.[3]

Heidegger's two initial venues, the Club zu Bremen and the Bühler Höhe, drew their membership from the upper crust of Germany's educated professionals and economic elite. One member of the audience characterized them, with some exaggeration, as "great merchants, export specialists, shipping and wharf directors, for whom the famous thinker is a fabulous creature or demigod."[4] They invited Heidegger at their own expense during a period when the Allies had forbidden him to lecture at German universities. Hugo Ott credits these private audiences with reinvigorating Heidegger after he had suffered a nervous breakdown shortly after the war's end.[5] Setting aside Heidegger's "demigod" status, why, we might ask, would a private audience of Germany's most elite bankers, civil servants, and industrialists *want* to listen to a mentally unstable philosophical *Schwätzer* (blabbermouth)? Heidegger, as we will see, not only used the venue to imply that they had *no* culture but that the work of their days and hands was responsible for the death of Being. Moreover, he reminded them pointedly, and not inaccurately, that they had shared responsibility for the gas chambers. Why was Heidegger invited at all?

The answer can illuminate why the Nazis' unique penchant for factory-like extermination has so preoccupied interpretations of the Holocaust and why many have found it so compelling to believe that things like technology or bureaucracy caused it—rather than, say, Germans, Nazis, or the SS. Beyond that, it is also an interesting example of West Germans' attempts to come to terms with, rather than "repress," the Nazi past in the immediate postwar years.

Heidegger's text starts with a kind of "world we have lost" meditation. It identifies typical processes of modernization as a new ontological dilemma facing humankind and sets out to define their essence. Heidegger here focuses upon the annihilation of time and space that modern technology makes possible. Though technology can bring that which is distant near, he argues, it by no means brings the "essence" of things to our attention; rather, it obscures what is essential. He contrasts this state of affairs to the ancient Greeks' conception of *poiesis,* which once made it possible for true craftsmen to synthesize heaven and earth, the godlike and the profane—all that is and was essential.[6] Thus Heidegger is willing to allow that true, meaningful culture and *Technik* (technology) are not necessarily antithetical. Yet, under prevailing conditions of modernity, their reconciliation has proven quite impossible. Technology and culture are sundered.

After repeatedly comparing valorous craftwork to modern science-based industry, the final version of this essay condemns modern physics for destroying *poiesis.* "Of what essence is modern technology then, that it could decay into such a state that it applies modern physics?" Heidegger asks. Technology once capable of glory in the hands of the Greeks has, in other words, degenerated under the dead hand of modern science.[7] This diatribe takes up the vast majority of the essay, especially its earliest drafts. Still, Heidegger ends on a surprising note. He proposes salvation through his now-famous *Kehre,* an unexpected "turn" *toward* the "essence" of modern technology itself.

To summarize the forbidding argument in this part of his essay, just as every destiny, or *Geschick,* manifests the Being of beings, he argued, so must the present epoch of modern science and technology. It must also carry within its ripening a new disclosure of Being. This new epoch inevitably needs humanity to wait in attendance at its birth, and Heidegger assured his audiences that renewal could only be born out of the current *Gestell* of modern technology. His essay makes clear his own distaste for contemporary technological society, but for him there was no sense swimming against the tide. There is no going back for Heidegger. Instead, he proposes a new vision of progress, understood ontologically. Even as he acknowledged modern society's culpability for the Holocaust, he also called upon it to evolve. Only by embracing technology's essence, its destiny, he argued, could it do so. As he would develop forcefully in other essays, Heidegger called upon his listeners to maintain a *Haltung* (attitude), a *Gelassenheit* (composure), an openness to this new, coming epoch of Being.[8] This "turning" at least partly explains his ready audience among industrialists and engineers. Rather than exclusively condemning (their) technology as a threat to culture (so common among humanists), Heidegger surprisingly offered this now-famous "turning" as an embrace of modern science and technology. Yet he did so even as he condemned modern industry for causing Auschwitz in the same breath!

Intellectual historians often record that Heidegger delivered his final reworked essay of 1953 at the Bayrische Akademie der schönen Künste. The academy did sponsor the event and published the proceedings, but in fact Heidegger spoke at the Polytechnical University of Munich, again seeking a mixed audience of technical professionals and humanists. It was an event common at engineering schools, which are often prompted to contemplate how to impart "culture" to their charges. Between 1945 and 1955 it was hardly unique. Rather, it was part of a widespread effort in postwar Germany to understand the relationship between technology and culture, often against the implicit (or not so implicit, in the case of Heidegger's earliest draft) background of Auschwitz. All seem to have shared a *mutual* concern for cultural regeneration and the role of organized capital in it, specifically, its unique ability to command modern technology.

In this context, Heidegger's own "turning" is all the more paradoxical when one considers that at Munich in 1953, most of the lectures delivered in conjunction with his own aimed to convince their audience that culture and engineering were scarcely miscible entities and, further, that the engineer threatened to cast the humanist into outer darkness. "What function is left at all to artistic being?" asked the convener of the Munich conference, Emil Preetorius. He went on to summarize in a more simplified form the themes upon which Heidegger (along with others) was to meditate: "Our world is increasingly technicized, rationalized, and forcibly dominated by the tendency to transform and dissolve by mechanization what was formerly understood as a whole, unified, that is, essentially 'individual' human being or object into a mere calculable function."[9]

The remedy, most German humanists argued, was to grant themselves a heroic role, a sentiment widely echoed in such venues. Artists, poets, philosophers—they alone were capable of saving modern society from the culturelessness of technical professionals.[10] To quote one later, well-known editor of the *Gesamtausgabe* (complete edition) of Heidegger's work: "In the midst of the dominance of the essence of technology, it may one day be granted to the arts to bring a saving 'flash of world light' [here obsequiously quoting Heidegger]."[11] This message seemed plausible to many who interpreted the Third Reich as a reign of cretins, contrary to all that was known then and now about the role that intellectuals played in the regime. And among compromised "bearers of culture," who was more prominent than Heidegger himself? Thus his discussion of a mystic *Kehre* fit well in early postwar venues that mixed academic humanists and industrial elites striving together to come to terms with their own role in Germany's catastrophic past.[12] In 1949 and 1950, Heidegger was issuing no less than a call for rebirth; and, contrary to the oft-repeated impression that he wished to reject modern technology, he called upon his audience to embrace it, albeit, again, simultaneously blaming the *Gestell* of modern technology for the Holocaust.

Such accounts as we have imply that these meditations were extraordinarily well received, despite the fact that Heidegger's first draft goes on for no fewer than eighty-one prolix pages![13] One can only imagine the plight of listeners barraged with entire paragraphs consisting of the extended ellipses and parataxis that have been ridiculed, gently or no, by everyone from José Ortega y Gasset to Thomas Sheehan to Rüdiger Safranski. A small sample suffices: "The jug is a thing in so far as it things. Out of the thinging of the thing also occurs and fixes first the presence of the presencing from out of the nature of the jug . . ."[14] When Heidegger delivered this lecture for the second time, on March 25 and 26, 1950, at the Bühler Höhe, the sanatorium's director, Gerhard Stroomann, proudly recorded fifteen hundred people in the audience spilling out into the hallways. Regarding another of Heidegger's talks there, the conservative newspaper *Deutsche Zeitung und Wirtschaftszeitung* warned dyspeptically, "We incline like no other people toward unconditionally raising a spiritual form as an absolute without critique," but in the end recorded the "remarkable response" to Heidegger's appearances.[15]

There seems to have been some disjunction between Heidegger's popularity as a public lecturer and his "official" reception among the "taste professionals" of the media and academia.[16] Whereas even one of his former students (Wilhelm Kamlah, incidentally a professor at a technical university) inveighed against his obtuseness, there is evidence that businessmen, engineers, and top managers found him stimulating. And this opinion seems to have been despite—or maybe even because of—the critical commentary of other, official pundits among what the Germans call the spiritual sciences (*Geisteswissenschaften*).[17] As Jonathan Wiesen notes, at this time German industrial elites were greatly concerned with the reconstitution of German society and worried about much more than the economy. They were hungry for new ways to understand their ethical and cultural role. Holding high a supposed independent spirit among entrepreneurs and already claiming that they, as rational industrialists, had resisted the irrationality of the Nazis in order to rescue the economy from Hitler, many saw themselves as new "bearers of culture" (*Kulturträger*). The "protection of Germany and Europe's cultural essence" fell to them.[18]

Eager attendance at the Club zu Bremen and the Bühler Höhe was not unique, nor was Heidegger the only guru sought out in these efforts to renegotiate postwar culture. There was also an active dialogue among Christians and among political figures, large and small, within all the major parties.[19] But the relationship between technology and modernity was very much a hot topic.[20]

The *Deutsche Zeitung und Wirtschaftzeitung* was intrigued enough by Heidegger's various meditations on technology to send a reporter to interview him in Totnauberg. Once again the paper warned of unbridled metaphysical speculation, but Heidegger's observations drew special interest when he implied that "man does not make technology; rather technology makes man."[21] Again and again in such venues, elites who, more than any others, actually exercised a great deal of command and control over technology still found it fascinating to be told that technology controlled them. This interest would seem to be part of a larger groundswell of sentiment in Germany, identified by Y. Michal Bodemann, in which Germans sought to attribute the recent catastrophe of the Nazi period to "anonymous powers and an inscrutable state machine."[22] But Heidegger was engaged in talk about technology of a much less metaphorical nature, and he addressed it to technical professionals. Just to cite another example, at the one hundredth anniversary of the Jugendstil artists colony of Mathildenhöhe, architects, civil engineers, philosophers, and civic leaders convened in Darmstadt in 1951. Heidegger spoke here alongside José Ortega y Gasset and a bevy of doctoral engineers from Germany's polytechnic universities. A plaque set at the entrance proclaimed, OUR AGE IS AN AGE OF TECHNOLOGY.[23]

Why this interest? My own tentative thesis is that given Germany's prostration after its defeat and occupation and its moral degradation in light of the Holocaust, Heidegger's appeals fell on fertile ground in a brief symbiosis between technologists—industrialists, business moguls, scientists, engineers—on the one hand and more traditional humanists on the other. All seemed more intent upon reworking the Nazi past, not repressing it, and it is tempting to see Heidegger's "turning" toward modern technology as part of what Alexander and Margarete Mitscherlich have called the "inability to mourn."[24] The Mitscherlichs' argument is not that Germans embraced postwar consumer culture in order to repress memory of the Holocaust, as it is commonly summarized, but that Germans could not mourn their *affection* for Adolf Hitler and National Socialism precisely *because* of their knowledge of the Holocaust. They repressed their own desire to mourn the Third Reich in their embrace (dare it be called *Gelassenheit*) of postwar "Americanization." This development took place in an environment in which, at least in the West, Germany was being pried open to rapid, widespread expansion of American-style corporations and new consumer goods. It displaced an economy of scarcity that had spanned fully three generations.

Volker Berghahn notes that whether German intellectuals identified themselves with the Left or the Right, all viewed the hegemony of American culture with trepidation, especially its overtures to the mass consumer. Germany's businessmen and industrialists were literally engineering this transformation, and it would be a mistake to believe that they were any less concerned than anyone else with the Nazi past and German culture. More than one historian has linked the coming of American-style consumer society to Germany with the "repression" of the memory of the Holocaust. Yet Heidegger's early postwar meditations on technology seem more intent upon reworking the Nazi past, not repressing it. This energy put into reworking the past is something that was more widespread initially than often supposed, and otherwise committed political enemies attacked the task from different angles. As Rüdiger Safranski points out, "The 50s and early 60s built up a discourse of catastrophe which coexisted peacefully with the ambition to rebuild, with the concern for social welfare, with happiness in small and short term things . . . with the sober businesslike manner of the prospering Federal Republic of Germany. . . . [Theodor] Adorno painted a picture of horrific capitalistic alienation and did so in order to attract attention once more to a [Frankfurt] Institute for Social Research that was now under the patronage of the business culture and leadership of Mannesmann; Heidegger turned edifying talk of technology against technology—in edifying talks."[25] Talks addressed to engineers and scientists, we might add; Mannesmann was not just sponsoring such venues, its managers were participating in them. The point is not to vilify Adorno—or Heidegger, for that matter—as a sellout by catching him in the act of accepting checks from German capitalists or accusing him of some kind of collusion with former National Socialists in corporations. Rather, these examples show how much mutual effort on the part of intellectuals and business elites was being poured into the reconstitution of German culture.

Berghahn dwells upon the massive funding of public institutions in which discussions of Germany's cultural rebirth *and* Americanization took place simultaneously. The American High Commission for Germany and the Ford Foundation, in particular, undertook to nurture the liberal Left, especially left-leaning former Communists-cum-anti-Communists.[26] The venues in which Heidegger participated were often privately funded, spontaneous initiatives rather than the mixed endeavors such as Berghahn identifies. They likely carried a slight flavor of defiance, as the ostentatious invitation of Heidegger to Bremen while the Allies had forbidden him to lecture elsewhere implies. Certainly this effort was not unique nor strictly defiant. German Christians of all denominations also founded Societies for German-Jewish Cooperation and invited lecturers on theology to address Germany's moral predicament.[27] We might plausibly count institutions like the Club zu Bremen or the Bühler Höhe as conservative, secular counterparts to these efforts to forge a new legitimacy for German culture. But they were undertaken in the spirit of a political religion.

Gerhard Stroomann, the sanatorium director of the Bühler Höhe, made it his explicit mission to rejuvenate German culture through the fine arts. He founded his weekly lecture series immediately upon the withdrawal of the French occupation. And the word "mission" was no metaphor for him, as he wrote in 1946, "given the course of contemporary events . . . how much of the holy flame [of the arts] remains, that depends upon the radiance and heat of this flame—of the pure priesthood—upon the greatness of talent, of genius and much else."[28] Stroomann organized fifty lectures on Wednesday evenings between July 1949 and April 1954. Heidegger participated no fewer than four times. In all such forums, much more than "repression" was going on. Direct allusions to the Holocaust were rare, but mention of the catastrophe of the recent German past was not.

Heidegger's inability to repent his own infatuation with Nazism or publicly condemn the Holocaust has often been taken as rather typical of "repressed memory."[29] If there can be little doubt that, as early as 1934, Heidegger began to struggle with the real, existing manifestations of Nazism itself, he is hardly a role model for any coming to terms with the past, much less for "resistance." As is now well known, his *Introduction to Metaphysics* (1953) and the famous 1966 interview in *Der Spiegel* (published posthumously in 1976) held firm to the "inner truth and greatness of this [National Socialist] movement."[30] Still, firm evidence demonstrates that his work struggles with the consequences of National Socialism—far more, it would seem, than such other prominent German intellectuals of his day as Werner Conze, Otto Brunner, and Theodor Schieder, the interdisciplinary sociologists and historians who would inspire Germany's Bielefeld school after the war.[31] And these figures had done much more than brood over Nietzsche on long walks through the woods. They had sent memorandums to organizations such as the SS's Reichskommissariat for the Strengthening of Germandom, only to chafe when they were ignored. Like Heidegger, they were wont to reinterpret their participation in the Third Reich after the war in terms of global, technological forces imposed externally on German society: "The fully evacuated man is, so to speak, the raw material out of which handymen and executioners of the extermination terror can be formed. He is only just another piece of rational-technical apparatus."[32]

Yet while the Holocaust is invoked often by the French philosophers of the 1970s and 1980s who made Heidegger into something of a grandfather of postmodernism, it disappears from his own work after the end of the 1940s. He already cut it from the 1953 draft of

"The Question Concerning Technology."[33] There he accuses his audience of causing the Death of Being, but not the death of real men and women in gas chambers.

The earliest draft of "Die Frage nach der Technik" thus shows Heidegger at work, risking more of a confrontation with the immediate Nazi past than he ever would before or after. Many critics have roundly condemned his facile and tasteless comparison of the Holocaust to the U.S. and Soviet nuclear weapons research or agribusiness (quoted earlier in this essay).[34] Rarer is any discussion of another passage, in which Heidegger condemns the factory-like extermination of human beings directly. Here he dwells upon the Holocaust with somewhat more sensitivity: "Hundreds of thousands die en masse. Do they die? . . . They become pieces of stock in the inventory of the fabrication of corpses. Do they die? They are liquidated without any notice in extermination camps. And also without such camps."[35] Few scholars would endorse Silvio Vietta's attempt to whitewash the philosopher by stating, "Heidegger expressed himself toward fascism wherever it was possible for him to do so with the philosophical means at his disposal and at the level of understanding that he himself saw as appropriate for Western history."[36] But Heidegger's passage about "extermination camps" in 1949 and 1950 can scarcely be construed as "repressed memory" or "silence."

Thus, by directly confronting himself and his audience with the Holocaust, Heidegger was doing something unusual, if not unheard of. How could he reconcile this condemnation of modernity, technology, and the Holocaust, on the one hand, with his simultaneous embrace of technology's "destiny" (*Geschick*)? And why did engineers, businessmen, and managers of German commerce provide such a ready audience for this message? We may perhaps draw upon the context of other arguments that differed only slightly from Heidegger's own. His assertion that modern, global technology "caused" the Holocaust quickly became a mainstay of academic theories of "functionalism" as well as popular misconceptions of the Holocaust throughout the latter half of the twentieth century. It would be an exaggeration to trace them all back to Heidegger. On the contrary, the widespread preoccupation in the 1950s with *both* technology and the Holocaust suggests that his thoughts on the matter were hardly unique. To put it simply, blaming anonymous forces of global science and technology for the Holocaust was "in the air" after 1945.[37] It is therefore interesting to note what an enormous exculpatory appeal this approach held for both German intellectuals and German businessmen and engineers.

The distinction between culture and modern technology that Heidegger and his humanist colleagues wished to make allowed managers, civil servants, and engineers who had served the Third Reich a philosophical golden parachute. They could escape judgment by pretending that they had "known not what they had done"; if "technology makes men," in other words, technology had made them do it. On the other hand, if technology, the *Gestell,* "standing reserve," and the like work their deeds by nullifying culture, profaning the spirit, reducing everything to industrial raw material and information rather than art and literature—in such a world, neither can Germany's traditional "bearers of culture" be considered part of the problem. They are rather its victims. Richard Wolin puts his finger on this issue directly in his book *The Heidegger Controversy:* "Since Nazism proves in the last analysis to be merely a particular outgrowth of the rise of 'planetary technology,' which itself is a mere 'symptom' of the 'forgetting of Being' that has victimized the history of the West since Plato, the historical specificity of the Hitler years becomes, in the overall scheme of things, *a minor episode*" [emphasis in original].[38]

What is fascinating is how much mutual cooperation and genuine work it required to construct separate spheres for modern technology and culture in order to make possible this escapism. By midcentury, the boundary line had long been blurred between simple technology—understood as artifacts—and complex systems of human knowledge, education, management, consumption, and any number of the other accoutrements of large, technological systems which are normally tallied not as "technology" but as "society" or "culture." The real boundaries between technology, ideology, politics, culture were all becoming impossibly intractable to definition at precisely the point that humanists began decrying the culturelessness of modern, technological society.[39] But insisting on separate spheres had obvious benefits, rhetorically, for both culpable engineers and culpable intellectuals, both of whom could then proceed to ignore each other with just a residual mutual resentment.

To name one cluster of examples, we might choose the leading representative of the German technical professions, Albert Speer. Next to him, we might select a humanist such as Joachim Fest (conservative) or Sebastian Haffner (liberal-Left). What is remarkable is the widespread consensus and even outright collusion among such figures. Haffner had written from exile in London as a war journalist, "Speer symbolizes a type which is becoming increasingly important in all the belligerent nations today: the pure technician, the classless, brilliant man without a past who knows no other goal than to make his way in the world through his technical and organizational abilities. . . . We may get rid of the Hitlers and the Himmlers, but the Speers, whatever happens to this particular man, will be with us a long time."[40] Speer's aides read this quotation in a British newspaper, and Speer's chronicler translated and kept the clipping.

A few years later, at Nuremberg, Speer was already blaming technology and technocrats for delivering Germany into the hands of a manipulating dictator in his closing defense statement: "The means of communication alone enable [the authoritarian system] to mechanize the work of the lower leadership. Thus the new type of uncritical receiver of orders is created. . . . The nightmare of many people, that peoples could be dominated by technology, was almost accomplished in Hitler's authoritarian system." Like Heidegger, Speer meant this lesson to apply to any society, not just Germany: "Every state in the world now faces the danger of being terrorized by technology."[41] In his Nuremberg testimony, Speer had not yet attributed any nefarious, anonymous agency to technology itself in the Holocaust. He had merely identified it as the means by which Adolf Hitler controlled the German people. In his memoirs and subsequent writings, however, he increasingly attributed agency to technology itself.[42] It is little known that the German journalist and historian Joachim Fest published articles on the technocratic mentality of National Socialism far in advance of Albert Speer's own memoirs. Then, years later, it was Fest who helped Speer copyedit and rewrite his best-selling memoirs, *Inside the Third Reich*.[43] These memoirs served to both confirm and popularize admonishments of Nazi technocrats.

The new technocrat as an amoral man, an apolitical man, was an invention of this period. Before 1933 the technocracy movement had been consciously political.[44] The postwar technocrat personified instead a divorce between technology and culture, one which divided technology—conceived as an amoral, apolitical, but above all aphilosophical state of mind—from culture, supposedly the sole repository of the virtuous contemplation of moral, political, in short, philosophical matters.

It is an argument of lasting endurance, and, once again, Joachim Fest's new biography of Albert Speer might serve as an example. Blithely dismissing two generations of scholarship and sanctimoniously chiding Gitta Sereny and Jan van der Vat for suggesting that Speer might have had any motives at all beyond those of an apolitical professional, Fest again presents a technocrat. This book found its way almost immediately into English translation, accompanied by favorable reviews from suitable American taste professionals. In the *New York Times Book Review,* Max Frankel rather preciously summarizes Fest's conclusions: "how easily . . . people will allow themselves to be mobilized into violence, abandoning the humanitarian traditions they have built up over centuries to protect themselves and each other."[45] This kind of pontification would scarcely be so annoying if not for the unquestioned assumption that Speer and others did what they did only because their technological work compelled the *abandonment* of "centuries old" culture. As Ingo Haar so depressingly points out, the Holocaust was brought about precisely by the *interdisciplinary* work of humanists and technically trained professionals.[46] Together they would continue to grope for some kind of viable German culture after the war.

Heidegger only enhanced the appeal of this syncretism, of which Speer, Haffner, and Fest are so exemplary, by arguing that a quasimystical embrace of technology's historic destiny might rescue humankind from the "forgetting" of Being. It is the forgetting of Being, not modern technology itself, that Heidegger blames for Auschwitz. He holds out the hope that a truly cultured people might rescue Being *through* modern technology. What could be more happily endorsed by leading industrialists at once eager to import the innovations of American capitalism and at the same time anxious about Elvis Presley, nylon stockings, and Hollywood? If they embraced Heidegger's "turn" (*Kehre*) in particular, they needed only to keep doing what they were already setting out to do anyway; they needed only to convince themselves of their sensitivity, their own *Gelassenheit* toward Being. Then, according to the philosopher, a *Kultur-Nation* might still be possible, as it had been among the ancient Greeks.

NOTES

Except where noted otherwise, all English translations from German sources in this essay are mine.

1. Martin Heidegger, "Einblick in das was ist," in *Bremer und Freiburger Vorträge,* vol. 1, *Einblick in das was ist: Bremer Vorträge 1949,* ed. Petra Jaeger (Frankfurt am Main: Vittorio Klostermann, 1994), 26; Rüdiger Safranski, *Ein Meister aus Deutschland: Heidegger und seine Zeit* (Frankfurt am Main: Fischer, 1997), 457; Michael Zimmerman, *Heidegger's Confrontation with Modernity: Technology, Politics, Art* (Bloomington: Indiana University Press, 1990), 43. See also Richard Wolin, ed., *The Heidegger Controversy* (Cambridge, MA: MIT Press, 1993), 15 and, for Heidegger's exchange of letters with Herbert Marcuse, 152–64. The Soviet Union had exploded its first atom bomb on August 29, only roughly three months before Heidegger gave this lecture first in Bremen.

2. Martin Heidegger, "Die Frage nach der Technik," in *Die Künste im technischen Zeitalter,* ed. Clemens Graf Podewils (Munich: R. Oldenbourg, 1954). It was reprinted by the Academy of Fine Arts in 1956 and 1966 but is most commonly cited from its 1962 publication in *Die Technik und die Kehre* (Pfullingen: Neske, 1962) or from the *Gesamtausgabe.*

3. Hans-Ulrich Wehler, "Deutsches Bürgertum nach 1945: Exitus oder Phönix aus der Asche?" *Geschichte und Gesellschaft* 27 (2001): 617–34.

4. Heinrich Petzet, *Auf einen Stern zugehen: Begegnungen und Gespräche mit Martin Heidegger 1929–1976* (Frankfurt am Main: Societäts Verlag; 1983), 59.

5. Hugo Ott, *Martin Heidegger: Unterwegs zu seiner Biographie* (Frankfurt am Main: Campus, 1992), 340–41. Petzet also notes that Bühler Höhe director Gerhard Stroomann was commemorated upon his death as one of the "true promoters of Martin Heidegger." Petzet, *Auf einen Stern zugehen,* 74.

6. Martin Heidegger, "Erde und Himmel, die Göttlichen und die Sterblichen," in *Bremer und Freiburger Vorträge,* 17.

7. Heidegger, "Die Frage nach der Technik," in Podewils, *Die Künste,* 27.

8. For example, Martin Heidegger, "Denken ist Andenken," in *Reden und andere Zeugnisse eines Lebensweges 1910–1976* (Frankfurt am Main: Vittorio Klostermann, 2000), esp. 527–28.

9. Emil Preetorius, "Eroeffnung der Vortragsreihe," in Podewils, *Die Künste,* 12. See Manfred Schroeter, "Bilanz der Technik," in Podewils, *Die Künste,* 189.

10. Gustav Fiek, "Begrüssungsansprache," in *Mensch und Raum,* ed. Otto Bartning (Darmstadt: Neuer Darmstädter Verlagsanstalt, 1952), 10.

11. Friedrich-Wilhelm von Hermann, "Technik und Kunst im seyns-

geschichtlichen Fragehorizont," in *Kunst und Technik,* ed. Walter Biemel and Friedrich-Wilhelm von Hermann (Frankfurt am Main: Vittorio Klostermann, 1989), 46.

12. The cryptic conclusion of "The Question Concerning Technology," reworked for the Technische Universität Munich in 1953, reduces the *Kehre* section of the 1949 essay to an almost vestigial discussion and closes instead with a quotation from Hölderlin's *Patmos:* "Wo aber Gefahr ist wächst / Das Rettende auch" (Heidegger, "Die Frage nach der Technik," in Podewils, *Die Künste*).

13. The Club zu Bremen apparently has no records of the event other than that it happened, for on December 1, 1949, when Heidegger was first invited, the club itself still lay in ruins and had to meet in the Bremer Rathaus. Its members had not yet restarted their newsletter, and, as it was an exclusive, private membership, no local press seems to have reported on it. Eckehart Löhr, Geschäftsführer des Clubs zu Bremen, to author, March 26, 2002, and telephone conversation of March 3, 2002.

14. Martin Heidegger, *Bremer und Freiburger Vorträge,* vol. 1, *Einblick in das was ist: Bremer Vorträge 1949,* ed. Petra Jaeger (Frankfurt am Main: Vittorio Klostermann, 1994), 16. Petzet, *Auf einen Stern zugehen,* 58–83.

15. A. F., "Bühler-Höhen-Luft," *Deutsche Zeitung und Wirtschaftszeitung,* October 14, 1950. See Gerhard Stroomann, *Aus meinem roten Notizbuch: Ein Leben als Arzt auf Bühlerhöhe,* ed. Heinrich Petzet (Frankfurt am Main: Societäts-Verlag, 1960), 206–7.

16. According to Heidegger's rather obsequious student Heinrich Petzet (*Auf ein Stern zugehen,* 59), the reception was also good.

17. Wilhelm Kamlah, "Martin Heidegger und die Technik, ein offener Brief," *Deutsche Universitäts Zeitung* 9, no. 11 (1954): 10–13; and, most bluntly, upon the occasion of Heidegger's 1953 publication of his *Einführung in die Metaphysik,* see Dolf Sternberger, "Martin Heidegger Bleibt unverständlich," *Die Gegenwart* 8 (1953): 639–42. Sternberger titled his sections "Wut" ("Rage"), "Pomp" ("Pomp"), "Orakel" ("Oracle"), and "Nebel" ("Fog"). Similarly, see Richard Scheffler, "Martin Heidegger und die Frage nach der Technik," *Zeitschrift für philosophische Forschung* 9 (1955): 116–27, which opposed Heidegger's perceived mysticism and lack of any concrete ethical pragmatism with Christian democracy.

18. Jonathan Wiesen, *West German Industry and the Challenge of the Nazi Past, 1945–55* (Chapel Hill: University of North Carolina Press, 2001), 160.

19. Frank Stern, *The Whitewashing of the Yellow Badge: Antisemitism and Philosemitism in Postwar Germany* (New York: Pergamon Press, 1992), 320–23.

20. Richard Beyler and Morris Low, "Science Policy in Post-1945 West

Germany and Japan," in Mark Walker, ed., *Science and Ideology: A Comparative History* (London: Routledge, 2003), 102–9.

21. "Martin Heidegger fühlt sich mißverstanden: Begegnung mit dem Philosophen, der kein 'Heideggerianer' ist," *Deutsche Zeitung und Wirtschaftszeitung,* February 17, 1951. I thank Frau M. Maasjosthusmann of the Wirtschaftsarchiv der Universität Köln who was kind enough to send me copies of these articles when no copies of the *Deutsche Zeitung und Wirtschaftszeitung* could be located in the United States.

22. Y. Michal Bodemann, "Eclipse of Memory: German Representations of Auschwitz in the Early Postwar Period," *New German Critique* 75 (1998): 67. I thank Dagmar Herzog for this reference.

23. Otto Bartning, *Mensch und Raum* (*Man and Space*) (Darmstadt: Neuer Darmstädter Verlagsanstalt, 1951), 33. This was the second in a series of Darmstädter Gespräche. The fourth was *Individuum und Organisation* (*Individual and Organization*). The sixth was *Ist der Mensch Messbar?* (*Is the Human Being Measurable?*) These early themes were indicative of the widespread interest in technology, modern organization, and culture.

24. Alexander and Margarete Mitscherlich, *Die Unfähigkeit zu Trauern: Grundlagen kollektiven Verhältens* (Munich: Piper, 1967).

25. Safranski, *Ein Meister aus Deutschland,* 453. See also Anson Rabinbach, *In the Shadow of Catastrophe: German Intellectuals Between Apocalypse and Enlightenment* (Berkeley and Los Angeles: University of California Press, 1997), 166–98.

26. Volker Berghahn, *America and the Intellectual Cold Wars in Europe* (Princeton, NJ: Princeton University Press, 2001).

27. Stern, *Whitewashing of Yellow Badge,* 320.

28. Stroomann, *Aus meinem roten Notizbuch,* 181.

29. Typical perhaps is the visit of Paul Celan to Heidegger's residence in Totnauberg, described in Ott, *Martin Heidegger,* 341–43. When confronted with the Nazi past by Jürgen Habermas, Heidegger also responded as most scholars do when condemned for handling the Holocaust ineptly; that is, having no argument, he resorted to character assassination of the author, suggesting that anyone who "misunderstood" his relationship to National Socialism had not "learned the craft of thinking." Wolin, *Heidegger Controversy,* 188, exchange with Habermas at 186–97, exchange with Herbert Marcuse at 152–64.

30. Martin Heidegger, *Introduction to Metaphysics,* trans. Gregory Fried and Richard Polt (New Haven, CT: Yale University Press, 2000), 213. *Der Spiegel* interview is published in Wolin, *Heidegger Controversy,* 91–115, esp. 103–4.

31. Götz Aly, "Theodor Schieder, Werner Conze oder die Vorstufen der physischen Vernichtung," in *Deutsche Historiker im Nationalsozialismus,* ed.

Winfried Schulze and Otto Gerhard Oexle (Frankfurt am Main: Fischer, 1999), 163–82; Ingo Haar, "'Kämpfende Wissenschaft' Entstehung und Nidergang der völkischen Geschichtswissenschaft im Wechsel der Systeme," in Schulze and Oexle, *Deutsche Historiker im Nationalsozialismus,* 215–40; James Melton, "From Folk History to Structural History: Otto Brunner (1898–1982) and the Radical-Conservative Roots of German Social History," in *Paths of Continuity: Central European Historiography from the 1930s to the 1950s,* ed. Melton and Hartmut Lehmann (Cambridge: Cambridge University Press, 1994), 263–92.

32. Aly, "Theodor Schieder," 175.

33. See, for example, Jean-François Lyotard, *The Differend: Phrases in Dispute* (Minneapolis: University of Minnesota Press, 1988), 43, 56–57, 89–110. "Auschwitz" is the ultimate "differend," the hole in our understanding that gives the lie to any absolute statements of truth and ultimately to the Enlightenment itself. Allusions to National Socialism are sprinkled throughout Michel Foucault's work as well as many others. For a good review, see Richard Wolin, "French Heidegger Wars," in Wolin, *Heidegger Controversy,* 272–300.

34. This comparison is a recurring preoccupation of Richard Wolin's. See his introduction to *Heidegger Controversy,* 15; Richard Wolin, *Heidegger's Children: Hannah Arendt, Karl Löwith, Hans Jonas, and Herbert Marcuse* (Princeton, NJ: Princeton University Press, 2001), 9–10, 13–14, 182, 193–99, 210. See also Michael Zimmerman, *Heidegger's Confrontation with Modernity: Technology, Politics, Art* (Bloomington: Indiana University Press, 1990), 43.

35. Heidegger, *Bremer und Freiburger Vorträge,* 56: "Darum vermag der Mensch den Tod nur und erst, wenn das Seyn selber aus der Wahrheit seines Wesens das Wesen des Menschen in das Wesen des Seyns vereignet. . . . Den Tod in seinem Wesen vermoegen, heisst: sterben koennen."

36. Silvio Vietta, *Heideggers Kritik am Nationalsozialismus und an der Technik* (Tübingen: Max Niemeyer Verlag, 1989), 9. Although elsewhere Heidegger typically equated Russian prisoner-of-war camps with concentration camps, nevertheless, here he identifies the abiding unique means of Nazi genocide as the most horrid instance in which humanity is alienated (*verstellt*) from the truth of being human. Concentration camps barred their victims from experiencing a human death.

37. Jeffrey Herf, "Belated Pessimism: Technology and Twentieth-Century German Conservative Intellectuals," in *Technology, Pessimism, and Postmodernism,* ed. Yaron Ezrahi, Everett Mendelsohn, and Howard Segal (Boston: Kluwer Academic Publishers, 1994), 115–32.

38. Wolin, "French Heidegger Wars," 290. See also Zimmerman, *Heidegger's Confrontation with Modernity,* 256.

39. See also Leo Marx, "The Idea of 'Technology' and Postmodern Pessimism," in Ezrahi, Mendelsohn, and Segal, *Technology, Pessimism, and Postmodernism,* 11–28; and Wiesen, *West German Industry,* 159.

40. Quoted after Werner Durth, *Deutsche Architekten: Biographische Verflechtungen 1900–1970* (Braunschweig: Friedrich Vieweg und Sohn, 1986), 202. I have had to retranslate back into English from Durth's German translation, so the original of Haffner's will not match.

41. Herf, "Belated Pessimism," 128.

42. Albert Speer, *Inside the Third Reich: Memoirs* (New York: Macmillan, 1970); and especially Albert Speer, *Sklavenstaat: Meine Auseinandersetzung mit der SS* (Stuttgart: Deutsche Verlagsanstalt, 1981).

43. Note the almost complete continuity between Fest's first biographical sketch of Albert Speer in Joachim Fest, "Albert Speer und die technizistische Unmoral," in *Das Gesicht des Dritten Reiches* (Munich: R. Piper, 1964), 271–85; Speer's own memoirs, *Inside the Third Reich: Memoirs,* which Fest helped edit with the author; and Fest's more recent work, Joachim Fest, *Speer: Eine Biographie* (Frankfurt am Main: Fischer, 1999). In 1999 Fest magisterially dismisses the original research pertaining to Speer over the previous two decades as not meeting the qualifications "einer annähernd zureichenden historischen Biographie" (of a remotely adequate historical biography) (*Speer,* 8).

44. Mark Walker and Monika Renneberg, "Naturwissenschaftler, Techniker und der Nationalsozialismus," in *Ich diente nur die Technik: Sieben Karrieren zwischen 1940 und 1950,* ed. Alfred Gottwaldt (Berlin: Nicolaische Verlagsbuchhandlung, 1995), 1–32.

45. Max Frankel, review of *Speer: Eine Biographie,* by Joachim Fest, *New York Times Book Review,* October 6, 2002.

46. Ingo Haar, "German 'Eastern Research' and Antisemitism" (paper presented at seventh Lessons and Legacies Conference, University of Minnesota, Minneapolis, November 2, 2002).

Suzanne Brown-Fleming

Recent Historiographical Contributions to the History of the Churches and the Holocaust: The Catholic Case

IN 2001, JAMES CARROLL, A FORMER ROMAN CATHOLIC PRIEST TURNED journalist and novelist, published a provocative book titled *Constantine's Sword: The Church and the Jews.* In a book that is part history, part memoir, and part theological treatise, Carroll makes the following point: "Hitler *had not started* the war on the Jews, even if it was his central purpose . . . to finish it."[1] Carroll states delicately what Daniel Jonah Goldhagen levies as a bold accusation in his recent article "What Would Jesus Have Done? Pope Pius XII, The Vatican, and the Holocaust," which appeared in a January 2002 issue of the *New Republic.* Goldhagen's central argument is this: "the main responsibility for producing this all-time leading Western hatred [of Jews] lies with Christianity. More specifically, with the [Roman] Catholic Church."[2] It seems fair to compare Goldhagen's thesis to a description of anti-Semitism that appeared in an 1892 edition of *L'Osservatore romano,* the Vatican's official daily newspaper founded in Rome in 1861 and owned by the Holy See. In an unsigned article on anti-Semitism in heavily Roman Catholic France, the following statement appeared: "true anti-Semitism is and can be in substance nothing other than Christianity, completed and perfected in Catholicism."[3] By the 1890s, writes sociologist and anthropologist David Kertzer in his devastating study of nineteenth-century anti-Judaism within the Holy See's Secretariat of State, the secretary of state himself "regularly authored unsigned articles in [*L'Osservatore romano*'s] pages, making known the Holy See's opinions on matters of current concern."[4] Kertzer argues that we can therefore view this 1892 statement (and the many others like it) as either coming directly from the secretary of state himself—who, in the Holy See's bureaucracy, is second only to the pope—or, at the very least, as having been vetted by the secretary of state.

Carroll's "war on the Jews," Goldhagen's "all-time leading Western hatred" for Jews, and *L'Osservatore romano*'s "true anti-Semitism" began twenty centuries ago, with the events of the crucifixion of the Jewish prophet Jesus of Nazareth by Roman authorities; the subsequent birth of the Jewish sectarian "Jesus movement"; and the gradual split between Judaism and Christianity. Carroll and Goldhagen argue that Christian anti-Judaism, with relentless and ever-increasing intensity, culminated (alongside other factors) in the Holocaust.[5] Until recently, scholarly debate had reached an uneasy stalemate on the subject. Scholars focused on religion-based anti-Judaism but separated it from supposedly more deadly forms of post-nineteenth-century anti-Semitism (racial, political, economic, cultural, etc.) and certainly from Daniel Goldhagen's uniquely German "eliminationist" anti-Semitism.[6] Walter Zwi Bacharach's characterization of Catholic-Jewish relations provides a good summary of the established canon on this subject. Christians persecuted Jews—that is, labeled them, ghettoized them, expelled them, and restricted their economic possibilities—through the centuries due to Jewish resistance to the practice of the Christian *religion*. Christians remained interested in the survival of Jews in order to convert them, while rejecting racist theories. Nazism, on the other hand, called for the physical annihilation of Jews and the total eradication of Judaism. For the Roman Catholic Church between the years 1933 and 1945, protection of Christians and promotion of the interests of the church took precedence over humanitarian concern for the fate of Jews. Bacharach writes that it is difficult to prove the existence of a direct link between Catholic anti-Judaism and Nazi anti-Semitism, though ideological continuity between Nazism and Catholic anti-Judaism existed in that Catholics played an important part in "disseminating the negative image of the Jew."[7]

An increasing number of scholars defy the canon that because Catholic anti-Judaism did not equal Nazi anti-Semitism, it should be viewed and studied separately from the events leading to the Holocaust. Recent work also questions other, related canons, and in the remainder of this brief essay, I shall address five of them specifically. These are: first, the fiction of supposed lack of Catholic support for the Nazi movement in the 1920s and early 1930s (a degree of support existed); second, the half-truth of a laudable Catholic "resistance" record vis-à-vis the Nazi regime (it only rarely had to do with Nazi anti-*Jewish* policy); third, the fiction of lacking Catholic participation in the crimes of the Holocaust (in recent case studies, Catholic perpetrators outnumbered Protestant perpetrators); fourth, the fiction that Catholic institutions were not involved in the use of forced and slave labor (they were); and, fifth and finally, the insensitivity and lack of full disclosure in Catholic statements about guilt and responsibility for Nazism in the first two decades after the war.

We turn first to the supposed lack of Catholic support for the Nazi movement in the 1920s and early 1930s. Due to traditional loyalties to the Catholic Center Party prior to its dissolution in 1933, as a rule Catholic electoral support for Nazism *was* weaker than was Protestant electoral support in the years leading up to 1933.[8] But its weakness relative to Protestantism did not *exclude* the possibility of Catholic electoral support for Nazism. In his 1998 study of the predominantly Catholic Black Forest–Baar region of southern Baden, German historian Oded Heilbronner found that as early as 1930, the Nazis won an above-average number of votes and significant support in a number of Catholic communities in that region. In this case, the long-held model that Catholic electoral support for Nazism was too nonexistent to be of importance did not apply.[9] Further regional studies are required in order to tell us whether other Catholic communities might also have supported Nazism to a previously unsuspected degree.

Second, the Catholic "resistance" record vis-à-vis the Nazi regime: new studies providing in-depth analysis of individual German bishops and priests confirm *acquiescence,* not resistance, in the face of Nazi officialdom, *except* in the face of anti-Catholic measures. New studies confirm enthusiasm for the potent nationalism, war aims, and anti-Judaism crucial to Nazi ideology, a finding first introduced to historians in the pathbreaking works of Saul Friedländer, Guenter Lewy, and Gordon Zahn in the 1960s.[10] In 2000, a dissertation entitled "Nationales Denken im Katholizmus der Weimarer Republik" by German theologian Reinhard Richter provided evidence that strongly nationalistic thinking as a vital part of the German Catholic worldview was not limited to bishops alone.[11] In another study, German historian Wolfgang Stücken examines the moral stewardship of Casper Klein, archbishop of Paderborn (1920–41), and Lorenz Jäger, his successor as archbishop (1941–73) during the Nazi era. Dr. Stücken's conclusions are distinctly unflattering. Both archbishops placed church political strategy and, as threats to the church increased, continued existence of the church and church life within the Nazi state above the fate of Jewish Germans or other victims. Reflecting on the collectively issued German bishops' Fulda pastoral letter of 1943,[12] which explicitly condemned the killing of "innocent persons of foreign races and ancestry," Archbishop Jäger insisted that the Catholic Church's proper concern should be limited to "our German brothers and sisters, who are of one blood with us."[13] Then and thereafter, Archbishop Jäger preached support for the German war as an epic defense of Christian civilization against Bolshevism.[14]

To take another example, Bishop Clemens August von Galen, who remains famous for his courageous stand against Nazi euthanasia policy, was not friendly toward beleaguered Jews. In her book *Bishop von Galen: German Catholicism and National Socialism,* published in 2002, Beth Griech-Polelle examines Bishop von Galen's use of Catholic values, theology, and ideology to oppose *selectively* certain elements of National Socialism, such as the euthanasia project, while *choosing to remain silent* on issues concerning the discrimination, ghettoization, deportation, and murder of Jews. Unlike earlier studies that place von Galen in the pantheon of resisters to Nazism, Professor Griech-Polelle's research reveals a more complex figure who moved *between* the boundary of dissent and complicity during the Nazi regime and who linked Jews to Bolshevism.[15]

Professor Kevin Spicer has identified and collected material on over two hundred Catholic priests, scattered across the dioceses of Berlin, Freiburg, Munich-Freising, Augsburg, Eichstätt, Paderborn, and Würzburg, who either belonged to the Nazi Party or publicly aligned themselves with the Hitler movement and its ideology. Professor Spicer's initial findings indicate that priests who supported National Socialism did so for a variety of reasons, which included anti-Semitism and nationalism but also included antiliberalism, anti-Bolshevism, opportunism, or alienation from their colleagues and church superiors.[16] In the diocese of Speyer, Thomas Fandel similarly discovered twenty-six priests who supported the Nazi Party outright among 346 personnel files he analyzed.[17]

Moving on to the third theme I would like briefly to address, I assert that being a Roman Catholic did *not,* as Pope Pius XII's June 1945 radio address from Vatican City might have one believe, exclude the possibility of becoming a Holocaust perpetrator. In his quantitative study of 1,581 men and women involved in Nazi genocide, Michael Mann concludes that among Holocaust perpetrators, a majority came from Catholic regions. Dr. Mann was able to determine the religion of the perpetrator's own family in 22 percent of his sample, and Catholics (especially Bavarians) were *over*represented.[18] Aleksander Lasik's study of Auschwitz SS men showed Catholics as *more* likely to become perpetrators than their Protestant counterparts. Throughout the camp's entire history, a total of 6,800 SS men and about 200 SS women supervisors served in the camp.[19] The personnel papers at Auschwitz contained a query about "religious persuasion," though, after 1937, SS leadership pressured its members to sever their affiliation with any organized religion by way of introducing a form pledging no religious denomination. Information about religious persuasion was available for 9 percent (roughly 630) of the 7,000 SS personnel under study. Of these 630, a total of 237 (nearly 40 percent) proclaimed themselves Catholic.[20]

Fourth, new research indicates that Roman Catholic institutions actively participated in the forced and slave labor system in Germany during World War II. According to Professor John Delaney's report in the June 2002 Association of Contemporary Church Historians Newsletter, news of utilization of forced labor by a Catholic seminary in Paderborn first surfaced in July 2000. In August 2000, following intensive (and laudable) research efforts by parishes, religious orders, Catholic institutions, dioceses, and archdioceses across Germany, the bishop of Mainz and current chair of the German Bishops' Conference Karl Lehmann announced that seven thousand foreign workers and prisoners of war had been used as forced labor in parishes, monasteries, abbeys, convents, and church educational and charitable institutions such as nursing homes, homes for the disabled, schools for troubled youth, vocational schools, Catholic schools, and hospitals in the diocese of Rottenburg-Stuttgart and the archdiocese of Munich-Freising. In October 2000, church officials increased their estimate of seven thousand forced laborers to ten thousand.[21]

Finally, I address the half-truths reflected in Catholic statements about guilt and responsibility for Nazism in the first two decades after the war. Professor Michael Phayer's book *The Catholic Church and the Holocaust*, published in 2000, contains documentary evidence of when, precisely, German bishops learned about the mass murder of

European Jewry;[22] what, if any, response they lodged to their superiors in Rome;[23] and, postwar, the manner in which fear of communism and latent anti-Jewish sentiments eclipsed already lukewarm endeavors to address Catholic accountability for the Holocaust. In this essay, I will briefly address Professor Phayer's discoveries concerning the debate surrounding the final version of the German Catholic bishops' August 1945 Fulda pastoral letter, which indirectly addressed the Holocaust. The pertinent paragraph reads as follows:

> We profoundly deplore the fact that many Germans, even in our own ranks, allowed themselves to be deceived by the false teachings of National Socialism, [and] remained indifferent to the crimes against human freedom and dignity; many by their attitude lent support to the crimes, many became criminals themselves. A heavy responsibility falls upon those who, because of their influence, could have prevented such crimes and did not do so but made these crimes possible and in this way associated themselves with the criminals.[24]

While this statement is in many ways impressive for its frank qualities, it did *not* reflect the sentiments of the majority of German Catholic bishops. Professor Phayer's research indicates that the German bishops debated *several* drafts of the Fulda pastoral before agreeing to the version that appeared in the public domain. The first draft "glossed over the Holocaust," calling it only a "dark chapter" in German history. But Bishop Konrad Preysing of Berlin demanded revisions, and Phayer credits Bishop Preysing, and Bishop Preysing alone, for the sentences noted in the quoted paragraph. Collectively, the bishops also edited certain passages *out* of the final draft, such as a section denying that Germans knew about specifics concerning atrocities, because, argues Professor Phayer, a number of German bishops *did* know. Finally, the bishops avoided the issues of anti-Semitism and Catholic enthusiasm for the war.[25] Indeed, the remainder of the five-page Fulda pastoral letter praised Catholics at large. It thanked the Catholic clergy and dioceses for the "loyalty" shown to their church during "hard times" via their circulation of "pastoral words from [the German bishops] that countered the errors and crimes of Nazism." The pastoral letter credited the German bishops with repelling the state's encroachment into religious life and "raising their voices against race hatred (*Rassendünkel und Völkerhass*)." Catholics at large were unblemished, argued the Fulda pastoral letter. "We are happy to say that in such great numbers [Catholics] kept free from the idolatry of brutal power. We are happy that so many believers never bowed before Baal.[26] We are happy that the godless and inhumane teachings were rejected across the great range of Catholic brethren," wrote the bishops.[27]

Regarding conversation among Catholic Church leaders about guilt and responsibility for Nazism in the first two decades after the war, I include a brief example from my research on Cardinal Aloisius Muench, Vatican papal emissary to Germany from 1946 until 1959.[28] On at least one occasion, then-Archbishop Muench and Pope Pius XII shared a Holocaust-related "witticism" during a private discussion. During an audience in May 1957, Pope Pius XII told Archbishop Muench a "story . . . with a great deal of delight." The story relayed to then-Archbishop Muench by the pope was as follows, as recounted by Muench in his private diary and also in a letter to close acquaintance Monsignor Joseph Adams of Chicago:

> Hitler died and somehow got into heaven. There, he met the Old Testament prophet Moses. Hitler apologized to Moses for his treatment of the European Jews. Moses replied that such things were forgiven and forgotten here in heaven. Hitler, relieved, said to Moses that he always wished to meet him in order to ask him an important question. Did Moses [also] set fire to the burning bush?[29]

"Our Holy Father told me the story with a big laugh," Muench told Monsignor Joseph Adams of Chicago.[30] The "delight" and "laughter" described by Muench indicates that neither man appeared to understand the inappropriateness of the story. This incident revealed how little importance either man placed on the Jewish experience under the Nazi onslaught.

To conclude, recent evidence suggests that the Roman Catholic Church as an institution as well as the German Catholic episcopate, clergy, and laity reacted to the Nazi regime and to the Holocaust with eager participation; collaboration; passive acquiescence; and, in some cases, resistance and heroism on behalf of Jews specifically. We need to address the denial or even falsification of a history that shows the all-too-human nature of an institution that claimed and still claims to follow a higher course. The Catholic Church must accept the responsibility of an honest accounting of its past and embrace truths of resistance and heroism *and failure, acquiescence, even elements of shared nationalistic and anti-Jewish ideology.* This lack of willingness to look at all truths—those that make us proud and those that make us ashamed—is what truly disturbs and angers those outside of the church and some within it. What is at stake is nothing less than the dignity and integrity of an institution that shows itself to be more human than divine.

NOTES

The views and opinions contained in this paper are solely my own and do not in any way represent the official policy, positions, or sentiments of the United States Holocaust Memorial Museum or its Center for Advanced Holocaust Studies.

1. James Carroll, *Constantine's Sword: The Church and the Jews* (Boston: Houghton Mifflin, 2001), 510.

2. Daniel Jonah Goldhagen, "What Would Jesus Have Done? Pope Pius XII, the Vatican, and the Holocaust," *New Republic,* January 21, 2002, 22.

3. Quoted in David I. Kertzer, *The Popes Against the Jews: The Vatican's Role in the Rise of Modern Anti-Semitism* (New York: Alfred A. Knopf, 2001), 146–48, 312n26. Kertzer cites his source as "L'antisemitismo in Francia," *L'Osservatore romano,* July 1, 1892, 1.

4. Kertzer, *Popes Against Jews,* 146–47.

5. Golgotha (also known as Calvary) is the site of Jesus Christ's execution under Roman orders. In 1979, in his visit to Kraków, Pope John Paul II called Auschwitz "the Golgotha of the modern world" (Carroll, *Constantine's Sword,* 3).

6. Kertzer, *Popes Against Jews,* 12–19.

7. See Walter Zwi Bacharach, "The Catholic Anti-Jewish Prejudice, Hitler, and the Jews," in *Probing the Depths of German Antisemitism: German Society and the Persecution of the Jews, 1933–1941,* ed. David Bankier (New York: Berghahn Books, 2000), 417.

8. See Martin Broszat, Elke Fröhlich, and Falk Wiesemann, *Bayern in der NS-Zeit,* 6 vols. (Munich: Oldenbourg, 1977–83).

9. See Oded Heilbronner, *Catholicism, Political Culture, and the Countryside: A Social History of the Nazi Party in South Germany* (Ann Arbor: University of Michigan Press, 1998).

10. The most important studies that pointed to Catholic cooperation with the Nazi state in the form of the concordat, the nascent anti-Judaism found in the pastoral writings of the German bishops, and the strong nationalism and support for the war by the majority of German Catholic bishops

were those by Saul Friedländer, *Pie XII et le IIIe Reich* (Paris: Editions du Seuil, 1964); Guenter Lewy, *The Catholic Church and Nazi Germany* (New York: McGraw-Hill, 1964); and Gordon Zahn, *German Catholics and Hitler's Wars* (New York: E. P. Dutton, 1969).

11. Reinhard Richter, "Nationales Denken im Katholizismus der Weimarer Republic" (Ph.D. diss., Universität Bochum, 2000).

12. A pastoral letter is a document issued by a bishop to address matters of concern in a diocese. The term "pastoral letter" also refers to similar documents issued by a conference (group) of bishops that deal with matters in the territory of a particular episcopal conference (an assembly of the bishops of a nation or region for the purpose of addressing issues affecting those nations or regions). I discuss the example of the Fulda pastoral letter issued by German Catholic bishops in August 1945.

13. Wolfgang Stücken, *Hirten unter Hitler: Die Rolle der Paderborner Erzbischöfe Caspar Klein und Lorenz Jäger in der NS-Zeit* (Essen: Klartext-Verlag, 1999), 165.

14. Ibid.

15. Beth Griech-Polelle, *Bishop von Galen: German Catholicism and National Socialism* (New Haven, CT: Yale University Press, 2002). Alternatively, see Joachim Kuropka with Gian Luigi Falchi, Franz-Josef Schröder, and Thomas Sternberg, *Clemens August Graf von Galen: Neue Forschungen zum Leben und Wirken des Bischofs von Münster* (Münster: Verlag Regensberg, 1998); and Joachim Kuropka and Maria-Anna Zumholz, eds., *Clemens August Graf von Galen: Sein Leben und Wirken in Bildern und Dokumenten* (Cloppenburg: G. Runge, 1992).

16. Kevin Spicer's manuscript, "Hitler's Priests: Catholic Clergy in the Nazi Party," is forthcoming in 2007. Also Kevin Spicer, ed., *Love Thy Neighbor? Antisemitism, Christian Ambivalence, and the Holocaust* (Bloomington: Indiana University Press, forthcoming 2007). For a discussion of how Berlin seminarians who were trained during the Weimar period understand the concept "who is neighbor," that is to say who was included in the category of neighbor and who was excluded, see Spicer, *Resisting the Third Reich: The Catholic Clergy in Hitler's Berlin* (DeKalb: Northern Illinois University Press, 2004), 129–31.

17. See Thomas Fandel, *Konfession und Nationalsozialismus: Evangelische und katholische Pfarrer in der Pfalz 1930–1939,* VKZ B76 (Paderborn: Ferdinand Schöningh, 1997).

18. Mann's subjects were German war criminals whose biographical data he has collected from published court accounts. Mann relied upon Fritz Bauer, ed., *Justiz und NS-Verbrechen: Sammlung deutscher Stafurteilte wegen national-sozialistischer Tötungsverbrechen 1945–1966,* 22 vols. (Amsterdam: University Press, 1968–81), among other sources. For his discussion of

religion as a factor in the likelihood of becoming a perpetrator, see Michael Mann, "Were the Perpetrators of Genocide Ordinary Men or Real Nazis? Results from Fifteen Hundred Biographies," *Holocaust and Genocide Studies* 14, no. 3 (Winter 2000): 347–49.

19. In 1940, the total number of SS staff members in Auschwitz did not exceed 500. On January 15, 1945, one day before the camp's evacuation, the number of SS personnel reached its peak of 4,481 SS men and 71 SS women supervisors. See Aleksander Lasik, "Historical-Sociological Profile of the Auschwitz SS," in *Anatomy of the Auschwitz Death Camp,* ed. Israel Gutman and Michael Berenbaum (Bloomington: Indiana University Press, in association with United States Holocaust Memorial Museum, 1998), 274–79.

20. Ibid., 280.

21. John Delaney, "Research Report: Recent Revelations Concerning the German Catholic Church and Nazi Forced Labor," Association for Contemporary Church Historians Newsletter 8, no. 6 (June 2002), http://www.calvin.edu/academic/cas/akz2206.htm.

22. For example, Bishop Wilhelm Berning of Osnabrück learned of plans to murder European Jewry as early as February 1942. See Michael Phayer, *The Catholic Church and the Holocaust, 1930–1965* (Bloomington: Indiana University Press, 2000), 68.

23. Bishop Konrad Preysing of Berlin (1880–1950) was unique among the German bishops in that he was the *only* one to try to defend *all* Jews, not just those who converted to Catholicism. Preysing's cousin was the famous Clemens August Count von Galen, the so-called Lion of Muenster. Preysing came to see the 1933 concordat as "a mistake," a view markedly different than that of Pope Pius XII. Preysing supported the work of Margarete Sommer, head of the Hilfswerk beim Ordinariat Berlin, a diocesan rescue operation for Berlin Jews (the only Catholic organization of its kind). In March 1943, Preysing wrote to Pius XII to describe the final roundup of Jews in Berlin (February 27–March 1), indicating that their deportation likely meant their death. In a series of thirteen letters over fifteen months (1943–44), he repeatedly urged the pope to recall Vatican Nuncio Orsenigo, break off diplomatic relations with the Nazis, and condemn the murder of the Jews. See Phayer, *Catholic Church and Holocaust,* 18, 49–50, 57, 69, 74, 81, 152.

24. Woldgang Löhr, ed., "Die deutschen Bischöfe: Erster gemeinsamer Hirtenbrief nach dem Krieg, Fulda, 23 August 1945," in *Dokumente deutscher Bischöfe: Hirtenbriefe und Ansprachen zu Gesellschaft und Politik 1945–1949* (Würzburg: Echter Verlag, 1985), 1:40–45.

25. See Phayer, *Catholic Church and Holocaust,* 135–39.

26. "Baal" is an Old Testament biblical reference to the Canaanite storm and fertility god.

27. Woldgang Löhr, ed., "Die deutschen Bischöfe," 40–41; my translation.

28. The Cardinal Muench Collection, located in the archives of the Catholic University of America in Washington, DC, occupies eighty-one linear feet of shelf space and numbers over 150,000 items. This author viewed the Cardinal Muench collection in its entirety, beginning in the fall of 1996; resuming during the spring of 1998 after a 1997–98 Friedrich-Ebert-Stiftung research fellowship in Munich, Germany; and continuing without interruption during the summer and fall of 1999 and the spring and early summer of 2000. I thank Dr. Timothy Maher, chief archivist, and William John Shepherd, assistant archivist, for their friendly and unfailing cooperation.

29. Moses was the leader of the Jewish Exodus from Egypt ca. 1300 BC and lawgiver of the Old Testament. According to scripture, "Moses was tending the flock of Jethro, his father-in-law, the priest of Midean, and he led the flock to the far side of the desert and came to Horeb, the mountain of God. There the angel of the Lord appeared to him in flames of fire from within a bush" (Exod. 3:1–2, *NIV Study Bible,* 90). This was the experience to which Hitler referred when he hinted that Moses had perhaps set the fire himself in order to invoke the authority of "God." On the evening of February 27, 1933, large parts of the Reichstag (parliament) building in Berlin were destroyed by fire. Though the arsonist was allegedly Dutch anarchist Marinus van der Lubbe, suspicions of the Nazis' own involvement circulated.

30. Muench recounts this audience in both a letter and in his diary. See diary entry, May 21, 1957, Muench Collection, vol. 21, p. 287. See also Archbishop Aloisius Muench, Bad Godesberg, to Monsignor Joseph Adams, Chicago, May 29, 1957, Muench Collection, HM 37/11/7, ACUA.

Bob Weinberg

The Politics of Remembering: The Treatment of the Holocaust in the Soviet Union

THE SECOND WORLD WAR WAS THE DEFINING MOMENT OF THE SOVIET Union. The war extracted an incredible toll on the Soviet Union: more than eight million soldiers and at least seventeen million civilians dead, close to two thousand towns and seventy thousand villages razed to the ground, and thirty thousand industrial enterprises destroyed. Millions of Soviet citizens survived the war as homeless refugees, and many others suffered permanent physical damage and lifelong psychological trauma as a result of the hostilities. But the Red Army's triumphant march into Berlin in late April 1945 and the unconditional surrender of Germany on May 9 prompted many Soviet citizens to attribute victory over fascism to the policies of Stalin. The Soviet Union's heroic effort to turn back the German invaders and then rout the enemy's retreating troops proved the mettle not only of the Stalinist system but also the Soviet people who collectively endured four years of war. To many Soviets, the sacrifices and bloodletting that characterized the building of socialism since the late 1920s had their payoff in the Soviet Union's defeat of Germany. As one Soviet friend told me while we watched fireworks televised on May 9, 1983, to commemorate the thirty-eighth anniversary of Germany's surrender, "except for defeating Hitler and his army, we Soviets have nothing to be proud of." Or consider the story told to me by an American colleague who, while riding a bus in Moscow in 1983, witnessed the following scene. An elderly woman, laden with several bags brimming over with potatoes and onions, boarded the crowded bus. She began berating a twentysomething man who did not relinquish his seat, insisting that she deserved a seat because she had liberated Berlin in 1945 just so he could live the good life in the early 1980s. At the same time, other passengers—young, middle-aged and old, men and women, some standing, some sitting—felt it was their civic duty to add their two cents and joined the ad hominem attack on the man. After enduring several minutes of this verbal lashing, the young man looked at the woman and shouted, "I've had enough talk about the war. I'm sick and tired of hearing how you saved the Soviet Union. I didn't ask you to march into Germany."

Similarly, the wartime experiences of those Soviet Jews who had the good fortune to survive Germany's war of annihilation served as a reference point for their post-1945 lives. As my elderly Russian aunt responded when my wife inquired in 1995 how life in post-Communist Russia was treating her, "What can be bad about my life now? The Germans aren't on their way, and there's no famine." Born in 1919, she spent most of the war years as an evacuee from Moscow in a town near Lake Baikal, several thousand miles from the atrocities of the Final Solution. Yet her comment underscores the extent to which she has carried throughout her adult life the memories of the tragedy that befell her country when she was a young woman.[1] Close to two million of the nearly six million Jews killed by the Germans lived on Soviet territory when the war broke out. Members of the Einsatzgruppen shot well over a million Jews, while hundreds of thousands died in ghettos, in transit to the camps, or in the extermination camps. Thus, the history of the Holocaust is integrally linked to the history of Soviet Jewry, and neither can be explored and understood in isolation.

Given the impact of the war on Soviet society, it is not surprising that the Kremlin mobilized its resources to memorialize the Soviet Union's heroic and triumphant efforts against Germany. A cottage industry of books, films, plays, and public ceremonies developed in the decades after 1945, reaching its apex in the late 1970s and early 1980s when the Brezhnev regime relied on the public commemoration of the war to provide the social and political cohesion that was sorely in need of bolstering.[2] But when it came to addressing the specifically anti-Jewish aspects of German policy and the particular suffering experienced by Soviet Jews, Soviet historians were, for the most part, silent. For a host of political reasons (as will be discussed), the Soviet authorities instructed historians to refrain from mentioning the specifically Jewish nature of the genocide carried out on Soviet territory. Historians either overlooked the attempted extermination of Soviet Jewry or submerged the trauma suffered by Jews in a grocery list of Soviet citizens of all nationalities and ethnicities who fell victim to the German invaders. The flap over the memorial at Babi Yar is undoubtedly the most publicized example of the Soviet Union's refusal to acknowledge the Jewish genocide. As Zvi Gitelman, a leading expert on the history of Soviet Jewry, asserts:

> I know of no book published in the USSR that sought to explain the Holocaust as *sui generis*. In fact, the term "Holocaust" is completely unknown in the Soviet literature. In discussions of the destruction of the Jews, terms "annihilation" (*unichtozhenie*) or "catastrophe" (*katastrofa*) have been used. It is only recently that the "Holocaust," transliterated from English, has appeared.[3]

Indeed, the scholarly interest in documenting and explaining the Holocaust, so widespread in the United States, Israel, and Europe, was virtually nonexistent during the Soviet era. One can search in vain high school and college textbooks and official histories of the war for any mention of Jews, anti-Semitism, and extermination camps.

Notwithstanding the desire to expunge from the historical record any mention of Jews, the Kremlin did not adopt a consistent policy of suppressing information about the Holocaust in the postwar era. Indeed, Soviet scholars did not avoid the topic altogether. This essay explores what Soviet historians wrote—and chose not to write—about the Holocaust from 1945 to 1991 in an effort to uncover the political and ideological calculus that shaped Soviet scholarship on the topic. Information about the Holocaust was available to Soviet citizens both during and after the war, though its amount and quality varied during the post-1945 period. The remainder of this essay focuses on how Soviet treatment of the killing of some two million of its Jewish citizens during World War II reflected the changing concerns of the Kremlin between 1945 and 1991. By American, Israeli, and Western European standards, Soviet scholarship fell way short of providing a satisfactory discussion and analysis of the Final Solution, and examination of the political concerns of the Soviet leadership sheds light on the selective memory of Soviet historians.[4]

Contrary to those accounts that stress the ignorance of Soviet Jews regarding what to expect from the Germans when they invaded in June 1941, Mordechai Altshuler notes that Soviet Jews did have access to information about the German government's persecution of Jews in countries under its control.[5] To be sure, no one inside the Soviet Union could have known about the planned annihilation of Soviet Jews because of the secrecy surrounding Operation Barbarossa. But as Altshuler argues, unofficial channels of transmitting news coexisted with the prohibition of publicizing the anti-Jewish policies of the Germans in the official media that was in effect between the signing of the Nazi-Soviet Non-Aggression Pact in mid-1939 and the outbreak of the war nearly two years later. For example, the Soviet occupation of eastern Poland in mid-September 1939 prompted hundreds of thousands of Polish Jews with firsthand experience of German cruelty to cross the new border into territory annexed by the Soviet Union. The same holds for those Polish Jews who escaped the Germans by seeking a safe haven in the Baltic countries that the Soviet Union annexed. Even after the Soviets and Germans sealed the borders of their newly acquired territories, Jews still found it possible to cross over to the Soviet Union with the help of smugglers. Many of these refugees subsequently obtained Soviet citizenship and moved elsewhere in the Soviet Union, where they told others of what life was like under the Germans. Moreover, letters and other accounts from people caught in German-controlled Poland still managed to find their way to friends and relatives on the other side of the border. Altshuler concludes that it "is hard to believe that this relatively large quantity of information, flowing through diverse channels (individuals, letters, attestations), remained hidden from very broad segments of the Jewish public."[6]

Altshuler also notes that prior to September 1939, the official Soviet media published accounts of the mistreatment of Jews in Germany, Austria, and Czechoslovakia. Articles appeared in the mainstream Russian-language press such as *Pravda* and *Izvestiia* as well as the Yiddish newspaper *Der Shtern,* where details of attacks on Jews, incarceration in concentration camps, burning of synagogues, and destruction of Jewish property were presented in graphic detail. The flow of this information picked up after Kristallnacht in November 1938 and no doubt served to make Soviet Jews aware of German brutality. In addition, the films *Professor Mamlok* and *The Family Oppenheim,* Soviet productions from 1938, were favorably reviewed by critics and ran in theaters and factories until the signing of the nonaggression pact in mid-1939 put an end to the appearance of negative news about the Soviet Union's new ally.[7]

Not surprisingly, the Kremlin lifted the prohibition on official information about the Germans' brutal treatment of Jews within days of the German invasion. Articles about the Germans' anti-Jewish atrocities quickly reappeared in the national and local press, and radio stations aired shows describing the travails endured by Jews in territories under German control. Moreover, the Germans themselves publicized what Soviet Jews could expect. Leaflets dropped from planes and radio broadcasts disseminated German propaganda, advertising the German military's intention to annihilate both Jews and Bolsheviks. In other words, neither the enemy nor the Soviet authorities tried to conceal the fact that Jews were in a dire situation. Altshuler concludes that "many Jews, before the German invasion of the Soviet Union and *a fortiori* afterward, were aware of the Nazis' discrimination against and persecution of Jews (although they had no information about genocide)."[8] To be sure, many civilians greeted such news with skepticism and preferred to believe that reports of German brutality were merely Kremlin propaganda. Still others, particularly those who could remember the Great War, had trouble reconciling these reports with their recollections of German rule a generation earlier. Finally, those Jews who considered Soviet power as their chief enemy reasoned that Hitler had to be a preferable ruler to Stalin.[9]

For the duration of the war, Soviet authorities did not conceal information about the genocide of the Jews. As Lukasz Hirszowicz points out, "a considerable amount of material about the Holocaust . . . appeared in the Soviet Union during the war and its immediate aftermath."[10] For example, the government instructed the writers Ilya Ehrenburg and Vasily Grossman to lead a commission devoted to the documentation of the German murder of Soviet Jewry. They printed a typescript of their findings (known as the *Black Book*) in 1946, but within a year the authorities decided to prohibit its publication because of the shift in the political and ideological climate. In 1948, the Kremlin ordered the destruction of all copies of the manuscript, along with the typescript, but the *Black Book* nonetheless soon appeared in Hebrew and English translations because the manuscript had already been sent abroad. An Israeli publisher also issued the Russian version, but the fact remains that no version of the *Black Book* was published in the Soviet Union.[11] In addition, the Jewish Anti-Fascist Committee, established in the middle of the war in order to drum up foreign support (financial and moral) for the Soviet Union, helped publicize the horrors of the Germans' concerted effort to kill all Soviet Jews.[12] Furthermore, details of the Nuremburg trials also appeared in the official media. In a similar vein, the Russian and Yiddish versions of the daily newspaper published in Birobidzhan, capital of the Jewish Autonomous Oblast, printed letters from displaced Soviet Jews who survived the German onslaught and were seeking a new life in Birobidzhan, the putative national enclave of Soviet Jewry. The Jewish theater troupe of Birobidzhan staged the production of *He Is from the Ghetto,* a play about the Jewish uprising in the Warsaw Ghetto.[13]

Notwithstanding these events, the suppression of the *Black Book* signaled the Kremlin's growing ambivalence and discomfort with any specific mention of the Holocaust. Undoubtedly, the anti-Semitic hysteria that had begun to characterize certain aspects of Stalin's domestic and foreign policies, and reached a crescendo in the campaign against "rootless cosmopolitans" and the Doctors' Plot during Stalin's final years, certainly played a role in the decision to downplay the special nature of the Germans' treatment of the Jews.[14] But several other issues merit consideration in any explanation of why the Soviet authorities silenced discussion of the Holocaust in the Soviet Union. First, publication and discussion of these materials, especially those compiled by Ehrenburg and Grossman, raised the very uncomfortable issue of collaboration by Soviet citizens, particularly those Ukrainian and Latvian civilians who assisted the Germans in their slaughter of Jews. The fact that significant numbers of Soviet citizens were traitors to the Soviet cause threw into doubt the Kremlin's claim that the Communist regime enjoyed the unconditional support of the populace.[15]

Second, the Soviet authorities realized that social and political cohesion would be better served by not treating the Jewish genocide as a unique phenomenon. As Solomon Schwarz noted more than fifty years ago, the Kremlin worried that highlighting Hitler's belief that the war against the Soviet Union stemmed from his war against the Jews would weaken "civilian and military morale."[16] In a sad commentary on the persistence of popular anti-Semitism, the Soviet leadership worried that non-Jewish Soviets would be susceptible to German propaganda and blame the Jews for the horrors visited upon all Soviet citizens, thereby weakening their resolve to combat the enemy. Put bluntly, the Kremlin did not want Soviet citizens to believe they were fighting to protect the Jews. It is therefore not surprising that already during the war the Soviet authorities took efforts to minimize the unique nature of the Germans' campaign to exterminate Soviet Jewry. For example, they instructed the commission set up to gather evidence of the Germans' murder of Jews to omit any mention that Jews were the victims. The Kremlin also told the commission to minimize the role played by Soviet citizens who collaborated with the Germans in the mass shootings and massacres of Jews.[17]

Finally, the elation with which many Soviet Jews greeted the establishment of the State of Israel in May 1948 and the enthusiastic welcome accorded Golda Meir, head of the Israeli legation that visited Moscow in the fall, bolstered suspicions among many in the Kremlin that Soviet Jewry was not loyal to the Soviet Union. In addition, the rising tide of official anti-Semitic policies and pronouncements gave many Soviet Jews good reason to take pride in Israel, particularly because they could not but notice that the regime had deliberately turned its back on them and had no interest in examining the wartime travails of Soviet Jewry.[18]

By the end of the 1940s, this tendency to avoid mentioning the German effort to annihilate Soviet Jewry had become the norm and remained as such until the collapse of the Soviet Union in 1991. The overwhelming number of books published about the war years, from memoirs and novels to document collections and monographs, maintained a silence regarding the genocide of Soviet Jews. In one incident, the Soviet censors excised from the diary of a Jewish girl who endured ghetto life any mention of her Jewishness.[19] Yet it bears noting that the Soviets never denied that the Germans murdered six million Jews. Nor did they deny that the Germans targeted European Jewry for extermination. Instead, Soviet treatments tended to conflate the victimization of Soviet Jewry with the sufferings endured by all Soviet citizens. Such an approach demystified the Holocaust and eliminated the need to explain the mass murder of six million Jews because the Final Solution "was seen as an integral part of a larger phenomenon—the murder of civilians—whether Russians, Ukrainians, Belorussians, Gypsies, or other nationalities. It was said to be a natural consequence of racist fascism," which in turn was the inevitable consequence of the paroxysms of capitalism in its death throes.[20] In other words, Soviet treatments of the war years universalized the murder of Soviet Jews, relegating them to a place on the list of Soviet victims of fascism and at times even erasing any mention of their Jewishness. It was common practice to refer to Jewish resistance fighters, soldiers, and victims as

"Soviet," thereby conveying the impression that Jews were not special targets of the Germans and may not have distinguished themselves in combat. From the perspective of the ideologues in the Kremlin, there was no need to point out what Jews experienced during the war, especially if the sense of Jewish victimhood could fuel Jewish national feelings and foster a sense of entitlement. The authorities also worried that underscoring the Jewish nature of the Final Solution could spark resentment among non-Jewish Soviets who also suffered at the hands of the Germans. All Soviet citizens were targets of Germany's racial profiling during the war, especially ethnic Russians, and Jews found themselves mentioned along with the myriad nationalities and ethnicities that also endured Germany's campaign for Lebensraum and destruction of communism.

Stalin's death in 1953 did very little to alter the general approach of Soviet treatments of the Holocaust. Still, this does not mean that all mention of Jews, including even highlighting the special treatment meted out to Jews, vanished. In the 1950s and 1960s, the Soviet media did not shy away from covering war crimes trials conducted in West Germany and even the Soviet Union. Along with the fascination generated by the capture and trial of Adolf Eichmann in the early 1960s, the specific nature of these trials made it difficult to avoid mention of the Jewish victims. In addition, *Sovetish heymland,* the Yiddish monthly published in Moscow from 1961 to 1991, saw fit to print stories, poems, memoirs, and documentary material on the Holocaust in "almost every issue."[21] But how many Soviet citizens, Jews and non-Jews, could read Yiddish? Only a few publications appeared in the post-Stalin years that offered honest assessments of the Final Solution on Soviet territory, with explicit attention paid to the Jewish ghettos and mass executions of Soviet Jews.[22] Still, the vast majority of publications erased any mention of the Jewishness of Soviet victims from the historical record.

However, it is the controversy over building a monument to the thirty-three thousand Jews of Kiev murdered at Babi Yar in September 1941 that best illustrates the desire to downplay public recognition of the Holocaust. The public clamor to erect a memorial at Babi Yar crystallized a movement demanding that the Kremlin acknowledge the existence of anti-Semitism and commemorate the murder of thirty-three thousand Soviet Jews. With his poem "Babi Yar," the poet Yevgeny Yevtushenko in the early 1960s catapulted the issue onto the world stage, opening a festering wound that Soviet society had been living with for nearly twenty years. The world-famous Dmitry Shostakovich also added his imprimatur to the incident by including Yevtushenko's poem in his Thirteenth Symphony and thereby earning the wrath of the authorities, who prohibited public performances of the composition for several years. While Yevtushenko and his supporters prevailed by convincing the Kremlin to establish a memorial at Babi Yar, their victory was a hollow one and fell short of what they wanted. The inscription refers to the one hundred thousand "citizens of Kiev and prisoners of war" who perished at the hands of German soldiers in 1941 and 1942 at Babi Yar. The authorities obviously did not want to sanctify Babi Yar as a site of Jewish victimization because doing so would run against the grain of policy and threaten to offend the sensibilities of non-Jewish Soviet citizens who also lost friends and relatives at Babi Yar. And when the Kremlin authorized performances of Shostakovich's Thirteenth Symphony, Yevtushenko first had to amend the poem to include mention of Russian and Ukrainian victims and highlight how Russia resisted the Germans. Not surprisingly, the authorities' decision inflamed Jewish sensibilities both inside and outside the Soviet Union, and the controversy continued until the end of the Communist regime. In the late 1980s, the city fathers added another plaque to the memorial. Written in Yiddish, the plaque amazingly does not mention Jews. It was only after the dissolution of the Soviet Union and the emergence of Ukraine as an independent country in 1991 that a fitting memorial commemorating the Jewish victims at Babi Yar was erected. This new memorial was in the shape of a menorah with Yiddish and Hebrew texts that refer to Jews. But it is located at a spot some distance from the original monument.[23]

The dissolution of the Soviet Union changed the political calculus of the successor states, including the Russian Federation, offering historians and politicians alike a chance to reconsider their countries' wartime experiences, especially in terms of their relationships toward Jews and Germans. But the collapse of communism did not mean that discussion of the Holocaust became depoliticized throughout the former Soviet Union. To the contrary, in some countries examination of what happened to Jews during World War II remained a sensitive and contentious matter, particularly when it intersected with the efforts of these newly independent states to reverse the effects of decades of Moscow rule. For example, Zvi Gitelman notes that in September 1991 the Lithuanian government, soon after the Kremlin recognized its independence, pardoned close to one thousand Lithuanians whom postwar Soviet tribunals found guilty of collaborating with the Germans. The approach adopted by the Lithuanian government was simple and direct: any Lithuanian judged guilty by the Soviet authorities must have been innocent. Not unexpectedly, Israeli and Jewish observers of these events protested and convinced the government to reconsider the rehabilitation of the collaborators. The government also established a joint commission of experts from Israel, the United States, and Lithuania to examine the records and trials of the convicted collaborators. But resolution of the issue has not been reached, largely because American and Israeli members of the commission refused to accept the Lithuanian proposal that equates Jewish and Lithuanian suffering during and after the war. In addition, the proposal also tries to expunge from the historical record the responsibility of Lithuania for the genocide of the Jews.[24]

Clearly, then, the issue of collaboration still resonates in the former Soviet Union, not only affecting Jewish-gentile relations but also highlighting the political capital that the Holocaust still possesses. For example, in Ukraine a number of independent Jewish researchers studying the fate of Ukrainian Jews during the war have published historical accounts of the Final Solution based on documents and interviews with survivors. But as Yohanan Petrovsky-Shtern points out in a recent essay, these researchers affix responsibility for the atrocities to Ukrainian nationalists who collaborated with the Germans. Furthermore, Petrovsky-Shtern believes that these independent scholars use the study of the Holocaust as a way to "attain political and social importance within the Jewish community and attract the attention of the Ukrainian authorities; . . . Holocaust studies are used as an instrument of struggle for power in the Jewish community in Ukraine at large."[25] In contrast to this self-serving effort to blame Ukrainian extremists as the instigators of the Final Solution, a group of presumably non-Jewish scholars connected to official institutions revert to the scholarly practices of the Soviet period and make no mention of the role of Ukrainian collaborators. According to Petrovsky-Shtern, a disturbing revisionist trend has emerged that seeks to sweep under the carpet the participation of Ukrainians in the Final Solution and promote a view of Ukrainian history in which Jews and Ukrainians lived in friendly, peaceful coexistence.[26]

On the other hand, since the early 1990s, the government of independent Ukraine has been sincerely trying to rectify the mistakes of the past. In Ukraine, where large numbers of Ukrainians collaborated with the Germans in liquidating ghettos, rounding up and executing Jews, and fighting the Red Army, the Ukrainian government has made a concerted effort to mend Jewish-Ukrainian relations. The government has helped sponsor annual commemorations of the Babi Yar massacre and has rejected the relativization of the Holocaust that characterized Soviet treatments of the subject.[27] In addition, officials in many of the major centers of Jewish residence during the Soviet period helped sponsor conferences, memorials, public gatherings, and other events commemorating the Holocaust.[28] Finally, Alfonsas Eidintas, Lithuania's ambassador to Israel in 2001, has edited a collection of documents and articles on the Holocaust in Lithuanian by prominent Lithuanian intellectuals of various political stripes.[29]

In post-Soviet Russia, the end of Communist rule provided favorable conditions for a burgeoning field of Holocaust studies. By the mid-1990s, local centers devoted to the study of the Holocaust had sprouted up, often at the behest of professional historians interested in publishing and educating the public about the genocide of Soviet Jews. The Center for Research and Education on the Holocaust, located in Moscow, established a series entitled The Russian Library of the Holocaust[30] and published the papers from a 1994 international symposium entitled Lessons of the Holocaust and Contemporary Russia.[31] Under the direction of Ilya Altman, the center has issued several document collections pertaining to the Holocaust, including one designed for pre-university-level teachers entitled *Istoriia Kholokosta, 1933–1945 gg.: Paket-komplekt dokumental'nykh materialov* (1995). Edited by D. I. Poltorak, the documents, which include selections from Hitler's *Mein Kampf,* along with diaries, memoirs, statistical records, official SS reports, and assorted photographs, come with lesson plans replete with discussion questions and possible assignments. The center has also organized traveling exhibitions and helped train teachers. In addition, the Institute of Jewish Studies in Kiev promotes research on the Holocaust in Ukraine.[32]

At the same time, the opening of the archives of the former Soviet Union and the ability of archivists at Yad Vashem in Israel and the

United States Holocaust Memorial Museum to microfilm materials from these repositories has been a boon to the study of the Holocaust on Soviet territory. Several journals from Russia, England, Israel, and the United States publish on a regular basis articles written by scholars from the former Soviet Union who utilize documents preserved in archives in Moscow, Kiev, Minsk, and the Baltic states.[33] In addition, Jewish Soviet war veterans have undertaken efforts to preserve the historical memory of the Holocaust, and Jewish researchers have published memorial books about the vanished Jewish communities. Complementing this flurry of interest in the Holocaust is the publication of books and articles by scholars investigating the Kremlin's policies toward Jews before, during, and after the war. Still, the ability to publish openly on the Holocaust has not led scholars in the former Soviet Union to break significant new ground and offer fresh analyses of the genocide of Soviet Jews.

Despite the recent advances, the dissemination of information about the Holocaust in the Soviet Union lags behind the explosive growth of Holocaust studies in the United States and elsewhere. Material on the Holocaust tends to appear in publications issued by Jewish organizations whose readership is primarily the small circle of scholars interested in the Final Solution in the Soviet Union. In addition, some of the articles that have appeared are Russian translations of articles written by American, English, and Israeli scholars. The following incident underscores the failure of the Soviet academic establishment to address the tragedy of the Holocaust. In July 1995, I spent some of my spare time perusing recent publications about Soviet history and World War II, interested in learning what the spate of books commemorating the fiftieth anniversary of the end of the war contained about the Holocaust. I browsed the offerings of the major bookstores in the city and came up empty-handed.

However, a more recent endeavor in May 2003 revealed that historians are now paying attention to the Holocaust in general and the killing of Soviet Jews in particular. For example, a textbook on the history of the Soviet Union designed for high school and college students offers a concise but accurate discussion of the genocide of Soviet Jews. Not only do the authors of the text note that Germany's war aims targeted "Jewish Bolshevism," but they assert that the German invasion of the Soviet Union coincided with the decision regarding the Final Solution. More significant is the authors' decision to underscore how many Soviet citizens, "especially those with strong antisemitic feelings," collaborated with the Germans. Unfortunately, the authors offer discredited information such as when they (on the one hand) assert that four million persons died at Auschwitz-Birkenau and (on the other hand) underestimate the number of Soviet Jews who perished at the hands of the Germans.[34] In addition, an April 2003 issue of *Novoe vremia*, the Russian equivalent of *Newsweek* or *Time*, published two articles discussing the Warsaw Ghetto and the 1943 uprising as well as the silence of Soviet historians regarding these events.[35] So it seems as if the Russian public is slowly but gradually receiving exposure to the history of the Holocaust, though it bears noting that a 2001 textbook on the history of Russia, also designed for high school and college students, does not mention the Holocaust or the fate of European and Soviet Jewry.[36]

Still, the progress post-Soviet scholars have made since the early 1990s is commendable and augurs well for the future treatment of the Holocaust. As historians reexamine and revise the old Soviet historiography of World War II, they will find it difficult to avoid giving the Final Solution on Soviet soil the attention that is long overdue. The national consolidation of the newly independent countries of the former Soviet Union will no doubt proceed apace and alleviate the perceived need to hold an honest assessment of the Holocaust hostage to the politics of nation building. One can hope that a more open and accurate reckoning of the Holocaust will prevail in the scholarship of historians working in the former Soviet Union.

NOTES

1. Questionnaires conducted in the 1990s indicate that remembrance of the Holocaust is a crucial element of identity among Jews in Russia and Ukraine. See Zvi Gitelman, "Thinking About Being Jewish in Russia and Ukraine," in *Jewish Life After the USSR,* ed. Zvi Gitelman (Bloomington: Indiana University Press, 2003), 49–60; and Zvi Gitelman, Valeriy Chervyakov, and Vladimir Shapiro, "*E Pluribus Unum?* Post-Soviet Identities and Their Implications for Communal Reconstruction," in Gitelman *Jewish Life After USSR,* 61–75.

2. See Nina Tumarkin, *The Living and the Dead: The Rise and Fall of the Cult of World War in Russia* (New York: Basic Books, 1994), for an insightful analysis.

3. Zvi Gitelman, "Politics and the Historiography of the Holocaust in

the Soviet Union" in *Bitter Legacy: Confronting the Holocaust in the USSR,* ed. Zvi Gitelman (Bloomington: Indiana University Press, 1997), 18–19.

4. For accounts of the genocide of Soviet Jewry, see the essays, many of them excellent, in Gitelman, *Bitter Legacy;* and Lucjan Dobroszycki and Jeffrey S. Gurock, eds., *The Holocaust in the Soviet Union: Studies and Sources on the Destruction of the Nazi-Occupied Territories of the USSR, 1941–1945* (Armonk, NY: M. E. Sharpe, 1993). In addition, see Nora Levin, *The Jews in the Soviet Union Since 1917,* 2 vols. (London: I. B. Tauris, 1988).

5. Mordechai Altshuler, "Escape and Evacuation of Soviet Jews at the Time of the Nazi Invasion: Policies and Realities," in Dobroszycki and Gurock, *Holocaust in the Soviet Union,* 77–104.

6. Ibid., 85.

7. Ibid., 84.

8. Ibid., 89.

9. Ibid.

10. Lukasz Hirszowicz, "The Holocaust in the Soviet Union," in Dobroszycki and Gurock, *Holocaust in the Soviet Union,* 31.

11. Gitelman, "Politics and Historiography," p. 19.

12. On the Jewish Anti-Fascist Committee, see Shimon Redlich, *War, Holocaust and Stalinism: A Documentary Study of the Jewish Anti-Fascist Committee in the USSR* (Luxembourg: Harwood Academic Publishers, 1995); Shimon Redlich, *Propaganda and Nationalism in Wartime Russia: The Jewish Anti-Fascist Committee in the USSR, 1941–1948* (Boulder, CO: East European Quarterly, 1982); Joshua Rubenstein, ed., *Stalin's Secret Pogrom: The Postwar Inquisition of the Jewish Anti-Fascist Committee* (New Haven, CT: Yale University Press, 2001); Gennadi Kostyrchenko, *V plenu u krasnogo Faraona* (Moscow: Mezhdunarodnye Otnosheniia, 1994); Gennadi Kostyrchenko, *Tainaia politika Stalinia: vlast' I antisemitizm* (Moscow: Mezhdunarodnye Otnosheniia, 2001); Arkadii Vaksberg, *Stalin Against the Jews* (New York: Knopf, 1994).

13. Robert Weinberg, "Jewish Revival in Birobidzhan in the Mirror of *Birobidzhanskaya zvezda,* 1946–49," *East European Jewish Affairs* 26, no. 1 (1996): 35–53.

14. See the books by Rubenstein and Kostyrchenko and Yehoshua Gilboa, *The Black Years of Soviet Jewry, 1939–1953* (Boston: Little, Brown, 1971).

15. For a fascinating analysis of the regime's attitudes and policies toward traitors, see Amir Weiner, *Making Sense of War: The Second World War and the Fate of the Bolshevik Revolution* (Princeton, NJ: Princeton University Press, 2001).

16. Solomon Schwarz, *The Jews in the Soviet Union* (Syracuse, NY: Syracuse University Press, 1951), 200.

17. Gitelman, "Politics and Historiography," 21.

18. Schwarz, *Jews in Soviet Union,* 198–201.

19. Gitelman, "Politics and Historiography," 24.

20. Ibid., 18.

21. Ibid., 25.

22. For example, see P. P. Lipilo and V. F. Romanovskii, eds., *Prestupleniia nemetsko-fashistikikh okkupantov v belorussii, 1941–1944* (Minsk, 1965); and V. I. Vinogradov, *Istoriia SSR v dokumentakh I illustratskikh* (Moscow, 1981).

23. On the controversy over Babi Yar, see William Korey, "A Monument Over Babi Yar?" in Dobroszycki and Gurock, *Holocaust in the Soviet Union,* 61–74; and Gitelman, "Politics and the Historiography," 20–21. A similar controversy broke out when Anatoly Kuznetsov published his novel *Babi Yar* in the mid-1960s.

24. Gitelman, "Politics and Historiography," 32–33.

25. Yohanan Petrovsky-Shtern, "The Revival of Academic Studies of Judaica in Independent Ukraine," in Gitelman, *Jewish Life After the USSR,* 160–61.

26. Ibid., 158–59, 161.

27. Gitelman, "Politics and Historiography," 34.

28. Ibid., 32.

29. Alfonsas Eidintas, ed., *Lietuvos zydu zudyniu byla: Dokumentu ir strapsniu rinkinys* (*The Case of the Massacre of Lithuanian Jews: Selected Documents and Articles*) (Vilnius: Vaga Publishing House, 2001).

30. The Jewish Heritage Society in Moscow (http://www.jewish-heritage .org) serves as an umbrella organization for many of the organizations devoted to the study of Jewish history and culture in the former Soviet Union. It publishes the research findings of historians studying the Holocaust on Soviet territory and is a partner with the Center for Research and Education on the Holocaust. The Jewish Heritage Society's Web site has an English-language list of its publications and activities.

31. The book contains remarks by Boris Yeltsin, who welcomed the symposium's participants and paid "tribute to the feat of the army of liberators who saved the Jews of Europe from full extermination." M. I. Gefter and I. Altman, eds., *Uroki kholokosta i sovremennaia Rossiia* (Moscow: Nauchno-prosvetotel'nyi tsentr "Kholokost," 1995). My translation.

32. See the Institute of Jewish Studies Web site, http://www.judaica .kiev.ua.

33. The list of journals includes *Vestnik evreiskogo universiteta v Moskve, Jews in Eastern Europe* (formerly *Jews and Jewish Life in Eastern Europe*), *East European Jewish Affairs,* and *Genocide and Holocaust Studies.*

34. A. K. Sokolov and V. S .Tiazhel'nikov, *Kurs sovetskoi istorii, 1941–1991* (Moscow: Vysshaia Shkola, 1999), 4–5, 48–49.

35. Iakov Ettinger, "Bunt obrechennykh," *Novoe vremia* 16 (April 20, 2003): 35; Petr Gorelik, "Krepost' masada v Varshave," *Novoe vremia* 16 (April 20, 2003): 37.

36. A. P. Derevianko and N. A. Shabel'nikov, *Istoriia Rossii s drevneskikh vremeni do kontsa XX veka,* 2nd edition (Moscow, 2001).

VI. D·O·C·U·M·E·N·T·A·R·Y

Stuart Liebman

Documenting the Liberation of the Camps:
The Case of Aleksander Ford's *Vernichtungslager
Majdanek—Cmentarzysko Europy* (1944)

OPERATION BAGRATION, THE GREAT OFFENSIVE AGAINST THE
Wehrmacht initiated by the Soviet general staff on June 23, 1944,
quickly proved to be an extraordinary success. By July 14, the Red
Army attacked south of the Pripet Marshes between Tarnapol and
Kovel, and on July 21, the army's right horn crossed the Bug River in
its advance through Poland toward the frontiers of Germany. They
stood on the threshold of one of the most significant discoveries of the
war. Within three days, Marshal Rokossovsky's units, soon followed
by elements of the Kosciuszko Division of General Berling's Polish
Army, entered Lublin, and for the very first time overran a German
concentration camp located on Polish territory.[1]

It was no ordinary camp but the infamous work and extermination camp, Majdanek. Himmler had designed it as a prison camp for
Soviet prisoners of war soon after the German armies overwhelmed
Russian defenses in 1941. By 1944, the complex within view of the
city of Lublin had expanded to accommodate new functions, including large-scale processing of stolen property, most of it from murdered
Jews, as well as the extermination by gas and shooting of Jews, Russian
soldiers, and some Poles. At its peak, the camp covered approximately
675 acres and encompassed six sections with twenty-four barracks in
each. Between twenty-five thousand and forty-five thousand prisoners
had been confined at any one time within its electrified barbed-wire
fences, although by December of 1943, the number had fallen to approximately six thousand.[2] When Red Army units overran Majdanek,
however, they found sections 3, 4, and 5 entirely abandoned because

the Germans, knowing the precariousness of their situation, had undertaken a massive evacuation of inmates during the late spring of 1944. Only 480 detainees, mostly invalid Soviet prisoners of war and a few Polish farmers, remained to greet their liberators.[3] Nevertheless, despite the Nazis' acute awareness of the need to eliminate traces of their crimes, as they had already done at Belzec, Sobibor, and Treblinka, the Russian assault had proceeded so quickly that the SS had insufficient time to remove all the incriminating evidence. Although the retreating Germans set the crematorium complex on fire on July 22, the Russians found the ovens still intact, with piles of ashes and bone shards lying in front of them. The principal crematorium chimney also remained as a distinctive marker visible from far across the flat fields surrounding it. About 820,000 pairs of shoes[4] and immense stores of clothing offered mute testimony to the countless victims who had suffered and been killed in the camp. Many mass graves containing thousands of rotting corpses would soon be exhumed.

As the Soviets immediately recognized, at Majdanek they had uncovered crimes against humanity more enormous and heinous than any of the many others that had come to light thus far during their march to the West.[5] At the time, a joint Polish-Soviet Extraordinary Commission concluded[6] that nearly 1.5 million victims from all across Europe had died in Majdanek, and that as many as 1,380,000 bodies had been burned, either in the crematoriums or on open pyres in the Krępiec Forest nearby.[7] Even as estimates of the dead have steadily fallen over the years, it is clear that since 1941, hundreds of thousands of prisoners, among them Soviet POWs, Polish and other European political prisoners, and preeminently, of course, Jews, died from starvation and disease or were shot or gassed at Majdanek.[8]

Accompanying the Russian and Polish army units were two teams of filmmakers charged with documenting the conditions they found, clearly with an eye toward the creation of cinematic war propaganda. Indeed, the film that was completed by the late autumn of 1944, *Vernichtungslager Majdanek—Cmentarzysko Europy* (*Majdanek Death Camp—The Cemetery of Europe*), is, in my opinion, one of the most important ever made about the Holocaust, not least because it has a legitimate claim to be the *first* such work. It has the dubious distinction, for example, of being the first film to develop visual and narrational strategies to dramatize the unprecedented story of German brutality in a camp as opposed to the more commonplace war crimes such as mass shootings of civilians and POWs that the Soviets had documented from the outset of the war. That it does so in original, visually striking ways is very much to the film's credit. Here, for the first time, are shots of the electrified barbed-wire fences, crematorium ovens, and gas chambers. Many of its images were, in fact, recycled in later films, suggesting that it contributed significantly to the developing visual discourse about crimes against humanity and, eventually, the Holocaust.[9]

For anyone concerned with charting the emergence of the representation of the Holocaust in film, however, its narrative is curiously unsettling. Without outrightly falsifying any details, the filmmakers chose to focus on certain images and to highlight certain voices that distort the reality of the camp in highly significant ways. Before the narrational strategies and ideological thrust of this first film about the Holocaust can be understood, one must analyze in detail a series of interlocked questions: How did *Vernichtungslager Majdanek* come to be made? Who made it? And, finally, to whom was the film addressed?

As I already noted, two production teams are mentioned in the credits for the film as having cooperated in its making. The Central Studio for Documentary Film in Moscow (Tsentral'noe Studio Dokumental'nogo Filma), a group headed by Roman Karmen, a leading Russian Jewish journalist and documentarian, is listed second.[10] The Russian cameramen under his command were almost certainly responsible for the aerial views of the camp since they were the ones most likely to have had access to Soviet Air Force planes. They may also have contributed some of the images of the city and the camp soon after they were liberated,[11] and their studio facilities in Moscow were essential for the completion of the work.

The first and, in my view, more important group, however, was the recently founded Wytwórnia Filmowej Wojska Polskiego, the Film Studio of the Polish Army, then headed by the well-known Polish Jewish director Aleksander Ford. His collaborators were several veteran cameramen, including Stanisław Wohl and the brothers Adolf and Władysław Forbert, all Jews and Communists who had been members of Ford's politically progressive avant-garde film group Start during the 1930s. Like Ford, they had found refuge in the Soviet Union during the war, and they would perform important services for the Communist-dominated Polish film industry in many areas for more than the next two decades.[12]

Both camera teams must have been present in Lublin shortly after the Red Army overran the city, because the film footage includes shots of Polish Army units entering Lublin and their moving fraternization with the local population, including sustained male kisses on the lips,[13] as well as the more familiar images of the tears of joy or sorrow shed by attractive women. Even more indicative of how closely the camera crews shadowed Soviet forces are the graphic pictures of the dozens of still-unburied corpses they recorded. These were the bodies of the approximately 450 Polish political prisoners who had been detained in the Lublin fortress and then executed shortly before the Germans withdrew. The gruesome shots were later intercut with the moving and pained expressions of Polish women grieving over the loss of their loved ones.

From these two initial sequences, the film abruptly shifts to the camp at Majdanek, introduced as its name is almost shouted by the film's narrator. After various striking compositions of the electrified barbed-wire fences, a long, traveling camera surveys a row of prisoners who are still lined up, silently, behind them. It is unclear when this shot was taken or whether the scene was staged.[14] What is clear is that these shots of survivors, as well as those of the crematoriums and gas chamber, are the first ever made of such installations from within the confines of a death camp.[15]

While preparing their text and organizing the production, Ford and scriptwriter Jerzy Bossak set up headquarters for several weeks in the former villa of the repellent SS criminal Odilo Globocnik, who had done so much to organize the mass murders in Polish camps.[16] From other images, moreover, we can deduce that the teams of film-makers or, more likely, the Polish camera crew remained in the Lublin area for some time, at least through the end of August, and possibly even into the first weeks of September. The shots of the impressive Catholic mass for the dead presided over by Prelate Kruszinski, for example, had to be made when it took place on August 6, 1944. The scenes of various exhumations that appear later were made as they were occurring during mid-to-late August 1944. The images of foreign journalists and, it would appear, of some Western military men examining the piles of shoes and other goods stolen from murdered civilians probably were recorded when the Soviet authorities allowed the journalists to visit on August 25, 1944. Finally, the images of the Extraordinary Commission at work had to have been made when its sessions commenced during August.[17] Filming may have even been extended through an early phase of the trial of the camp guards, which began in Lublin on September 12, 1944.[18] The film's editing was completed in Moscow under Ford's direction sometime during the late autumn of 1944. According to Władysław Jewsiewicki, it premiered at the Apollo and Bałtyk movie houses in Lublin in late November, shortly before the trial of the camp guards began.[19]

The motion picture shots Ford's team recorded provided a kind of "dress rehearsal" for the British and American cinematic (and photographic) coverage of the concentration camps in the West nearly a year later.[20] They had to solve many problems, some practical, others conceptual. What visual elements could best convey the look and "feel" of a camp? How could the inhuman brutality of the "German fascists" be suggested? How could the enormous scale of the killings be dramatized? How could the complexity of the systematic murder operations be communicated? How could one give voice to both the perpetrators and the survivors? The Polish team's solutions, often rooted in the practice of Soviet war documentaries, were not entirely novel, but the results remain gripping.

Perhaps the easiest problem to solve was the development of an iconography, a set of characteristic metonymies that quickly came to define visual representations of the camps. For example, the electrified barbed-wire fences, filmed to highlight their articulation in layers, communicated the sinister obstacles placed between an inmate and freedom. Victims frozen in their death agonies, caught at close range from oblique angles in such a way as to complicate a viewer's spatial orientation, forcefully conveyed the grotesque spectacles the liberators witnessed. Low-angle shots of the mountains of mismatched shoes, over which the camera then tilted up to reveal a seemingly endless stream of wayward leather, set precedents for the way such stores would later be filmed by the Russians at Auschwitz and other camps. As interesting, perhaps, is the way Ford and Bossak skillfully provided a forum for a spectrum of participants, from expert witnesses and commission members to surviving prisoners and even some of the perpetrators themselves. They testify to then-hard-to-believe stories of cruelty that had occurred on an unimaginable scale. In such a context, the guards' evasive denials, also caught on camera, are easily exposed as lies.

One may distinguish eight major narrative segments in all. Although a different, slightly more complex segmentation might be made, the sections can be most easily summarized as follows:

1. The arrival of Polish troops in Lublin and their fraternization with the inhabitants.

2. The slaughtered Polish prisoners in the city's fortress prison and those who mourn them.

3. The camp at Majdanek, articulated by familiar icons of barbed-wire fences, passports and photos, piles of shoes, stunned prisoners, etc.

4. The interrogation of two SS guards (*Obersturmführer* SS Thernes and *Rottenführer* Schöllen)[21] and testimony of other witnesses in front of the Extraordinary Commission.

5. The exhumation of mass graves.

6. At Majdanek camp, the gassing process, and the array of signs of the victims, such as eyeglasses, shoes, dresses, toys, etc.

7. Testimonies of four former prisoners, a Dutchman (speaking in German), a Frenchman, a Flemish-speaking Belgian, and an Austrian.

8. The Catholic last rites given to the hundreds of Polish victims.[22]

Over the course of less than twenty-five minutes, *Vernichtungslager Majdanek's* narrative moves from panoramic views of the city and a striking low-angle close-up of an unfurled Polish flag to joyous scenes of the local population at their liberation. Then, the scene abruptly shifts to a vivid depiction of the crimes committed, *against ethnic Poles,* in the fortress of Lublin. Next, the account proceeds to the camp itself, the investigations undertaken by the Extraordinary Commission and its more extended examination of the German methods of mass murder, including the gas chamber and scenes of the disinterment of victims. After a brief section in which four foreign survivors offer brief testimonies about their experiences, the film is capped by the spectacular Catholic funeral mass, accompanied by the old Polish patriotic hymn "Rota" ("The Oath").

There are many crucial features of *Vernichtungslager Majdanek's* selection of incidents, representative individuals, and overall narrative. One striking aspect is its appeal to the rule of law, which is most apparent in the fourth, fifth, and sixth sections. These sections provide a careful account of the investigation process, carried out with appropriately dignified formality by the Extraordinary Commission. Notable, too, is the lengthy attention given over to statements by the accused who, while denying their responsibility for mass murder, willingly testify to the existence of the awful crimes that occurred in the camp on a gigantic scale. The filmmakers, in short, wished to portray the Communist-dominated commission members as civilized seekers of truth and not merely as vengeful victors. However, they also evidently needed to convey a satisfying conclusion to the drama, both for the Poles and for an imagined international community. In this respect, the Majdanek film is incomplete, for it does not show the ultimate fate of those put on trial.

That task was taken up in a pendant film, *Swastyka i Szubienica* (*Swastika and Gallows*), which was also produced by the Film Studio of the Polish Army, also shot by the Forbert brothers and Stanisław Wohl, directed by Kazimierz Czyński, and edited by Włacław Kaźmierczak.[23] *Swastyka i Szubienica* covered public aspects of the trial in Lublin of the former German camp guards rounded up in the vicinity of the city. Begun on November 30, 1944, the trial lasted three days, and sentences were handed down on December 2. The filmmakers provided extended excerpts of testimony by various witnesses, along with statements by the accused and the chief judge, as well as the prosecuting attorney's highly emotional concluding plea. The film's aim was clearly to provide key information to far larger audiences than could actually be present. In so doing, the filmmakers obviously sought to sway public opinion. The conspicuous presence of a large, rapt public, our surrogates in the crowded courtroom, as well as of Polish and foreign journalists who were reporting on the trial for the local and world media, is also noteworthy for the way it buttresses the idea that Communist justice was not only eminently fair but also exceedingly swift. At the film's end, five of the defendants are brought to an imposing set of gallows in the middle of a large crowd.[24] We know the date—December 4, 1944—and the location: a space immediately adjacent to the crematorium in the camp.[25] The last images we see are of the bodies of five German guards swinging in the wind, as a voice-over points up the intended message: "This is not an act of revenge, but a simple act of justice."[26]

Taken together, the overarching narrative of *Vernichtungslager Majdanek* and *Swastyka i Szubienica* may be said to reflect a "crime-investigation-punishment" pattern developed in earlier Soviet war documentaries. To date, I have located only a single title, a documentary called *Prigovor Naroda* (*Verdict of the People,* 1943), but it provides an important model. *Verdict of the People* chronicles the crimes committed in the Krasnodar region and the ensuing trial of Soviet collaborators that began on July 14, 1943, in the city of Krasnodar. The film premiered in Moscow on August 19, 1943, and ends, as does *Swastyka i Szubienica,* in a graphically illustrated public hanging of the alleged perpetrators.[27]

But for all its commendable successes in trenchantly indicting German crimes and effectively conveying them in cinematic terms, *Vernichtungslager Majdanek* remains unsettling. No more than the Soviet documentary, which focused on the treason of Soviet citizens and was only obliquely about the Holocaust, does Ford's film take up the burden of representing the particular fate of the Jews in the German persecutions. It is true that Jews are mentioned in passing, but merely as one group of victims among many. This neglect was deliberate. The marginalization of Jewish victims reflects the well-known, ideologically motivated reluctance of the Communists, both Soviet and Polish, to single out the Jews despite the especially egregious losses they were known to have endured.

In fact, the stories told and the evidence adduced in *Vernichtungslager Majdanek* modify the conclusions of the Extraordinary Commission. Even while the commission's authors claimed that "the enslavement and extermination of the leading and active part of the *Slavic* peoples" was a major German war aim, they were at least candid in their blunt acknowledgment that the Nazis sought the "wholesale extermination of the Jews."[28] And the report also candidly acknowledged the ethnic background of a Corporal Resnick, a Jew who served in the Polish Army, who testified about his experiences in the camp. Now, thanks to the discoveries by the von zur Mühlens in Russian archives, we even know that actual footage of Corporal Resnick's testimony existed, but Ford and Bossak did not include it, even though he was one of the very few of the four thousand Polish Jewish soldiers who survived the camp. Nor did Ford mention the fact that the young Dutch man speaking about the loss of his parents in a monotonous, affectless German was also a Jew, Anton Benem.

The conspicuous downplaying of Jewish suffering when Jews almost certainly constituted the major group of victims at Majdanek is clearly connected with the audience that the Polski Komitet Wyzwolenia Narodowego (PKWN), or Polish Committee of National Liberation, the organization ultimately backing the filmmakers, wished primarily to address. Newly established and certainly not widely popular among the population they wished to control, the Communist-dominated PKWN above all needed to engage their *Polish* compatriots by underscoring that crucible of bitter experience shared by those who had remained in Poland and those like themselves who had fled their homeland during the German occupation. The gruesome images of the mass murder of non-Jewish Polish citizens and political resisters at the Lublin Castle—almost certainly among the first the formerly captive local Polish populations would have seen on film—would have been extremely important in the effort to create such emotional bonds. Their sympathetic portrayal was a sine qua non for the Communists to base an appeal for a shared patriotic effort to fight against the Germans. Interestingly, Bossak's narration over the victims at Lublin Castle was cannily gauged to appeal to the Poles by specifically invoking the memory of those Polish officers who had allegedly been murdered by the "Hitlerites" at Katyn Forest. This widely disseminated Communist propaganda charge was, of course, false, since the Russians themselves had killed them. (In fairness, it is not clear if Bossak was aware of this fact.) This stress on Polish suffering, therefore, was of strategic political importance to the Communists. Stress on Jewish experience, because it was even more devastating than that of the Poles, would have only gotten in the way. While fully aware of and not entirely indifferent to the fate meted out to the Jews, most Poles, as is well known, did not look forward to welcoming Jews back from the camps and exile. The Polish Jewish makers of the film would have been all too aware of this situation, and that is why they represent the Jews only as a kind of afterthought, as merely one of a class of victims who, *after the Poles,* are all treated as equal in stature.[29]

Ford and his coworkers also made the film with other propaganda intentions in mind. That is why the international dimensions of German aggression and the vital, larger context of the Soviet struggle were also not neglected. The short speeches (subtitled in Polish) given by the four former prisoners, each clearly labeled by his nationality, served as a vital reminder to Poles that they were not alone in their struggle, even as such testimonies may have been intended to remind Western audiences of the ties of blood that morally bound them to their Soviet allies. Their inclusion certainly suggests that the filmmakers and their political masters may very well have conceived the film for export abroad.[30] The rhetoric of universal suffering they used was, in any case, consistent with that routinely invoked in Communist-inspired reporting on the war in general and, after Majdanek, the camps in particular.

The last sequence is perhaps most telling about the film's unabashed effort to appeal to the Polish population. Here, the filmmakers attempted to "speak" in a sympathetic idiom to Poles legitimately skeptical of Communist intentions. By portraying in a dignified way a most un-Communist mourning ceremony, they went out of their way conspicuously to respect the Catholic religious orientation of the overwhelming majority of their compatriots. Prominently displayed are images of nuns and the revered icon, the Black Madonna of Częstochowa. Meanwhile, on the soundtrack, audiences were offered the familiar strains of the Polish hymn "Rota," albeit as sung by a Red Army military choir recruited and recorded by Ford and Bossak in Moscow.[31]

One may correctly say, of course, that in its identification of the victims with immediately recognizable Christian icons, the film is of its time. However much the reasons may vary, such an identification of the victims, one which entailed an evasion or even a suppression of recognition of how much and, often, how differently the Jews had suffered, was, in fact, a major feature of nearly all the postwar documentaries about the camps made in both East and West and, somewhat later, about the international criminal trials, too. Clearly, despite their ideological antipathies to religious observance, Polish and Russian Communist filmmakers evidently wished strategically to oppose the cross and the swastika, that is, an allegedly benign historical Christianity and Nazi paganism which, as Sylvie Lindeperg has observed in her recent book *Clio de 5 à 7,* often characterized Western Christian responses to Nazism.[32]

The prominent positions given to the Catholic burial ceremonies and Christian icons at the end of the film, however, also directly supported an emerging discourse that occluded the awful facts of the massive destruction of the Jewish community by using the emblems of Christianity. Many of the other documentary films made over the next few years were similarly marked by the display of Christian religious symbols. Consider, for example, the prominent burial scenes in the film about the concentration camp at Gardelegen, *Todesmühlen*

(*Death Mills,* 1946), or Roman Karmen's *Oświęcim* (*Auschwitz,* 1945), as well as the ending of such fictional films as Wolfgang Staudte's *Die Mörder sind unter uns* (*The Murderers Are Among Us,* 1946) and the Czech director Alfred Radok's *Dáleka Cesta* (*Distant Journey,* 1949). If one did not know better, one might conclude that the Nazis' primary victims were Christian. Clearly, such an emphasis calls for explanations which, however, cannot be offered in the space of this short essay.

We still know relatively little about how widely distributed *Vernichtungslager Majdanek* was, either in Eastern or Western Europe or in the United States. Mention has already been made of the film's exhibition in Lublin in November 1944, and one can assume that it was shown elsewhere in the Polish territories later "liberated" by the Russians. More work in Polish archives will undoubtedly confirm more extensive screenings than we now know of. Jewsiewicki comments on several documentary films shown in London (*Poland Fights On* and *Monte Cassino*) that portrayed Polish valor but does not mention Ford's work.[33]

Several studies have recently suggested that *some form* of the film was distributed in both the United States and France. Indeed, my research has confirmed that what was referred to as "a Russian news film of the 'Nazi death factory' at Maidanek," with a voice-over by William S. Gailmor, had its premiere at the Embassy Newsreel Theatre and at the Stanley Theatres in New York City on April 27, 1945.[34] The film's length, however, was only fourteen minutes, that is, one reel, about half of the Polish original. Contemporary accounts conclusively indicate, moreover, that material from *Swastyka i Szubienica,* specifically the hanging of the camp guards, was included in the distributed American version. The advertisements I already cited confirm this.[35] It remains uncertain what images this film contained or what story it told. We cannot know for certain since a film called *Maidanek Death Camp,* described as "sensational pictures of the Nazi Prison Camp," is listed—but only once—in an undated catalog of Artkino, a well-known American distributor of Soviet feature and documentary films.[36] It was soon dropped from the catalog and appears to be lost.

It is unclear whether this is the same Artkino film Soviet authorities presented under the title *Nazi Atrocities* in New York on April 26, 1945.[37] According to Delage, this film apparently also contained images of Auschwitz, which had been overrun by the Red Army in late January 1945, six months after Majdanek. Images of Auschwitz, however, are not mentioned in any of the accounts of the film I have located, as they almost certainly would have been. The ads for the distributed Majdanek film were, moreover, often boldly headlined "Nazi Atrocities," as were some for the American Signal Corps footage that was disseminated in late April in New York City and elsewhere across the country. This duplication may have led to some confusion.[38] It is doubtful, in any case, that this Soviet compilation and the possible bid for recognition of suffering on the eastern front it represented would have stood out amid the flood of even more ghastly images of violence and degradation then just beginning to appear in Western newsreels and photographs of the newly uncovered camps in Germany.[39] Majdanek as a symbol of ineffable evil was already giving way in the popular imagination to the even more graphic and shocking horrors portrayed by the first British newsreel images from Bergen-Belsen.

Our understanding of the Majdanek film's distribution in newly liberated France is also still sketchy. Christian Delporte notes that the discovery of the Eastern camps by the Soviets was not prominent in the recently liberated French newsreels, and their diffusion was, in any case, limited by lack of film stock.[40] Sylvie Lindeperg, however, provides evidence that some version of the film was distributed. She observes that French military censors suspended the public projection of a film entitled *Maïdanek* on April 12, 1945. The reason given was the possible demoralization of French families waiting for their loved ones to return from German captivity.[41] Once again, it is not clear what this version contained. Even more explicit confirmation of the screening of an eighteen-minute-long version of *Maïdanek* comes from Claudine Drame. After having been temporarily forbidden, she writes, the French authorities granted it a "*visa d'exploitation*" on April 30, 1945, but she also notes that it was never screened with the newsreels then beginning to flood French cinemas.[42] Where it was seen, by whom, and with what effect, she does not say. What seems clear from Lindeperg's and Drame's account is that some version of Ford's film containing the first images of the Eastern death camps was very likely seen in France, but questions about how widely it was seen, how much the French public was aware of the distinctions between extermination and other types of camps, and what responses the film provoked remain to be researched more thoroughly.

In short, the impact of Ford's *Vernichtungslager Majdanek* on Western filmmakers as well as on their local and broader European and American audiences cannot be accurately assessed at the present time. If the film presented what would become all-too-familiar material in vivid ways that later filmmakers, consciously or unconsciously, would respond to, I do not mean to claim for it a direct influence larger than it had. Certainly, more work needs to be done in the Polish archives to map its distribution in the Soviet occupation zones and the USSR, if, in fact, it was ever screened in a Soviet Union never eager to officially recognize the systematic extermination of the Jews and increasingly dominated by Stalinist anti-Semitism. More research is also needed to explore the film's influence on what I am convinced was its primary intended audience—the Poles just released from the German yoke.

In conclusion, one may appropriately praise *Vernichtungslager Majdanek* for being the first film to treat the Holocaust in considerable depth. As such, its stature and significance are undeniable. If its skillful narration and image making deserve to be commended, however, its sidestepping of Jewish suffering simultaneously highlights the constraints that political factors—in the Soviet-dominated Eastern bloc but not, it must be said, exclusively confined to it—exerted on the representation of the Holocaust when the cinema first assumed the burden of doing so.

NOTES

French historian Christian Delage first invited me to present my research on the Majdanek film at a conference he organized with Professor Anne Grynberg at the Musée du Judaïsme in Paris in June 2001. I am grateful to him for this opportunity and for the many discussions we have had on this topic. I would also like to thank my research assistant, Nat Trotman, Ph.D. candidate in art history at the City University of New York (CUNY) Graduate Center, for his help researching the American newspaper archives. My friend Professor Emeritus Krystyna Prendowska located and translated several crucial items from Polish film archives and libraries. Finally, my colleague Professor Dan Gerould of the Ph.D. program in theater at the CUNY Graduate Center and the writer and translator Jadwiga Kosicka corrected errors in Polish spelling in an earlier version of this essay.

1. B. H. Liddell Hart, *History of the Second World War* (New York: G. P. Putnam and Sons, 1971), 581. See also Gerhard L. Weinberg, *A World at Arms: A Global History of World War II* (New York: Cambridge University Press, 1994), 658, 708.

2. See Raul Hilberg, *The Destruction of the European Jews* (Chicago: Quadrangle, 1961), 580.

3. Józef Marszałek, *Majdanek: Konzentrationslager Lublin* (Warsaw: Interpress, 1984), 189. See also Konnilyn G. Feig, *Hitler's Death Camps: The Sanity of Madness* (New York: Holmes and Meier, 1981), 317ff. Alexander Donat provides a particularly vivid account of life in Majdanek in *The Holocaust Kingdom* (New York: Holt, Rinehart and Winston, 1963), 161–216. Soviet journalist Konstantin Simonov wrote the first extended account after the war. See *Maïdanek: un camp d'extermination* (Paris: Éditions Sociales, 1945). The short monograph was also published in several other languages. An English translation by Anatol Kagan is now available in Ilia Ehrenburg and Konstantin Simonov, eds., *In One Newspaper: A Chronicle of Unforgettable Years* (New York: Sphinx Press, 1985), 405–30.

4. "Report of the Polish-Soviet Extraordinary Commission for the Investigation of Crimes Committed by the German-Fascist Invaders in the Extermination Camp at Majdanek in the Town of Lublin," in *Soviet Government Statements on Nazi Atrocities* (London: Hutchinson, 1946), 222. First published in *Soviet War News* 965 (September 19, 1944).

5. For a selection of communiqués about earlier discoveries, see *Soviet Government Statements*. Such opinions were communicated to the English-language press by, among others, Roman Karmen, the Soviet journalist and documentary filmmaker. See Roman Karmen, "Lublin Extermination Camp Called 'Worst Yet' by Writer," *Daily Worker,* August 14, 1944, 8. The great novelist Vasily Grossman seconded Karmen's view in the *Daily Worker* on August 20, 1944. Western reporters following in the wake of Soviet forces echoed these opinions. See especially John Gibbons's reports in the *Daily Worker* on August 16 and 31 and September 1, 1944. Mainstream newspapermen such as the *New York Times* writer W. H. Lawrence commented, "After inspection of Maidanek, I am now prepared to believe any story of German atrocities, no matter how savage, cruel and depraved" ("Nazi Mass Killing Laid Bare in Camp," *New York Times,* August 30, 1944, 1, 9). The Majdanek crimes are also presented against the background of other war crimes in the film entitled *The Atrocities of the German-Fascist Invaders* that the Soviet prosecution team presented at the Nuremberg trial on February 19, 1946. It can be seen in the archives of the Centre de Documentation Juive Contemporaine in Paris. I thank Professor Delage for alerting me to this film's existence and Madame Karen Taieb of the Centre de Documentation for making it available to me. For more about it, see Christian Delage, "L'Image comme preuve," *Vingtième Siècle* 72 (October–December 2001): 63–78.

6. The Extraordinary Commission took up its work at the behest of Nikolai Bulganin, a higher-echelon member of the Soviet leadership, and

Edward Osóbka-Morawski, head of the Polish Committee of National Liberation (Polski Komitet Wyzwolenia Narodowego, or PKWN) in Lublin in August 1944. The commission's leaders included Andrzej Witos, who was then vice president of the PKWN. Witos, an NKVD prisoner since 1939, was a member of the Peasant Party and the brother of Peasant Party leader Wincenty Witos, who had been Polish prime minister three times between the wars. Also included in the leadership were Dr. Emil Sommerstein, a right-wing Zionist, who had become a member of the PKWN, and Catholic Prelate Kruszyński of Lublin. General Kudryatsev, a ubiquitous member of such investigative commissions, led the Russian delegation.

7. "Report of Polish-Soviet Extraordinary Commission," 222. Note that the Polish prosecuting attorney at the Majdanek trial in November 1944 offered an estimate as high as two million. These numbers may well have been exaggerated for propaganda purposes.

8. Hilberg maintains the surprisingly low estimate of 50,000 Jews killed even in the third volume of the revised edition of his *The Destruction of the European Jews* (New York: Holmes and Meier, 1985), 880, 1219. Leni Yahil cites an unspecified "official Polish estimate" of 200,000 individuals killed at Majdanek, of whom 125,000 were Jews. See Leni Yahil, *The Holocaust: The Fate of European Jewry* (New York: Oxford University Press, 1990), 363. Marszałek provides what is perhaps the most accurate estimate. He asserts that 360,000 were killed in the camp; 59.8 percent of the victims were Poles. Of course the majority of the Poles who died were Polish Jews, not to mention the large numbers of Dutch and other West European Jews who were also slaughtered. See Marszałek, *Majdanek*, 71, 192.

9. For example, some images were recycled by Hans Bürger [aka Hanuš Burger] in *Todesmühlen* (*Death Mills*, 1946), a film made for the American occupation forces in Germany; by the Russians in their compilation film, *Crimes of the German-Fascist Invaders*, presented in 1946 at Nuremberg; and by the French director Alain Resnais in his celebrated *Nuit et Brouillard* (*Night and Fog*, 1956), among others. A video version of *Todesmühlen* is available from the National Center for Jewish Film, Lown 102, M5053, Waltham, MA 02454.

10. Roman Karmen's group later produced the first documentary film about Auschwitz. See their *Oświęcim* (*Auschwitz*, 1945). A video version of the film is available from the National Center for Jewish Film.

11. In the production credits of the copy of *Vernichtungslager Majdanek* in the archive of the Wytwórnia Filmów Dokumentalnych i Fabularnych in Warsaw, two Russian cameramen, Wiktor Sztatland and Awenir Sofin, are listed who do not appear in the credits of the Internet Movie Database (http://www.imdb.com). See next note for more details about the production crews.

12. Wohl and the Forbert brothers were active cameramen for the Polish newsreels as well as for feature films. Ford was one of the key organizers of the state-controlled Film Polski company. Other names listed in the credits are: Jerzy Bossak (script), Olga Mińska, Ludmilla Niekrasowa, and Ludwik Perski (assistant directors); Olgierd Samucewicz (cameraman); W. Kotow and S. Sienkiewicz (sound); Sergiusz J. Potocki [Sergei Potozky] (music); and Władysław Krasnowiecki (narrator). The Internet Movie Database also lists Eugeniusz Jefimow [Evgenii Efimov] as a cameraman, though he does not appear in the Wytwórnia Filmów print's credits. Ironically, in the last spasm of the anti-Semitic purges in 1968, the Polish government singled out most of the Jewish Poles who had so loyally served the regime in the film industry since its inception after World War II. Ford, Bossak, and the Forbert brothers, along with the noted film historian and rector of the Film Academy in Łódź Jerzy Toeplitz, who, with Ford, had been prominent in the organization of Film Polski after the war, were all forced into exile. See Josef Banas, *The Scapegoats: The Exodus of the Remnants of Polish Jewry,* trans. Tadeusz Szafar (London: Weidenfeld and Nicholson, 1979), 146.

13. The German documentary filmmakers Bengt and Irmgard von zur Mühlen identify the Polish Army officer who receives the crowds' affection as a Captain Kamińsky. See their film *Maidanek 1944* (1986), a substantially reedited version of Ford's film and the later *Swastyka i Szubienica* (1945), compiled by Kazimierz Czyński from newsreel materials, which recounts the trial and hanging of the German camp guards.

14. We know that the Soviets did stage scenes in the camps to construct ideological messages. See, for example, the footage, purportedly of the "liberation of Auschwitz," by the cameraman Vorontsov. These scenes and Vorontsov's later comments are included in the film by Irmgard von zur Mühlen, *The Liberation of Auschwitz, 1945* (1985).

15. In his article in the Polish journal *Film,* Stanisław Wohl claims to have been the first on the scene: "We entered Majdanek a few minutes after the Nazis left. Hitler's crematoria still smouldered. Live prisoners in their state of extreme biological and psychological exhaustion, wanted to greet us. But they had no strength to raise their hands or cross themselves." Cited in Stanisław Ozimek, "The Polish Newsreel in 1945: The Bitter Victory," in *Hitler's Fall: The Newsreel Witness,* ed. K. R. M. Short and Stephan Dolezel (London: Croom and Helm, 1988), 72, from original source "w Chelmie i Lubline," *Film* 28, no. 9 (1969). Wohl is quoted somewhat differently but to the same effect in Stanisław Ozimek, *Film Polski w Wojennej Potrzebie* (Warsaw: Instytut Wydawniczy, 1972), 195; and Ozimek there also cites the contributions of the Forbert brothers and Samucewicz. Władysław Jewsiewicki also notes Forbert's participation in filming the camp; see Władysław Jewsiewicki, *Polscy Filmowcy na Frontach Drugiej Wojny Światowej* (Warsaw:

Wydawnictwa Artystyczne i Filmowe, 1972), 174. I thank Professor Krystyna Prendowska for these two references.

16. "Ozimek," Polish Newsreel in 1945, 72.

17. Writers for *Pravda* and *Red Star,* such as Konstantin Simonov, began their reports on the camp by August 10, while the BBC refused Alexander Werth's accounts, at least initially, as unbelievable. Soviet journalists as well as the American correspondent John Gibbons reported on the inquest for United States audiences in the *Daily Worker.* See Vasily Grossman's report on August 13, 1944, and his article "Poland's Years of Blood," in the issue of August 20, 1944. The latter is illustrated with images of Prelate Kruziński celebrating the funeral mass on August 6. In general, see the excellent account of press coverage of Majdanek in Barbie Zelizer, *Remembering to Forget: Holocaust Memory Through the Camera's Eye* (Chicago: University of Chicago Press, 1998), 49–61. Curiously, however, she does not even mention Ford's film.

18. According to the *New York Times,* the trial commenced in Lublin on November 30, 1944. See the brief notices on November 28 and December 3, 1944.

19. See Jewsiewicki, *Polscy Filmowcy,* 177.

20. The formulation is Zelizer's (*Remembering to Forget,* 49).

21. Also called Shollen and Shallen in various reports.

22. The von zur Mühlens identify some of the former prisoners as Anton Benem, a Dutch Jew; Corentin Le Dû, a French resistance fighter; Ludwig Tomashek, the Austrian who speaks in front of the crematorium chimney; and Tadeusz Udzin, a Polish Army officer.

23. This film, 709 meters in length and lasting approximately twenty-five minutes, was completed in early 1945. It can be seen as inventory number 8232 in the collections of the Wytwórnia Filmów Dokumentalnych i Fabularnych in Warsaw.

24. Six Germans, four SS men and two *Kapos,* were sentenced: Hermann Vogel, Anton Thernes, Theodor Schöllen, Wilhelm Karl Gerstenmaier, Edmund Pohlmann, and Karlheinz Stahl. Only five were actually executed since, as the *New York Times* reported on December 3, "Polmann" hanged himself in his cell, probably on December 1. Several others connected with the trial, including the infamously brutal SS men Thumann and Muhsfeldt, were killed or caught and tried later.

25. Marszałek, *Majdanek,* 193.

26. It would seem that the Soviets were taking a strong position in advance *against* the call to vengeance that the American film critic James Agee feared was implicit in the wave of "atrocity films" that swept American movie screens in April and May 1945. See James Agee, "Atrocity Films," *Nation,* May 19, 1945. Reprinted in James Agee, *Agee on Film* (Boston: Beacon

Press, 1958), 161–62. Note that Agee admits that he had not actually seen *any* of these films.

27. Among other details, the film offers the first account I have located of mass murder by means of mobile gas vans, in this case, products of the German firm Saurer und Diamant. This is, therefore, perhaps the earliest film to attempt to represent that process of *industrialized* mass murder that some scholars insist marks the Holocaust as unique. For more on the trial itself, see *The Trial in the Case of the Atrocities Committed by the German Fascist Invaders and Their Accomplices in Krasnodar and Krasnodar Territory* (Moscow: Foreign Languages Publishing House, 1943).

28. See the Extraordinary Commission's comments in *Soviet Government Statements,* 214–15; my emphasis.

29. In writing this, I do not mean in any way to diminish the vast extent of Polish losses. Rather, I simply want to underscore what is now generally accepted as the even greater dimension of horrors the Germans wreaked on the Jews. Incidentally, the downplaying of the Jewishness of the camp victims is also a notable feature of Western newsreels and documentaries about the camp when they were produced after April 1945. This fact deserves greater consideration elsewhere.

30. Interestingly, shortly after the dissemination of the basic facts of Majdanek became known, an American reader of the *Daily Worker,* M. Kubit, explicitly called for a movie about the camp. "Graphic description such as one never believed possible outside of the anti-fascist press has spread the news of the horror perpetuated. But the reams written and the radio stories broadcast are as nothing compared to the visual medium of the nation's cinemas. . . . Mere words are as nothing compared with the visual education inherent in the 'movies.' Only by showing our people the visual horrors that met the eyes of the correspondents at Lublin can we ever get across to them the immensity of the crime committed. I urge, therefore, that you do all in your power to see that such a film is made, distributed and shown." M. Kubit, "Film Front," *Daily Worker,* September 11, 1944, 11.

31. As Ozimek notes, between August and November 1944, it was impossible to bring out a regular newsreel because there was no way to make sound copies. "Rota" and the film's voice-over commentary were recorded at the central newsreel studio Soyuzkinochronika in Moscow. See Ozimek, "Polish Newsreel in 1945," 73.

32. Sylvie Lindeperg, *Clio de 5 à 7* (Paris: CNRS Éditions, 2000), 170–71.

33. Jewsiewici, *Polscy Filmowcy,* 177. Nicholas Pronay, "Defeated Germany in British Newsreels: 1944–25," in Short and Doelzel, *Hitler's Fall,* 28–49, also does not take note of Ford's film. His judgment that footage of the camps taken before the horrible images of Belsen by British Army

units did not have much impact in Britain is confirmed by Hannah Caven, "Horror in Our Time: Images of the Concentration Camps in the British Media, 1945," in *Historical Journal of Film, Radio and Television* 21, no. 3 (2001): 205–53.

34. See "Nazi Death Factory Shown in Film Here," *New York Times,* April 28, 1945, 6; see also Dave Platt, "Maidanek Horrors Stun Audience at Film Opening Here," *Daily Worker,* April 28, 1945, 12. Advertisements appearing in the *Daily Worker* over subsequent weeks refer to the film as "Maidanek S.S. Guards Executed." See the issues of May 4 and 5, for example.

35. For the length, see "Nazi Death Factory Shown in Film Here." A published comment by a member of the public, H. Meyer, also confirms the hanging scene: "Did you hear the applause when the Russians hanged the Nazis at Maidanek?" See "Moviegoers Hit Ban on Atrocity Film," *Daily Worker,* May 3, 1945, 5.

36. The catalogs are in the archives of the Museum of Modern Art in New York. The citation is from the second catalog, p. 14. The catalog probably dates from the mid-1940s.

37. Christian Delage mentions it; see Delage, "L'Image comme preuve," 66.

38. The famous Radio City Music Hall, by the way, refused to show the American footage, supposedly because the venue was a theater catering to families. See Samuel Sillen, "Why Does Radio City Censor Army Films on Nazi Atrocities?" *Daily Worker,* May 4, 1945, 11.

39. See Zelizer, *Remembering to Forget;* and also Robert H. Abzug, *Inside the Vicious Heart* (New York: Oxford University Press, 1985). For more detailed information about Western newsreels about the camps, see George Raynor Thompson and Dixie R. Harris, *The Signal Corps: The Outcome, Mid-1943 Through 1945* (Washington, DC: Office of the Chief of Military History, 1966).

40. "Les médias et la découverte des camps (presse, radio, actualités filmées)," in *La Déportation et le système concentrationnaire nazi* (Paris: Musée d'histoire contemporaine, BDIC, 1995), 205.

41. Lindeperg, *Clio de 5 à 7,* 164. She mentions that the Majdanek film was "directed [compiled] by the Soviet J. Setkiva" (ibid., my translation). The identity of this individual is unclear. Most likely, this individual was Irina Setkina, the well-known Soviet editor and director of documentary films.

42. Claudine Drame, "Représenter l'irreprésentable: les camps nazis dans les actualités françaises de 1945," *Cinémathèque,* no. 10 (Fall 1996): 27.

Christian Delage

Alain Resnais's *Night and Fog:* A Turning Point in the History of the Holocaust in France

NIGHT AND FOG IS THE FIRST MAJOR FRENCH FILM ABOUT THE concentration camps. Since its initial release as *Nuit et Brouillard* in 1956, its short running time of thirty-two minutes has made it possible for it to be played in both commercial and art theaters. Moreover, some demanding teachers, among them Henri Agel, organized screenings of the film in their classrooms even before French authorities required the film to be screened in schools.[1] Since then, it has become a sort of compulsory reference point for educators when dealing with the Holocaust, as well as a tool to combat the resurgence of anti-Semitism in French society.[2]

This official recognition might lead us to believe that Resnais's work, produced by Anatole Dauman for Argos Pictures, received an enthusiastic welcome as soon as it was released and that a consensus has emerged over the years about—and in no small part owing to—the gravity of the film's purpose and the aesthetic and ethical framework within which it was made. Actually, it proved to be problematic in 1956, and it still is even today.

No sooner had it been completed, and despite the Prix Jean Vigo it received,[3] the film had to deal with the French government's Board of Censors, which wanted to cut some shots of bodies it considered too horrifying. The board also insisted that a still picture of a French gendarme surveilling the Pithiviers camp had to be removed, because it would explicitly show the participation of the Vichy regime in the deportation of the Jews.[4] Then, when the film was close to being selected as one of the French motion pictures for the Cannes Film Festival, it became involved in a diplomatic and political imbroglio. The

West German Embassy tried to reverse the decision to select the film, arguing that, according to one of the festival's rules, its national pride would be compromised.[5] Having begun its life in such a stormy manner, the film's subsequent career has been marked by a second wave of criticism focusing on its account of the genocide of the Jews:

> Serge Klarsfeld said recently that if, at the time of *Night and Fog*'s initial release, the film had deeply touched him, . . . today it may be seen differently since it is a film whose major flaw is not to correctly convey the singularity of the Jews' fate. In the years since 1975, what has emerged most clearly is the difference between the prisoners interned because they were political opponents of Nazism and those who were interned because they were born Jews.[6]

In the 1990s, Georges Bensoussan underlines, "the genocide of the Jews is almost absent from the film,"[7] while, even more definitively, Annette Wieviorka states, "This film is not at all concerned with the genocide of the Jews."[8]

These are strong and in some ways understandable comments. However, my hypothesis is that the collective experience of *Night and Fog* may be seen today as an important step in the work of remembering those dark years as well as in the historical development of the study of the Final Solution. By reconstructing the process of making the film, I will explain how the team involved in the writing and filming of *Night and Fog* constantly tried to combine different aspects of the Nazi concentration camp system. This, I think, has been the source of a great deal of the confusion about their intentions.

FROM EXHIBITION TO FILM

The year 1954 witnessed a number of initiatives that modulated France's official memory of the camps. In anticipation of the tenth anniversary of the liberation of France, a bill was passed on April 14 to institute a National Day of Remembrance of the Victims and Heroes of the Deportation. On November 10, the Pedagogical Museum in Paris opened an exhibition entitled Resistance–Liberation–Deportation. Inaugurated by the minister of national education, it welcomed some sixty thousand visitors; among them were some thirty thousand Parisian secondary-school students. Designed by the Committee for the History of the Second World War (Comité d'Histoire de la Deuxième Guerre Mondiale, or CHDGM) headed by Henri Michel, this exhibition occupies a significant place in the chain of transmission of memories of the war and the deportation. Just after the exhibition ended, the city council of Paris decided to assemble the archives shown at the exhibition in order to preserve them in a City Museum for the Resistance, Liberation, and Deportation. A similar bill was proposed by Madame de Lipovsky, a member of the National Assembly. The exhibition was supposed to close at the beginning of the new year. However, at the request of the French premier, Pierre Mendès-France,[9] who happened to be Jewish, the run was extended until January 23, 1955. The extension helped bring two events together. The year 1954 would be dedicated to memories of the liberation; 1955 would commemorate the opening of the camps.

The exhibition was welcomed by the newspapers, both national and worldwide, for the importance of the issues it raised. The *New York Times* simply stated that "the visitor learns how the Nazis behaved in France; in it, one can find once more the spirit of the struggle for the Liberation." The *Times* also underscored the objectivity of the exhibition's discourse: "In addition to the tribute to the Resistance, this exhibition provides an objective commentary on the Nazi methods in the French occupied zone and in the concentration camps." In France, *Déportation et Liberté* stated that "it was a good thing that such an exhibition attempted to show a large audience what the concentration camps were like, using images to explain how what happened in them was a deliberate execution of a plan that was fortunately stopped."[10]

In addition to the photographic images, relevant films were screened each day, focusing both on the Resistance and the deportation. After visiting the exhibition, the producer Anatole Dauman agreed with Henri Michel about the necessity of making a new film to commemorate the tenth anniversary of the liberation of the camps. In the exhibition, the evocation of the camps was made possible thanks to an edited documentary based on newsreels, *Les camps de la mort* (*The Death Camps*), and a Polish feature film, Wanda Jakubowska's *Ostatni Etap* (*The Last Stop*).[11] These cinematic documents were among the first to be seen by the future producers of *Night and Fog* as they prepared to make their film. Coming from France and Poland, these two films give an indication of the future partnership of the two countries in the production of *Night and Fog:* in France, the CHDGM and the

French Ministry of War Veterans; in Poland, the Zbowid (Union of War Veterans Fighting for Liberty and Democracy), a governmental association of former POWs and war heroes now involved in building a democratic Poland.

THE ISSUE OF THE "ATROCITY" PICTURES

In early January 1955, Henri Michel announced that "a film dealing with the subject of the concentration camps" was in preparation. He said that he had spoken about this project with the producer Anatole Dauman and his two associates, Philippe Lifchitz and Sylvain Halfon, during a special tour of the exhibition. During the visit, their attention focused on the special room dedicated to the deportation, which evoked the "fate of those who, put in prison because of their political commitments or for reasons of race, had to endure torture or death; or, who left French prisons only to be sent into camps in the Greater Reich." Access to this special room was prohibited to people younger than seventeen "because of the tragic aspect of numerous documents exhibited." A short review in the French newspaper *Le Monde* said:

> The exhibition will show the twenty-five thousand students who will visit it—and most of them were not born at the time—how the victory of 1944 was won. Visitors under seventeen will not have access to the room devoted to the deportation, and that's for the better. They wouldn't be able to draw the necessary lessons that adults can; they would only leave with incomprehensible, nightmarish visions. Nothing of the tragedy of the concentration camps has been left in the dark: the bathtub the Gestapo used at its Avenue Foch headquarters; personal objects belonging to prisoners; a desk blotter made of human skin; items from the gas chamber; photographs of living ghosts and mass graves. . . . Films inspired by the Resistance and the war will be screened throughout the exhibition.[12]

The historians involved in the writing of the film were concerned about showing atrocity pictures. In one of his first memos, dated March 3, 1955, Henri Michel wrote:

> The subject, the nature of the material collected, provides every guarantee of a serious treatment, but the film directors are aware of the

danger of forcing the spectators to endure too much horror. What matters is not so much the *sadistic, war crime, inhuman atrocity* side of it, but to make a sociological explanation the focus of image and text. When watching this film, the former prisoners interned in the concentration camps must recognize their own ordeals. Ordinary people should also understand how systematic, how cruel and scientific, the process of the concentration camps was.[13]

Two demands were made on the filmmakers. The first was pedagogical: the historians wanted to provide greater knowledge of the concentration camps. The second mainly focused on the issue of memory, of fidelity to the survivors. In doing so, it was necessary to take into account the gap between the generations. Quite clearly, the film's producers understood that young people were to be the main target.

Some of the first French viewers of *Night and Fog* thought Alain Resnais had deliberately chosen milder depictions of the camps, as he himself stated in 1986 in an interview with Richard Raskin:

> Some people had seen the film in private screenings and many said to me: "Of course, you were afraid to use violent pictures. So you did not include the terrible images we saw at the Liberation, etc." This is not true at all. I had access to all the French films shown at the time of the Liberation, and I did not suppress any violent footage. It's just that they imagined they saw things in 1944 and 1945 that had shocked them. But the legend has it that I deliberately toned down the film so that it could be more commercial. Not true. I didn't try to include extremely violent footage. It's just that I never came across any. I don't know what I would have done if I had. Legends were created: rumor had it that some shots showed what happened in a gas chamber at the moment of killing, that these had been shot by the Germans. I think this is a legend. Anyway, I never came across such documents.[14]

Fear that the violence in the images from the camps would be represented in a voyeuristic manner seems to have led the filmmakers to tone down the images, at least according to those first spectators from 1945. It is obvious that, ten years after the first filmic accounts of the concentration camps seen at the very moment when they were freed by the Allies, the memory of the event had grown, having been reinforced by the publication of thousands of written testimonies, many exhibitions, and even dramatic reconstitutions. Instead of gain-ing in distance from what happened, the reconstruction of the fate of the prisoners interned in concentration camps would seem to have reinforced the ordeal endured in 1945, thereby increasing the impact of the images. Some of their components—the barbed wire, the bodies, the skeletal survivors—had become icons, both factual and symbolic. This is a very interesting statement, for it emphasizes one of the principal problems in the film, namely, its representation of atrocity. Many such images were shot at the time of the liberation, but they only partially accounted for what happened when the camps were in full operation. The atrocities recorded in these images echoed the lack of belief that prevailed throughout the war regarding the information Allied embassies received about Nazi extermination policies. How could there even be images that confirmed written information that was beyond all comprehension?

Such disbelief must be considered from the perspective of the legacy of World War I. At that time, there had been intense contact between the front lines and the rear, accentuated by soldiers taking leave, going back and forth from home, and so on. Post-1918 witnesses were everywhere in society, and their memory was highly formalized and institutionalized; the war experience became a major subject in literature. The society that went into World War II was filled with images of war violence. The war experiences of the British and French—not to mention other countries—were, however, on a totally different scale after 1940. In collective representation, the mass graves of the concentration camps took the place of the mass graves of the trenches, in a complex system of symbolic correspondence. Yet this time, there was very little exchange—no letter writing, very few survivors who made it out of this new hell. There was an unprecedented problem in the transmission as well as the credibility of information which film would solve only after the war. When, for example, the Soviets showed their first newsreel about the Majdanek and Auschwitz camps (in the film named *Nazi Atrocities*) on April 26, 1945, in New York, there was general skepticism about witnesses who spoke about the camps as well as, in the United States, distrust of anything the Soviets had to say. The Americans had to see what their own cameramen had shot before they gave credit to the images shown by Artkino, the American distributor of Soviet materials. Only after similar newsreels by Americans were shown could the editor of the *Boston Globe* write, "Now we know that the Russians told the truth."[15]

One other problem is the lack of distinction between concentration and extermination camps, which is tantamount to overlooking the systematic policy of exterminating the European Jews. That is why historians and filmmakers criticized the film, although one should point out that the emergence of an accurate history of the Holocaust occurred many years later. I will return to this point.

THE RESEARCH IN FILM ARCHIVES

What did Resnais find in the archives? We could summarize what he discovered as follows. He could easily obtain photographs and films that were available from the museums at Auschwitz and Majdanek, which he visited with Michel and Wormser. He was also supplied with documents found by Michel in Holland. What he didn't have access to were British archives. "We were told," he said later, "that they did not want to make any document available to us."[16] He also could not gain access to American materials because he thought they "would have cost too much." However, when questioned years later, he remarked that he did not remember being denied access to material.[17] As for German archives, Resnais noted that he had only "what the Germans had given to the Committee for the History of the Second World War, or what that Committee had been able to obtain."[18]

He did watch, but could not acquire, images from French archives. "We visited the Film Department of the French Army which, I must admit, didn't have much to show. Still, I had chosen a shot, the unveiling of a war memorial, something like that, which I thought might be useful and which I ordered from them. But they never sent it to me. Instead I got a letter stating that, *because of the nature of the film,* no document from their department could be supplied to us."[19]

Resnais actually researched very few archives. His sources of film footage were surprisingly limited (and such material was mostly obtained secondhand, namely, from Soviet archives kept by the Poles, British archives kept in Holland, etc.), which is why the shots he gathered were often in poor condition and did not have their original titles.

In addition to the lack of footage, there was, "given the nature of the film," the censorship imposed by the French Army Photographic Branch (Service Cinématographique des Armées, or SCA). This attitude may appear strange, since the picture—which, at that time, was still at the writing stage—had received the support and even a grant from the Ministry for War Veterans. Alain Resnais had, indeed, just made *Statues Also Die,* a short film about African art which had already been censored because of its anticolonial tone. Moreover, he shared certain political attitudes with the producers of *Night and Fog,* namely, he wanted to inject the memory of the concentration camps into contemporary debates about the war in Algeria. In fact, since November 1954, newspapers had revealed to French audiences the torture methods employed against Algerian nationalists and linked them to those utilized by the Nazis during the Second World War.[20] Jean Cayrol, the writer of *Night and Fog*'s voice-over commentary, would say on the very day of the film's premiere:

> Memory remains only for as long as it illuminates the present. If the crematoria are now nothing more than derisory skeletons, if silence falls, like a shroud, on the overgrown grass of the former campgrounds, let us not forget that our own country is not immune to the scandal of racism.[21]

Even though they had selected only a limited number of films in the SCA archives, the Argos company tried to get the SCA to reverse its decision not to provide them. The company's efforts were unsuccessful. In the end, Resnais, who had seen some Buchenwald footage at the SCA, was given a copy from the Gaumont cinematheque. He even found some unedited footage in the Gaumont vaults.[22]

Once he secured Jean Cayrol's agreement to collaborate with him, the filmmaker wanted to explore "the notion of stupidity with a capital S. Stupidity as something terrifying. The horror of human stupidity."[23] He said he was determined not to make a film that looked like a "war memorial." Then he chose three strategies for his documentary, which are apparent to anyone who watches the film. First, he mixed archival footage and stills with contemporary shots of Auschwitz and Mauthausen. In fact, he organized the comparison between both sets of images by modeling several shots on some of the archival footage. Second, he emphasized the contrast between past and present by opposing color shots with the black-and-white archival footage. Finally, he carefully edited both sets of contrasting images with Jean Cayrol's commentary and Hans Eisler's music.

THE ROLE OF THE HISTORICAL CONSULTANTS

What role did the historical consultants of the film play in its creation, since at the time they were working not only on the Resistance and concentration camps but also on the special fate of the European Jews during World War II? In October 1944, following the same model as that established after the First World War, the Provisional Government of the French Republic set up a Commission on the Occupation and Liberation of France, an agency of the Education Ministry. The new unit was to focus on the history of the Resistance. There was also a Committee for the History of the War, closely affiliated with the governing council that attended to the work of collecting archival materials. The two groups merged in 1945 and became the Committee for the History of the Second World War, which in turn created a special commission dedicated to the history of the deportation. Henri Michel and Olga Wormser were members of this committee. Both consultants worked in an intellectual context, in which, according to Henry Rousso, there was "very little interest in the history of the Vichy regime, hardly any interest at all in its anti-Jewish policy, but a lot of interest in the history of the Resistance, deportation (though not in its racial dimension) and German repression."[24]

In 1950, Henri Michel, the director of the CHDGM, published the first mass-market book dedicated to the history of the Resistance.[25] Then, in 1954, in collaboration with Olga Wormser, he published an anthology of 190 texts entitled *Tragédie de la déportation 1940–1945: Témoignages de survivants des camps de concentration allemands* (*Tragedy of the Deportation 1940–1945: Testimonials of Survivors of German Concentration Camps*). In the introduction, it may appear as if the authors are writing this history along the lines that Henry Rousso, quoted earlier, had noted. They expressed their hope to preserve the "memory of these millions of martyrs, who belonged to all social classes and religions, from all political parties, the citizens of 22 nations."[26] However, at another point, Michel and Wormser wrote, "The individual executions produced an unsatisfactory result, given the number of prisoners and the goal established by the SS, [namely] the extermination of inferior races (Jews and Gypsies) and the enemies of the Reich. That is why the cover-up of the murders is one of the most striking facts about the organization of the camps. Never in the history of any country did there exist a more perfect and murderous way of killing than the camp and crematorium at Auschwitz. There was no need of any pretext, of some physical or mental deficiency, of old age or the breaking of discipline. The prisoners of Auschwitz (except the hundreds of politicals, Aryans who, by the way, also died in large numbers) had to die because they were Jews."[27] This statement quite clearly highlights the problem of the specificity of the Jewish genocide and of the Auschwitz camp.

By the way, it was not Alain Resnais himself who decided to shoot in the Majdanek and Auschwitz camps, even though it was he who finally chose to use color stock for these images. Rather, it was Henri Michel. In a memo sent by one of the producers to Resnais, dated May 3, 1955, that is, three weeks after signing his contract, the producer reported,

> Mr. Henri Michel recently paid a visit to us and gave us good news concerning the forthcoming production of the film, thanks to our recent trip to Poland. He was deeply moved by the visit he paid to the deportation camps, made in the company of survivors. He thinks that the sight of the empty camps, and of the museums where the belongings, the relics of the prisoners are preserved, won't fail to move you in such a way that it would have a great influence on your conception of the film.[28]

The film, it seems, was to have two purposes in describing the history of the camps. First and foremost, the makers wished to give an account of the whole community formed by the prisoners in the camps and their tragic fate. Second, they wished also to focus on the genocide of the Jews. This double focus can also be identified in the two special issues of the journal of the CHDGM, published just before and after the production of the film. The first, released in 1954, is dedicated to the history of the "German system of concentration camps"; it focuses on the concentration camps. One of the texts published there is about the special fate of the "Nacht und Nebel" prisoners. As a matter of fact, we can find a similar interest in this special status in another text, a poem, that appears in the anthology published by Michel and Wormser. Written by Jean Cayrol, a former Mauthausen prisoner who in 1946 published his *Poèmes de la nuit et du brouillard* (*Poems of the Night and Fog*), the poem evokes what he had to endure as a *N.N.* (*Nacht und Nebel*) *Schutzhäftling.*[29] The *Nacht und Nebel* (night and fog) decree specified that offenses committed by the inhabitants of occupied territories were to result in the secret deportation of the offenders without trial. In this way, terror would be spread as persons mysteriously vanished without any indications as to what had happened to them.

The second special issue published by the CHDGM focuses on "The Condition of the Jews." In the foreword, Henri Michel pays tribute to the work accomplished in this field by the Centre de Documentation Juive Contemporaine and relates that the estimate of the number of Jews killed in the camps is close to six million: "It is the monstrousness of this number that makes this Nazi crime something new. . . . 'The Final Solution' of the 'Jewish problem' implemented by Himmler is only comprehensible against the background of the global Nazi ideology, of which it is one of the culminations."[30]

Not only is the genocide of the Jews clearly stated and the number of victims essentially accurate, even the responsibility of the Vichy regime is sharply underscored. "A major fact: the manifestation by the Vichy Governments of their independence led them to anticipate and to be ahead of the occupation authorities in the measures taken against the Jews."[31]

These publications provide a clear indication of how the film script was then about to be written. One need pay attention only to the successive tentative titles given by the producer to the project. On March 1, 1955, it is called "Film About the Deportation." On March 3, "Film About the System of the Camps." Then, on May 20, "Resistance and Deportation." Finally, on May 24, it has become "Night and Fog." On the other hand, the first memo written by the historical consultants developed their idea of summarizing the prisoners' fate as "the Stations of the Cross." However, even in this highly Christianized vision of the Calvary the deportees experienced, the mention of the particular fate of the Jews was not forgotten. In the preamble to the script, their situation is related to the presence of the Germans in France: "The Fate of the Jews (the census; the Yellow Star; the despoliation; the internment camps; a roundup)." And these images are then tied, at least implicitly, to Nazi ideology: "Flashback: Nazi parade in Nuremberg, Hitler, Himmler, Göring.

Sentences of *Mein Kampf* about the extermination of opponents and inferior races."[32]

WHAT HAPPENED TO THE MENTION OF THE JEWISH GENOCIDE?

In one of the first drafts of the film script, the events of early 1942 are formulated as follows:

> The second visit of Himmler in 1942. The German war effort. The growth of the camps starting from this visit on. The twenty-two countries. "Tens of thousands of Russian women for digging anti-tank ditches, etc." The "Final Solution of the Jewish Question," decided in 1942. "The inferior races must work for us. The Jews, the Poles, the Gypsies and the Russians must be annihilated, but productively. Annihilation through labor is more productive," etc.[33]

The historians of the CHDGM, who agreed to the synopsis by putting their official stamp on it, asked for some changes to the three first sentences:

> The second visit of Himmler in 1942 [in Auschwitz]. The German war effort. The growth of *the camps* [words cut, replaced by: "Kommandos and crematoriums"] starting from this visit on.

Then the moment after the shooting of the film arrived, when Jean Cayrol was about to write the commentary.[34] A special screening was organized for him. At its end, Cayrol was shocked; he said to Resnais that it was too hard for him to go back to these memories and that he preferred to withdraw from the project. Chris Marker, who had made possible the meeting between Resnais and Cayrol, however, insisted that he continue. Finally, Cayrol agreed, but only on the condition that he write his text without seeing the film for a second time. It is Marker who will put the words of Cayrol on top of the images, trying to preserve the poetic character of the writing. Here is the way the year 1942 is evoked in the final version:

> 1942. A visit from Himmler. "We must destroy, but productively." Leaving the production aspects to his technicians, Himmler concentrates on destruction. Plans, models are studied. They are carried out; the deportees themselves take part in the work. A crematorium can be made to look like a picture postcard. Today, tourists

have themselves photographed in front of them. Deportation extends to all of Europe.[35]

The reference to what Resnais had himself put in quotations marks, as a kind of historical fact ("The 'Final solution to the Jewish Question,' decided in 1942") disappeared. This cut is certainly related to Cayrol's style of writing, more literary than historical. Cayrol, in any case, wished to make a more general statement about the experience of the camps rather than to focus more specifically on the Jewish question, as Resnais had apparently envisioned.

It is important to remember, too, that Cayrol, like Resnais and the other producers, also wanted to insert the memory of the concentration camps into the history of contemporary France; that is, they wished to link the memory of the camps with the war in Algeria. Because he was the last to intervene in the process of making the film, it would seem that the mention of the Final Solution was cut from the commentary only at the very last moment.

I think I have offered some explanations for why this ultimate cut was made. For his part, Alain Resnais is the first to recognize the burden of the material, intellectual, and emotional constraints he had to cope with. With great humility, he says he regrets not having had the time necessary to do further research before shooting. For us today, there is no doubt that he really succeeded in offering a film equal in gravity to its subject by finding an appropriate aesthetic and ethical framework for it. He was, moreover, dependent on Jean Cayrol's own experience, although Cayrol had been in a concentration camp, not in a death camp. Having to rely on Henri Michel and Olga Wormser, he could only follow the historiographical trends of the time, which did not put the genocide of the Jews at the center of historical research. But, as I explained, the years 1954 and 1955 are far from being an idle time in the evolution of both the history and the memory of the genocide of the Jews and of the responsibility of the Vichy regime for the Final Solution. On the contrary, they represent a turning point.

For all these reasons, *Night and Fog* is a document deeply rooted in the context of its making. Because it is, it may be regarded as a text that teachers or filmmakers can examine as an adaptation to ever-changing patterns in the history of and education about the Holocaust. *Night and Fog,* in other words, is not just a "representation of" historical facts; rather, it is a construction of the past, based on the viewpoints of individuals who did not share the same experience of the war and who were then engaged in the process of negotiating the meaning of the camps by making the film.

The Christian Jean Cayrol was deported because he was a *résistant* (resister), which explains why he wanted to focus on the daily life of prisoners in the camp; the film producer, Anatole Dauman, born in 1925 inside the Jewish Russo-Polish community of Warsaw, was also strongly committed to fighting for the liberation of France, which explains why he would afterward prefer to declare himself a resister rather than a Jew. The historians of the CHDGM, Henri Michel and Olga Wormser, who happened to have contributed much to research about the war and the Holocaust during the 1950s, had confidence in the power of film—something not that common, even today—and they tried to promote a dispassionate and well-documented writing of history in the new medium. Finally, Alain Resnais's dual identity as an attentive viewer and an experienced filmmaker helped incarnate their ideas in a vivid and memorable way. Whatever limitations the film may rightly be said to have, it remains a model of serious collaboration between filmmakers and historians.

NOTES

This essay was translated from the French by Stuart Liebman, in consultation with the author. The essay has been made possible by Madame Florence Dauman, who provided special access to the archives of Argos Films at the Institut Lumière in Lyon, France. Thanks are also due to Thierry Frémaux and Nicolas Riedel of the Institut Lumière. A longer, slightly modified version of this text appears in my book (coauthored with Vincent Guigueno) *L'Historien et le film* (Paris: Gallimard, 2004). ARTE Video released a DVD edition of *Nuit et Brouillard* in March 2003.

1. "Henri Agel, a French teacher of literature at the Lycée Voltaire, was one of these peculiar borderline figures," writes French critic Serge Daney. "To avoid the toil of Latin class, for himself as well as for us, he used to have us vote on the following: whether to work an hour on a text by Livy or to watch films. The class voted for the motion pictures, and regularly left the dilapidated film club thoughtful and engaged. Somewhat sadistically, and because he obviously had some prints available, Agel screened short films designed to take away the teenagers' innocence. [He showed] Georges Franju's *Le Sang des bêtes* [*The Blood of the Beasts*] and, above all, Alain Resnais' *Night and Fog*." Serge Daney, "Le Travelling de *Kapo*," *Trafic* 4 (1992): 7.

2. It was, for example, broadcast on all TV channels after the desecration of the Jewish cemetery in Carpentras in 1990.

3. The Prix Jean Vigo was awarded on January 31, 1956. Resnais had already won the award two years earlier for his *Les Statues meurent aussi* (*Statues Also Die*), which did not prevent the film from being banned in 1956.

4. "Resnais was forced to remove an offending gendarme's *képi,* which appeared in a shot of the transit camp at Pithiviers, a camp set up by the Germans but administrated by the French. The censors thus obliterated not the filmmaker's words or images but an actual historical detail, an incontestable fact." Henry Rousso, *The Vichy Syndrome: History and Memory in France Since 1944,* trans. Arthur Goldhammer, foreword by Stanley Hoffmann (Cambridge, MA: Harvard University Press, 1991), 230.

5. See Richard Raskin, *Alain Resnais's* Nuit et Brouillard: *On the Making, Reception and Functions of a Major Documentary Film, Including a New Interview with Alain Resnais* (Aarhus, Denmark: Aarhus University Press, 1987), 33–45. When it was released in Germany, the film could be shown only to adults over the age of eighteen.

6. André Heinrich, interview by Nicole Vuillaume, "*Nuit et Brouillard* au-delà de la censure," radio program, France Culture, August 6, 1994.

7. Georges Bensoussan, *Auschwitz en héritage? D'un bon usage de la mémoire* (Paris: Éditions des Mille et une Nuits, 1998), 44.

8. Annette Wieviorka, *Déportation et génocide. Entre la mémoire et l'oubli* (Paris: Plon, 1992), 223.

9. Pierre Mendès-France was born in Paris in 1907. He joined the Radical Party and entered parliament in 1932. An opponent of the Vichy government, he was stripped of public office because he was a Jew and imprisoned in 1940. He escaped the following year and went to England to join the Free French forces. In 1945, he was appointed minister for national economy under Charles de Gaulle. He became prime minister in 1954 but was forced to resign the following year over his North African policy.

10. Press articles quoted in the exhibition catalog *Résistance, Libération et Déportation* (Paris: Musée Pédagogique, 1954). Files of the Institut d'histoire du temps présent, Centre national de la recherche scientifique, File Nr. RF 527, 3.

11. On this film, read Stuart Liebman, "Les Premières constellations du discours sur l'Holocauste dans le cinéma polonais," in *De l'histoire au cinéma,* ed. Antoine de Baecque and Christian Delage (Brussels: Éditions Complexe, 1998), 193–216. See also Annette Wieviorka, "*La Dernière étape:* un film entre témoignage et fiction," in Wieviorka, *Déportation et génocide,* 293–312.

12. Quoted in Raskin, *Alain Resnais's* Nuit et Brouillard, 27.

13. "Film documentaire sur le 'système concentrationnaire allemand,'"

n.d., 2 pp., Files Argos Films, Institut Lumière, Lyon (hereafter cited as Argos Files).

14. Quoted in Raskin, *Alain Resnais's* Nuit et Brouillard, 57–58.

15. Uncle Dudley, "Bedeviled Germans," *Boston Globe,* quoted by Barbie Zelizer in *Remembering to Forget* (Chicago: Chicago University Press, 1998), 62.

16. Quoted in Raskin, *Alain Resnais's* Nuit et Brouillard, 53.

17. Heinrich interview.

18. Ibid.

19. Ibid.

20. Raphaëlle Branche reports that in January 1955, "it was Claude Bourdet and François Mauriac who revealed these practices to French audiences in articles with titles as provocative as they were troubling: 'Your Gestapo in Algeria' and 'The Question.' They denounced the torture to which the General Secretary of the MTLD, Moulay Merbah, had been subjected." Raphaëlle Branche, *La Torture et l'armée pendant la guerre d'Algérie, 1954–1962* (Paris: Gallimard, 2001), 32–33.

21. Jean Cayrol, "We Conceived of *Night and Fog* as a Warning Device," *Les Lettres françaises,* no. 606 (February 9, 1956). For its producer, Anatole Dauman, the film aimed at a special target, which also suited the Polish Communist organizations involved in the project: "Explain clearly how the system of the concentration camps (its economic side) results from fascism. Evoke the start of the camps at the same time as the victory of the Nazis in 1933. . . . Be careful: 'fascism is always possible.'" Notes on the meeting of Saturday, May 28, 1955, Argos Files.

22. Specifically, the following two documents: "Procès de Buchenwald et de Dachau" (1947–NU-301) and "Tribunal Buchenwald" (1947–NU-578); the abbreviation *NU* stands for *Not Utilized.*

23. First draft of the script, Anatole Dauman's *Night and Fog* Files, Institut Lumera, Lyon.

24. Henry Rousso, *La Hantise du passé* (Paris: Textuel, 1998), 72–73.

25. Henri Michel, *Histoire de la Résistance* (Paris: Presses Universitaires de France, 1950).

26. Henri Michel and Olga Wormser, *Tragédie de la déportation 1940–1945: Témoignages de survivants des camps de concentration allemands* (Paris: Hachette, 1954), 10.

27. Ibid., 401–2.

28. Philippe Lifchitz to Alain Resnais, May 3, 1955, Argos Files.

29. Jean Cayrol, *Lazare parmi nous* (Neufchâtel: Éditions de la Baconnière, 1950), quoted in Michel and Wormser, *Tragédie de la déportation,* 136–37.

30. Henri Michel, foreword to special issue "La Condition des Juifs,"

Revue d'histoire de la Deuxième Guerre mondiale, no. 24 (October 1956): 2–3.

31. Ibid.

32. All memos in Anatole Dauman's *Night and Fog* Files, Institut Lumera, Lyon.

33. *Nuit et Brouillard,* script, March–April 1955, Argos Files.

34. We should also mention the role of the music written by Hanns Eisler. Its double-edged tone, both ironic and desolate, pays tribute to the softness desired by Resnais. The music would later be used by the German filmmaker Alexander Kluge in *Die Patriotin* (*The Patriot;* 1979), albeit one which entailed a shift from its original meaning.

35. *Nuit et Brouillard,* film commentary, December 1955, Argos Files.

Lawrence Douglas

Trial as Documentary: Images of Eichmann

IN EXAMINING DOCUMENTARIES OF THE 1961 ADOLF EICHMANN TRIAL in Jerusalem, my interest is in exploring the role that film plays in transforming historic trials into historical events. In so doing, I want to consider how trials staged to define the terms of responsible remembrance have themselves become digested into collective memory.

The Eichmann trial provides an exemplary subject for such a study inasmuch as the trial marked an unprecedented intrusion of television-video technology into a legal setting. As is well known, Capital Cities, an American film and television company, agreed to film the trial in its entirety. The judges, concerned that the presence of movie cameras might diminish the dignity of a proceeding already troubled by the specter of the carnivalesque—the zoolike glass booth designed to protect the defendant, the reconverted theater in which the trial was staged—granted permission to Capital, but only after the production company convinced the tribunal that its four hidden cameras and newly developed sound-dampened equipment wouldn't disturb the proceeding. (In the pretrial hearing to consider the feasibility of filming, Capital surprised the judges by revealing that the hearing itself had been filmed using the very stealth technology that would be used at trial.)[1] Capital also decided to use another new technology—videotape, which could be quickly copied and distributed to broadcasting outlets around the globe. Capital did this all as a public service, offering copies to broadcasters at no profit and supplying the court with a complete set at no cost. And so the Eichmann proceeding became the first televised trial. Long before Court TV, long before O.J., there was Eichmann. (In Israel, however, the fledgling communications infrastructure didn't include television, and so the trial was broadcast live on radio—also, for the time, an unprecedented event.)[2]

Unprecedented as it was, the filming and televising of the trial was no mere ancillary or idiosyncratic feature of the proceeding. The trial, as many have noted, was staged not simply to submit the crimes of the Holocaust to legal judgment but also for didactic reasons. In the words of Israeli attorney general and chief prosecutor Gideon Hausner, the trial intended to provide a younger generation of Israelis with "real knowledge . . . of the way in which their own flesh and blood had perished."[3] As a second matter, the trial meant to educate the world at large, "which had so lightly and happily forgotten the horrors that occurred before its eyes, to such a degree that it even begrudged us the trial of a perpetrator."[4] Broadcasting the event was thus instrumentally of a piece with the very pedagogical ends the trial meant to serve.

Whether the ends of justice and didactic history are compatible is, of course, a matter of controversy. Hannah Arendt, in her famous critique of the Eichmann proceeding, argued that the "purpose of a trial is to render justice, and nothing else."[5] We must be wary, Arendt insisted, of subjecting the trial to pressures that may distort the solemn dictates of justice. The danger of turning a trial into a pedagogical spectacle is that it becomes a legal farce, a show trial lacking the element of "irreducible risk" that Otto Kirchheimer identified as the sine qua non of a just legal proceeding.[6] Other scholars, however, such as Michael Marrus, have offered a critique that is the obverse of Arendt's.[7] Here the argument is not that law's tutelary role will distort its solemn responsibility to do justice to the accused. Rather, it is that when called upon to clarify the past, trials fail to do justice to the historical record. However we might feel about these matters—my recent book, *The Memory of Judgment,* treats them in some depth—they underscore the point that the filming of the trial was a critical extension and manifestation of the logic of the trial itself: to create a record of the Holocaust for the present and posterity.[8]

It is hardly a surprise, then, that a trial that accepted, if not invited, cameras into the courtroom has been the subject of a number of film documentaries. My interest is in considering four: *Verdict for Tomorrow,* created and broadcast at the time of the trial itself, in 1961; *Witnesses to the Holocaust,* produced roughly a quarter of a century later, in 1987; *The Trial of Adolf Eichmann,* a PBS-ABC collaboration of a decade after that, 1997; and finally, *The Specialist,* an independent film released by an Israeli-French film team in 1999. While each film relies on a particular documentary idiom for the purposes of capturing the trial, together they dramatize evolving understandings of the meaning and nature of the proceeding, and in so doing, they highlight and underscore both the attractions and dangers of turning courtrooms into filmic events.

Verdict for Tomorrow, with a running time of thirty minutes, was the first documentary made about the Eichmann trial.[9] Produced by the Anti-Defamation League and Capital Broadcasting, it was directed by Leo Hurwitz, who, with producer Milton Fruchtman, had arranged and overseen the filming of the trial by Capital. An early member of the leftist Film and Photo League, Hurwitz had made his name during the 1930s with a number of edgy documentaries exploring hunger, oppression, and racial intolerance in the United States during the Depression. They included his famous examination of civil rights, *Native Land,* made with Paul Strand and narrated by Paul Robeson.[10] His contempt of Hollywood and his interest in using film as a tool of social justice earned him a blacklisting in the 1950s, though he continued to find work with certain outlets such as Capital.

Verdict for Tomorrow, which received Emmy and Peabody awards, was completed and screened between the conclusion of the trial phase of the Eichmann proceeding in August 1961 and the delivery of the court's judgment several months later, in December. Narrated by Lowell Thomas, a pioneering broadcaster best known for his work in radio, the documentary explicitly understands both the trial and its filming as instruments of legal justice. Beginning with archival images from Kristallnacht and concluding with pictures of corpses discovered in the "liberated" camps, the film uses the camera both to track the course of the trial and to link it to evidence of criminality captured filmically at both the onset and the conclusion of the Nazi campaign against the Jews. The camera in *Verdict for Tomorrow* serves, then, as the tool of justice in a double sense: it both displays the drama of legality as it unfolded in Jerusalem and indexically supplies, through archival crosscutting, evidence of the very crimes for which Eichmann was being tried. The documentary supplements this material by providing extended excerpts from the testimony of two survivor witnesses who, while within the documentary remaining nameless, provided the trial with two of its most spectacular testimonial moments: in the first, we witness Yehiel Dinur, better known by his pen name Katzetnik—a novelist and writer who wrote chilling accounts of life on "planet

Auschwitz"—collapse in the stand; in the second, we watch Rivka Yoselewska, who suffered a mild heart attack on the eve of the day she was originally scheduled to testify, describe how she climbed out of a mass grave after being left naked and for dead during a mass killing. Within the context of the documentary, both testimonial gestures are offered as evidence of the accused's crimes, though conceived strictly as a juridical matter, Dinur's and Yoselewska's appearances can be understood to complicate rather than simplify the legal task that faced the prosecution.[11] Dinur's collapse, in this regard, stands as a powerful reminder of the difficulty of translating Holocaust trauma into legally digestible narrative, while Yoselewska's hellish tale widens, rather than bridges, the gulf between personal experience and probative proof.

These problems, which loomed large at trial and would play a critical role in Arendt's famous critique, are resolved within the documentary by the narration, which gradually assumes the burden of presenting the state's case. Remarkably, then, the documentary is structured in such a way that Lowell Thomas gradually takes over the role of prosecutor from Gideon Hausner. The film shows clips from Gideon Hausner's opening address, and his famous words, "Here we encounter a new kind of killer, one who sits behind a desk."[12] It then cuts to Lowell Thomas, who essentially completes the prosecutor's statement. Thomas stands directly before the camera; he addresses us in the same incredulous and sardonic tones that Attorney General Hausner reserved for Eichmann. "And what explanation did Eichmann have?" Thomas asks, contemptuously: "I was the little man." Later, commenting on Eichmann's cross-examination by the attorney general, Thomas observes, "A pattern emerges: when Eichmann couldn't deny the facts, he denied responsibility." The film relies, then, on a technique described by Bill Nichols as "evidentiary editing": "two pieces of space"—here the shots of the courtroom and those taken from wartime archives—"are joined together to give the impression of one continuous argument."[13]

In turning the narrator into a proxy for the prosecution, the documentary turns the viewers into surrogate judges, a point made explicitly in Thomas's concluding remarks, a court summation of sorts: "What will the verdict be? What purpose has the trial served? . . . We hope this has made you stop and think, so as to render your own final verdict." The judgment requested of the viewer contains, then, two distinct aspects: we are asked to return a verdict both on the accused and on the trial itself, which, the film has reminded us, was staged against the backdrop of myriad jurisdictional and procedural challenges. Just as we are urged to return a guilty verdict against the accused, we are asked to acquit the trial, as the film ends by defending the integrity of the proceeding, reminding us that it has been fairly and scrupulously conducted—in short, that it was no show trial, a fact complicated, if not belied, by the very existence of the documentary. Yet the appeal to the viewer to serve as judge complexly serves to justify the trial by reminding us that, weight of the evidence notwithstanding, the verdict has not been fixed or predetermined; each of us is free to reach our own principled judgment. In this final remarkable way, the film serves not simply to document a landmark juridical proceeding but to legitimate it. The film is no mere witness to a trial; it is an instrument of the prosecution.

If *Verdict for Tomorrow* turns the documentary into a prosecutorial weapon, *Witnesses to the Holocaust* presents the trial in its didactic role as a teacher of history.[14] Produced in 1987 by the Jewish Museum of New York in cooperation with Yad Vashem, the Israeli state-supported Holocaust research institute, *Witnesses to the Holocaust* relies on an idiom of documentary representation significantly different from *Verdict for Tomorrow*. Instead of immediately confronting us with images of violent crimes, *Witnesses to the Holocaust* begins with a scrolled text that summarizes the understanding of the trial that will be presented in the remaining ninety minutes of the film:

> The Trial of Adolf Eichmann was more than just the trial of a single man. The eyewitness testimony gathered for the trial and video-taped for posterity examines the entire apparatus of persecution during the Holocaust.

The documentary's focus on the trial as history lesson structures the film. The narrator, in this case, the actor Joel Grey, never appears before the camera as did Lowell Thomas; instead, his presence is limited to a conventional voice-over: his is a disembodied, roving omniscience, occupying a position of neutral detachment, a formal analogue to the hovering but invisible presence of the professional historian in his or her text. Having described the trial as an exercise in recording history through survivor testimony, the film, recapitulating the gesture of *Verdict for Tomorrow*, immediately identifies itself with the ambitions of the trial itself; in this case, however, the end is pedagogical, not prosecutorial. The documentary, Grey's narration reminds us, seeks to "educate a new generation" to the history of the Holocaust so that "once more the world should not forget." Such invocations are, of course, familiar, particularly at the present moment, as the last expressions of exigent memory are gradually absorbed into history. Yet they sounded with particular force at the time of the documentary's production in 1987. In 1985, on the fortieth anniversary of the end of the Second World War, U.S. President Ronald Reagan visited a German military cemetery at Bitburg. For many, the president's words and actions "reflected an erosion of historical memory and a desire to have the past press less demandingly on contemporary consciousness."[15] During the 1987 trial of Ivan Demjanjuk in Jerusalem, prosecutors likewise bemoaned, "the Holocaust seems to have been forgotten from the collective memory."[16]

Witnesses to the Holocaust gives voice to this sense of urgent remembrance, however, in a strangely self-referential fashion. For it is not the vanishing of the witnesses that troubles the film, but the vanishing of *film itself.* After presenting a glimpse of Hausner's opening statement, the documentary tells us, via Grey's narration, that of the five hundred hours of film originally prepared by Hurwitz for Capital Broadcasting, less than a third, only some 170 hours, remain. (As we shall see, this statement was later proved incorrect.) The temporal vulnerability of video to decay and destruction thus stands as a trope for the passing of the witnesses themselves. Saving the film of the trial from further erosion and the complementary gesture of preserving memory from forgetfulness describe the documentary's urgent logic.

By using the trial as a means of teaching the history of the Holocaust, the film remains faithful to one of the principal goals of the trial itself. The trial presented the history of the Holocaust in discrete chapters—persecution, ghettoization, extermination—and by following the chronology of the trial, *Witnesses to the Holocaust* is able to present the underlying chronology of the Holocaust itself. The witnesses serve as mouthpieces of the larger general history related in Grey's impersonal narration. The relationship between history and testimony is made explicit by the film's heavy use of crosscutting from footage of survivors telling their stories on the stand to archival material. Thus, for example, Abraham Aviel's shocking description of surviving an *Aktion* is interspersed with photographs of Einsatzgruppen killings.[17] Later

Yitzhak Zuckerman's description of resistance in the Warsaw Ghetto is punctuated with images of the ghetto uprising.[18]

This use of archival footage serves not simply to supplement or illustrate survivor stories. Again, by supplying a visual corollary of the spoken word, this technique importantly serves to translate testimony into a historical document, establishing an irrefutable indexical referent for narratives shaped by memory. The conclusion of the film both underscores and enlarges this point. The judges rise; Eichmann exits the glass booth; and the narrator explains the tribunal's judgment and the method of the accused's execution. But the documentary does not end with the end of the trial. Instead it circles back to Abraham Aviel, the survivor of the Einsatzgruppen action. Now, however, Aviel describes not how he escaped but how he was sustained by the idea of sharing his story. "It was always my thought: one must survive, one must remain behind . . . so he can tell what happened." If the survivor is the living embodiment of traumatic history, then the trial and now the film serve as the means of history's transmission to a new generation. The trial, which created the first public opportunity to teach Holocaust history through survivor testimony, is now passed on again through the vehicle of the documentary. Here then the indexical quality of documentary comes to embrace the survivors themselves: they are the authentic artifacts of history. The documentary thus offers itself as an instrument of the selfsame pedagogical mission of the trial.

And so we come to appreciate the interesting ambiguity of the film's title: At first glance, the title, *Witnesses to the Holocaust,* seemingly refers to the survivors who testified in Jerusalem. By the film's end, however, we realize that the title also names the film's viewers, who, like the original spectators of the proceeding, have learned history from being made into witnesses of the witnesses.

A decade later, in 1997, the third important documentary appears, *The Trial of Adolf Eichmann,* a two-hour coproduction of PBS and ABC, broadcast on PBS.[19] Like its 1987 precursor, the PBS documentary relies heavily on a technique of crosscutting from trial to archival footage. And like *Witnesses to the Holocaust, The Trial of Adolf Eichmann* uses a narratorial voice-over, in this case supplied by David Brinkley. *The Trial of Adolf Eichmann* begins, however, not with Brinkley's sonorous voice but with melodious, dimly melancholy chords of a piano. The use of a musical sound track is striking, if only because it is so deeply conventional. Like a standard Hollywood feature or a televised Olympic moment, the PBS documentary deploys sound to prepare, stimulate, and organize the viewer's emotional response to the film's words and images. When the defendant delivers a crisp "*Ja wohl*" in response to the court's question, "Are you Adolf Eichmann?" the accused's words are underscored by an ominous drumroll meant to remind us, if somehow it weren't already clear, that the moment when the defendant first faced his judges was one of high drama.

The use of sound is novel in a second regard. In *Verdict for Tomorrow* and *Witnesses to the Holocaust,* the voices we hear issuing from the court are those of the simultaneous interpreters rendering the polygot tongues spoken at trial into imperfect English. In *The Trial of Adolf Eichmann,* the court interpreter has been replaced by professional actors. Ed Asner provides the English of Robert Servatius, Eichmann's lead counsel; Eli Wallach supplies the voice of David Ben-Gurion; and the likes of Eric Bogosian and Tony Roberts speak for the various witnesses. Here then we find a splintering of the indexical and the representational, as the documentary threatens to transform itself into a re-creation, a restaging of the original trial.

And yet the film's use of crosscutting serves to verify the authenticity of the proceeding from such destabilizations. The cuts in *Witnesses to the Holocaust,* we recall, were always to antecedent archival material; this technique, I have argued, offers an indexical referent, a visual corroboration, of the history told at trial in testimonial form. In *The Trial of Adolf Eichmann,* however, the crosscutting is both retrospective, to archival images of the Holocaust, and *prospective,* to posttrial interviews with various participants in the proceedings. On one level, these juxtapositions—between the black-and-white footage from the courtroom and the full-color interviews—serves to transform the trial itself into an article of history, placing it in the context of its staging. Yaakov Baror, for example, the assistant state's attorney at the trial, confesses in an interview that at the beginning of the case, the prosecutors themselves knew little about the Holocaust; they, too, had to "learn to never forget." Gabriel Bach, at the time also an assistant prosecutor and later a justice on the Israeli Supreme Court, offers a poignant story of his struggle to maintain composure during the testimony of Auschwitz survivor Martin Földi.[20] As he tells the story, the camera cuts from the present-day interview with the elderly Bach back to the courtroom, where we see the young assistant prosecutor briefly faltering. Eliahu Rosenberg, a trial witness, describes in another present-day interview how prior to the proceeding, Israelis used to call Holocaust survivors "cowards, pieces of soap." The commentary is often fascinating, enriching an understanding of the trial as a historic undertaking.

But as opposed to *Witnesses to the Holocaust*, *The Trial of Adolf Eichmann* does not use the proceeding to teach afresh the underlying history of the Holocaust; nor is the goal simply to offer a history of the trial itself. Instead, the complex crosscutting from trial to archival footage to recent interviews serves another distinct end: it turns the film into a continuation of the drama of remembrance staged at the trial. The subsequent interviews, particularly those with survivors, serve less to historicize the trial than to keep it fresh in collective memory. When trial witness Israel Guttman, in an interview, describes how many of the witnesses were reluctant to testify, it's as if he were once again on the stand, extending and supplementing the testimony he offered decades before.

The film's end, a concluding interview with Michael Goldman, most dramatically accomplishes this purpose. Goldman, an officer in the special 06 division of the Israeli police responsible for investigating Nazi crimes and himself a famous figure of survival at Auschwitz by virtue of Haim Gouri's 1974 documentary, *The Eighty-First Blow*, was responsible for throwing Eichmann's ashes into the Mediterranean.[21] In relating this story, one which brings final closure to the trial, Goldman reveals that the act of handling Eichmann's ashes suddenly reminded him of a moment at Auschwitz, when he came upon a veritable mountain of cremated human remains. "When I saw the remains of Adolf Eichmann," that small pile, Goldman says, "I knew how many hundreds of thousands had been in the Auschwitz mound." Watching Goldman tell his story, we forget we are listening to an agent of the state describing the aftermath of the condemned's execution. Instead, we can't help but feel that we're watching a clip from the trial, listening to the difficult testimony of yet another survivor-witness. Although Goldman's story means to provide the concluding chapter to the Eichmann affair—the criminal is seemingly laid to rest—it also bears witness to the continuing legacy of the executed man's crimes, how they remain vitally alive in the memory of the survivors. The act of bearing witness, of keeping memory alive, is thus vital and ongoing: a project stimulated by the trial and continued by the documentary about it.

In this final regard, the documentary's most objectionable features—its use of a heavy-handed sound track and actors to supply the voices of historical figures—can be grasped as not a trivialization of the juridical project but very much in its spirit. For just as the prosecution strived to turn bleak tales of Holocaust survival into displays of heroic memory, the documentary likewise labors to confer poignancy and meaning to the memories captured in its frame.

Altogether different are the representational strategies of *The Specialist*.[22] Directed by Eyal Sivan, an Israeli-French filmmaker, and written by Rony Braman, likewise an Israeli-born resident of France, and released in 1999, *The Specialist* is in many ways the most interesting, complex, intriguing, and problematic of the documentaries about the Eichmann trial.

In contrast to its documentary predecessors, *The Specialist* entirely eschews the use of a narratorial voice-over responsible for organizing and explaining the film's images. Moreover, the film presents no archival footage of the Holocaust; nor does it include any material compiled in the decades after the trial. The absence of a voice-over and of archival material invites immediate comparisons with Claude Lanzmann's *Shoah,* arguably the greatest documentary ever made about the Holocaust.[23] In the case of Lanzmann's masterpiece, however, the eschewal of archival material supports the central problematic of the film—the "historical crisis of witnessing," explored by critics such as Shoshana Felman and Dominick LaCapra.[24] While *The Specialist* relies on a similar representational strategy, one seemingly influenced by Lanzmann, the logic behind such documentary austerity is far from clear. The entire 150 minutes of film remain within the confines of the proceeding; the camera never exits the courtroom. The effect is a bit claustrophobic, though the footage is frequently striking, at least in part because it includes much material not seen in the earlier documentaries: Sivan and Braman, after a Sisyphean struggle with the Israel State Archives, discovered nearly twice as much film as previously had been thought to have survived. Unfortunately, much of this material was in terrible condition, the result of decades of neglectful storage. As Stuart Liebman has noted, the footage had to be reformatted and digitally enhanced, and the soundtrack had to be overdubbed, in places, with the radio transmissions from the trial.[25]

These elaborate techniques, however, do as much to problematize and reconfigure the original as they do to restore it. Though *The Specialist* never leaves the theater-turned-courtroom, a logic of theatricality controls its images, as the film relies on techniques far more stylized than those deployed in its documentary predecessors. In the earlier films, evidentiary editing is used to create the semblance of a coherent argument; here the crosscutting serves to disrupt the trial's chronology. Moreover, the very technology that made possible the recovery of the footage is deployed to transform its content. Through digital manipulation, reflections of the courtroom are projected onto the accused's glass booth. Voices are overdubbed, creating menacing cacophony. The musical sound track is arresting. In contrast to the innocuous dulcet chords of the PBS film, the sound track of *The Specialist* is like a composition of high modernism: strident bow work, plucked strings, random notes—sounds of discord, disruption, and disharmony.

The use of these elaborate techniques along with the curious absence of any narrative or supplementary images make *The Specialist* a more difficult film to read, and even the knowledge, supplied in the credits, that it was inspired by Arendt's *Eichmann in Jerusalem* hardly simplifies the matter. Certainly the connection to Arendt helps explain certain of the film's more heavy-handed moments. Arendt has very little good to say about lead prosecutor Gideon Hausner, and the film likewise portrays him as a histrionic figure, given to bloated rhetoric and melodramatic poses. (The film amplifies and overdubs his voice, creating an incoherent acoustic wave of accusation.) The concluding shot also finds its inspiration in Arendt: digital technology is used to make the surrounding courtroom, the golem-like guards, and the glass booth slowly vanish, so that finally Eichmann sits alone before a desk—an image which is then colorized, presumably to remind us that a similarly bland bureaucrat can be found virtually anywhere (a point, I should add, that does not really find support in Arendt's controversial text).

Still, the film cannot be seen simply as a documentary illustration of Arendt's banality thesis. In particular, the absence of a voice-over finds little analogue in Arendt's book, which is very much about *voice*. The book condemns both the prosecution and, to a lesser extent, the court for failing to frame Eichmann's offenses in an adequate legal idiom, and the book ends with a remarkable inversion, in which Arendt substitutes her voice for the court's, supplying the very terms of judgment she found wanting in the court's opinion.[26] The film's silences, if they deconstruct the prosecution's and the court's controlling narratives, provide no substitute framework, no rival interpretation of the trial. On the contrary, the film's highly stylized documentary idiom is significant not because it offers a particularly interesting reading of the trial but because it rejects the framing logic of both the trial *and* Arendt.

In this regard, *The Specialist* represents a powerful reorientation of film's relationship to the proceeding. In the first three Eichmann documentaries, trial footage is worked *with* to invite judgment or to teach history, or to sacralize memory; now the footage is worked *upon*. In *The Specialist* the trial has passed from occasion to object, and the accused appears not as index or juridical trope but as a cultural icon. Here again the film is notable for many of its omissions and exclusions. In contrast to the other documentaries, the survivor-witnesses play a marginal role in *The Specialist*. If one of the aims of the trial was to puncture the numbing anonymity of genocide by providing witnesses an opportunity to present narratives of their victimization, resistance, and survival, the film rejects this gesture, rendering the voice of memory disembodied and incoherent.[27] In one sequence, the testimony of numerous witnesses is run together through a series of quick cuts, their elaborate stories reduced to disjointed, fragmented, and isolated utterances:

> "Eichmann"
> ". . . a head, a foot . . ."
> ". . . keep beating us . . ."
> ". . . dead!"
> "I don't sleep . . ."

Likewise, the spectators at the trial, who in the earlier documentaries are often captured reacting to the words either of a witness or of the accused, barely appear. The banishment of the witnesses and the spectators to the margins of the film places the defendant all the more in the center: in *The Specialist*, Eichmann is very much the star of his trial and the documentary. His gestures are exaggerated: as the camera focuses on him cleaning his glasses, the squeak of cloth on lens is digitally enhanced. Close-ups likewise track his copious note taking, the scratch of pen on pad building ominously in volume, slowly drowning out the speech in the courtroom.

Not all the effects are born of digital manipulation. In a remarkable sequence, footage captures Eichmann's exiting the glass booth to better explain the logistics of the deportations. He stands before a large map of Europe, pointer in hand, and close beside him stands Attorney General Hausner. With their backs to the camera, the men—balding, bespectacled, of identical height—look virtually like twins. It is an astonishing moment, but little more or less than that. For beyond noting the odd instant of forced kinship, we are not moved to make any grander or more profound observations beyond the relatively banal one—though not in the sense intended by Arendt—that all human beings look more or less alike. Any deeper reading of the image would be tendentious, if not perverse.

More interesting is the footage of Eichmann responding directly to questions from the bench. In contrast to the exchanges between prosecutor Hausner and Eichmann—Hausner's blustery challenges, sarcastic asides, and impatient interruptions; Eichmann's defensive evasions and bureaucratic hairsplitting—the exchanges between the accused and the judges are characterized by a peculiar delicacy. The judges, dispensing with the artifice of simultaneous interpretation, address Eichmann in the language that is both the defendant's mother tongue and theirs as well. They do not seek out eye contact, but they also don't refuse it, and they speak in calm, even tones. Eichmann, visibly relieved to be free, at least for the moment, from Hausner's verbal pummeling, answers courteously—respectfully, even. Still, these exchanges provide no deeper insight into the character of the accused. There is no moment of epiphany when the man suddenly reveals himself; nor can the absence of revelation be construed as essentially revealing. At most, the exchanges direct attention to an aspect of the trial not typically associated with a spectacular criminal proceeding: its capacity to create moments of intimate exchange.

Yet the refusal of the film to sponsor any deeper reading of the trial is, I believe, not its failure but its most interesting signature—the surest indication of the documentary's transformation of the proceeding into pure representation. To this extent, the absence of archival or supplementary footage is hardly accidental, for it has the effect of releasing the proceeding from the pressures of time and place. By remaining in the courtroom, *The Specialist* turns the trial into an object of art—a thing not to be understood, contextualized, or assessed but to be manipulated, appropriated, acted upon. Here we can appreciate the irony implicit in the filmmakers' avowal of their indebtedness to Arendt. For far from revealing the banality and extreme limitations of the accused, the film, by microexamining his skewed grimace, nervous blinking, compulsive note taking, and attentive responses, transforms Eichmann into icon. This is not to say the film endows Eichmann with complexity; on the contrary, he strikes the viewer as neither banal nor malignant, neither veracious nor duplicitous. Instead, like Marcus Harvey's oversize painting of convicted murderess Myra Hindley, Eichmann remains a cipher—a pure trope of our cultural overinvestment in images of extreme criminality.[28]

Trials are not about the production of rival meanings. Though numerous commentators have noted that trials provide a site of contestation, an arena in which narratives compete and clash, the very intensity of this competition is born of the fact that each story strives for dominance, aims to be inscribed as authoritative in the court's judgment.[29] As I've noted, Arendt faults the court not for silencing rival narratives but for championing the wrong one. *The Specialist,* by contrast, does not condemn the trial—condemnation implies argument; the film's ultimate gesture of antagonism toward the trial is its refusal to indulge simple critique. Ultimately, then, the film challenges the trial in a far more radical fashion: by aestheticizing it. In *The Specialist,* the trial is no longer in control of its meaning.

This point is underscored in the film's concluding shots, in which footage of Eichmann is interspersed with the credits. For the first time we see the defendant smiling, smirking perhaps, and the sound track, departing from its signature discordant chords, now plays Tom Waitt's jaunty *Russian March.* Accustomed as we are to the defendant's dour bank-teller appearance, we are unprepared for his smile and are discomfited by it—not because it suddenly humanizes him but because it testifies to the strange power of film to manipulate our responses by marrying image with sound. The jaunty tunes and the sly smile suggest Eichmann has outfoxed the court. And in a sense he has—through the instrument of the film itself. By turning the accused into pure representation, the film frees Eichmann, both literally and figuratively, from the juridical box in which the trial tried to contain him. It is an ironic acquittal.

The documentary forerunners of *The Specialist* all recapitulate the essential gesture of the trial: they are structured as arguments. In *Verdict for Tomorrow,* we encountered the documentary as the ally of the trial, a tool of the prosecution. *Witnesses to the Holocaust* similarly turned itself into a tool of the trial by dedicating itself to the proceeding's ulterior project of teaching traumatic history. *Eichmann on Trial* conjured the proceeding as a means of preserving memory, a goal to which the film also pledged its assistance. Each film, through different effects, captured a single aspect of the competing purposes that were provocatively pursued and balanced in the Jerusalem court; and in so doing, it underscored the affinities between the didactic aims of law and documentary film.

With *The Specialist,* however, we move beyond law, history, and memory. Here documentary no longer serves as a tool of paraphrase or even critique. Its hostility to the trial is the hostility of image to word, of art to law: not a simple binary antagonism but a complex collision over the control of meaning. The film liberates Eichmann from the debilitations of history, law, and memory; he is now free to circulate in our culture as sheer image.

NOTES

1. Moshe Pearlman, *The Capture and Trial of Adolf Eichmann* (New York, 1963).

2. Tom Segev, *The Seventh Million: The Israelis and the Holocaust* (New York, 1993), 350.

3. Gideon Hausner, *Justice in Jerusalem* (New York, 1966), 291.

4. Ibid.

5. Hannah Arendt, *Eichmann in Jerusalem: A Report on the Banality of Evil* (New York, 1963), 254.

6. Ibid., 244.

7. Michael Marrus, "History and the Holocaust in the Courtroom," in *Le Génocide des Juifs entre process et historie,* ed. F. Brayard (Paris, 2000); Mark Osiel, *Mass Atrocity, Collective Memory and the Law* (New Brunswick, NJ, 1997). See also Donald Bloxham, *Genocide on Trial: War Crimes Trials and the Formation of Holocaust History and Memory* (Oxford, 2001).

8. Lawrence Douglas, *The Memory of Judgment: Making Law and History in the Trials of the Holocaust* (New Haven, CT, 2001).

9. *Verdict for Tomorrow,* videocassette, directed by Leo Hurwitz (1961; New York: ADL Media, 1988).

10. See William Alexander, *Film on the Left: American Documentary Film from 1931 to 1942* (Princeton, NJ, 1981).

11. For a more in-depth discussion of this point, see Douglas, *Memory of Judgment.*

12. *The Trial of Adolf Eichmann: Record of the Proceedings in the District Court of Jerusalem,* 6 vols. (Jerusalem: Ministry of Justice, State of Israel, 1992–95), 3. Hereafter cited as *TAE.*

13. Bill Nichols, *Representing Reality: Issues and Concepts in Documentary* (Bloomington, IN, 1991), 20.

14. *Witnesses to the Holocaust: The Trial of Adolf Eichmann* (1987; New York: Jewish Media Fund, 1997).

15. Alvin H. Rosenfeld, "Another Revisionism: Popular Culture and the Changing Image of the Holocaust," in *Bitburg in Moral and Political Perspective,* ed. G. Hartman (Bloomington, IN, 1986), 97.

16. Quoted in Tom Teicholz, *The Trial of Ivan the Terrible: State of Israel v. John Demjanjuk* (New York, 1990), 269.

17. For a transcript of Aviel's testimony, see *TAE,* 495–99.

18. For a transcript of Zuckerman's testimony, see *TAE,* 409–20.

19. *The Trial of Adolf Eichmann* (1997; Alexandria, VA: PBS Home Video, 1997).

20. See Douglas, *Memory of Judgment,* 162–65.

21. *The Eighty-First Blow,* directed by Haim Gouri (1974; Teaneck, NJ: Ergo Media, 1987).

22. *The Specialist,* directed by Eyal Sivan (1999; New York: Kino International, 1999).

23. *Shoah,* videocassette, directed by Claude Lanzmann (1985; Hollywood: Paramount Video, 1986).

24. Shoshana Felman, "The Return of the Voice: Claude Lanzmann's *Shoah,*" in *Testimony: Crises of Witnessing in Literature, Psychoanalysis, and History,* ed. Shoshana Felman and Dori Laub (London, 1992); Dominick LaCapra, *History and Memory After Auschwitz* (Ithaca, NY, 1998).

25. Stuart Liebman, "'If This Be a Man . . .' Eichmann on Trial in *The Specialist,*" *Cineaste* 27, no. 2 (2002): 40–42.

26. See Arendt, *Eichmann in Jerusalem,* 254–56.

27. For a detailed discussion of the complex and contested role that survivor testimony played at the trial, see Douglas, *Memory of Judgment,* 150–82.

28. See Anthony Julius, *Transgressions: The Offenses of Art* (London, 2002); see also Sandra Kemp, "'Myra, Myra on the Wall': The Fascination of Faces," *Critical Quarterly* 40, no. 1 (Spring 1998).

29. See generally the essays in Paul Gerirtz and Peter Brooks, eds., *Law's Stories: Narrative and Rhetoric in the Law* (New Haven, CT, 1996).

VII. H·I·S·T·O·R·I·O·G·R·A·P·H·Y A·N·D P·E·D·A·G·O·G·Y

Piotr Wróbel

Polish-Jewish Relations and *Neighbors* by Jan T. Gross: Politics, Public Opinion, and Historical Methodology

LIKE MOST POLISH HISTORIANS SPECIALIZING IN MODERN HISTORY, I have also participated in the Jedwabne polemic. Initially, I belonged among those scholars who believed that this controversy constituted one of the most important Polish national debates during the contemporary post-Communist era. The Polish-language version of *Neighbors,* published in May 2000, caused a moral earthquake in Poland. Every newspaper produced articles on the book, with the two largest Warsaw dailies—*Rzeczpospolita* (*Republic*) and *Gazeta Wyborcza* (*Electoral Gazette*)—printing more than fifty articles each. *Neighbors* became a hot political issue, dividing families and friends. The most radical critics claimed that the book was a perfidious fabrication concocted to support Jewish financial claims vis-à-vis Poland. Many people accepted the moral point of the book but questioned its scholarly value and discussed the allegedly untrue details. Numerous readers, especially those from among the intelligentsia stratum, rejected any critique of the book and fully accepted its message. Most people were confused and lost among three important aspects of the issue: moral, political, and historical. Politicians of the Right found in their opposition to the book a new unifying force.

Archivists were looking for new documents that might shed further light on the matter, and historians began writing about other pogroms and different national minorities persecuted in Poland after World War II. The foreign media have joined the debate, too. The largest Western European newspapers, for example, have published numerous articles about *Neighbors.* On March 12, 2001, the *New Yorker* presented an abbreviated version of the book. In April 2001, the English-language edition of the book appeared in the United States and started a North American phase of the debate, also fierce and highly politicized. Recently, German and French versions have been issued.

Participating in the debate, I published an enthusiastic review of the book and spoke highly about it during several scholarly conferences. After the first reading of *Neighbors,* I was numbed and outraged that a group of Polish people behaved like vicious beasts in Jedwabne. I was also frustrated that the issue had been waiting almost sixty years to be acknowledged. I believed that this silence constituted a part of the crime and that people responsible for it should be punished if they were still alive. I emphasized that as a Pole, I was ashamed that this heinous crime happened in my country and that I felt personally tainted by it. I expressed my satisfaction that the president, the prime minister, and the primate of Poland publicly apologized for it and that the Instytut Pamięci Narodowej (Institute of National Remembrance) started an official and thorough investigation in order to verify all the details and to allow the guilty persons to be punished. I concluded my presentations with a statement that *Neighbors* is a brilliant historical essay, stimulating and provocative; that it shows clearly once again that the history of Poland and most Eastern European nations has to be rewritten. Occupied and persecuted for centuries, the Poles believed during World War II that they were threatened with extinction. In defense, they have developed a simplified, bipolar interpretation of their wartime history, which shows them as victims and depicts everybody else as oppressors and enemies. Gross has demonstrated that the victims can also be victimizers.

Among my professional colleagues and fellow Poles, I belonged to the most energetic defenders of Jan T. Gross and his book. Now, two years, hundreds of articles, and several conferences later, I am not so certain about my initial enthusiasm. I still consider *Neighbors* an outstanding and important book, but my reservations, which existed from the very beginning of the debate, have not disappeared. On the contrary, I now have greater doubts than I had before. I am uncomfortable with the fact that throughout the text, Gross assumes too high a moral ground in his descriptions, and I do not believe that accusing or judging historical characters is the most important role of the historian. Our task, rather, is to describe and explain historical events accurately.

The Gross book accuses but does not explain too much. Edward H. Carr wrote in his classic book on history that "the study of history is a study of causes."[1] In other words, historians, above all, are supposed to answer two main questions: "What happened?" and "Why did it happen?" or, to quote Carr again, "Why individuals acted as they did?" and "What lies behind the act?" I would gladly see more "study of causes" in the Gross book. "Before the War" and "Soviet occupation, 1939–1941" are short (22 pages out of 218) and rather sketchy. Yet, without a solid historical and contextual background, it is difficult to understand the Jedwabne crime. It was completely irrelevant to the victims, but it should not be irrelevant to us: the killers of Jedwabne were not vicious beasts by nature. They became vicious beasts due to a variety of circumstances. It is very important to explain these circumstances and to note, too, that explanation is not the same as justification.

From the very beginning, I had methodological reservations. *Neighbors,* a powerful and momentous book, includes several statements difficult to accept, especially for professional historians. "To begin with," writes Jan Gross,

> I suggest that we should modify our approach to sources for the period. When considering survivors' testimonies, we would be well advised to change the starting premise in appraisal of their evidentiary contribution from a priori critical to in principle affirmative. By accepting what we read in a particular account as fact *until we find persuasive arguments to the contrary,* we would avoid more mistakes than we are likely to commit by adopting the opposite approach, which calls for cautious skepticism toward any testimony *until an independent confirmation of its content has been found* [italics in the original].[2]

The author's intentions here are clear: survivors are less and less numerous, their voices are drowned by other comments, and those who were killed in the Holocaust are unable to speak for themselves. Yet, no professional historian can accept the aforementioned methodological statement. The postulate that Jan Gross wants to eliminate belongs among the most basic rules of our profession. There is no touchstone for historical truth besides the commitment to basic standards of historical veridicality, the commitment to accuracy and to the procedures of verification and documentation. In addition, witnesses' testimonies are sometimes mutually exclusive. For example, the Jedwabne pogrom survivors Rivka Fogel and Itzchak Yaacov (Yanek) Neumark, whose testimonies have been published in a volume edited by the brothers Julius and Jacob Baker, *Yedwabne: History and Memorial Book,*[3] describe some parts of the pogrom differently than does Szmul Wasserstein, the key witness for Jan Gross. Sometimes these differences are significant. For example, Wasserstein wrote, "They [two Jewish women] put their children in the water and drowned them with their own hands: then Baśka Binsztajn jumped in and immediately went to the bottom, while Chaja Kubrzańska suffered for a couple of hours. Assembled hooligans made a spectacle of this. They advised her to lie face down in the water, so that she would drown faster."[4] Fogel described the same scene in the following way: "They exchanged the children between themselves and together they jumped into deep water. Gentiles standing nearby pulled them out, but they managed to jump in again and were drowned."[5] In spite of this and other similar differences, Gross claims that Wasserstein's deposition "has to be taken literally."[6]

The author's attitude toward primary sources assumes disturbing forms on many pages of the book. We can read there that in Jedwabne "the Polish half of a town's population murders its Jewish half."[7] This is a powerful accusation and a catchy phrase, but primary sources give us no evidence to support it. On the contrary, Wasserstein and other survivors call the perpetrators "local hooligans."[8] Neumark, who managed to escape from the burning barn, claims in his testimony published by the Baker brothers that some Poles did not want to participate in the crime.[9] Neumark mentions a prewar Polish police chief who opposed it and another gentile Pole who escaped to Warsaw after he had protested against the pogrom. It would also be very interesting to explain a most surprising statement by Neumark: "An American gentile who did not want to take part in the slaughter was also thrown into the flaming barn."[10] All these pieces of information do not appear in the Wasserstein text.

Leaving aside the controversial issue of German participation, it seems that, indeed, a large group of local Poles and numerous peasants from the nearby villages, altogether probably more than one hundred persons, took part in the pogrom and terrorized the town so efficiently that nobody dared protest or oppose them. This is shameful enough, but it is not identical to "the Polish half of a town's population murders its Jewish half."

Neighbors is based on several sources: the Wasserstein testimony; the documentations of the 1949 and 1953 trials of the participants of the Jedwabne pogrom; the Bakers' 1980 *Memorial Book;* and the interviews recorded by the filmmaker Agnieszka Arnold and by Jan Gross himself. The interviews, conducted in the late 1990s, cannot be considered reliable sources, especially regarding the details of the crime. Similarly, the *Memorial Book,* prepared more than thirty years after the war, can serve only as supplementary evidence. The postwar trials were "hastily arranged" and involved typical Stalinist interrogation methods such as beating and torturing the suspects. It is therefore difficult to agree with Jan Gross's statement that their documentation "can serve us well."[11] In addition, both trials were triggered by and based on the Wasserstein testimony. This deposition, given four years after the crime, is in fact the only historical primary source that can be considered sufficiently reliable.

It is unfortunate, however, that this is the only source of this kind. In 1966, the late Szymon Datner, the most outstanding Polish specialist on the Holocaust in Poland ever, published a long article on "The Extermination of the Jewish Population in the District of Białystok."[12] This article also mentions Jedwabne. However, Szymon Datner could not write openly about the anti-Jewish pogroms because of censorship in Communist Poland. Nevertheless, analyzing the Jedwabne crime, Datner used several testimonies deposited in the Archives of the Jewish Historical Institute in Warsaw and given not only by Szmul Wasserstein but also by other survivors from Jedwabne, Abraham Belawicki and Abraham Śniadowicz. It appears that to Datner the testimonies of Belawicki and Śniadowicz were more important than the Wasserstein deposition. Why did Jan Gross ignore these sources entirely? Finally, although oral history is in vogue today, we have to be very careful with testimonies given several—or even worse—dozens of years after the fact. An Israeli scholar, Ben-Cion Pinchuk, writes in the introduction to his book on the Jews under Soviet occupation: "It is clear that the presence of the narrator on the spot at the time does not itself guarantee authenticity. Given the strong tendency to reconstruct the past from the vantage point of the present, and the very high possibility of forgetting many details, one has to be very careful in using the evidence."[13]

Szymon Datner is worth mentioning also for another reason. A survivor himself, he deposited his own testimony at the Jewish Historical Commission in Białystok on September 28, 1946,[14] which means that he was talking to the same people at the same time as was Szmul Wasserstein. Contrary to Wasserstein, however, Datner was not present in Jedwabne in 1941. Yet Datner's testimony is very similar to the Wasserstein text. Six or seven other testimonies from Jedwabne, mentioned before and kept in the Archives of the Jewish Historical Institute in Warsaw, also are very similar. It is very likely, therefore, that the survivors, who met in Białystok (the greatest and the safest town of their native region) in 1946, talked a lot about Jedwabne events and created a "common" version, not necessarily quite true. They did not do so purposely or even consciously. They just talked a lot about their terrifying war experiences and emphasized and memorized common fragments of their stories.

It is unfortunate as well that Jan Gross neglected the German part of his research. During the last ten years in particular, numerous books have appeared that focus on the Nazi occupation of and on the Nazi crimes in the prewar Eastern Polish territories. Such scholars as Bernhard Chiari,[15] Christian Gerlach,[16] Wolfgang Benz, Jürgen Matthäus,[17] Shalom Cholawsky,[18] and Martin Dean[19] show that the Germans planned the extermination of the Jews before the invasion of the Soviet Union and that after it, they provoked and encouraged the local population to participate in the operations of Einsatzgruppen and Eisatzkommandos. In his book, Martin Dean writes, "Dr. Walther Stahlecker, the commander of *Einsatzgruppe A,* confirmed in his report that it was deliberate policy to incite pogroms in the first days of German rule. The pogroms gave the appearance of popular support for the measures against the Jews. Care was to be taken, however, to ensure that Germans were not seen to be coordinating these actions."[20] We also know that Heinrich Himmler and Reinhard Heydrich gave orders to organize "popular pogroms" but cautioned that the SS should leave "no trace" of its involvement in them. In addition, Gross wrongly calls German-appointed "authorities" led by a *Volksdeutsch* Karolak a town council.[21]

Alexander B. Rossino, a scholar at the United States Holocaust Memorial Museum, carried out research in German sources, missing in Gross's work, and presented it during a panel at the museum in April 2001 and in an article in *Polin: Studies in Polish Jewry.*[22] According to Rossino, the pogroms in Jedwabne and other towns of the Białystok District were organized by Sonderkommandos led by SS officers Adolf

Bonifer, Erich Engels, Johannes Bohm, and Wolfgang Birkner. This conclusion agrees with reconstructions of the July 1941 events given by several other scholars, who add the name of SS-Hauptsturmführer Hermann Schaper and his Kommando. Szymon Datner stated very clearly that German units sometimes carefully prepared pogroms but did not participate in the atrocities themselves.[23] The most outstanding Holocaust scholars in the West also believe that pogroms were provoked by the Einsatzgruppen.[24] And yet, in my opinion, since we do not have a single credible primary source, confirming that the Poles of Jedwabne had been forced by the Germans to kill the Jews (as the opponents of Gross imply), there is no significant difference from the moral point of view whether the Jedwabne pogrom had been prepared by a dozen policemen stationed in the town, as Jan Gross shows it to have been, or by these policemen and an additional special unit.

Among the many elements in the historical context of the Jedwabne crime, there is one of special importance: the Soviet occupation of Eastern Poland from 1939 through 1941. Some historians, particularly from the "Jewish camp (though not all Jewish scholars belong to it)," to use Ezra Mendelsohn's term,[25] claim that this period was irrelevant or not very important to the explanation of the Jedwabne crime. It appears that Jan Gross's book also underestimates the importance of this period. There is no place here to discuss the issue of Jewish collaboration with the Soviets. It is a large and complicated matter that requires a major book. To me, there is no doubt, however, that we cannot accept some conclusions of Jan Gross's book regarding this issue, such as: "To put it simply, enthusiastic Jewish response to entering Red Army units was not a widespread phenomenon at all."[26] This conclusion is unacceptable not only to the members of the "Polish camp (though not all its adherents are Poles)," to use Mendelssohn's term again,[27] but also to Jewish scholars working on this issue, such as Ben-Cion Pinchuk,[28] Dov Levin,[29] Shalom Cholawsky,[30] or even Jan Gross himself in his earlier works.[31]

The Soviet occupation from 1939 through 1941 was important not only in the context of Jewish activities. It was also crucial to what happened to the Christian Poles at that time. The Soviets deported from Eastern Poland to Siberia hundreds of thousands of Polish citizens; a substantial part of the entire population. The deportees were mostly educated members of the local elites: town council, professionals, community leaders, teachers, policemen, and army officers. This meant that the society of Eastern Poland in general, and of Jedwabne in particular, was "decapitated" and divided by the Soviet divide et impera policy. Leaving aside the minuscule group of real Communists (the prewar Communist Party of Poland had never had more than ten thousand members, and with its autonomous affiliates, it reached about sixteen thousand), the new Soviet apparatus was based on the worst opportunists and even criminals. Leaving aside prewar anti-Semitism and the long and difficult history of Polish-Jewish relations, a brutalization and barbarization of the Jedwabne society started before the German attack on the Soviet Union. It is absolutely clear that the Jedwabne tragedy would not have happened if there had been no German occupation of Poland. I also believe that it would not have happened if German occupation had not been preceded by the Soviet one.

Even more difficult to accept is Jan Gross's hypothesis about the postwar social support for Stalinism:

> One may also reflect in this light about the process of the imposition of communist rule from the vantage point of society rather than that of the apparatus of power. From this point of view, I would propose that communities where Jews had been murdered by local inhabitants during the war were especially vulnerable to sovietization. . . . The issue can best be taken up as a factual question, to be resolved by empirical research. But at this stage it suggests a very intriguing hypothesis, which inverts a well-established cliché about this period by positing that *anti-Semites rather than Jews were instrumental in establishing the Communist regime in Poland after the war* [italics in the original].[32]

The chapter speculating on this issue not only lacks evidence but also does not fit into the structure of the book and is not necessary to support the presented reconstruction of the Jedwabne crime.

In my opinion, this reconstruction does need some additional support, or, in other words, the book would benefit not only from more research but also from more analysis. Gross evaded complexity, did not discuss multiple interpretations, and presented one rather simplistic version of the Jedwabne events: the Poles hated the Jews and killed them when an opportunity arose. Perhaps application of elements of crowd psychology and crowd sociology would help explain the crime. Even the classic works in these fields give us arguments applicable to the Jedwabne event.[33] The German anti-Semitic propaganda was especially dangerous in such regions as the Jedwabne area, one of the most backward in Poland, with the lowest level of education and right-wing political domination before the war. It would be beneficial to the book, as well, to compare the Jedwabne event to other pogroms that took place at the same time in the region, in Radziłów, Rutki, Wizna, Zambrów, Wąsosz, Łomża, and Tykocin. It seems that they were quite similar. On June 27, 1941, more than seven hundred Jews of Białystok were burned in their largest synagogue. This crime, in which the participation of the German Police Battalion 309 is unquestionable, could have been a pattern for the following extermination operations.[34] Quite frequently, the pogroms were filmed by German camera crews.[35] Even a more careful analysis of the Jedwabne pogrom alone would produce additional interesting conclusions. A Polish historian, Dariusz Stola, shows in his article that the pogrom was not that chaotic and that there was in fact a plan. The killers gathered the Jews in the main square of the town, while the strongest men were selected, isolated, and killed to avoid resistance and fighting. On the day of the pogrom, there was only limited plunder of private Jewish property, and, unlike in most spontaneous pogroms, almost all the Jews of the town were killed.[36]

Jan Gross has touched the most sensitive elements of contemporary Polish identity and self-understanding. He has annihilated the myth that the Poles had never collaborated with the Germans. Even if he wrote a methodologically and technically perfect book, there would always be a group of offended and angry people, attacking him to defend a "good image of Poland" (as they understand it). On the other hand, however, the Gross book is not a sacred writing, and we should discuss it. An absence of controversies and doubts is a clear symptom of stagnation in historiography. It is important that we talk about the Jedwabne case. "Now the pressure is on the historians"—wrote the *Economist*.[37] The debate, provoked by the first Polish edition of the book, influenced the opinions of Jan Gross himself, who has changed some small but important details in the following English edition. The last sentence of the Polish version claimed, for example, that the Jews of Jedwabne were killed by the Polish *społeczeństwo*—"society" or "community."[38] The last sentence of the English text says that the Jews were killed by "their neighbors."[39] This is not only a question of translation. "Neighbors" are a specific group of people; "society" or "community" has a broader and heavier meaning. Yet, Gross does not emphasize this change and, even though every new edition and translation gives him a chance to add an updated clarified introduction or epilogue, he refuses to do so.

I hope that the Jedwabne debate will help change a scandalous situation in which Poland, so important to the history of the Holocaust and so distinctly shaped by it, has not a single scholarly center which specializes in Holocaust studies. There is also hope that Polish educational programs, not satisfactory in this respect, will be changed.[40] *Neighbors* has reopened the discussion on Polish-Jewish relations, especially during World War II. As a by-product, the Jedwabne debate has created a new question regarding the social responsibility of historians. The debate has demonstrated clearly a conflict between collective memory and history in Poland.[41] Should historians serve as myth destroyers? How dangerous can bad history be? Can a suppressed history "explode"? Is Jan Gross's book such an "explosion"? What can replace a discredited history? How can historians contribute to the shaping of historical conscience? How can historians dissociate themselves from the deformations of collective memory and, at the same time, preserve respect for their discipline and support of their audience? Is a historian allowed to produce a methodologically controversial book to support a right cause? How can one produce a historical text which will be both intelligible and convincing in several different societies simultaneously? Proportions and arguments used by Gross resonate differently with the Polish audiences than they do with North American readers. Now, most North Americans, especially young ones, associate Polish-Jewish relations during World War II with one phenomenon: the Gross version of the Jedwabne events. It is also striking that now scholars who are skeptical about Gross's approach are more numerous than at the beginning of the debate. I am one of them. Let's put emotions and stereotypes aside; let's follow the generally accepted rules of the historical profession as a guarantee of impartiality; let's avoid generalizations and bad journalistic methods; let's keep a sense of proportions; let's put the Holocaust into a broader historical context; let's analyze causes first before we discuss guilt; and let's write another book about Jedwabne.

NOTES

1. Edward Hallett Carr, *What Is History?* (New York: Penguin Books, 1965), 87.

2. Jan T. Gross, *Neighbors: The Destruction of the Jewish Community in Jedwabne, Poland* (Princeton, NJ: Princeton University Press, 2001), 139.

3. Julius L. Baker and Jacob L. Baker, eds., *Yedwabne: History and Memorial Book* (New York: Yedwabner Societies in Israel and in the U.S., 1980).

4. Gross, *Neighbors,* 17.

5. Baker and Baker, *Yedwabne,* 101.

6. Gross, *Neighbors,* 22.

7. Ibid., 9. On page 7: "half of the population of a small East European town murdered the other half."

8. Ibid., 19, 57: also Menachem Finkelsztajn used the word "hooligans," describing the pogrom of Radziłów, 57.

9. Baker and Baker, *Yedwabne,* 116.

10. Ibid.

11. Gross, *Neighbors,* 32.

12. Szymon Datner, "Eksterminacja ludności żydowskiej w Okregu Białostockim," *Biuletyn Zydowskiego Instytutu Historycznego* [*Bulletin of the Jewish Historical Institute,* Warsaw], no. 60 (October–December 1966): 3–29.

13. Ben-Cion Pinchuk, *Shtetl Jews Under Soviet Rule: Eastern Poland on the Eve of the Holocaust* (Oxford: Basil Blackwell, 1990), 1.

14. Archiwum Żydowskiego Instytutu Historycznego w Warszawie [Archives of the Jewish Historical Institute in Warsaw], Relacje [Testimonies], file 1995, pp. 1–5.

15. Bernhard Chiari, "Deutsche Zivilverwaltung in Weissrussland 1941–44: Die lokale Perspektive der Besatzungsgeschichte" ["German Civilian Administration of Belorussia 1941–44: A Local Perspective of the History of the Occupation"], in *Militärgeschichtliche Mitteilungen* 52, no. 1 (1993); Bernhard Chiari, *Alltag hinter der Front: Besatzung: Kollaboration und Widerstand in Weissrussland, 1941–1944* [*Everyday Life behind the Front: Occupation, Collaboration and Resisatnec in Belorussia, 1941–1944*] (Düsseldorf: Droste Verlag, 1998).

16. Christian Gerlach, *Kalkulierte Morde: Die Deutsche Wirtschafts- und Vernichtungspolitik in Weissrussland 1941 bis 1944* [*Premeditated Murder: German Economic and Genocide Policies in Belorussia, 1941–1944*] (Hamburg: HIS Verlag, 1999); Christian Gerlach, "Deutsche Wirtschaftsinteressen, Besatzungspolitik und der Mord an der Juden in Weissrussland, 1941–1943" ["German Economic Interests, Occupation Policy, and Extermination of the Jews in Belorussia, 1941–1943"], in *Nationalsozialistische Vernichtungs-*

politik 1939–1945 [*Nazi Genocide Policy 1939–1945*], ed. Ulrich Herbert (Frankfurt am Main: Fischer Taschenbuch Verlag, 1998).

17. Wolfgang Benz, Konrad Kwiet, and Jürgen Matthäus, eds., *Einsatz im "Reichskommissariat Ostland": Dokumente zur Völkermord im Baltikum und in Weissrussland, 1941–1944* [*Operations in "Reichskommissariat Ostland": Documents on the Genocide in the Baltic Countries and Belorussia, 1941–1944*] (Berlin: Metropol Verlag, 1998).

18. Shalom Cholawsky, *The Jews of Bielorussia During World War II* (Amsterdam: Harwood, 1998).

19. Martin Dean, *Collaboration in the Holocaust: Crimes of the Local Police in Belorussia and Ukraine, 1941–44* (New York: St. Martin's Press, 2000).

20. Ibid., 21.

21. *Rzeczpospolita,* May 12, 2001; *Gazeta Wyborcza,* May 12, 2001.

22. Alexander B. Rossino, "Polish 'Neighbors' and German Invaders: Contextualizing Anti-Jewish Violence in the Bialystok District During the Opening Weeks of Operation Barbarossa," in *Polin: Studies in Polish Jewry* 16 (2003).

23. Datner, "Eksterminacja," 19. Datner writes about the German units operating in the Białystok District: "Sometimes these units, using the worst instincts [of the local population], organized the outburst of the 'popular anger.' They did not participate in the massacre but delivered weapons and gave instructions. As a rule, they photographed the atrocities, to have proof that the Jews were hated not only by the Germans."

24. Andrzej Żbikowski, "Lokalne pogromy Żydów w czerwcu i lipcu 1941 roku na wschodnich rubieżach II Rzeczpospolitej" ["Local Pogroms of the Jews in June and July 1941 in the Eastern Borderlands of the II Republic"], in *Biuletyn Żydowskiego Instytutu Historycznego* [*Bulletin of the Jewish Historical Institute,* Warsaw], no. 2–3 (1992): 5.

25. Ezra Mendelsohn, "Interwar Poland: Good for the Jews or Bad for the Jews?" in *The Jews in Poland,* ed. Chimen Abramsky, Maciej Jachimczyk, and Antony Polonsky (Oxford: Basil Blackwell, 1986), 130.

26. Gross, *Neighbors,* 155.

27. Mendelsohn, "Interwar Poland," 130.

28. Pinchuk, *Shtetl Jews:* "An outburst of joy and relief was the overwhelming reaction of the Jews in the many shtetlach of Eastern Poland to the entry of the Soviet army" (21); "The unanimity of Jewish reaction, in spite of differences in tone and enthusiasm, was noticed by many and was particularly resented by the Polish population" (22); "Jews participated in disproportionate numbers in the Soviet-established institutions during the first few weeks of the new regime" (26); and so forth.

29. Dov Levin, *The Lesser of Two Evils: Eastern European Jewry Under Soviet Rule, 1939–1941* (Philadelphia: Jewish Publication Society, 1995), 33: "Thus the Jews of Eastern Poland had good reason to greet the Red Army with relief. A Jew from the Eastern Galician city of Tarnopol described this sensation aptly: 'All the Jews in town greeted the Soviet army with satisfaction and relief.' . . . Various accounts attest to the joyous welcome that the Red Army received almost everywhere."

30. Cholawsky, *Jews of Belorussia,* 3: "The Jewish population in Western Belorussia received the Red Army with great joy. This spontaneous reaction included almost all sections of the population."

31. Jan T. Gross, "The Sovietisation of Western Ukraine and Western Byelorussia, " in *Jews in Eastern Poland and the USSR, 1939–46,* ed. Norman Davies and Antony Polonsky (London: Macmillan, 1991), 66. This entire article is written in a completely different tone than *Neighbors.*

32. Gross, *Neighbors,* 166–67.

33. Gustave Le Bon, *The Crowd: A Study of the Popular Mind* (Dunwoody, GA: Norman S. Berg, 1968), 6, 12, 22.

34. Heiner Lichtenstein, *Himmlers grüne Helfer: Die Schutz und Ordnungspolizei im "Dritten Reich"* [*Himmler's Green Helpers: The Defense and Order Police in the Third Reich*] (Cologne: Bund-Verlag, 1990), 13–78.

35. Michel Mielnicki, as told to John Munro, *Bialystok to Birkenau: The Holocaust Journey of Michel Mielnicki* (Vancouver: Ronsdale Press, 2000), 103–7.

36. Dariusz Stola, "Pomnik ze słów" ["A Monument Built Out of Words"], *Rzeczpospolita,* June 1–2, 2001.

37. "It Wasn't Just Germans," *Economist,* April 26, 2001.

38. Jan Tomasz Gross, *Sąsiedzi: Historia zagłady żydowskiego miasteczka* (Sejny: Pogranicze, 2000), 115.

39. Gross, *Neighbors,* 170.

40. Jolanta Ambrosewicz-Jacobs, "Teaching the Holocaust in Post-Communist Poland," *Jews in Eastern Europe* 36, no. 2 (Fall 1998): 5–18.

41. The issue is described in Michael C. Steinlauf, *Bondage to the Dead: Poland and the Memory of the Holocaust* (Syracuse: Syracuse University Press, 1997).

Gavriel D. Rosenfeld

The Normalization of Memory: Saul Friedländer's *Reflections of Nazism* Twenty Years Later

WHEREVER ONE LOOKS TODAY, SIGNS OF THE NORMALIZATION OF THE Nazi past abound in contemporary culture. Italian wine marketed in bottles featuring the image of Hitler. Teenagers quaffing beers beneath swastika banners at a Nazi-themed pub in Seoul, South Korea. Avant-garde artists irreverently exploiting Nazi imagery at the *Mirroring Evil* exhibition at New York City's Jewish Museum. Films and television specials dedicated to exploring Hitler's "human" side. Hitler in comic books. Nazis in video games.[1] As these examples undeniably demonstrate, Hitler and the Nazis not only continue to fascinate, they continue to garner attention, and they continue to sell.

In attempting to make sense of this trend, we owe a great debt of gratitude to one of the pioneering scholars who first directed our attention to it—Saul Friedländer. Among his many achievements, Friedländer has notably helped make us aware of a phenomenon that is now commonly referred to as "the normalization of memory."[2] He is probably our most perceptive analyst of the phenomenon of normalization, having examined its diverse manifestations in contemporary political, academic, and cultural life. As is well known, Friedländer commented widely on the political normalization of the Nazi past in Germany in the 1980s, in such episodes as the Bitburg controversy and the Historians' Debate.[3] Thereafter, he became involved in discussing the phenomenon of academic normalization in his debate with Martin Broszat over "historicizing" the Nazi past and in his seminal edited work on "probing the limits" of representing the Holocaust.[4] But his first analytical foray into the subject of normalization dates back even further, to the year 1982, when he published his pathbreaking study

on what might be called the aesthetic or cultural form of normalization—*Reflections of Nazism: An Essay on Kitsch and Death.*[5] Some
twenty years after the appearance of this seminal study, it seems timely
to revisit Friedländer's work and see what insights it can provide us in
our attempt to understand how contemporary culture has continued
to deal with the legacy of the Third Reich.

Reflections of Nazism tackled a simple yet vexing question: What
explained the striking shift in the representation of the Third Reich in
works of European high culture during the 1970s? An avid filmgoer in
Paris and Geneva, Friedländer first began to notice this shift in such
films as Luchino Visconti's *The Damned* (1969), Liliana Cavani's *The
Night Porter* (1973), and Hans-Jürgen Syberberg's *Hitler: Ein Film aus
Deutschland* (1977). At the same time, he identified similar patterns
of representation in works of literature, such as Michel Tournier's *The
Ogre* (1972) and George Steiner's *The Portage to San Cristobal of A.H.*
(1982), as well as in works of history, such as Albert Speer's memoir,
Inside the Third Reich (1970), and Werner Maser's *Hitler: Legend,
Myth, and Reality* (1973). These and other works were all linked by
their abandonment of prior modes of depicting the Nazi era. During the first decades of the postwar era, Friedländer argued, Nazism
had been overwhelmingly perceived as the "damned part of Western
civilization, the symbol of evil. Everything the Nazis had done was
condemned; whatever they touched defiled."[6] After the late 1960s and
early 1970s, however, the image of Nazism began to change. Instead
of moralistically condemning the perpetrators, various novelistic, cinematic, and historical works expressed a more detached and at times
prurient fascination with their lurid world of violence and degradation.
"Attention has gradually shifted," he noted, "from the horror and the
pain . . . to voluptuous anguish and ravishing images."[7] In short, it
was the aestheticizing of atrocity that constituted what Friedländer
called a "new discourse" on the subject of Nazism.[8]

In attempting to explain the origins of the new discourse, Friedländer abandoned the conventional historical methodology of his prior
studies and embarked upon a more novel form of extended cultural
criticism. His new approach was demonstrated in *Reflections of Nazism*'s
structure, which was less a fully fleshed-out work of history than an
extended essay. The primary reason for this shift in scholarly approach
was Friedländer's conviction that conventional social, political, and
economic explanations were insufficient for explaining the ongoing

presence of the Nazi past in contemporary cultural life. With the social, political, and economic conditions for Nazism no longer existing in the postwar world, Friedländer concluded that it was far more likely that a certain psychological climate was involved. This possibility seemed especially likely since the new narratives transcended political affiliation, coming from both the Left and the Right.[9] As such, he adopted a psychoanalytic approach of sorts to make sense of the new discourse. In so doing, Friedländer arrived at his most controversial conclusion, namely, that the contemporary reevocation of the Nazi era was rooted in the same psychological forces that initially attracted people to Nazism in the 1930s. As he put it, just as "Nazism's attraction lay less in any explicit ideology than in the power of emotions, images, and phantasms," the reappearance of these same emotions, images, and phantasms constituted "reflections of Nazism" in the present that could "help us better understand the past itself."[10] Friedländer devoted the central chapters of *Reflections of Nazism* to exploring three specific dimensions of the contemporary fascination with the Third Reich: "the beginning of a frisson, the presence of a desire, [and] the workings of an exorcism."[11]

The first theme—the beginning of a "frisson"—referred to the emotional thrill that ensued from the provocative manner in which the works of the "new discourse" juxtaposed images of "kitsch and death." For Friedländer, works such as *The Damned* offered images of pseudomythical heroism and camaraderie, on the one hand, together with portrayals of "ritualized, stylized, and aestheticized death," on the other. Significantly, both were depicted through an "overload of symbols" and repetitive images in such a way as to express some of the core features of Nazism's appeal at the time of its existence. Indeed, as Friedländer argued, the combination of kitsch and death—of "harmony" and "terror"—explained why so many Germans were drawn to Nazism in the first place.[12]

This attraction to Nazism was best illustrated by Friedländer's second theme, the "presence of a desire" surrounding Hitler in the new discourse that resembled that which existed during the Nazi years. According to Friedländer, just as the German people in the 1930s were attracted by Hitler's odd pairing of petit bourgeois kitsch sentimentality and yearning for absolute destruction, the works of the 1970s were far more seduced than repulsed by it. Werner Maser's Hitler biography, Albert Speer's memoirs, and Hans-Jürgen Syberberg's film expressed a deep interest in Hitler's pedestrian human side—the fact, for example, that he loved secret nighttime walks, dabbled in architecture and music, and could not match his socks with his suits. At the same time, these and other works expressed an attraction to his destructive personality. Prime examples here include Speer's wistful reminiscences of Hitler discussing the coming war against the backdrop of a bloodred sunset in Berchtesgaden and George Steiner's depiction of Hitler's passionate self-defense on his Brazilian jungle witness stand.[13]

Finally, Friedländer perceived in the works of the "new discourse" the "workings of an exorcism." This process, for Friedländer, was highly ambiguous, for while it superficially appeared to constitute a "confrontation" with the past, it actually remained "an evasion." Indeed, in attempting to expel the demons of Nazism by reevoking their spell, the proponents of exorcism fell prey to them. Syberberg's barrage of images, for example, may well have intended to confront and condemn Hitler's legacy, but in Friedländer's view, they ultimately functioned as "an ever more effective screen hiding the past." Syberberg's visual feast ultimately failed to offer a rational explanation for Nazism and ended up merely perpetuating the fascination with its perverse spectacle. To a degree, Friedländer recognized that the inability of Syberberg's words and images to convey a sense of Nazism's historical horror was part of a larger problem of language itself to represent atrocity. This difficulty reflected the frustrated realization of artists who saw realism as incapable of meeting the challenge of representation and instead sought refuge in the imagination as the best solution. Yet, Friedländer observes, the result was the aestheticization of a subject that called for "restraint." This result, however, was far from being an accidental by-product of the limits of language. Indeed, it revealed a degree of intentionality. For as Friedländer concluded, by dwelling on the "aesthetic element," the works of the "new discourse" revealed the influence of a certain "type of 'affect neutralization,'" which reflected an inability to confront what was most unbearable about the Third Reich. As he put it, the "fundamental characteristic of this exorcism . . . [is] to put the [Nazi] past back into bearable dimensions, . . . put it in the identifiable course of things, into the unmysterious march of ordinary history, into the reassuring rules that are the basis of our society." Each interpretation of Nazism in the new discourse, he concluded, "easily turns into a rationalization that normalizes, smoothes, and neutralizes our vision of the past."[14]

In arriving at this important conclusion, *Reflections of Nazism* emerged as one of the first texts to examine the phenomenon of aesthetic normalization. Although Friedländer used the term "normalization" only once—preferring the term "neutralization" throughout the text—he provided an innovative and insightful interpretation of a phenomenon that very few other scholars had given much thought to at that point. That Friedländer indeed had produced a pathbreaking and innovative analysis was confirmed by enthusiastic reviewers who described his argument as "brilliant" and praised his writing as full of "dazzle."[15] The book's appearance in four languages and its frequent citation over the years by cultural historians, literary scholars, and cultural critics provide further evidence of its considerable significance.[16]

Twenty-odd years later, however, what can we usefully take from the book? In light of recent trends in the representation of the Nazi past, how applicable do its insights remain? To begin with, one obvious point to note is that the narratives promoting an aesthetic version of normalization have changed. While Friedländer largely examined how works of high culture represented the Nazi past, it is arguably the case today that the process of normalization is being advanced more relentlessly in the realm of popular culture. The exploitation of the Nazi past in popular culture existed as a trend back in the 1970s as well, of course, as was skillfully analyzed by such figures as Susan Sontag and Alvin Rosenfeld.[17] But it may well be more powerful today due to popular culture's greater status, presence, and visibility in our increasingly media-saturated world. To be sure, the blurring of the line between high and low culture in our postmodern era makes it difficult to decisively classify works as belonging to either category, but the presence of Nazi themes today in mass-market novels, films, comic books, music lyrics, video games, and Internet Web sites unmistakably testifies to the significance of popular culture and underscores the need to grant it careful study. Such is especially the case given the fact that the field of popular culture is governed by different underlying forces and motives than high culture. While Friedländer identified an enduring psychological attraction to, or fascination with, Nazism as involved in the normalization of the past, today, commercial considerations are equally involved in normalizing Nazism. Given our awareness that images of Hitler and Nazism reap instant attention and easily sell, it is clear that Friedländer's largely psychoanalytic methodology could be profitably supplemented by considering the economic imperatives behind the broader commodification and resulting normalization of the Nazi era.

To be sure, why consumers continue to be drawn to the Nazi era also remains a psychological issue. But if *Reflections of Nazism* were written today, it would have to consider a second question, namely, what explains the Third Reich's ongoing fascination across successive generations? It has been said that every generation rediscovers Hitler for itself. Added to this truism is the obvious point that every generation reinterprets him in light of its own experiences. Significantly, many of the figures whose work Friedländer discussed were born in the 1930s or earlier and personally lived through the Nazi years.[18] This fact of biographical background stands in stark contrast to the situation today, in which the producers of narratives have no personal experiences of the era itself and are largely communicating the "vicarious" memories of the Nazi years.[19] Today, adding a generational component to the study of Nazism's ongoing fascination would deepen our understanding of whether the reasons for it have changed or remained constant. It may well be the case that audiences today remain drawn to Nazism's unique combination of kitsch and death. Some of the works displayed at the *Mirroring Evil* exhibit in New York, for example, would initially seem to suggest this interest by virtue of their highly ambiguous representation of the perpetrators.[20] Yet, upon closer examination, many of the works are less concerned with exploring the sordid reality of the Nazi past for its own sake than universalizing the Nazi past to make comments about largely unrelated issues, such as the totalitarian potential of the fashion, advertising, or toy industries.[21] The apparent persistence of fascination with the Nazi past today thus may well be somewhat more calculated and opportunistic today in comparison with the more visceral attention of the 1970s.

Other recent trends in the representation of Nazism further suggest shifting views toward it. In many ways, the narratives of recent years have ceased concentrating on Nazism's destructive features and have instead begun to adopt new and highly unconventional modes of depicting the Nazi era. Some works, for example, have utilized humor as a strategy of representation. They include such works as Roberto Benigni's film *Life is Beautiful* (1997); the recent theatrical musical adaptation of Mel Brooks's 1968 film comedy *The Producers* [a film version of which was released in 2005, also titled *The Producers*]; the

German comic book series by Walter Moers, *Adolf, Die Nazi-Sau;* Achim Greiser's book of Hitler cartoons, *Der Führer Privat* (2000); and the German satirical film *Goebbels und Geduldig* (2000).[22] Far from dwelling on images of violence and degradation, these are works that have tempered such horror through the means of satire—itself, to be sure, a sign of normalization. Other unconventional strategies have been visible in the many works of alternate history that have explored "what if?" questions pertaining to the Nazi past. These works have also normalized the Nazi era in offering speculative conclusions about how its historical course might have evolved in different fashion under different conditions. Narratives that have portrayed a Nazi victory in World War II, for example, such as American science fiction writer Philip K. Dick's 1962 novel *The Man in the High Castle,* originally depicted a Nazi-ruled world as a dystopia, while more recent works, such as historian John Lukacs's 1979 essay, "What If Adolf Hitler Had Won the Second World War?" or German historian Alexander Demandt's 1995 essay, "Wenn Hitler gesiegt hätte," depicted it as a relatively tolerable place.[23] Similarly, while Hitler's elimination from history was originally portrayed by such works as American writer Jerry Yulsman's 1984 novel *Elleander Morning* as improving it, most later tales, such as British writer Stephen Fry's 1996 novel *Making History,* consistently portrayed Hitler's elimination as making history turn out for the worse.[24]

The phenomenon of alternate history raises a third question pertaining to the ongoing normalization of the Nazi past: the national origin of the narratives themselves. While the vast majority of alternate histories of Nazism have emanated from the Anglo-American cultural realm, *Reflections of Nazism* focused nearly exclusively on the European continent, examining French, German, and Italian narratives. Would the conclusions of Friedländer's study have been different had he consulted American and British sources? Anglo-American narratives, of course, have also normalized the Nazi era, but less in the realm of high culture examined by Friedländer than in popular culture. These examples, however, which include such well-known works as Ira Levin's 1976 novel *The Boys from Brazil* and Jack Higgins's 1975 novel *The Eagle Has Landed,* have to a greater extent remained squarely within simplistic moralistic frameworks and have demonstrated less of the striving for exorcism identified by Friedländer in more highbrow European works.[25] Further research is necessary to adequately flesh this point out, but a possible reason for this difference between American and European tales is most likely their differing historical experiences of the Nazi era. Friedländer's own analysis would suggest that if, in fact, American tales have exhibited fewer yearnings to exorcise the demons of Nazism than have European texts, it may well stem from the fact that they have lacked the same degree of historical guilt for producing or collaborating with Nazism in the first place. The psychological motives behind works that seem to normalize the Nazi past, in short, may vary according to national context. To point out that Americans have less at stake psychologically or emotionally in representing the Nazi past, of course, is not to absolve them of any responsibility for normalizing it. But it is unlikely that the aestheticizing of the Nazi era in American works reflects the same worrisome yearnings Friedländer feared might exist in Europe. Distinguishing between the differing national backgrounds and motives of the producers of fictional representations of the Nazi era thus may yield a more differentiated understanding of normalization.

Overall, then, where does Friedländer's analysis of the 1970s leave us as we try to understand the phenomenon of normalization today? Friedländer's main concern a generation ago revolved around the motives that were driving European writers, filmmakers, and historians to produce the so-called new discourse on the Nazi past. Friedländer feared these works might reflect the enduring appeal of Nazi ideas in the present and a loosening of moral inhibitions about once more flirting with them. As he put it, the works of the era possibly reflected the persistence of a psychological disposition in modern society that was willing to risk "annihilation" for the sake of "the dream of all-powerfulness."[26] Today, by contrast, with the Nazi era having retreated a generation further into the past and with the end of the cold war having eliminated the immediate threat of nuclear annihilation, we can hopefully assert with confidence that we have less need to be on guard against what Friedländer called "the supreme transgression" of omnipotence. September 11 may have changed this—it is still unclear. But at present, the main concern related to normalization is different. At the risk of overgeneralizing, it does not so much revolve around the fear that people have continued to find Nazism appealing as the fear that they have largely lost sight of its inherent inhumanity and horror. The turn to humor, the instrumentalized use of the Nazi era for unrelated ends and the playful reconfiguration of its historical reality suggest that the historical experience of the Third Reich has become a reservoir of images and ideas to be exploited by anyone for any purpose. The future treatment of the Nazi era is impossible to predict. But in outlining a generation ago the distinct abandonment of a moralistic perspective toward it, Saul Friedländer sensitized us all to the unpredictable phenomenon of normalization. For providing us with the tools necessary for charting the ongoing evolution of the past in the present, we all owe him a debt of thanks.

NOTES

1. Ruth E. Gruber, "Jews Do Not Cheer Wine Bearing Faces of Dictators," *Jewish Telegraphic Agency,* May 1, 1995, 10. On the Korean Nazi-themed bar, see David Cohen, "The Rise and Fall of the Third Reich Café," *Jerusalem Report,* May 22, 2000, 42. The 2002 exhibit at New York's Jewish Museum, *Mirroring Evil,* raised charges that artists were instrumentalizing the Nazi past in irresponsible fashion; see, among many others, Edward Rothstein, "Artists Seeking Their Inner Nazi," *New York Times,* February 2, 2002, B9. Menno Meyjes's 2002 film *Max,* starring John Cusack and Noah Taylor, is a fictionalized account of the young Hitler's relationship with a Jewish artist in Munich after World War I; see "Portrait of the Führer as a Young Man," *Forward,* December 20, 2002. CBS announced in mid-2002 plans for a four-hour miniseries on Hitler's life up to the year 1933, based in part upon the study of Ian Kershaw; see Richard Weinraub, "Planned Mini-Series on Hitler's Early Life Brings Criticism," *New York Times,* August 20, 2002, E1; and, generally, Julie Salamon, "Is a Demon Humanized No Longer a Demon?" *New York Times,* February 2, 2003, 13, 19. Grant Morrison's 1991 comic book series, *The New Adventures of Hitler,* portrayed Hitler as a disgruntled young man living in Liverpool in 1912; see Rob Rodi, "Cruel Britannia," *Comics Journal,* June 1991, 41–47. On Nazis in video games, see Jonathan Kay, "Defying a Taboo, Nazi Protagonists Invade Video Games," *New York Times,* January 3, 2002, G6.

2. The concept of normalization is regularly invoked by scholars—especially scholars of modern German history and memory—but has only seldom been explored from a theoretically rigorous perspective. Among the few who have made efforts to discuss the term conceptually are Aleida Assmann and Ute Frevert, *Geschichtsvergessenheit, Geschichtsversessenheit: Vom Umgang mit deutschen Vergangenheiten nach 1945* (Stuttgart, 1999), 59–63; and Jeffrey K. Olick, "What Does It Mean to Normalize the Past?" *Social Science History* (Winter 1998): 547–71. Among many other scholars who

have recently utilized the term, see Stefan Berger, *The Search for Normalcy: National Identity and Historical Consciousness in Germany Since 1800* (Providence, RI, 1997); and Siobhan Kattago, *Ambiguous Memory: The Nazi Past and German National Identity* (Westport, CT, 2001).

3. See, for example, Saul Friedländer, "Some German Struggles with Memory," in *Bitburg in Moral and Political Perspective,* ed. Geoffrey Hartman (Bloomington, IN, 1986), 27–42.

4. For Friedländer's discussion with Broszat, see the contributions in Peter Baldwin, *Reworking the Past: Hitler, the Holocaust, and the Historians' Debate* (Boston, 1990); and Saul Friedländer, ed., *Probing the Limits of Representation: Nazism and the "Final Solution"* (Cambridge, MA, 1992).

5. Saul Friedländer, *Reflections of Nazism: An Essay on Kitsch and Death* (New York, 1984). This English translation appeared two years after the French original, *Reflets zu Nazisme.*

6. Friedländer, *Reflections of Nazism,* 11–12.

7. Ibid., 21.

8. Ibid., 12.

9. Ibid., 13.

10. Ibid., 14, 17–18.

11. Ibid., 18.

12. Ibid., 25, 43, 45, 50.

13. Ibid., 63, 28, 113–14.

14. Ibid., 86, 97, 96, 95, 107, 102.

15. Most effusive was Alan Mintz's review of *Reflections of Nazism* in the *New Republic,* October 1, 1984, 40–42.

16. See, for example, many of the essays in Bernd Ogan and Wolfgang W. Weiß, eds., *Faszination und Gewalt: Zur politischen Ästhetik des Nationalsozialismus* (Nuremberg, 1992); and, more recently, Norman Kleeblatt, *Mirroring Evil: Nazi Imagery/Recent Art* (New Brunswick, NJ, 2001).

17. Susan Sontag, "Fascinating Fascism," in *Under the Sign of Saturn* (New York, 1980), 73–105; Alvin H. Rosenfeld, *Imagining Hitler* (Bloomington, IN, 1985).

18. These figures include Albert Speer (born in 1905), Luchino Visconti (1906), Werner Maser (1922), George Steiner (1929), Michel Tournier (1932), Liliana Cavani (1933), and Hans-Jürgen Syberberg (1935). Also included in this group is French filmmaker Louis Malle (1932), whose work Friedländer also discusses.

19. James Young discusses the concept of vicarious memory in his recent book *At Memory's Edge: After-Images of the Holocaust in Contemporary Art and Architecture* (New Haven, CT, 2000).

20. See, for example, the work of Piotr Uklanski, *The Nazis* (1998),

which displayed 166 full-color photographs of Hollywood actors dressed up as Nazi officers for various feature films. For several discussions, see Kleeblatt, *Mirroring Evil.*

21. This was particularly true of the work of artists Tom Sachs, Maciej Toporowicz, and Zbigniew Libera. For a thoughtful discussion, see Walter Reich, "Appropriating the Holocaust," *New York Times,* March 15, 2002, A23, in which he quotes Sachs as saying, "I'm using the iconography of the Holocaust to bring attention to fashion. Fashion, like fascism, is about loss of identity."

22. Walter Moers, *Adolf* (Frankfurt am Main, 1998); Walter Moers, *Adolf: Teil 2* (Frankfurt am Main, 1999); Achim Greiser, *Der Führer Privat* (Bittermann, 2000). *Goebbels und Geduldig* (2000) was directed by Kai Wessel and aired on German television in late 2002.

23. Philip K. Dick, *The Man in the High Castle* (New York, 1992); John Lukacs, "What If Hitler Had Won the Second World War?" in *The People's Almanac,* vol. 2, ed. David Wallechinsky (New York, 1978), 396–98; Alexander Demandt, "Wenn Hitler gewonnen hätte? *Tango,* no. 18 (1995): 20–27.

24. Jerry Yulsman, *Elleander Morning* (New York, 1984); Stephen Fry, *Making History* (London, 1996).

25. Ira Levin, *The Boys from Brazil* (New York, 1976); Jack Higgins, *The Eagle Has Landed* (London, 1975).

26. Friedländer, *Reflections of Nazism,* 135.

Eric D. Weitz

The Holocaust and Comparative Genocide

I HAVE NEVER TAUGHT A HOLOCAUST COURSE. I HAVE, MORE TIMES than I care to count, taught the history of Nazi Germany. The students might not understand the distinction when they register for the class, but they probably come to recognize the point fairly quickly as they peruse the syllabus and see that it takes about one third of the semester just to get the Nazis to power. I also tell them in the first minutes that my goal is to teach many aspects of the history, from high-level politics to the social lives of youth and families under the Nazi regime, from diplomatic and military maneuvers to the course of racial policies. The last third of the course focuses on war and the Holocaust, and issues of representation and memory are never far behind.

In whatever format I have taught it, as a seminar for first-year students at a liberal arts college or as a lecture course at a large public university, Nazi Germany and Hitler's Europe has been popular. Almost any course with "Hitler" or "Nazi" in the title will attract hordes of students, generally for the best reasons—because they have an intense desire to learn about a regime that systematically repressed and annihilated people and about a history that figures so prominently in our public culture.

Yet over the years I have become increasingly discontented with the nearly exclusive focus on Nazi Germany and the Holocaust in my teaching and research and in relation to public and political discussions both in the United States and in Germany. I am by training and inclination a historian of modern Germany. It is what I know best. Yet the narrowness of perspective gnaws at me, and I find unconvincing and unsatisfying the sheer unwillingness to move beyond the German national frame and the fate of Jews under the Third Reich. I need to be very clear here. The Holocaust was an atrocity of monumental proportions and the greatest tragedy in Jewish history. Yet the Holocaust was also one of a number of genocides that have occurred in the twentieth century. It had its particular characteristics, as do all historical events, as does every genocide. Those particularities had to do with Germany's highly developed bureaucratic and military culture, which constituted one (though certainly not the only) very powerful strand of the German tradition. Once the Nazis had seized power, they were able to draw upon and further develop bureaucratic and military practices in the drive to annihilate Jews. The other particularity had to do with Germany's great power status, which contributed to very grand territorial ambitions in Europe, much grander than most other dictatorial systems. But there was, unfortunately, *nothing exceptional* in the Nazis' utopian drive to create homogeneity, *nothing unusual* in their deployment of the ideology of race to classify, purge, and kill defined groups of people.

If this is indeed the case, then we need to be very cautious about positioning the Holocaust as *the* decisive event of the twentieth century, *the* singular, exclusive "civilization rupture," to use Dan Diner's phrase.[1] It is, of course, fully understandable why the Holocaust has come to play that powerful role in Western societies. The Holocaust occurred in Europe in a war that involved all the major Western powers. It was unprecedented in its dimensions, so much so that even Jews in its midst could not fully comprehend what awaited them. Yet the Armenian genocide was also unprecedented. Despite past instances of violence, some of which had taken tens and hundreds of thousands of lives, nothing had quite prepared Armenians for the organized, systematic, and total attack on their very existence by the Ottoman state and emergent Republican Turkey from 1915 to 1923. In Rwanda, Hutus and Tutsis had fought with one another previously, but the 1994 genocide was also unprecedented. Never before had Hutu leaders sought the elimination in total of the Tutsi population.

No case of genocidal politics has been as extensively researched and written about as that of the Third Reich. The literature of all sorts—scholarly studies, memoirs, novels, philosophical explorations—not to speak of film and other media, is so immense that no single individual can master it all. Yet at least in terms of the historiography, the singular focus on the Nazi regime and the Holocaust has probably gone as far as it can. Of course, very important individual studies are still being published. Many of them draw on the newly opened archives of the former Soviet bloc countries and are the work of a new generation of historians, many of them German, who have learned Polish, Russian, or other Slavic languages. Clearly, there will still be very important debates sparked by works like Jan Gross's *Neighbors* or by continued investigations into the timing of the Holocaust.[2] But at this point, it is hard to imagine any paradigm-shifting study that will emerge. While predictions are always hazardous, it seems to me that a certain exhaustion of research is setting in, as is typical (and not to be mourned) of any field that undergoes explosive growth and inspires countless researchers to set off on the archival trail. If the founding of scholarly societies and journals constitutes one sign of emerging fields, then the establishment of the International Association of Genocide Scholars in 1994 and of the *Journal of Genocide Research* and the *Zeitschrift für Genozidforschung,* both in 1999, is an indication that comparative approaches have arrived. So is the publication of a variety of books that adopt an explicitly comparative approach, such as Norman M. Naimark's very important study, *Fires of Hatred: Ethnic Cleansing in Twentieth-Century Europe;* the Pulitzer Prize–winning work of Samantha Power, *"A Problem from Hell": America and the Age of Genocide;* and my own *A Century of Genocide: Utopias of Race and Nation.*[3]

The move in scholarly discussions toward placing the Holocaust in a comparative context therefore requires some rethinking on the part of teachers, no matter what their discipline. I am not at all suggesting that we abandon courses and research on the Holocaust and on Nazi Germany. I will continue to teach my own course on the Third Reich and others that relate specifically to Germany. At the same time, I do want to suggest that on the larger canvas of school and university curricula and of research, the singular focus on the Holocaust no longer suffices.

It is all well and good, perhaps not even that controversial, to talk about the virtues of a comparative approach. Certainly, there have been courses for some time now at a variety of universities on comparative genocide. But the problem remains: How does one do it? What are the criteria of comparison? And how does one compare in a way that is attentive to and respectful of the particular dimensions of the Holocaust and other cases? How does one compare without falling into the trap of suggesting that there have been other atrocities in history so what is so bad about the Holocaust or, even worse, that the Holocaust was merely a defensive reaction on the part of Germany? And how does one compare in such a way that we do not fall into that other trap, comparative suffering or the body-count approach to history? That approach also gets us nowhere in terms of understanding—communism killed eighty million or one hundred million and National Socialism "only" six million, or maybe it is thirty-eight million or fifty million if we count the war as well. Those figures are facts that constitute part of our efforts to understand the tragedies of the twentieth century; they do not provide, in and of themselves, conclusions of any sort.

Let me suggest a few criteria that guide my research and teaching about genocides, the Holocaust and others.

IDEOLOGIES OF RACE AND NATION

There exists a very large, sophisticated body of scholarly literature on nation building and nationalism. There is another large, sophisticated body of scholarly literature on racial formation. One of the most general conclusions to be drawn from that literature is that nations and races are constructions and the process of "making" nations and races is historically contingent and never complete. Races and nations are always in the process of being made. At the same time, every genocide entails first the act of classification, of identifying and categorizing populations, those who are targeted for annihilation as well as those whose efflorescence is seen to depend upon the removal of the dangerous group.[4] Every categorization is an ideological and political act; there is nothing "natural" about classifications.

But when we get to the actual events of the Third Reich and other genocidal systems, we tend to abandon historicity and talk about the Germans, the Jews, and the Poles; or the Serbs, the Croats, and the Muslims; and so on, as if these were unproblematic designations for homogeneous and ahistorical collectives. At the ultimate moment of roundups, deportations, and killings, those identities have indeed become fixed. But until that moment, we need always to be attentive to the historical—and therefore contingent—nature of the very categories of race and nation. The word "race" did not even exist in the European languages until the late fourteenth century and did not become common until the sixteenth century.[5] Race thinking emerged around 1500 with the European explorations. It developed in tandem with New World slavery and especially with eighteenth-century scientific, social, and political developments. The word "nation" has a much longer lineage, of course, but its meaning became transformed in the modern era from the French Revolution onward.[6]

While there is no unmediated, direct connection between these categories and genocide—many national and racial systems are "merely" discriminatory rather than murderous, and in each of the cases, many other historical factors have to be taken into account—they lie at the heart of the Holocaust and the other genocides of the twentieth century. In acting upon the ideologies of race and nation, the genocidal regimes of the twentieth century drew upon Enlightenment conceptions of human progress and nineteenth-century scientific advances that posited the possibility—indeed, the desirability—of improving society by shaping its very composition. By the turn into the twentieth century, there were increasingly loud claims that some categories of the population were incapable of improvement and constituted a drag on the well-being of the population as a whole. Depending on who was speaking and where, the lower classes generally, promiscuous women, African-descended peoples, Jews, criminals, the mentally ill, or some combination of all of these might be identified as the threatening group. The future progress of society, in this view, depended upon protecting enterprising, productive people from the negative influences of dissolute and degenerate ones.[7] When such ideas were linked to racial and national identities, as they so often were, then entire populations could be categorized as dangers to the well-being of the dominant group. Genocide in the twentieth century was the ultimate expression of this perspective, a policy of working on the population to shape its literal character by the forced, violent elimination of groups defined as "alien" and threatening.

By categorizing and purging populations in this fashion, genocidal regimes function as radical simplifiers. They reduce the variety of human identities to one single form of race or religion or nation, which are supposedly natural and eternal categories—until the enemy is removed from the face of the earth. Invariably the regimes in question employed the powerful metaphors of "cleanness" and "purity" as well as "productivity" in relation to the honored groups. "Cleanness" and "purity" are terms that, necessarily, signify their binary opposites, the unclean and the impure. Those who were considered unclean were an active source of pollution that threatened to contaminate the clean and the pure. For some of the powerful systems of the twentieth century, the dirt that Mary Douglas famously described as "matter out of place" was, in fact, human matter, and it had to be eradicated through political action. In excluding "dirt," these systems were "positively reordering [the] environment, making it conform to an idea."[8]

So the first criterion of comparison, it seems to me, is about the ideologies of race and nation. The first couple of days of my course on comparative genocides are spent on definitions of genocide, ethnic cleansing, and human rights, and then we launch into two weeks of readings, discussions, and lectures on the theory and historical development of race and nation. There are quite a number of good anthologies that provide students with excerpts from major contemporary theorists as well as from primary sources authored by the ideologues of race and nation.[9] A number of good general histories also exist, and I use Phillip Yale Nicholson's *Who Do We Think We Are?* which serves almost as a companion piece to lectures and discussions in the first few weeks of class.[10] Over the course of the semester, as we proceed through various cases of genocide, we examine, in each case, how regimes constructed and enforced categories of identities. I also bring the students back to the topic of the first few weeks of class, both to remind them that race and nation are political and ideological constructions and also to deepen their acquaintance with major theorists by reading excerpts from Max Weber, Ernest Gellner, and Benedict Anderson.

This procedure also enables me to follow and expand upon one of Hannah Arendt's key insights in *The Origins of Totalitarianism:* that an inextricable link existed between the racism that developed with European colonial empires and anti-Semitism, that the Holocaust was, in some senses, the coming back into Europe of imperialism.[11] It has taken about forty years for historians, literary scholars, and others to follow up on her insight and to start providing its empirical underpinnings. Working off Arendt's position opens up a global perspective. It enables us to explore how European ideas and political models traveled into the colonies and then back into Europe in more radicalized fashion, or how indigenous racial concepts became intermingled with European ideas about race. Examples abound: the lessons that German military and civilian officials derived from the genocide of the Herero in Southwest Africa (present-day Namibia) and of the Armenians in the late Ottoman Empire; the blending of indigenous Khmer and

French colonial understandings of race; the Belgians' establishment of racial categories between Hutus and Tutsis.

REVOLUTIONARY REGIMES AND UTOPIAN GOALS

In most cases of twentieth-century genocides, political leaders were animated by powerful visions of the future and sought to create a utopia in the here and now. To be sure, the content of the utopias differed significantly, from the explicitly Aryan future that the Nazis posited to the supposedly classless, egalitarian societies of the Soviet Union and Cambodia. But all of these regimes launched massive projects, from economic development, such as forced collectivization, forest clearings, and canal constructions, to the total restructuring of education. They were "project states" or, in the words of James C. Scott, authoritarian "high modernist" regimes.[12]

An absolutely central aspect of these projects entailed collective population politics on a vast scale, the refashioning of individual consciousness and the reshaping of the very composition of society. In the drive to create a homogeneous population of one sort or another, the regimes classified people sometimes by their social class background and political orientation; sometimes by religion, race, or nation; sometimes by a blending of all of these categories.

By striving to remake the nature of society so thoroughly, by so utterly transforming the conditions of life for so many people, these regimes, rightist and leftist, required the organizing capacities of the modern state, its bureaucracies that slotted people into defined categories and its security forces that imprisoned and killed members of the targeted populations. Because these regimes asserted total claims over society, obliterating, at least theoretically, the distinction between public and private realms that is a defining feature of liberalism, they recognized no inherent limits to their intention to remake society. The possession of state power and the ideological conviction of utopia gave them license to launch all sorts of huge projects, from the construction of dams through the massive deployment of human labor to reshaping the very composition of society by granting the honored members privileged access to resources and by interning, deporting, and, ultimately, killing the dishonored ones.[13]

So the second criterion of comparison entails an examination of regime ideologies and structures. Mostly it is conveyed to students in my lectures, with extensive quotes from primary sources—political leaders from Lenin to Pol Pot and Miloševic, party and state journals, images of propaganda posters. All these sources give students a sense of the regimes: What were the visions of the future that regimes sought to implement? What were their ideologies? And how was the state organized to carry out such policies? To understand genocides, students (and the rest of us) need to understand something about the nature of the regimes in question. The comparative approach broadens their horizons and is, perhaps, a cautionary tale, for they see a variety of formal ideological and political systems at work that carried out the worst forms of population politics.

THE CRISIS SITUATIONS OF WAR AND INTERNAL SOCIAL UPHEAVAL

Not every revolutionary regime has committed ethnic cleansings and genocides. Even the Holocaust was not predetermined, if one follows the current scholarly consensus. Some form of exclusion of Jews was inevitable once the Nazis had seized power, but not necessarily physical annihilation. For all the importance of contextual factors, a high level of contingency is present in every case of genocide. Only at moments of extreme societal crisis—often self-generated—of immense internal upheaval and war, of great opportunities but also dread dangers, did regimes initiate the most extreme form of population politics and "tip over" from pursuing discrimination and partial killings to perpetrating the more systematic and deadly policies of genocide.

The connection between genocides and extreme societal crisis is so critical because both war and revolution break standard codes of human interaction. Revolutions by definition overthrow the legal norms of a polity and, in the process, undermine existing legal and cultural constraints on human behavior. In wartime, states typically impose emergency conditions that give officials the freedom to act in ways they would not dare venture in peacetime. The upheavals of revolution and war heighten the sense of insecurity, leading to calls for swift and forceful actions to remove those who are seen as dangers to the national cause or to the creation of the new society. At the same time, wars open up vistas of pleasure in the future and present great opportunities for vast restructurings of societies and populations. Wars and revolutions are by definition also violent acts; they create cultures of violence and killing. Such was especially the case in the twentieth century because total war required the mobilization of entire societies in the enterprise of violence. The battlefields of World War I set standards of violence that revolutionary states sought to replicate in their deliberate purges of defined population groups.

In every case of genocide that I teach, we move from broad analysis of the nature of regimes to the very specific political decisions that culminated in genocide. I hope that the students grasp the human dimension of these events, including the ever-present possibilities that they did not have to happen. That is a far more unsettling perspective than, for example, Daniel Goldhagen's notion that all of modern German history was on a course to the Holocaust, that virtually all Germans wanted Jews eliminated and Hitler only implemented their deepest desires.[14]

To introduce students to these themes, I have them read toward the beginning of the course all of Naimark's important comparative study *Fires of Hatred*.[15] Naimark's book is very good at identifying the broad contextual as well as immediate political factors that led to the atrocities in each of the cases he studies in detail. Discussions on the book also introduce students to comparative methodology and provide concrete historical examples that allow the class to venture deeper into the problem of defining and classifying genocide, ethnic cleansing, and other forms of human rights abuses. Then there are additional sources on some (not all) of the specific cases, for example, an edited book by Richard Hovannisian on the Armenian genocide and a brief but excellent film produced by the BBC on the Rwanda crisis.[16] In some cases I also use memoirs (discussed subsequently), such as Loung Ung's *First They Killed My Father* about Cambodia, as a basis for analyzing the regime.[17] With the students I try to work back from her account of specific incidents—the family's deportation from Phnom Penh, her younger brother's efforts to procure food for the family—to an analysis of the nature of the Khmer Rouge system.

POPULAR MOBILIZATION

From something of a political science approach focused on the nature of regimes and moments of crisis, we then move to social history. Genocides are the result of state policies. But genocides in the twentieth century became so extensive and systematic because the regimes engaged massive social projects that mobilized people for all sorts of activities. The literal reshaping of the population could not simply be decreed and could not happen overnight; it had to be created by the hard work of thousands and thousands of people, whether obtained through force, begrudging compliance, enthusiastic support, or the innumerable forms in between. As Alf Lüdtke writes specifically about the Third Reich, but with words that can be generalized to the other cases:

> The gruesome attraction of complicity [*Mitmachen*] operates in relation to exclusions and suppressions—and ultimately to murder actions. Participation [*Mit-Täterschaft*] in tormenting other human beings became an integral part of the "work of domination," such that the boundary between the guilt of a few and the innocence of many blended away.[18]

Rituals of violence became the mechanisms for carrying out the deadly policies of these systems and a way of binding people to the regimes. States organized people to serve as brigade leaders, social workers, and pioneers, but also as the jail keepers, guards, torturers, and killers who invented and implemented the brutalities of genocide. In all cases, the circle of complicity extended still further to the population at large to include those, for example, who watched gleefully as the Nazis or their auxiliaries killed Jews in market squares and synagogues or as Serbian forces killed Muslims. Neighbors and bystanders seized the properties of Jews, Crimean Tatars, Chechens, Vietnamese, or Bosnian Muslims and forced them out of their homes. Genocides on the scale of the twentieth century were possible only with the participation of these many thousands, some of whom were active agents in mass killings, others of whom reaped the benefits, material and otherwise, of the removal of their neighbors.

In exploring this dimension of genocides with students, I find that literature, films, memoirs, and trial testimonies are particularly helpful. They direct attention at both state policies and the individuals who were their enactors. Memoirs describe in intricate and painful detail the herding of people into train cars, the blows that rained down upon bodies, the separation of women and children from men. These kinds of sources depict the social character of genocides. They can be difficult materials to watch and to read, as we all know. But after weeks of more abstract historical and social scientific discussions, it is critical that students read and see the searing brutality of genocides. It is often the moment in the semester—hearing the stories of Armenian survivors, viewing an excerpt from the film *Shoah,* reading Loung Ung's description of life in Democratic Kampuchea—when students seem to grasp the enormous dimensions of what we have been discussing.[19]

MEMORY

Genocides are deadly to the victims; they are also events whose corrupting character travels deep into the population. The successors to the societies that have been consumed by mass violence cannot escape the legacy; they remain overburdened by the past, precisely because of the participatory nature of genocides in the modern era.

In the last two weeks of the course, we discuss memory and also the various forms of human rights enforcement: tribunals, military interventions, truth and reconciliation commissions. By this point in the semester, students have little time for extensive readings. The case study approach has gotten exhausting and emotionally draining. But images of memorial sites and museums provide an important opening for discussion, as do excerpts from memoirs, novels, and poems.[20] The very inconclusiveness of the politics of memory leaves many students unsettled, but it also impresses upon them how much the events of the past continue to reverberate in individual and collective lives and in contemporary politics.

There have been genocides for as long as recorded history. In the twentieth century, genocides and related human rights violations, such as ethnic cleansings, became more extensive, more systematic, and more deadly. The Holocaust was one case among a general class of extreme population politics carried out by modern states. *Vergleich ist nicht Gleichsetzung,* as Germans say: comparison does not mean equivalencies. Comparison heightens the attentiveness for similarities and differences within a class of common events or situations. The comparative method enables us to see how political ideas and models travel, sometimes to unexpected places. It opens up a transnational and even global perspective, an approach, a few years into the twenty-first century, more needed than ever.

NOTES

Some of the passages here are drawn from my book, Eric D. Weitz, *A Century of Genocide: Utopias of Race and Nation* (Princeton, NJ: Princeton University Press, 2003).

1. Dan Diner, *Beyond the Conceivable: Studies on Germany, Nazism, and the Holocaust* (Berkeley and Los Angeles: University of California Press, 2000).

2. Jan T. Gross, *Neighbors: The Destruction of the Jewish Community in Jedwabne, Poland* (Princeton, NJ: Princeton University Press, 2001).

3. Norman M. Naimark, *Fires of Hatred: Ethnic Cleansing in Twentieth-Century Europe* (Cambridge, MA: Harvard University Press, 2001); Samantha Power, *"A Problem from Hell": America and the Age of Genocide* (New York: Basic Books, 2002); Weitz, *Century of Genocide.*

4. See the classic study of Raul Hilberg, *The Destruction of the European Jews* (Chicago: Quadrangle, 1961).

5. Werner Conze, "Rasse," in *Geschichtliche Grundbegriffe: Historisches Lexikon zur politisch-sozialen Sprache in Deutschland,* vol. 5, ed. Otto Brunner, Werner Conze, and Reinhard Koselleck (Stuttgart: Ernst Klett, 1984), 135–78.

6. Guido Zernatto, "Nation: The History of a Word," *Review of Politics* 6, no. 3 (1944): 351–66.

7. Amir Weiner, ed., *Landscaping the Human Garden: Twentieth-Century Population Management in a Comparative Framework* (Stanford, CA: Stanford University Press, 2003).

8. Mary Douglas, *Purity and Danger: An Analysis of the Concepts of Pollution and Taboo* (1966; London: Routledge, 1996), 2, 36.

9. Emmanuel Chukwudi Eze, ed., *Race and the Enlightenment: A Reader* (Cambridge, MA: Blackwell, 1997); Montserrat Guibernau and John Rex, eds., *The Ethnicity Reader: Nationalism, Multiculturalism and Migration* (Cambridge, UK: Polity, 1997).

10. Phillip Yale Nicholson, *Who Do We Think We Are? Race and Nation in the Modern World* (Armonk, NY: M. E. Sharpe, 2001).

11. Hannah Arendt, *The Origins of Totalitarianism* (1951; Cleveland: Meridian Books, 1958).

12. James C. Scott, *Seeing Like a State: How Certain Schemes to Improve the Human Condition Have Failed* (New Haven, CT: Yale University Press, 1996); see also Tim Mason, *Nazism, Fascism and the Working Class: Essays by Tim Mason,* ed. Jane Caplan (Cambridge: Cambridge University Press, 1995); and Charles Maier, *Dissolution: The Crisis of Communism and the End of East Germany* (Princeton, NJ: Princeton University Press; 1997).

13. On Cambodia, see David P. Chandler, *The Tragedy of Cambodian*

History: Politics, War, and Reconstruction Since 1945 (New Haven, CT: Yale University Press, 1991); David P. Chandler, *Voices from S-21: Terror and History in Pol Pot's Secret Prison* (Berkeley and Los Angeles: University of California Press, 1999); and Ben Kiernan, *The Pol Pot Regime: Race, Power, and Genocide in Cambodia Under the Khmer Rouge, 1975–79* (New Haven, CT: Yale University Press, 1996). On Rwanda, see Mahmood Mamdani, *When Victims Become Killers: Colonialism, Nativism, and the Genocide in Rwanda* (Princeton, NJ: Princeton University Press, 2001).

14. Daniel Jonah Goldhagen, *Hitler's Willing Executioners: Ordinary Germans and the Holocaust* (New York: Alfred A. Knopf, 1996).

15. Naimark, *Fires of Hatred.*

16. Richard Hovannisian, ed. *Remembrance and Denial: The Case of the Armenian Genocide* (Detroit: Wayne State University Press, 1999).

17. Loung Ung, *First They Killed My Father: A Daughter of Cambodia Remembers* (New York: Perennial, 2001).

18. Alf Lüdtke, "Einleitung: Herrschaft als soziale Praxis," in *Herrschaft als soziale Praxis: Historische und sozial-anthropologische Studien,* ed. Alf Lüdtke (Göttingen: Vandenhoeck und Ruprecht, 1991), 44; my translation.

19. Hovannisian, *Remembrance and Denial; Shoah,* videocassette, directed by Claude Lanzmann (1985; Hollywood: Paramount Video, 1986); Ung, *First They Killed My Father.*

20. Anna Akhmatova, *Requiem and Poem Without a Hero,* trans. D. M. Thomas (Athens: Ohio University Press, 1976); Franz Werfel, *The Forty Days of Musa Dagh* (1933; Carroll and Graf, 2002).

Notes on Contributors

GERARD AALDERS is a senior researcher at the Netherlands Institute for War Documentation (NIOD). He has published a trilogy of books and several articles on looting and restitution.

MICHAEL THAD ALLEN is the author of *The Business of Genocide: The SS, Slave Labor, and the Concentration Camps,* which won the German Studies Association-DAAD Best Book Prize in 2002. He is currently working on a history of Auschwitz.

HARVEY ASHER is a professor emeritus of history at Drury University in Springfield, Missouri. He is currently writing a popular history, *Things Could Always Be Worse—And They Were!*

FRANK BAJOHR is a senior researcher at the Forschungsstelle für Zeitgeschichte in Hamburg and the author of several books on National Socialism, the Holocaust, and anti-Semitism, including *"Aryanization" in Hamburg: The Economic Exclusion of Jews and the Confiscation of Their Property in Nazi Germany.*

OMER BARTOV is John P. Birkelund Distinguished Professor of European History at Brown University. His books include *Hitler's Army, Murder in Our Midst, Mirrors of Destruction, Germany's War and the Holocaust,* and *The "Jew" in Cinema.* He is currently writing a book on the interethnic town of Buczacz in East Galicia.

DORIS L. BERGEN is a professor of history at the University of Notre Dame. She is the author of *Twisted Cross: The German Christian Movement in the Third Reich, War and Genocide: A Concise History of the*

Holocaust, and numerous articles and essays on religion, gender, and ethnicity in Nazi Germany and Europe. Bergen edited *The Sword of the Lord: Military Chaplains from the First to the Twenty-First Century* and will edit *Lessons and Legacies VIII: From Generation to Generation* (Evanston, IL: Northwestern University Press, forthcoming). She is currently writing a monograph on Wehrmacht chaplains in World War II and the Holocaust.

SUZANNE BROWN-FLEMING is a senior program officer in the University Programs Division of the United States Holocaust Memorial Museum's Center for Advanced Holocaust Studies in Washington, DC. She is author of *The Holocaust and Catholic Conscience: Cardinal Aloisius Muench and the Guilt Question in Germany.* Her new project, "The Vatican-German Relationship Reexamined, 1922–1939," utilizes the recently released records of the Vatican nunciatures in Munich and Berlin and of Eugenio Pacelli's tenure as secretary of state.

MARTIN DEAN is an applied research scholar at the United States Holocaust Memorial Museum's Center for Advanced Holocaust Studies in Washington, DC. He received his Ph.D. from Queens' College, Cambridge, in 1989, and worked as the senior historian for the Metropolitan Police War Crimes Unit in London from 1992 to 1997. His publications include *Collaboration in the Holocaust: Crimes of the Local Police in Belorussia and Ukraine, 1941–44* and "Local Collaboration in the Holocaust" in *The Historiography of the Holocaust.*

CHRISTIAN DELAGE is a historian who teaches at the University of Paris 8 and at the École des hautes études en sciences sociales, also in Paris. He is the author of *La Vision nazie de l'histoire; Chaplin, la grande histoire; L'Historien et le film* (with Vincent Guigueno); and *La Vérité par l'image: De Nuremberg à Milosevic.* He is also a filmmaker; recently, he directed a 90-minute documentary, *Nuremberg: The Nazis on Trial and the Emergence of the Genocide of the Jews,* for the French and German cultural channel ARTE.

LAWRENCE DOUGLAS is a professor of law, jurisprudence, and social thought at Amherst College. He is the author of a study of war crimes trials, *The Memory of Judgment: Making Law and History in the Trials of the Holocaust;* a book of humor, *Sense and Nonsensibility: Lampoons of Literature and Learning* (with Alexander George); and a novel, *The Catastrophist.* He has contributed to numerous publications, including the *Yale Law Journal,* the *Washington Post,* the *New York Times Book Review,* and the *Times Literary Supplement.* He is currently writing a book titled *Reflections on the Glass Booth: The Cultural Afterlife of War Crimes Trials.*

REBECCA GOLBERT received her doctorate in social anthropology from the University of Oxford. Her research has focused on facets of Jewish memory and identity in post-Soviet Ukraine, both among the younger generation and among Holocaust survivors. Her preliminary research on the Pechora camp in the Romanian-occupied zone of Transnistria was published in *Holocaust and Genocide Studies.* Her forthcoming article on Holocaust memorials and memorialization practices in Ukraine is to be published in *Polin: Studies in Polish Jewry.*

JAN T. GROSS is a professor of history and Norman Tomlinson '16 and '48 Professor of War and Society at Princeton University. He is the author of *Neighbors: The Destruction of the Jewish Community in Jedwabne, Poland; Revolution from Abroad: The Soviet Conquest of Poland's Western Ukraine and Western Belorussia;* and *Polish Society Under German Occupation: The Generalgouvernement, 1935–1944.*

JEFFREY HERF is a professor of modern European history at the University of Maryland in College Park. His books include *Reactionary Modernism: Technology, Culture and Politics in Weimar and the Third Reich; Divided Memory: The Nazi Past in the Two Germanys;* and *The Jewish Enemy: Nazi Propaganda During World War II and the Holocaust.*

DAGMAR HERZOG is a professor of history and Daniel Rose Faculty Scholar at the Graduate Center, City University of New York. She is the author of *Sex After Fascism: Memory and Morality in Twentieth-Century Germany* and *Intimacy and Exclusion: Religious Politics in Pre-Revolutionary Baden* as well as the editor of *Sexuality and German Fascism* and coeditor of *Sexuality in Austria,* a special issue of *Contemporary Austrian Studies.*

STUART LIEBMAN is a professor of film studies at Queens College and the City University of New York Graduate Center. He edited a forthcoming anthology on Claude Lanzmann's *Shoah* and was named one of two Academy Film Scholars for 2006 by the Academy of Motion Picture Arts and Sciences.

JÜRGEN MATTHÄUS is a scholar at the United States Holocaust Memorial Museum's Center for Advanced Holocaust Studies in Washington, DC. He has taught in the United States, Germany, and Australia, and he is coauthor of *The Origins of the Final Solution: The Evolution of Nazi Jewish Policy, September 1939–March 1942* and coeditor of *Contemporary Responses to the Holocaust*.

THOMAS PEGELOW is an assistant professor in the history department of Grinnell College. He has published articles in *Central European History* and *Contemporary European History* and is currently working on the book *Linguistic Violence: Language, Power, and Separation in the Fate of Germans of Jewish Ancestry, 1928–48*.

JONATHAN PETROPOULOS is the John V. Croul Professor of European History at Claremont McKenna College in Southern California. He is the author of *Art as Politics in the Third Reich, The Faustian Bargain: The Art World in Nazi Germany,* and *Royals and the Reich: The Princes von Hessen in Nazi Germany,* as well as coeditor of *A User's Guide to German Cultural Studies* and *Gray Zones: Ambiguity and Compromise in the Holocaust and Its Aftermath*. As research director for art and cultural property on the Presidential Commission on Holocaust Assets in the United States, he helped draft the report *Restitution and Plunder: The U.S. and Holocaust Victims' Assets*.

GAVRIEL D. ROSENFELD is an associate professor of history at Fairfield University and the author of *The World Hitler Never Made: Alternate History and the Memory of Nazism* and *Munich and Memory: Architecture, Monuments, and the Legacy of the Third Reich*. He is currently working on a study of postwar Jewish architecture and the memory of the Holocaust.

ROCHELLE G. SAIDEL is founder and executive director of the Remember the Women Institute in New York, which is dedicated to integrating women into history. She is the author of *The Jewish Women of Ravensbrück Concentration Camp* and other Holocaust-related books. A political scientist, she is also a senior researcher at the Center for the Study of Women and Gender at the University of São Paulo, Brazil.

CHRISTA SCHIKORRA is a researcher and curator at the House of the Wannsee Conference in Berlin. She is the author of *Kontinuitäten der Ausgrenzung: "Asoziale" Häftlinge im Frauen-KZ Ravensbrück* as well as essays on women and youth in Nazi concentration camps; psychiatry and welfare under Nazism; Jewish survivors; and Holocaust memory.

PATRICIA SZOBAR is a translator and a doctoral candidate in history at Rutgers University. She lives and works in Berlin.

JAMES WALLER is Edward B. Lindaman Chair and Professor of Psychology at Whitworth University in Spokane, Washington. He is the author of *Face to Face: The Changing State of Racism Across America, Prejudice Across America,* and *Becoming Evil: How Ordinary People Commit Genocide and Mass Killing.*

BOB WEINBERG teaches at Swarthmore College and is the author of *The Revolution of 1905 in Odessa, Stalin's Forgotten Zion: Birobidzhan and the Making of a Soviet Jewish Homeland,* and *The Russian Revolution: A History in Documents* (with Laurie Bernstein).

ERIC D. WEITZ is a professor of history at the University of Minnesota, where he also holds the Arsham and Charlotte Ohanessian Chair in the College of Liberal Arts and directs the Center for German and European Studies. His books include *Creating German Communism, 1890–1990; A Century of Genocide: Utopias of Race and Nation;* and the forthcoming *Weimar Germany: Living with Modernity.*

EDWARD B. WESTERMANN is a senior military professor at the United States Air Force Academy. He has published several articles on the German police as well as a book, *Hitler's Police Battalions: Enforcing Racial War in the East.*

PIOTR WRÓBEL is an associate professor and Konstanty Reynert Chair of Polish History at the University of Toronto. He is coeditor of *Nation and History: Polish Historians from the Enlightenment to the Second World War.* His current project is devoted to the radical left-wing underground in the Warsaw Ghetto.